REVOLUTIONS IN SOVEREIGNTY

PRINCETON STUDIES IN

INTERNATIONAL HISTORY AND POLITICS

Series Editors
Jack L. Snyder
Marc Trachtenberg
Fareed Zakaria

Recent Titles:

Revolutions in Sovereignty: How Ideas Shaped Modern International Relations by Daniel Philpott

After Victory: Institutions, Strategic Restraint, and the Rebuilding of Order after Major Wars by G. John Ikenberry

Stay the Hand of Vengeance: The Politics of War Crimes Tribunals by Gary Jonathan Bass

War and Punishment: The Causes of War Termination and the First World War by H. E. Goemans

In the Shadow of the Garrison State: America's Anti-Statism and Its Cold War Grand Strategy by Aaron L. Friedberg

States and Power in Africa: Comparative Lessons in Authority and Control by Jeffrey Herbst

Entangling Relations: American Foreign Policy in Its Century by David A. Lake

The Moral Purpose of the State: Culture, Social Identity, and Institutional Rationality in International Relations by Christian Reus-Smit

A Constructed Peace: The Making of the European Settlement, 1945–1963 by Marc Trachtenberg

Regional Orders at Century's Dawn: Global and Domestic Influences on Grand Strategy by Etel Solingen

From Wealth to Power: The Unusual Origins of America's World Role by Fareed Zakaria

Changing Course: Ideas, Politics, and the Soviet Withdrawal from Afghanistan by Sarah E. Mendelson

Disarming Strangers: Nuclear Diplomacy with North Korea by Leon V. Sigal

REVOLUTIONS IN SOVEREIGNTY

HOW IDEAS SHAPED MODERN INTERNATIONAL RELATIONS

Daniel Philpott

PRINCETON UNIVERSITY PRESS

PRINCETON AND OXFORD

PUBLISHED BY PRINCETON UNIVERSITY PRESS, 41 WILLIAM STREET,
PRINCETON, NEW JERSEY 08540
IN THE UNITED KINGDOM: PRINCETON UNIVERSITY PRESS,
3 MARKET PLACE, WOODSTOCK, OXFORDSHIRE OX20 1SY

LIBRARY OF CONGRESS CATALOGING-IN-PUBLICATION DATA

PHILPOTT, DANIEL, 1967–
REVOLUTIONS IN SOVEREIGNTY: HOW IDEAS SHAPED MODERN
INTERNATIONAL RELATIONS / DANIEL PHILPOTT.
P. CM.
INCLUDES BIBLIOGRAPHICAL REFERENCES AND INDEX.
ISBN 0-691-05746-X (CL : ALK. PAPER)—
ISBN 0-691-05747-8
(PB : ALK. PAPER)
1. SOVEREIGNTY. 2. INTERNATIONAL RELATIONS. I. TITLE
JZ4034.P48 2001
320.1'5—DC21 00-059826

THIS BOOK HAS BEEN COMPOSED IN GALLIARD

PRINTED ON ACID-FREE PAPER ∞
WWW.PUP.PRINCETON.EDU

PRINTED IN THE UNITED STATES OF AMERICA

1 3 5 7 9 10 8 6 4 2
3 5 7 9 10 8 6 4 2 (PBK.)

To Mom, Dad, and Grandmother

CONTENTS

Tables and Figures ix

Preface xi

PART ONE: REVOLUTIONS IN SOVEREIGNTY 1

ONE
Introduction: Revolutions in Sovereignty 3

TWO
The Constitution of International Society 11

THREE
A Brief History of Constitutions of International Society in the West 28

FOUR
How Revolutions in Ideas Bring Revolutions in Sovereignty 46

PART TWO: THE FOUNDING OF THE SOVEREIGN STATES SYSTEM AT WESTPHALIA 73

FIVE
Westphalia as Origin 75

SIX
The Origin of Westphalia 97

SEVEN
The Power of Protestant Propositions 123

PART THREE: THE REVOLUTION OF COLONIAL INDEPENDENCE: THE GLOBAL EXPANSION OF WESTPHALIA 151

EIGHT
Ideas and the End of Empire 153

NINE
The End of the British Empire: Cashing Out the Promise of Self-Government 168

TEN
Revolutionary Ideas in the British Colonies 190

ELEVEN
Britain's Burden of Empire 203

TWELVE
The Fall of Greater France 220

PART FOUR: THE REVOLUTIONS CONSIDERED TOGETHER 251

THIRTEEN
Conclusion: Two Revolutions, One Movement 253

Notes 263

Bibliography 309

Index 331

TABLES AND FIGURES

Tables

2.1	Characteristics of International Behavior	24
3.1	Major Constitutional Revolutions Since the Middle Ages	31
4.1	Summary: Three Versions of the Two Roles of Ideas	68
6.1	The Correlation Summarized	111
12.1	Public Opinion Poll on Favored Solution for Algeria	231
12.2	France's and Britain's Trade with Africa as a Percentage of Their Total Trade	244
12.3	Settler Populations in the Colonies	248

Figures

4.1	The Two Roles of Ideas	50
4.2	Structural Skepticism of the First Role of Ideas	56
4.3	Structural Skepticism of the Second Role of Ideas	66
7.1	The Causal Pathways of the Influence of Protestantism	126
8.1	Explaining the Pattern of Colonial Independence	165

PREFACE

SCHOLARS EASILY underestimate the dependence of knowledge upon community and friendship. In publishing this first book, I want to acknowledge the fellowship that prepared me for it and accompanied me in writing it. It was a high school teacher, Sally Durrant, who first showed me that studying politics could be rigorous and exuberant. I am ever awed by her passion for the *polis* and her courage against adversity—intimations of Socrates. Two professors at the University of Virginia then inspired me to study and teach politics as a vocation. Michael Joseph Smith's kind mentorship and commitment to the study of ethics in international relations were formative. Kenneth Elzinga's example of teacher as servant proposed an attractive vision, too. My advisers in graduate school at Harvard University inspired me both through their own formidable scholarship and their conscientious commitment to my project. Stanley Hoffmann's humanistic learning, Robert Keohane's methodological rigor, Andrew Moravcsik's tenacity, and Bryan Hehir's leadership in integrating faith, learning, and politics all shaped the endeavor. Deeply formative, too, were my friendships in the Graduate Christian Fellowship at Harvard, and in the national graduate ministry of InterVarsity Christian Fellowship. It was there that I gained my deepest sense of vocation. I thank, too, my unusually supportive colleagues and friends in the Political Science Department at the University of California, Santa Barbara. I especially appreciate the help of our chair, Stephen Weatherford, in securing for me an early sabbatical leave.

Many colleagues read and commented upon some portion of the manuscript. I am grateful to them all: Samuel Barkin, Aaron Belkin, Sheri Berman, Allan Castle, Vikram Chand, Houchang Chehabi, Jarat Chopra, Benjamin Cohen, Bruce Cronin, Michael Desch, George Downs, Michael Doyle, Sally Durrant, Colin Elman, Martha Finnemore, Gregory Fox, Aaron Friedberg, Michael Gordon, Rodney Bruce Hall, Chris Hardy, Sohail Hashmi, Kevin Hula, Samuel Huntington, Andrew Hurrell, Robert Jackson, Gary King, Stephen Kocs, Stephen Krasner, Friedrich Kratochwil, William Roger Louis, Kate McNamara, John Mearsheimer, Henry Nau, Brent Nelson, John Owen, Dani Reiter, Timothy Shah, Anne-Marie Slaughter, Daniel Thomas, Stephen Van Evera, Barbara Walter, Alexander Wendt, William Wohlforth, Patrick Wolf, Stewart Wood, Phoebe Yang, and two anonymous reviewers for Princeton University Press. Even where these interlocutors have disagreed with my arguments, I have profited enormously from their reactions. All are responsible for some of the book's insights, none for any of its errors.

For financial and institutional support, I thank the Weatherhead Center for International Affairs at Harvard University; the Center for European Studies, Harvard University; the John M. Olin Institute for Strategic Studies, Harvard University; the Research Program on International Security at the Center of International Studies at Princeton University; the Erasmus Institute at the University of Notre Dame; and the Faculty Senate at the University of California, Santa Barbara. For crucial logistical support, I thank the staff at the Institute for Commonwealth Studies, London; the administrators at the Public Records Office, London; and Steve Ashton and Philip Murphy, the assistants at the Bodleian Library and Rhodes House Library, Oxford University. For valuable research assistance, I thank Michael Hall. For helpful proofreading, I thank Jessica Vasquez and Samar Mansour. Finally, I thank Charles Myers at Princeton University Press for his conscientious editorial work, and Joan Hunter for her virtuoso copy editing.

What is remarkably apparent to me about all of this fellowship is how little I planned, pursued, or, still less, earned it, and how it always came to me, not I to it. It can only be grace.

Revealing the gift of fellowship most fully of all is my family, whose love for education, travel, and challenges of all sorts eased naturally into their love for me. I dedicate the book to my father, my mother, and my grandmother.

For permission to publish parts of work that I have previously published, I thank:

Johns Hopkins University Press for permission to borrow portions of "The Religious Roots of Modern International Relations," *World Politics* 52 (January 2000): 206–45.

The Political Studies Association for permission to borrow portions of "Westphalia and Authority in International Society," *Political Studies* 47, no. 3 (Annual 1999), 566–89.

The *Journal of International Affairs* for permission to borrow portions of "Sovereignty: An Introduction and Brief History," *Journal of International Affairs* 48, no. 2 (Winter 1995), 353–69.

Pennsylvania State University Press for permission to borrow portions of "Ideas and the Evolution of Sovereignty," in Sohail H. Hashmi, ed., *State Sovereignty: Change and Persistence in International Relations* (University Park, Pa.: Pennsylvania State University Press, 1997), 15–49.

PART ONE

REVOLUTIONS IN SOVEREIGNTY

ONE

INTRODUCTION: REVOLUTIONS IN SOVEREIGNTY

VIRTUALLY ALL OF the earth's land is parceled by lines, invisible lines that we call borders. Within these borders, supreme political authority typically lies in a single source—a liberal constitution, a military dictatorship, a theocracy, a communist regime. This is sovereignty. Hobbes and Bodin and Grotius first wrote of the modern version of the principle in the sixteenth and seventeenth centuries; by the middle of the seventeenth century, states across Europe practiced it. A generation ago, the sovereign state captured nearly the entire land surface of the globe when European colonies received their independence. Sovereignty has come closer to enjoying universal explicit assent than any other principle of political organization in history.

But sovereignty is again the issue. During the past decade, the United Nations has lent its imprimatur to intervention in war-torn, malnourished, dictatorial, and minority-persecuting states, in Iraq, Somalia, Haiti, Rwanda, Bosnia, Cambodia, Liberia, and elsewhere. Fifteen European states have formed a European Union, creating among other things a common currency among eleven of these states, continuing an amalgamation of governance begun in 1950 with the founding of the European Coal and Steel Community. Intervention, integration—both challenge the sovereign state's territorial supremacy. They are conspicuous challenges—"revolutions in sovereignty," as I will call them. They overthrow some of the basic rules of authority that define international relations, rules that I will call "the constitution of international society."

When a political order ruptures, in international politics as in national politics, its rivaling factions will send their scribes to seek out the order's origins—conservatives, to fortify its pedigree; revolutionaries, to expose its flawed foundations. More measured scholars will also interest themselves in the order, but will eschew declaiming, seeking instead simply to understand what sorts of winds first brought it about and what sorts are now carrying it away. Mine is this task of understanding. If our sovereign states system is cracking, how did it ever come to be?

That is the question that I propose to answer in this book. My premise: The sovereign states system arrived most commandingly through revolutions. Through two prominent ones in particular. The first is what political scientist John Gerard Ruggie describes as "the most important contextual change in international politics in this *millennium*"—the shift in Europe from the medieval world to the modern international system, which took full shape at the Peace of Westphalia in 1648.[1] The system then spread, rapidly expanding across the globe when the colonial empires collapsed after World War II. Colonial independence is the second revolution. These forging moments, which successively wrought the sovereign state system, were both the yield of volcanic periods, ones of wars, crises, and imbroglios that in the end amounted to refining furnaces, casting an apparatus so hardy that it came to organize every piece of land on the globe, an apparatus that has only now begun to crack. It is these casting moments whose causes I want to discover. I want to discover the origins of international revolutions just as historians and sociologists seek the origins of the French, American, and Russian revolutions.

My central claim: Revolutions in sovereignty result from prior revolutions in ideas about justice and political authority. What revolutions in ideas bring are crises of pluralism. Iconoclastic propositions challenge the legitimacy of an existing international order, a contradiction that erupts in the volcano—the wars, the riots, the protests, the politics—that then brings in the new order. This, through a typical chain of events: The ideas convert hearers; these converts amass their ranks; they then demand new international orders; they protest and lobby and rebel to bring about these orders; there emerges a social dissonance between the iconoclasm and the existing order; a new order results. In early modern Europe, it was the Protestant Reformation that brought a century of war, culminating in the Thirty Years' War (1618–1648), which in turn brought about a system of sovereign states. In the twentieth century, it was nationalism and racial equality that brought the revolts, protests, and colonial wars that extended the system globally. For both revolutions, international agreement upon sovereign statehood was the terms on which a crisis of pluralism was settled.

My claim, too, is about what revolutions in sovereignty are not. That is, they are not merely the aftereffects of the rise and fall of great powers, or of slow shifts in class structure or political structure, in technology, commerce or industrial production, or in the division of labor, methods of warfare, or population size. Such forces contribute to the upheavals but do not solely bring them about. It takes a revolution in ideas to bring a revolution in sovereignty.

I suspect, though, that most citizens of most international societies would find the very idea of an international revolution a bizarre notion, a malapropism. Why? Because they widely believe that politics within borders and politics between polities are two sorts of realms with two sorts of habits. Within borders there are constitutions and there are revolutions. We enjoy civic familiarity; we fly flags symbolizing our common life; we recall, in eulogy or censure, a revolution, a founding moment, one that we remember through paintings, monuments, oratory, and criticism, through lessons and stories about battles, debates, heroes, and traitors. We speak of 1776, 1789, or 1917, of the spirit of the revolution, of the intentions of founders. We do not, however, exalt, versify, or acclaim in reverent public ritual the 1648 Peace of Westphalia, which christened modern international relations, nor repeat lore to schoolchildren about the early 1960s, when Britain, France, and Belgium freed their colonies.[2] Only scholars write of such things, and they do so cooly to categorize and chronicle, not to pronounce or polemicize.

The eccentricity of international revolutions, the reluctance to remember them, I further suspect, lies in the strangeness of the very idea of an international constitution, an order that arranges the authority of states, empires, colonies, nations, the United Nations, and the European Union much as a domestic constitution establishes courts, the powers of presidents, and the federal rights of regions. That there are others states, empires, and the like, each having its own authority and having the authority to trade and negotiate and fight with each other, is something that most citizens of most states during most times take for granted, and do not consider the product of anyone's design or the work of architects or framers. In fighting, trading, and negotiating, states and their citizens reflect upon these rules no more than baseball players reflect upon the underlying rules of the game when they throw to first base or steal second base. Fighting, trading, negotiating, they believe, is the real business of nations.

Behind the perceived eccentricity of both the revolutions and the constitutions, I finally suspect, lies beliefs about what kinds of forces dominate the two realms, domestic and international politics. Within borders, we more readily believe that notions of justice, both laudable and damnable, energize politics. Beyond, we are more awed by power—military, economic, political, and technological. Marxists, materialists, prophets of technology, and mavens of other academic schools have posed variants of this view. But the most widespread version, not only among scholars but also, I think, among statespersons and many citizens, has been the Realist school, which regards wars, alliances, balances of power, and the rises and falls of states and empires as the germane international events, and which holds that the contest over the international distribution of military and economic power is what propels these events. The separation is not hermetic. There are materialists and even Realists who grant significance to domestic politics; and there are idealists in international politics. But the emphases are clear. In international relations scholarship, 92 percent of hypotheses and 94 percent of variables used by scholars were Realist, according to one analyst.[3]

Publics determine their canons of memory according to what forces they think influential. We would more likely remember orders and revolutions if we thought them the fruit of will and design, ideas and vision. Otherwise, why take seriously the founders, speeches, and battles? But if we think ideas infirm and the drive for material power eclipsing, we will also think that rules and orders are deceptive emissions, forgettable surface reflections, and that references to them are strange usages, fragments of false grammar. Here lies the link between the eccentricity of the revolutions and constitutions, and skepticism toward ideas as their cause. Rather than the rule of nonintervention established at Westphalia or the 1960 United Nations resolution that declared colonies free, we are more likely to remember the longbow at Agincourt, the rise of French armies and finance under Richelieu, the rise of Germany, the decline of the British Empire, and other rises and falls, alliances and balances, and wars. It is inside the state where constitutions matter, where ideas hold sway, where the order was once different but then altered by wise founders or reckless revolutionaries; outside the realm, ideas are muffled by necessity, by the workings of colossal, impersonal forces.

This view I want to challenge. What happens between states is less the handiwork of impersonal forces and more like the idea-infused polity than we are used to thinking. International relations has always had a constitution, an order defining the very entities that rise, fall, ally, balance, negotiate, make war, and make peace, decreeing whether the world is organized into a system of states rather than a Holy Roman Empire, a European Union rather than a simple system of states, whether states may hold colonies, whether stateless nations may become states, and whether states may intervene in one another's affairs. Publics in most times and places may take for granted the significance of these orders. But at particular charged times and places, aristocrats, liberals, Protestants, Catholics, nationalists, and colonists have shouted and fought both for and against their provisions. For such parties, the basic rules of authority around which the international world is organized represent exaltations or denials of justice.

It could turn out, though, that this advocacy and laud and protest and outrage amount to what Marx called false consciousness. Taking a long view, perhaps the beliefs of particular strata in the justice or injustice of international rules of authority are of little importance, and new orders emerge or fade only when armies, economies, and military technology first emerge or fade. This thinking, too, I want to challenge. The moral ideas of Protestants, nationalists, and liberal democrats, about rights to worship, self-determination, racial equality, and human rights are not just assessments that we now call "political philosophy," but are effectual in creating new authority. Tumultuous disputation yields novel orthodoxy; revolutions in ideas bring revolutions in sovereignty; and so the revolutions are worth remembering.

My argument will likely encounter two sorts of critics, each stirred by opposite convictions, both difficult to satisfy at once. One sort is the skeptic who doubts ideas' influence on politics. Ideas, for this doubter, may adhesively bind the joints of political structures by inducing people to think them just or satisfactory, or they may inspire this or that politician's zeal, but on balance, in the aggregate, on the big events, they have little effect. This view reaches back to Karl Marx, who replaced Hegel's history of the unfolding of spirit with a history driven by class conflict, and to Emile Durkheim, who thought a society's politics, religion, and philosophy to be mostly the products of its underlying division of labor.[4] It finds resonance, too, in much of historical sociology of the past generation, which finds huge structures of class and state institutions behind large historical developments—the formation of the state, social revolutions, and the development of democracy and dictatorship. We find the view, finally, in the long tradition of *realpolitik*, in which international orders are fashioned by the competition for wealth, land, and power, particularly between states.[5]

Meeting such skepticism invokes the book's project: a demonstration of ideas' influence. I want to show that revolutions in sovereignty, Westphalia and colonial independence, occur when ideas arrive on the scene, and proceed most vigorously in those locales where ideas are most voluble. Likewise, revolutions do not correspond well enough in time and place with the skeptic's structures—class, technology, the balance of power—to earn these structures the bulk of the credit for causing the revolutions. Along with asserting these correlations of time and place, I will also offer an account of the events, incidents, movements, and methods by which ideas moved politics—that is, a story of how revolutions in sovereignty result from revolutions in ideas. Through these methods, I will engage this skepticism, posing its plausible account of each revolution, but seeking to reveal its inadequacy for explanation.

The other sort of criticism doubts the value of this engagement. The view of these critics is quite opposite to the skeptics'. To them, the influence of ideas is not dubious, but unexceptional. It requires no proof, but is obvious to anyone who has ever considered the matter. The demonstration, then, is unnecessary. If these critics implacably insist that skepticism of ideas is implausible, it will be difficult to answer them. But we may nonetheless ask them to account for the tenacious prestige of such skepticism. It rolls forward, after all, inside and outside the academy. Realism, as I have mentioned, persists formidably in the academic study of international relations, but it is also voiced, again and again, in policy journals, in opinion pieces, in the State Department, Defense Department, and White

House, in the Congress, and in the foreign counterparts of these institutions, behind closed doors, out in public, pervasively. It is true that during the past decade, more and more scholars in international relations have turned back to ideas, arguing for their influence upon foreign aid policy, states' responses to outside threats, nuclear weapons policy, the end of the Cold War, and other international phenomena. Many call themselves "constructivists," emphasizing that national interests are defined or "constructed," not fixed, and that ideas, meanings, and discourses contribute to this definition of interests. Nearly all of these scholars, though, treat seriously the Realist hypothesis that the apparent handiwork of ideas is instead the fruit of the state pursuing material interests. They consider this argument, they provide evidence against it, and in so doing they implicitly pay tribute to its stature.[6] This combination of respect for and dissent from skepticism of ideas is what I adopt here.

To explain how revolutions in ideas brought the revolutions in sovereignty that brought us the system of sovereign states that so essentially defines world politics today, even if certain trends now depart from it, is my central purpose in this book. Making the case will require fashioning a couple of tools, which are important aims of the book, too. First, I describe that which is revolutionized: the constitution of international society. Only if we know just what an international constitution is can we identify and compare revolutions in sovereignty. This description appears in chapter 2. In chapter 3, I tell a brief history of constitutions of international society in the West, illustrating them and identifying their key revolutions. The second tool is an account of how ideas exert influence in international relations, and even more generally, in politics. In chapter 4 I develop a framework to describe this influence, one that asserts two crucial roles for ideas: as shapers of identities and as forms of social power.

In the ensuing chapters, I then make the historical case for ideas as causes of revolutions in sovereignty. Chapters 5, 6, and 7 are about the rise of the sovereign states system in early modern Europe. In chapter 5, I assert the Peace of Westphalia as the origin of modern international relations. In chapters 6 and 7, I argue for the efficacy of the Protestant Reformation in bringing about the revolution at Westphalia. Here, I challenge leading accounts of the formation of the state system, ones that stress the state's successful adaptation to technological, military, and economic change.

I allege instead the role of religious ideas. This particular kind of idea, too, poses a challenge. If international relations scholars today are coming to acknowledge the influence of ideas in general, few of them acknowledge the importance of religion. There are prominent exceptions, most notably Samuel Huntington in his *Clash of Civilizations.* Claiming that the major armed conflicts after the Cold War will be fought between religiously defined civilizations, Huntington's thesis created an uproar, coming to be attacked and defended in the media and in universities, foreign ministries, and other forums around the globe.[7] Yet, the very attention that far-flung publics gave to Huntington's thesis, to religion, accents how little attention political scientists who study international relations give to religion. Huntington first published his thesis in the prestigious and widely read *Foreign Affairs*, and then published the book version with a trade press. Meanwhile, scholarly journals in political science have virtually ignored religion. My own survey of four leading international relations journals, *International Organization*, *International Studies Quarterly*, *World Politics*, and *International Security*, reveals that in the entire period 1980–1999, only six or so articles featured religion as an important influence in international relations. A glance at world affairs during the sane period reveals the myopia of the omission. By 1994, Gilles Kepel could write of "The Revenge of God," shorthand for the resurgence of Islam, Christianity, and Judaism, a trend realized wherever these faiths exist, save only among Western Europe's publics and, not surprisingly, Western intellectuals.[8] Meanwhile, the revenge plays itself out in Northern Ireland, Bosnia, Kosovo, and Sudan, in radical Islamic and other authoritarian regimes that have increasingly cracked down on religious freedom, in countries like India, where religious minorities are more and more afflicted, in clashes over population policy at United Nations conferences in Cairo and Beijing, and even in the growth of religious freedom as a foreign policy issue in the United States. Here, I look at none of these contemporary contests, but rather seek to show that the very system of sovereign states, the world of international relations where such conflicts occur, is itself in large part the product of religious ideas. But if the place of religion at the origin of international relations becomes more clear, then perhaps its place in international relations today will be taken more seriously.

Chapters 8 through 12 then look at the revolution of colonial independence, which extended the sovereign states system to the rest of the globe. Chapter 8 describes this revolution and its importance. Chapters 9 through 12 argue for the force of colonial nationalism and racial equality in bringing about this revolution—chapters 9, 10, and 11 in Britain, chapter 12 in France. In both cases, I dispute that the collapse of empires was solely a product of their increased expense, in money and lives.

These two revolutions, Westphalia and colonial independence, I discuss as separate events, as two separate stages in the formation of a global sovereign states system. They came in very different eras, amidst very different languages, circumstances, causes, and understandings. But there are important connections between them. Through both revolutions, the liberation of peoples from empires unfolded, a freedom that modern liberals would come to name self-determination. Both sets of ideas behind these two revolutions, although addressed to different peoples and different empires, themselves called for this liberation, advancing its logic through history. These connections, I will draw out in chapter 13.

But there is a paradox to the liberation. If the sovereign state provides a people with one sort of liberty, it also provides a carapace under which regimes may, and have, suppressed liberal and democratic rights, other forms of liberty. Ideas directed at these injustices are also concerned with liberation. Their calls for international institutions that would restrict the authority of sovereigns on behalf of the liberties of their subjects may well be the seeds of the more recent revolutions in sovereignty which have begun to circumscribe the global system of sovereign states. To this paradox, I also draw attention in chapter 13.

The first twelve chapters, though, are concerned with how the ubiquitous though now disputed sovereign states system came to be. How did this constitution of international society develop? What caused the revolutions through which this development took place? We begin with the thing revolutionized.

TWO

THE CONSTITUTION OF INTERNATIONAL SOCIETY

BEHIND WARS AND COMMERCE and investment and immigration, prior to alliances, leagues, concerts, and balances of power, beneath agreements governing trade, armaments, and the environment, is the constitution of international society. Foundational, the constitution defines the political authorities—the states, the empires, the international organizations—who govern trade, regulate money and investment, invade each other, ally, intervene, build weapons, restrict drug flow and immigration, topple one another's governments, attempt to prevent environmental destruction, and undertake countless other ends.

Most academic scholarship on international relations has concerned itself with these ends, not with the rules that constitute the authorities who undertake them. The same goes for most makers of policy. Again, it may seem strange to speak of a constitution on the international level. But I contend that there are such constitutions, that they give international politics its form, that politicians and citizens often recognize them implicitly, that there are times of upheaval when people are intensely concerned about them, and that we ought to be concerned with how they operate and how they come about. At Westphalia, the constitution emerged as a system of sovereign states. Through colonial independence, this system became global. But states are not the only possible forms of authority, and they do not have to be absolutely sovereign. During the Middle Ages, whose long, slow death Westphalia consolidated, authorities and their privileges were profoundly variegated. Today, the European Union is an alternative to the state and limits its member states' sovereignty. The United Nations now limits some states' sovereignty when it intervenes in their borders to stop wars, deliver humanitarian supplies, and arrest war criminals. What constitutions are, how they differ, what is unique about today's—these are the concerns of this chapter.

The Constitution of International Society

Constitutions of international society are authors of orders, prescribing the polities that carry on business and war; they are etchers of blueprints, resembling the rules of baseball, defining the nine players, their strictures and allowances, the meaning and regulation of pitches, outs, strikes, steals, and balls. More precisely, *a constitution of international society is a set of norms, mutually agreed upon by polities who are members of the society, that define the holders of authority and their prerogatives, specifically in answer to three questions: Who are the legitimate polities? What are the rules for becoming one of these polities? And, what are the basic prerogatives of these polities? Constitutions of international society are both legitimate—that is, sanctioned by authoritative agreements—and practiced, generally respected by all polities that are powerful enough regularly to violate them.* The terms "international society," "norms," and each part of this definition, I will probe more deeply. What I now want to stress is the foundational nature of these constitutions.

One of the reasons that "constitution" seems odd in the international context is that we are most familiar with constitutions as single documents to which people give the name. This is what we find in the domestic context, after all. There, constitutions are most developed, rich, complex, and respected. On the international level, constitutions are rarely explicitly called such, and are often strewn among separate treaties, conventions, and customary law. But they are constitutive, foundational, in this essential respect: they define the polities and their basic powers with respect to one another. More specifically and familiarly, they define internationally the traditional troika of executive, legislative, and judicial powers. When imperial diplomats arrived at the halls of Münster and Osnabrück to negotiate the Peace of Westphalia, they still wanted to preserve something of medieval Christendom, where the pope and the emperor would pronounce laws and enforce Catholic uniformity, where the imperial legislature would pass laws, where the Church's and the empire's courts held session. Instead, sovereign princes came to monopolize this constitutional troika; all three kinds of powers were to be exercised at the state level according to the state's particular constitution. The British Empire asserted, then lost, all three kinds of powers over its colonies; the European Union possesses some measure of all three; and current debates over humanitarian intervention are essentially about the executive power of the United Nations. These are powers of the most basic sort.

As they are international in character, these constitutions refrain from defining all authority, at every level. Most international constitutions create polities that have internal realms, whose inhabitants in turn define their own constitutional authority. The modern state, as it emerged out of the Middle Ages, is such a polity. Over the years, its architects have rendered it monarchical, communist, social democratic, and the like. The international constitution's vital work is to found the scheme of authority that creates internal and external realms in the first place. It is like a town's property laws, which define where its residents may live, but leave them to govern their households as they see fit. It is more than simply the collection of its individual polities and their individual constitutions, then. It is the wide, mutual agreement among political authorities to recognize one another's powers in the first place. Without this mutual recognition, the internal authority of individual polities would mean little. Prior to Westphalia, rulers in the Netherlands and the German states sought a monopoly of constitutional powers—the status of a sovereign state—just like the one their counterparts elsewhere in Europe already enjoyed. But they could not enjoy these powers until they had achieved freedom from the rival authority of the Holy Roman Empire and the Catholic Church, which had once legislated, judged, and enforced laws and religious uniformity within the would-be states' territories. Likewise, a colony's freedom depends on having its former imperial ruler cease to govern its economy, its defense, its infrastructure, and the like. A polity's practice of its authority on the inside requires the recognition of this authority from the outside.[1]

Polities mutually recognizing one another's authority, and a scheme that defines and links the polities, suggest that those living under an international constitution view themselves as part of a common association. That is, they live in a society, an international society. It was Australian scholar Hedley Bull who first introduced the concept of international society to the academic field of international relations. He wanted to describe a world of political entities that are separate yet recognize common rules and institutions. With his colleague Adam Watson, he defined international society widely and broadly: "a group of states (or, more generally, a group of independent political communities) which . . . have established by dialogue and consent common rules and institutions for the conduct of their relations, and recognise their common interest in maintaining these arrangements."[2] The rules and common institutions are important, for they link the society's polities together. Bull and Watson understand them to include international law, norms of diplomacy, and tacit understandings about how to conduct war or trade. Of an international society's entire set of common rules and institutions, the international constitution is only a portion, just as a domestic constitution is only a portion of a single polity's entirety of laws and ordinances. In either setting, the constitution is the portion that defines the basic, foundational, constitutional authority that I have been describing.

The international constitution, then, is a constitution of international society. Although I am interested here in constitutions originating in modernity and the West, constitutions are exclusive to neither. We find them scattered throughout the globe and history, in great variety. International societies have most familiarly comprised sovereign states, but have also included city-states, empires, suzerains, consuls, dukes, barons, knights, or some combination of such authorities, and have existed in ancient Greece,

Sumeria, China, Rome, India, Persia, medieval Europe, and Renaissance Italy, and in the Americas prior to the arrival of Columbus. The type of polity that makes up an international society is indeed one way in which societies vary.[3]

International societies also differ in how their polities are separated. The fact that polities are separated is essential; it is what makes the societies international, rather than unified, like a city, a state, or an empire. But separation can range from the complete independence of states, to the distinct but overlapping authority of kings, nobles, pope, and emperor in medieval Europe, to the partially autonomous regions of a loosely centralized empire. The norms that separate the polities of a society may well create a ranking among them, rather than leaving them as equals. The medieval system was quintessential for its hierarchies. The Westphalian system, too, has embodied hierarchies. Although states are legal equals, some of them may enjoy privileged positions in international organizations—the members of the United Nations Security Council or the most powerful members of the World Bank. Westphalian norms have also sanctioned the holding of colonies, and the partition of nonmember polities into spheres of influence, as Western states did China in the nineteenth century. The norms of international societies, then, separate polities differently, and often hierarchically.

International societies differ, too, in their expanse. They are often geographically bounded and confined to a single civilization, as were ones in classical Greece, China, Sumeria, and medieval Europe, but they could also be global, as the current society of sovereign states has been since the fall of the European colonial empires. Or, a geographically bounded constitution might coexist with a worldwide one; the member states of the European Union, for instance, are also members of the global international society of sovereign states. There is one last variant, one much more common in ages before technology and communication became strong and dense global ligatures. That is, separate international societies might themselves carry on business between one another. Medieval Europe, China, India, and the Ottoman Empire, Greece, Persia, and Rome occasionally fought, sometimes traded, from time to time exchanged emissaries, and developed loose rules to govern this interaction. But these relationships were too distant to compose an international society. Labeled "secondary systems of states" by scholar Martin Wight, they involved no mutual acknowledgment of fundamental rules of authority—the essence of a constitution of international society.[4]

In the chapters that follow, I will concern myself with constitutions of international society within a particular time period and a certain place. I will chart first the constitution that emerged in Europe out of the Middle Ages, then the extension of this constitution, the sovereign states system, to the globe. Other constitutions have existed in other times and places, which we should not forget. But this constitution occupies an important time and place—our time and place. It warrants special attention.

The Three Faces of Authority

Constitutions of international society, then, define authority. But this authority is never plain. It is not simple, unchanging, or ubiquitously uniform, but is intricate, unfolding, and various, just as domestic constitutions are complex in connecting courts to parliaments to executives to citizens. Westphalia and colonial independence, the revolutions that brought us our sovereign states system, both changed the constitution of international society, but differently and complexly. To understand how constitutions differ and how they change, we need to understand better the nuances of authority in international politics. We need to see, I propose, that international authority appears in three faces. All constitutions contain all three faces; every constitution's depiction of them is its unique signature. Each face answers a different question about authority. The first face answers, What are the polities in a given international society? The second face answers, Which polities may belong to the society? And who may become one of these legitimate polities? The third face answers, What are the essential prerogatives of these polities? Together, these faces define constitutional authority for any international society. They allow us to distinguish constitutions, and provide a criterion for change. A revolution in the constitution of international relations, I will argue, involves a change in at least one of these three faces.

The First Face of Authority

Most fundamentally, international constitutions prescribe the legitimate polities of an international society. A legitimate polity is simply one that the members of a society recognize as properly participating in the society. What is a legitimate polity? The question is analogous to asking who is a citizen in a domestic society. Since Westphalia, in the West, and later throughout the globe, international constitutions have defined the legitimate polities mainly as states, possessing the quality of sovereignty. In this world, Burundi has a status that California does not, entitling Burundi to diplomatic privileges and membership in international organizations. The state, of course, is not the only possible form of legitimate polity, for other constitutions have prescribed other sorts of polities. Medieval Islam apportioned authority among a caliph and scores of geographically far flung lesser figures, while high medieval Christendom admitted hundreds of diverse authorities, few of them sovereign, all linked together by unique privileges and prerogatives.[5] But it is the sovereign state whose authority so pervades the globe today and whose status as legitimate polity I seek to account for. What, then, is the meaning of sovereignty, this idea that has long dominated the first face of authority?

Sovereignty

Sovereignty has suffered a troubled intellectual history. It has evolved over four centuries, philosophers have continually disputed its definition, and now even some international lawyers have become skeptical of the concept, having exhausted themselves of delineating, demarcating, explicating, and making distinctions.[6] Yet because sovereignty has so often been voiced and contested, in polemics and preambles, by statespersons, diplomats, members of parliament, or anyone protective of his or her authority, because it is the concept that first established international relations in the twilight of the Middle Ages and without which modern international relations does not exist, we cannot scuttle it.

But sovereignty sorely needs definition. Its tortuous evolution since its first recorded usage in the thirteenth century renders quixotic the attempt to find a single, specific, historically valid formulation.[7] The absolute sovereignty of early modern philosophers, like Bodin and Hobbes, conceived to contain religious bedlam in England and France, Jean-Jacques Rousseau's popular sovereignty of the Enlightenment, modern constitutional sovereignty, and the international lawyer's state sovereignty—the definitions vary widely. But I want to argue that there is yet a formulation broad enough to encompass much of the diversity, but discrete enough to be useful: supreme authority within a territory.[8]

Each element of the definition is crucial. One who is sovereign is firstly one with authority. Authority, in one philosopher's definition, is "the right to command and correlatively, the right to be obeyed."[9] As "right" suggests, authority is a matter of legitimacy. The holders of sovereignty do not just prod, coerce, assert their will, or force their way, but rule according to natural law, divine mandate, a communal law or tradition, a constitution, or international law—the sources of sovereignty.[10] "The breath of worldly man cannot depose / The deputy elected by the lord," illustrates Shakespeare's Richard II.[11] Since the Enlightenment, the source of sovereignty has increasingly been a constitution or an agreed-upon body of law such as international law. Today, law is sovereignty's universal basis.

But the definition is still too broad. A police chief, priest, and corporate executive all have authority; rarely do we call them sovereigns. Sovereignty has always involved another ingredient: supremacy. In the chain of authority by which I look to a higher authority, who in turn looks to a higher one, the holder of sovereignty is highest. No one may question it; no one may legitimately oppose it. Such supremacy is what both Bodin and Hobbes had in mind, and it anchors most subsequent definitions.

Finally, territoriality is crucial. This is a principle that defines the set of people over whom the holder of sovereignty rules. They are to be identified, territoriality says, by virtue of their location within borders. The people within these borders may not necessarily conceive of themselves as a "people" or a "nation" with a common identity. In the century of Westphalia, they rarely did. But their location within boundaries requires their allegiance to their sovereign. Territoriality is so deeply enmeshed in virtually all contemporary authority that it is difficult to imagine authority otherwise. Prior to modernity, though, other principles connected people to their rulers. Most opposite territoriality are the ties of a wandering tribe, whose authority has nothing to do with a particular piece of land. But even people who live stably on a piece of land are not necessarily politically matched with their authorities by virtue of living on that piece of land. It may instead be their family kinship, their religious or tribal affiliation, or feudal ties that link them with their rulers. The question to which territoriality provides an answer is, By virtue of what quality are citizens subject to their governing authority? By virtue of their religion? Tribe? Family? Nationality? No, territoriality says, It is by virtue of their residence in a state, one demarcated by boundaries, by lines drawn in the sand, or through woods, or along a river, or at the extent of a general's conquest.[12] Today, virtually all political authority is territorial. Even such institutions as the European Union or the United Nations are composed of territorial member states, rendering their authority territorially derived, too.

These are the limits of specificity, for within the broad definition of supreme authority within a territory, all historical uses of the term have meant a particular form of sovereignty, reflecting one or another philosophy in one or another epoch: sovereignty is never without an adjective. A compendium of these adjectives I cannot offer here. It would be massive and diverse.

But three categories of adjectives capture quite well sovereignty's variants. The first describes *holders* of sovereignty. Sovereignty need not lie in a single individual, as Bodin thought, or in a body above the law, as both Bodin and Hobbes thought.[13] It could also reside in a triumvirate, a committee of public safety, the people united in a General Will (as Rousseau thought), the people ruling through a constitution, or the law of the European Union. Popular constitutional rule governs the majority of modern states, although even here, in some matters, international law or European Union law may be sovereign. In all cases, who holds sovereignty depends on the prevailing philosophy of rule. On one reading, medieval and modern political philosophy has been a debate about the holders of sovereignty.[14]

Another relevant sort of adjective is the pair "internal" and "external," which are not distinct types of sovereignty, but complementary, always coexistent, aspects of sovereignty.[15] Supreme authority within a territory may evoke for us sovereignty within borders, but it equally implies immunity from external interference. All holders of sovereignty are Janus-faced, staring inward at their ruled subjects, and outward beyond the polity's walls, where they see no robed eccelesiasts who claim temporal authority within their borders, no orbed monarchs or inspired ideologues entitled to send troops into their polity to change the way their inhabitants are governed. Since Westphalia, the state has been the chief holder of external sovereignty. It was in the wake of this settlement that it became illegitimate to interfere in other states to influence their governance, especially of religion. The external sovereignty of the state is what international lawyers have in mind when they speak of sovereignty, and what the United Nations Charter means by "political independence and territorial integrity."[16] External sovereignty echoes political scientist Alan James's notion of sovereignty as constitutional independence.[17] The key here is constitutional authority: a sovereign constitution is supreme within borders and independent of all other constitutional authorities. To James's notion, I add only that this independence depends on its recognition by outsiders, entailed in the international constitution. This recognition, to borrow an analogy used by other scholars, is to states what a no-trespassing law is to private property—the broad societal agreement that bequeaths to property, or the state, its inviolability.[18]

External sovereignty is also what political scientists mean when they speak of international relations as anarchy, which means not necessarily chaos, violence, and riot, but simply the lack of a government, the absence of a higher authority that makes claims upon those who live under it. The external sovereignty of the state is compatible with a variety of holders of internal sovereignty. A monarch, the people, a constitution, a dictatorship, a theocracy, can each represent the state within borders and be immune from external intervention. Compared with internal sovereignty, external sovereignty has remained relatively constant—not unrevised, but steady like a suit of armor whose plates and hinges are only occasionally updated, while the personality inside changes often, from reform to reform, from revolution to revolution.

A final relevant pair of adjectives for describing kinds of sovereignty is "absolute" and "nonabsolute." At first, the possibility of nonabsoluteness might seem to contradict sovereignty's essential quality of supremacy. If sovereignty is supreme, how can it be anything but absolute? This is James's objection: Sovereignty, like pregnancy, is either present or absent, never only partially realized.[19] I understand absoluteness, though, to refer not to the quality or magnitude of sovereignty, for if sovereignty were less than supreme in any particular matter, it would not be sovereignty at all. But a holder of sovereignty need not be sovereign over all matters. Absoluteness is a measure of the scope of affairs over which a sovereign body governs within a particular territory. Is it supreme over all matters or merely some? In those matters to which a sovereign state's authority does not extend, sovereignty typically lies in the international law or institution that prescribes how authority is to be shared. The government of France is supreme in defense policy but not in trade, which it governs jointly with other European Union members as prescribed by EU law. The French constitution's sovereignty is nonabsolute. For Bodin and Hobbes, by contrast, sovereignty means authority over all matters; it is absolute, unconditionally.[20] The absolute sovereignty of the state is archetypical modern sovereignty; it is the norm to which the European Union and the emerging legitimacy of intervention sanctioned by the United Nations are two exceptions. It renders international relations anarchical, making states wholly autonomous, not required to yield or genuflect to any outside authority. It is the sort of sovereignty with which we are most familiar.

It is both its contemporary global prestige and its urgent need of definition that merits sovereignty such involved discussion. When sovereignty colors the first face of authority, the international constitution defines sovereignty's specifics, that is, who its holders are, the meaning of its internal and external dimensions, and how absolute it is. In the post-Westphalian era, constitutions of international society have bestowed sovereignty upon the state while leaving open the question of who holds sovereignty within the state, has given the state supremacy within its borders and independence from outside interference, and has usually allowed the state to be absolutely sovereign, although with significant exceptions. The exceptions—the European Union and the United Nations in certain capacities, for instance—show that the state is not the only possible holder of sovereignty, nor is its sovereignty necessarily absolute. Constitutions of international society can also define the first face of authority with polities that do not enjoy sovereignty at all. But these constitutions are, to us, mostly foreign and forgotten.

The Second Face of Authority

Every club has rules for membership, and these rules are tied closely to what it means to be a member. International societies, too, have rules that determine who enjoys, and can attain, the status of the legitimate polity, entitled to all of the privileges that legitimate polities enjoy. This is the second face of authority. The second face requires a prior definition of the first face. Given that we know what the legitimate polities are, it answers, who is entitled to recognition as one of these polities? If states are the legitimate polity, then who is considered a state? Who may become a state? Nations that have no state and aspire to one? Colonies?

The second face includes and excludes. According to its rules, international societies grant their own members a thicker set of privileges—diplomatic immunities, commitments to consultation, restraint from intervention—than they grant to those they deem outsiders. Medieval Islamic legal theorists, for instance, divided the world into two realms, *dar al-Islam* (the realm of Islam) and *dar al-harb* (the realm of war).[21] Medieval Christendom practiced similar standards toward the rest of the world. Even Westphalia's signers still intended to create a constitution for Christian Europe, one whose provisions would apply only to Christian states, and not, for instance, to the Ottoman Empire. The Treaty of Münster begins, "In the name of the most holy and individual Trinity."[22] Today, the European Union, secular, defined by intricate modern law, purveys elaborate application procedures that compose its standards of membership, this constitution's second face.

Along with distinguishing insiders and outsiders, the second face of authority proposes terms for dealing with outsiders. Many medieval Islamic theorists thought that members of the Islamic state were called to wage *jihad*, through both military and nonmilitary means, against outsiders in order to expand the sphere of *dar al-Islam*. But they also forged a third realm, *dar al-sulh*, for outside states with which Muslims developed treaty obligations. With them, *jihad* was to be postponed. Societies almost always trade, ally, and negotiate with outsiders. But outsiders are still not legitimate polities, entitled to full privileges.

A revolution in the second face is a revolution in the rules for membership. Colonial independence was a revolution of this sort. Prior to it, colonies had no legitimate, internationally recognized claim to independence. They could only plead, protest, and fight for their freedom, and they won it only when their metropole conceded it. The revolution came through a 1960 UN declaration that granted all colonial peoples a right to independence, regardless of their level of advancement or internal political control. They were now entitled to become members of the system of sovereign states without further qualification.

The Third Face of Authority

Once we know who are the legitimate polities and who may become one, we then need to know what they may do. What are their basic prerogatives as members? Such standing prerogatives are constitutional; they define fundamental powers of states, of the European Union, of any legitimate polity; they compose the third face of authority. They differ from the rules of the first face in that they are not essential to the legitimate polity's definition. Just as a president could be a president without a line-item veto power, a state could be a state even if nonintervention were not absolute. But if standing prerogatives are not essential, they are also steady and basic, existing prior to the commitments that states contract into, such as alliances, trade agreements, and sundry pacts governing sundry matters. In the eighteenth century, Vattel depicted the third face of authority when he defined international society as one of equal sovereign states, whose prerogatives included the right to send diplomats and enter treaties, the duty not to invade, and, most of all, the obligation not to intervene.[23] Another enduring core prerogative of states is *pacta sunt servanda*, the principle that states ought to keep their treaty commitments.[24] In a society of states, the third face tells us whether sovereignty is absolute or nonabsolute, and if nonabsolute, in which respects the state is sovereign.[25] Haiti, for instance, is sovereign in most matters, but its maintenance of democratic government is now subject to the oversight of the UN, which monitored its democratic elections in 1990. This is a matter for the third face of authority, the face that fills out the constitution of international society.

Revolutions in Sovereignty

If the three faces of authority define international constitutions, then the definition of revolutions of these constitutions follows as a major change in at least one of these faces. As constitutional revolutions since Westphalia have either established or diminished the sovereign state, I call them revolutions in sovereignty. In chapter 3, I chart these revolutions in sovereignty, noting which face they revised and how. They are the phenomena for which the rest of the book seeks to account.

What Exactly *Are* Constitutions of International Society?

Constitutions of international society define constitutional authority, according to the three faces of authority. This is what they *do*. But it still may not be clear exactly what they *are*. Are they laws? Morals? Norms? The habitual behavior of polities? How are they different from common agreements between polities that are not constitutional? Are constitutions still valid if violated? Do they amount to anything more than mere power? On these questions hinge constitutions' very distinctiveness.

Above all, constitutions of international society are sets of norms. By this hazardously contested, sometimes cryptic term, I mean rules that are viewed as obligatory by the broad majority of people living under them, and that are usually, customarily, practiced.[26] What makes constitutional norms unique is that they constitute polities and endow them with their basic prerogatives. They are the specific rules that inscribe the three faces of authority for any international constitution. This is what the norms are like: The legitimate polity is a state. Nations have no international right to secede from larger states unless they hold the status of a colony. The pope may adjudicate conflicts between princes only with their consent. States may intervene to promote human rights when they obtain the approval of the UN Security Council. And so on.

Constitutional norms have two essential features: their legitimacy and their practice. By legitimate, I mean perceived to be obligatory, worthy of assent, by the polities living under the norm. Norms are much like law. Polities speak of them as something they are mutually obligated to respect, and view the polity that violates them as one that breaches a promise. Connoting obligation, norms are more than behavior that polities merely desire. In a world where norms render state sovereignty sacrosanct, if France were to attack Austria-Hungary on account of Austria-Hungary's threats against Germany or Italy, Austria-Hungary would doubtless view France as hostile, but France would not be a violator of norms. But if France were to intervene in Austria-Hungary to counter creeping Protestantism or to liberate the Serbian nation, France would be a violator of the legitimate rules of the game.

Norms are also more than habitual behavior. Britain's nineteenth-century role as "holder of the balance," a doctrine that called for using military force on the European continent only to parry excessive great power expansion, was, no matter how consistent or wise, never seen as an obligation, either by Britain or by continental European powers. It was not a constitutional norm. Had Britain intervened in the Austrian empire in order to overthrow a monarch or to liberate a nation, by contrast, Britain would have violated the constitutional provision of nonintervention.

Finally, we must admit one feature of norms that departs from the domestic constitutional analogy: Even though norms are obligating, they are not necessarily enforced, whereas in the domestic realm we normally expect violators of constitutions to be punished. As in other respects, the contrast between international and domestic is not absolute: international authority is often respected; civil wars and anarchy are hardly foreign to the domestic realm. In any case, the lack of a central enforcer does not mean the lack of obligation. Polities may well perceive and adhere to their obligations out of a variety of motives ranging from the purely instrumental to altruistic. Indeed, many activities of polities reveal the regularity of their perception of obligation. When a secretary of state visits a foreign minister or when a papal nuncio visits an Islamic caliph, a recognition of constitutional authority—the authority for which the diplomat speaks—is implied.

How do we identify legitimate constitutional provisions? How do we know when polities recognize obligation and which obligations they recognize? We simply look at the claims about obligation that the polities agree upon. In the modern West, provisions of international constitutions are usually codified; they can be discovered in founding charters and major treaties, and are regularly reaffirmed and reinforced in protocols, pacts, and pronouncements. Colonial independence was legitimated in a 1960 UN declaration; the laws of the European Community were approved in the 1950 Treaty of Paris and revised in the 1957 Treaty of Rome and the 1991 Maastricht Treaty. Sometimes, as with Westphalia's elevation of sovereign statehood, we must look beyond the mere text of a treaty to the signers' shared understandings of the treaty, just as judges in domestic society will look beyond the text of a law to the intentions of its signers. More rarely, constitutional provisions are matters of "customary law," whose obligatory character is revealed in certain kinds of actions. For instance, the permissibility of intervention since the end of the Cold War has not been codified in a UN declaration, but has achieved its legitimacy through several instances of the Security Council's approval of actual interventions. Constitutional norms that are embodied in customary law or primarily in the understanding of states are no less binding or forceful for not being codified. They are analogous to the British constitution, which, though unwritten, carries formidable consensus.[27]

That constitutional provisions are expressed as obligation in codification or custom distinguishes them not only from mere habitual behavior but also from mere moral ideas, which need exist only in human minds, and which find their expression in books, speeches, or conversations. Constitutional provisions are not moral laws, natural laws, or God's laws; nor are they the notions of Luther, Kant, Rousseau, or Madison, or even the ideas of such philosophers of international relations as Grotius, Vattel, or Suarez, although they may be consistent with, and inspired by, any of these ideas.

Constitutional provisions must not only be legitimate, but they must also generally be adhered to, or their constitutional status—the distinction between mere moral ideas and constitutional provisions—would mean very little. That is, the authority that the norms prescribe must correspond to actual practice. With the UN declaration on colonies came the actual freeing of colonies. Following Westphalia, only states exercised significant power, and they rarely forcibly interfered in one another's religious affairs. The Holy Roman Empire, by contrast, still enjoyed codified constitutional powers after 1648, but states contemptuously ignored these powers; the empire did not practice sovereignty in any meaningful way. With the criterion of practice, we can eliminate as constitutional norms rules that are bare paper provisions. Table 2.1 shows international behaviors that share

TABLE 2.1
Characteristics of International Behavior

Characteristics of Rules	*Legitimate*	*Not Legitimate*
Practiced	Constitutional norms	Patterned behavior (Britain's role as holder of the balance)
Not practiced	Merely formal constitutional provisions (The Holy Roman Empire's sovereign prerogatives after Westphalia)	Normatively unpatterned behavior (Any number of events in international relations; e.g., wars)

various combinations of legitimacy and practice, and it identifies constitutions as possessing both features.

That international constitutions are both legitimate and practiced echoes what many scholars claim about sovereignty, that it has both de jure and de facto aspects. Some dissenters, though, want to define constitutions and sovereignty as matters of mere coercive power. The state's loss of control over trade, communication, multinational corporations, the defense of its borders, and flows of people, money, and drugs across its borders is, to them, the decline, the twilight, the downfall of sovereignty.[28]

For several reasons, I think this judgment is mistaken. First, it elides the insight of constructivist scholars that authority is constituted at least in part by mutual recognition: A state does not practice sovereign powers, for instance, unless it is surrounded by a community of states that recognizes these powers.[29]

Second, we lose the ability to describe situations in which constitutional authority is constant, yet power varies. During three centuries of a European sovereign state system, the holder of hegemony, the polar distribution of power, metamorphosed several times with only occasional changes in the faces of authority. Today, even if state power is challenged by corporations, immigrants, and money flows, these trends have brought little change in constitutional authority. Or, we can imagine Burundi and Japan, two equally sovereign states, that enjoy similar diplomatic privileges, but differ wildly in their economic and military size. Such distinctions would hardly be intelligible if power were inseparable from sovereignty.

Third, an equation of constitutions with power would rob the constitution of its very distinctiveness. It would omit sovereignty's most characteristic feature: that it does not just command obedience, but defines prerogatives, the privileges and roles that make a president a president, not a prince; a state a state, not an empire. It would also make sovereignty something that exists on a continuum, realized to greater and lesser degrees, whereas for most of sovereignty's conceptual history, its articulators have thought it to be the sort of quality that either exists or does not exist. Power, by contrast, ranges across an infinite continuum along which even the most powerful rulers are somewhat limited in what they can do. The extent of this limit will depend on fate, ability, and countless circumstances, military, economic, social, psychological, at home and abroad. To include all of these circumstances in measuring sovereignty would extend the study of sovereignty to all of politics; it would tell us little of unique importance. This is why it is unhelpful to refer to states' loss of control over trade, communication, multinational corporations, and other cross-border flows within recent decades as losses of sovereignty. A state's sovereignty is eroded only when it cannot practice constitutional prerogatives that it legitimately enjoys, not when it loses control over matters that have little to do with its legitimate prerogatives.[30]

Constitutions are not matters of mere power. Nor are they other phenomena with which we should also not confuse constitutions. They are not agreements between already constituted polities, regulating their arms, trade, religion, environment, treatment of criminals, or thousand of other matters, agreements obligating them to perform certain actions under certain conditions, but which do not cede any standing constitutional authority.[31] Most international laws that commit states to arbitration of disputes, and most multilateral organizations, although important to the character of international relations, acquire no constitutional authority from states. The collective security function of the United Nations, for instance, allows states to determine for themselves when they will participate in a war of enforcement, leaving their executive authority completely intact.

We must also distinguish constitutions from their exceptions, aberrations, and violations. Indeed, constitutions can be violated, and can experience aberrations and exceptions, without losing their status as constitutions. When compromised, they nevertheless continue to constitute the authority of polities, the very authority that is compromised.[32] What are some forms of this compromise? Some agreements do cede constitutional authority, but are signed between only two or a few polities, not the collectivity of polities in an international society, and thus fall short of revising an international constitution. Panama leased its Canal Zone to the United States government; nineteenth-century Britain maintained a sphere of influence in China, subject only to limited Chinese governance; the United States maintained the right to intervene in Cuba; the Soviet Union treated Eastern European states as semisovereign satellites according to its Brezhnev Doctrine.[33] All of these are aberrations, not constitutional revisions.

Polities also violate international constitutions. States intervene in other states; medieval barons violated the terms of dukes' authority; perhaps states continue to hold colonies after colonies have become illegitimate. When a polity violates a constitutional norm occasionally, in isolable instances, then the violation is just that, a violation, and not an annulment or revision of the norm. But if there exist revisionist states that reject a norm and constantly violate it, then the norm effectively does not exist—it is not practiced. Revisionist states are powerful states, ones that can prevent the norm's practice or force other states to fight to preserve it. Their existence and their actions mean that at least one major state in the international society does not adhere to one of the society's major norms. Eras of their reign are ones of "contested constitutions," meaning not that the old constitutional norm has been supplanted by a new one, but that no norm elicits general support at all. Although the 1555 Treaty of Augsburg prescribed sovereignty over religious matters within the Holy Roman Empire, neither Catholic nor Protestant powers accepted its terms, and in fact continued literally to invade one another's religious privacy. Only after 1648 was princes' sovereignty over religious practice accepted and respected and practiced. During revolutionary and Napoleonic France and the expansion of Nazi Germany, the prohibition of intervention was constantly violated, while an aspiring empire challenged the state as the legitimate polity. These were times of contested constitutions.

Even when constitutions are respected, though, we should not make the mistake of thinking that they will necessarily be tranquil. International constitutions create international orders, but not necessarily orderliness, or peace. Stable, uncontested constitutions are perfectly compatible with conflict, competition, even the worst sort of death and disaster, cruelty and holocaust, all of which occur within agreed-upon, legitimate norms of authority. Constitutions are often less like the script of a choreographed dance, a routine that performers follow cooperatively, than they are like the rules of a jousting match or bullfight, regulators of deathly competition. They do not eliminate conflict, but structure who fights it, and on what terms.

A final plea against exaggerating the idealism of international constitutions: That constitutions are matters of legitimacy as well as practice, that they involve perceived obligation, implies no conclusion about whether the obligations expressed in treaty and custom are the products of ideas or material circumstances. The point is important, for it would make little sense to argue that international revolutions are the result of new ideas if the answer were already implied in the definition of international constitutions. Ideas are matters of thought; the norms that make up constitutions are matters of word and deed. Whether there is a causal connection between ideas and norms is, at this point, an open question. It could be that legitimacy is little more than legitimation, that expressions of obligation are little more than moral dressing for material interests. Or perhaps polities express constitutional norms as obligation for rule-utilitarian reasons, believing that if the norm is generally followed within the international community, they will best realize their long-term material interests.[34] It is also possible that polities adhere to constitutional norms because their leaders or their publics demand compliance out of their moral beliefs.

Whether they turn out to be reflections of military and economic interests or the creation of new notions, even if their expressed legitimacy amounts to very little, constitutions of international society are still important, if for no other reason than that they have been considered important, in diverse times and places, by Protestants, Catholics, aristocrats, liberals, nationalists, colonists, human rights advocates, and countless other constituencies in the same way that domestic constitutions are important to these same groups. Whether the Holy Roman Empire practices intervention to enforce religious uniformity in the territory of European princes, whether sovereign states enjoy absolute sovereignty, whether colonies are held in empires or achieve independence, or nations may become states, whether the European Union decides the commercial affairs of otherwise sovereign states—these prerogatives can mean political deliverance or ruined destiny for factions, parties, classes, and strata just as can the democratic, monarchical, or constitutional character of domestic regimes. Again, the mere presence of these preferences, these passions, does not translate to efficacy. Analogously, if one agreed with Marx, one can believe that the revolution of the proletariat will be entirely the outworking of underlying shifts in the mode of production, and yet also recognize and sympathize with the proletariat's sense of injustice. Because international constitutions create authority, and because authority is always a matter of great justice and injustice, they have at times elicited great interest from those who seek to influence the course of politics.

So, too, they are worthy of our interest. If we want to understand international relations, we must understand the constitutions that create the very authority structures behind international relations. I have been describing what constitutions of international society and revolutions in sovereignty are—how they constitute authority, how they vary, how they change. We may now ask what actual historical constitutions have looked like. Chapter 3 describes how the three faces of authority have changed, from early modern Europe up through today. It is a brief history of constitutions of international society, of revolutions in sovereignty, since the Middle Ages.

THREE

A BRIEF HISTORY OF CONSTITUTIONS OF INTERNATIONAL SOCIETY IN THE WEST

A PARTNER TO REALIST SKEPTICISM toward international orders is a Realist international history. Machiavelli penned its first modern recitation, looking past controversies over medieval laws of warfare and the authority of the pope or the emperor, to ancient Rome, where he found model polities: well governed, militarily mighty, and prosperous. Since Machiavelli, historians of international politics have told again and again about the rise of states that expanded economically, seized technology to build up armies and navies, and governed themselves efficiently, as well as the fall of states that suffered military collapse, economic atrophy, and administrative desuetude, and conflicts between the rising and the falling.[1]

The relevance of these histories is indisputable. But international constitutions suggest a complementary international history. It is also one of rises and falls, but of authority, not power, authority in the form of Catholic empire, sovereign states, nations, colonies, minorities, the European Union, and the international protection of human rights. It is also one of conflict, but again, of conflict over authority, not material ascendancy. We may tell this history according to its revolutions, those crises in which old constitutions are discarded and new ones established.

Characterizing Revolutions in Sovereignty

In chapter 2, I proposed that a revolution in sovereignty is a major change in at least one of the three faces of authority—who the legitimate polities are, who may become one, and what their prerogatives are. In our history, then, we may characterize history's revolutions by how they redraw the three faces of authority—all of these faces, or some of these faces, in different manners and degrees. Two other standards also help us to describe a constitution. One is its geographic boundaries. Is it global or regional? If regional, where exactly does the region lie? The other standard is vital but imprecise: the constitution's intrinsic significance. Criteria here are much more subjective. One might be, How many people are affected by a constitutional change? On this score, the revolution of colonial independence is perhaps the most significant, for it placed much of Africa, Asia, and Central America under statehood. We could also ask about a constitution's intrinsic justice (or injustice). Colonial freedom, freedom from the rule of the Catholic empire, the diminishing of Catholic authority, the promotion of human rights, or the European Union's centralization of political authority could all be seen as the moral (or immoral) work of a constitution, depending on one's perspective. Or we could judge a constitution by its innovation and its promise of future change. Here, Westphalia and the 1950 founding of the European Coal and Steel Community, the prototype for the European Community, and later, the European Union, rank highly.

Below, I sketch a history of international constitutions for the international society of states as it has evolved since the Middle Ages—first in the West, then globally. My history must be brief; a comprehensive history requires its own volume. I describe summarily the major revolutions in sovereignty, their alteration of the three faces of authority, their geographic scope, and their intrinsic significance. As I mentioned in chapter 2, we could also tell similar histories of international constitutions in Islam, India, ancient Greece, ancient China, and elsewhere.[2] I focus on the West and the comparatively recent, though, because this history tells of the changes that brought the globe to its present condition—a universal system of sovereign states, but one that has begun to fracture. It is the origins of our order in which I am interested.

That today's international constitution both has a long history of development and has begun to encounter breaches over the past century suggests a way of telling the history of constitutional revolutions. That is, as a double movement, one of historical momentum in one direction, then a reversal of that same momentum. In the first movement, the sovereign state system took over Europe, then the world. In the second, sovereignty began to be circumscribed, largely during the twentieth century. Toward sovereignty, away from sovereignty—each movement involves a few major revolutions. It was Westphalia, then colonial independence around 1960, that introduced and globalized the system of sovereign states. It was the rise of minority treaties in the late nineteenth and early twentieth centuries, the founding of the European Coal and Steel Community, and the rise of internationally sanctioned intervention that have come to challenge it. How each revolution revised sovereignty's three faces, and each constitution's geographic boundaries, I summarize in table 3.1. These features, as well as each constitution's intrinsic significance, are then the subject of the brief history that follows.

Toward a System of Sovereign States

A constitution that prescribes a system of sovereign states in its purest form is one that holds that the sovereign state is the sole legitimate form of polity within a society, and that prescribes basic criteria for a polity to be recognized as a sovereign state—usually, that it possess a government that is in control of a people within a territory, and is capable of entering into international agreements. And it posits nonintervention as the basic prerogative of sovereign states. I doubt that such a pure system has ever existed. But something roughly like it emerged at the Peace of Westphalia, then gradually spread outwards, finally becoming globally legitimized and practiced through the revolution of colonial independence in the decade surrounding 1960.

The Revolution at Westphalia

The Peace of Westphalia of 1648 is the origin of modern international relations. In chapter 5, I will defend this claim in more detail. The claim is controversial and begs careful support, with qualifications, through historical nuances. I will point out that the break between the medieval and modern world is not a perfectly neat one. But the essentials of the argument for Westphalia are not hard to summarize. What Westphalia superseded was the Europe of the Middle Ages, at the peak of which no ruler enjoyed supremacy with a territory, no ruler enjoyed sovereignty. Then, out of the diverse and overlapping authorities of the *Respublica Christiana*, there grew up polities whose powers approached sovereignty, in England and France, then in Sweden. But as late as the eve of the Protestant Reformation, the Holy Roman Empire, an institution medieval in form, held significant, but not sovereign, powers in the Netherlands, in Germany, and throughout Central Europe. It was only over the following 130 years of religious wars, culminating in the continental Thirty Years' War, that the powers of the empire to interfere in the affairs of governments within territories were neutralized. The Peace of Westphalia was the settlement that ended this war of three decades, and this crisis of a century.

In several respects, the settlement established the state as the legitimate European polity—the first face of authority. Running as leitmotifs through the settlement were the principles of autonomy and equality for states, and the principle of a European equilibrium, a balance of power, that implied independent action among independent European states. Following the settlement, the Holy Roman Empire continued to exist, but it became largely a deliberative body, little different from a contemporary

TABLE 3.1
Major Constitutional Revolutions Since the Middle Ages

Revolution in Sovereignty	*Revision of First Face*	*Revision of Second Face*	*Revision of Third Face*	*Geographical Boundaries*
Westphalia (1648)	States replace Holy Roman Empire as holders of sovereignty	Polity must have basic characteristics of a state and be Christian	Government within state enjoys absolute sovereignty; nonintervention	Europe
Minority Treaties (1878, post World War One)	League of Nations judicial and oversight functions	Minority agreements criterion for recognition as states	States subject to oversight of minority treatment	Eastern Europe
European Integration (1950, later expanded)	EU institutions "pool" the sovereignty of states	Membership criteria as specified by EU law	States no longer sovereign in areas specified by EU law	European member states
Colonial Independence (early 1960's)	None	Colonies are entitled to statehood	None	Global
Intervention (Post–Cold War)	UN attains executive authority to enforce human rights and justice	None	States subject to outside enforcement of human rights practices	Potentially global

alliance among sovereign states. The authority of the emperor himself was effectively reduced to that of another sovereign, supreme within his central European Habsburg lands. The pope, too, saw his political power eviscerated. One of the settlement's most important provisions decriminalized the right of German princes to ally outside the empire. Elsewhere, statehood was simply recognized. The settlement effectively made the Swiss Confederation independent; a separate treaty recognized the sovereign independence of the Netherlands. Most crucially, Westphalia's prescription for politics and religion helped to ensconce state sovereignty. Although princes signed an international agreement to respect the right to worship of dissenters within their territories, after Westphalia, no authority, neither princes nor the emperor, would intervene to contest religion within another prince's territory. States whose rulers were territorially supreme were now the legitimate polity, prevailing as the new template for political authority in Europe.

What about the second face of authority? The practice of granting new states membership in the states system would become a precedent. By the eighteenth century, the criteria for membership were that new states should have the fundamental attributes of statehood—a viable government, control within their territory, the ability to make and carry out treaties. At the time of Westphalia, a Christian culture was required, too: Russia and Poland, but not the Ottoman Empire, were admitted, and given full diplomatic privileges. This requirement was gradually dropped over the following couple of centuries, as the second face of authority took on its modern form.

By contrast, the third face of authority, like the first face, took its modern form almost immediately after Westphalia. Nonintervention, the key prerogative of sovereign states, was not explicitly stated in the settlement, and would not be openly espoused by lawyers and philosophers until the eighteenth century. But nonintervention became standard and expected state practice as religious war and Habsburg intervention exited European history. Over the following three centuries, nonintervention persisted, not unchallenged, not always respected—both Hitler and Napoleon attempted to overthrow these practices, and many states would intervene—but perduring as normal, expected behavior. It perdures today, even if it is beginning to crack.

Geographically, the Westphalian system was a European system. European states made up the international society that this constitution governed. Its signers—almost all of Europe's powers, 145 in all—explicitly recognized as much, conceiving themselves as the "senate of the Christian world."[3] (The major absentee was England, whose civil war kept it out of the Thirty Years' War.) But if the society of sovereign states' extent was European, its influence and implications were global. Europe's colonies in North America, South America, Africa, and Asia came under the control of sovereign states, making them effective extensions of the system. Europe's trade and war with other parts of the world—Islam, China, and other systems and empires—formed a vast, global "secondary system of sovereign states," to borrow Martin Wight's term.[4] Though most of the globe was not part of a system of sovereign states, most of its polities bore some relationship to one.

Westphalia remains the most significant revolution in sovereignty to date. It revised all three faces of authority, and established constitutional authority in the form of the sovereign states system. This sweep is its most intrinsically significant feature. Westphalia is also significant as a template. Every subsequent constitutional revolution has revised Westphalia, geographically extending the states system, altering the criteria for being recognized as a state, curtailing the state's absolute sovereignty, all making Westphalia a benchmark, a standard, the subject that undergoes change, the thing to be revised. Even the European Union, an alternative to the state as a supranational form of institution, still involves states as states, treating them as constituent polities rather than replacing or wholly subsuming them into something other. Westphalia is also significant as a historical fulcrum. It brought to an end the significant temporal authority of Christendom's rival institutions, the papacy and the Holy Roman Empire, thus consolidating the long decline of the Middle Ages. It established a system of sovereign states that would accrue strength and gradually expand to the rest of the globe. Its just character? It depends on one's perspective. Destroyer of Christian unity, bringer of peace, provider of stability, a stepping-stone to religious pluralism, a carapace that shields sovereign states, even violators of human rights, from outside criticism—all of these labels, its chroniclers have applied.

Westphalia Europe and the Rest of the World

Over the ensuing three hundred years, the history of the sovereign states system is largely the history of Westphalia's geographic extension. Until this extension was completed through the revolution of colonial independence in the 1960s, polities outside the European international society generally held one of three kinds of status in relation to Europe. Some were rivals and trading partners with Europe, but not ruled or monopolized by Europe: the East Indies and China in the seventeenth and eighteenth centuries, the Ottoman Empire up through the nineteenth century. Although Europe shared with these polities at least certain principles like *pact sunt servanda*—the sanctity of treaties—it did not recognize them as states or accord them the privileges of statehood, and neither did these polities, for that matter, grant Europeans equal status. To Ottoman Muslims or the Chinese, Europeans were infidels or vassals.[5] No constitution of international society was mutually, explicitly, agreed upon.

A second category of non-European, nonsovereign polities included those that Europe treated as less than equal, but not as wholly subordinate, such as a colony. In both China and the Ottoman Empire during the last half of the nineteenth century and the first part of the twentieth, in areas of Africa, Asia, and the Middle East such as postindependence Egypt and Iran, in portions of Latin America, in the eastern European states that became independent in the nineteenth century—in all these polities, European powers exercised authority over assorted affairs that Westphalian states normally govern themselves. Europeans partitioned these lands into spheres of influence for trade; they maintained rights to military bases; they governed strategic plots of territory such as the Suez Canal zone;

they took over the collection of debts and customs or even intervened to collect debts; and they exercised other sorts of authority. The rulers of such territories were autonomous in many other matters, but these significant exceptions to their absolute sovereignty, combined with the lack of international assent to their sovereign status, made them less than Westphalian sovereign states.[6]

Wholly ruled, completely subordinated, entirely under the sovereign rule of European states was a third category—colonies, which the British, the French, the Dutch, the Portuguese, the Belgians, the Americans, and the Germans held in the Americas, Asia, the Middle East, and Africa. In effect, colonies were extensions of Westphalian sovereign states. Their rulers were ultimately accountable to European rulers; other European powers could not legitimately intervene in their affairs; and their European rulers could bargain their fate with other European powers. Colonial regions were indeed often the site of wars between European great powers. Of course, the inhabitants of colonies were not treated as equally as the members of metropolitan states, a disparity that only increased as European populations gained the franchise and other rights in the nineteenth and twentieth centuries.

These three categories of polities existed in different proportions at different moments in the three centuries after Westphalia.[7] Over time, the virtual partners declined, while the subordinated and colonized polities of the globe multiplied, culminating in the nineteenth century with the colonization of much of Africa, Asia, Central America, and the Middle East. During these centuries, a few polities also moved up the ladder, some from colonies to subordinate states, some to full membership in the Westphalian system. Many Latin American states became independent in the 1820s, although they were still subject to regular intervention when they defaulted on their loans, and were not included in conferences on peace and international law until the early twentieth century.[8] In the latter decades of the nineteenth century, Eastern European states became independent, although their statehood was subject to agreements regulating their treatment of minorities within their borders. Others advanced to full Westphalian status—the United States in 1783, Canada in 1867, and China and Japan by the early twentieth century, for instance.[9]

But none of these developments was a constitutional revolution. For a polity to advance out of colonial status or become Westphalian, there needed to be no change in membership criteria, no change in the Westphalian constitution; the polity merely acceded according to the set criteria. But did the standards themselves ever change? In one sense the rules for membership, the second face, evolved. European states no longer demanded Christianity, but instead a secularized "standard of civilization" for aspiring states. The standard meant that a polity would not be treated as a full member of the Westphalian system, entitled to nonintervention, allowed fully to govern its own affairs, until it met certain criteria. It had to guarantee basic rights—of life, property, travel, commerce—to both its own people and foreign nations; it had to have an organized government and capacity for self-defense; it had to adhere generally to international law as well as provide a domestic system of justice; it had to maintain diplomatic representation; and, more vaguely, it had to conform to the norms and practices of civilized international society.[10] In practice, such a requirement was little different from the earlier Christian standard. It was at most an evolution, not a revolution, in the international constitution. The second face, like the other faces, remained rather steady into the first half of the twentieth century. Indeed, both the League of Nations and the United Nations, the first global organizations and attempts to institutionalize international law, incorporated the Westphalian rendering of all three faces into their charters.

The Rise of Colonial Independence

The radical revolution in the second face, of authority which permitted all colonies to become full sovereign states, did not arrive until around 1960. I describe this revolution in more detail in chapter 8. As it was similar to Westphalia, though, we can summarize its essentials. As a widening and weakening of the previous criteria for being recognized as a state, the new norm of colonial independence held that colonies were entitled to statehood however weak their government, however scant their control over their territory, however inchoate their people.[11] In international constitutional history, this was the first victory of the principle of self-determination, holding that a people without a state, and aspiring to statehood, is entitled to attain statehood. General colonial independence won legitimacy through a 1960 UN declaration: "All peoples have the right to self-determination," it held. "Inadequacy of political, economic, and social and educational preparedness should never serve as a pretext for delaying independence." The resolution condemned colonialism as "alien subjugation, domination, and exploitation . . . a denial of fundamental human rights."[12] In the surrounding decade, colonial independence was practiced as Britain, France, and Belgium granted independence to the preponderance of their remaining colonies, just as the United States and the Netherlands had freed their colonies during the previous two decades, and as Germany and Spain had lost their empires a good bit earlier. Once independent, colonies became full members of an international society whose terms were now prescribed formally by the United Nations Charter, a constitution that granted states full legal equality.

Like Westphalia, the transition was not divinely neat: Some colonies had already been freed; others would trickle into independence during the next two decades; most egregiously, Portugal clung to Angola and Mozambique. But in the thought, word, and deed of the United Nations and the vast majority of states, including most of the colonial powers, it was now illegitimate for a state to govern a colony. Self-determination, though, had its limits. Only colonies became entitled to statehood, not nations or tribes, either within colonies or within other states.

Colonial independence revised only the second face of authority. The sovereign state remained the legitimate form of polity; and the new states attained all of the privileges of sovereignty. This revolution's geographical scope was one of its most remarkable features. For the first time, the entire globe came under a single international constitution, a sovereign states system. The revolution's intrinsic significance lies in the magnitude of the change required to complete this global extension. In 1914, more than 72,000 square kilometers across Asia, Africa, Latin America, and the Middle East, and more than 560 million people, a third of the world's population, were under colonial rule. Between 1955 and 1970, 78 colonies were released from political dependency, their populations becoming citizens of independent state, not of ruled colonies. To any colonist who regarded his subordination as unjust this new status was a dear acquirement. This is not to ignore what dependency theorists stress—the persistence, perhaps constancy, of structures of economic subordination into the independence era. It is only to say that political independence was far from a legal formality, and indeed entailed a jettisoning of intrinsic subordination, in the eyes of the colonial nationalists who demanded it.[13]

Away from a System of Sovereign States

Through Westphalia in Europe, through the spread of states outward from Europe, through the breakdown of European empires in the revolution of colonial independence, the sovereign state system spread so widely, so thoroughly, that this manner of organizing politics came to cover almost every inch of land on the globe. Today, nearly everyone everywhere belongs to a sovereign state; those who do not are refugees, and that we consider their status exceptional and troubled only testifies to the normalcy of belonging to a state. Toward sovereignty—this is the first movement in the history of postmedieval constitutions of international relations.

The first movement has only recently been consummated. No more than a generation has passed since sovereign statehood was globalized. But even prior to the first movement's completion, a second movement began, fragmentarily in the nineteenth century, more resolutely in the twentieth.

A reversal of momentum, it is the circumscription of sovereignty. This movement has not returned us to the Middle Ages, for it has not replaced or eviscerated the state, but it evokes medieval Christendom in its limitation of state sovereignty on behalf of transnational ideals, here human rights and European unity. This movement has consisted of three major revolutions—the rise of minority treaties in the nineteenth and twentieth centuries; European integration, beginning with the European Coal and Steel Community of 1950 and proceeding through the European Union of today; and the rise of internationally sanctioned intervention following the Cold War. Of the three revolutions, minority treaties have disappeared, while the other two continue in full swing.

Minority Treaties

Sovereigns, as long as they have existed in the West, have committed a certain kind of evil behind their shield of immunity from external constitutional authority: they have persecuted their minorities. As long as sovereigns have abused minorities, they have also encountered critics who would perforate their shield, asking them to answer for, and halt, this practice. European states have received this criticism most notoriously, although they are hardly the exclusive practitioners of the abuse. It is also European national and religious minorities, most egregiously the Jews in Nazi Germany, whose persecution has been recognized most prominently. But, dating from Westphalia itself, European sovereigns have agreed, from time to time, at least on paper, to tolerate certain minorities in their midst, to allow them to practice freely their language, education, and religion. The Treaty of Osnabrück, and then several subsequent treaties during the eighteenth century, granted Catholics, Lutherans, and Calvinists freedom to practice their faith in regions where their faith was neither official nor in the majority. The 1815 Congress of Vienna Final Act, which settled the Napoleonic Wars, for the first time made special provisions for a national minority, the Poles, who were stranded in Austria, Prussia, and Russia after losing their own state in 1795.[14]

While important in the history of minority treatment, such agreements rarely limited sovereignty, and thus hardly amended the constitution of international society. In chapter 2, I stress that far from all agreements among states amount to constitutional amendments, but only those that alter states' constitutional authority. An agreement making respect for minorities a condition of statehood would be such an amendment, this one a revision of the second face of authority. An agreement creating a standing international body to monitor and adjudicate minority treatment would also qualify, this one as a revision of the first and third faces of authority. The agreements up through the Congress of Vienna did neither.

When Britain, France, and Russia granted independence to Greece in an 1830 protocol, Britain imposed the condition that Greece protect the religious rights of Turks. In the Treaty of Paris in 1865, Britain, France, and Austria-Hungary, the victors of the Crimean War, mandated similar conditions upon Moldova and Wallachia, who became independent under the suzerainty of the Ottoman Empire. But it was not until 1878 that all of the major European powers—Britain, France, Prussia, Russia, Austria-Hungary, and the Ottoman Empire—agreed that minority protection would be a normal requirement placed on new European states. The 1878 Congress of Berlin granted independence to Serbia, Montenegro, Romania, and Bulgaria (the latter as a tributary state to the Ottoman Empire) on the condition that these states protect their religious minorities, mostly Jews and Muslims. It required the Ottoman Empire to respect the rights of Armenians as well. The trend culminated in the settlement of World War I, which included several provisions to protect minorities. With both the defeated states, Austria, Hungary, Bulgaria, and Turkey, as well as with the new or enlarged states, including Poland, Czechoslovakia, Yugoslavia, Rumania, and Greece, the victorious allies signed treaties that guaranteed minority rights. It thus was in 1878 at Berlin, and then in the treaties that ended World War I, that minority provisions first fulfilled the conditions of international constitutional change. They revised the second face of authority, the conditions for becoming a member of the international society. In the League of Nations Covenant, the victors of World War I also created a provision to guarantee the rights of "racial, religious, or linguistic minorities," to be monitored and enforced through a League judicial arbitration system. As states were now regularly subject to the oversight of a standing international body, and as their authority over their minority affairs was subject to outside restriction, the League provisions revised the first and third faces of authority as well.[15]

These minority treaties were a constitutional norm, but a limited one. Limited in geography: They were applied only by European states, and only to aspirants to statehood in Eastern Europe. Britain and France, for instance, never consented to international oversight of their treatment of the Irish or the Basques. They were limited also in time; by the mid-1930s, Poland and Germany had renounced their treaty obligations, and by World War II the treaties were defunct. Viewing minority rights schemes as a failure, the framers of the United Nations Charter did not aspire to recreate such a system.

What of the treaties' intrinsic significance? In some respects, this was limited, too. They restricted only a small portion of new states' constitutional powers, leaving these states nonabsolute, but nearly absolute in their sovereignty. The great powers' enforcement of these provisions was also weak. From 1894 on, the Turks killed Armenians with impunity; in 1915, they massacred a million. Nor did the powers enforce the rights of Jews, who were denied citizenship in Romania. Under the League arbitration scheme, many conflicts over minorities were successfully resolved, yet prominent persecution of minorities continued, especially in Poland.[16] In the history of the international constitution, though, the treaties are conceptually important. In their abridgment of absolute sovereignty lies a recognition that state governments ought to be accountable for the treatment of their individual citizens. Although minority treaties would not reappear, during the second half of the century an expanded concept asserted the same accountability, but much more broadly and robustly. This is universal human rights, the legatee of minority rights.[17]

The Return of European Unity

If Westphalia's significance lies in its revision of each of the three faces of authority, all toward the abolition of medieval European unity and its replacement with separate sovereign states, then the most significant revolution in the movement away from sovereignty is one that also revised all three faces, but toward the restoration of this unity. Such was the 1950 creation of the European Coal and Steel Community, which later expanded into the European Community and eventually the European Union. This institution's legal powers have always been defined through treaties signed by its member states, treaties whose explicitness and thoroughness make them the sort of constitution of international society that most resembles a domestic constitution. The 1991 Maastricht Treaty, which reconfigured the institution as the European Union, is the most recent version. It is a constitution that coexists with the larger international society of sovereign states of which its members are still a part.

For the first time since the demise of the Holy Roman Empire, a significant political authority other than the state, one with formal sovereign prerogatives, became legitimate within the boundaries of the Westphalia system—a revision of the first face of authority. The European Union does not replace states, but rather "pools" their sovereignty into a common "supranational" institution in which they no longer make decisions independently.[18] The union's constitution creates executive, legislative, and judicial powers. The European Commission, a largely executive arm, is the part of the union that operates most independently of states, proposing legislation and administering the union's day-to-day affairs through a large bureaucracy. The Council of Ministers, which votes the union's most important laws into existence, consists of states, but ones that no longer have individual veto power over the council's decisions, an important limit on their sovereignty. The members of the European Parliament, also legislative but not nearly as powerful as the council, are selected directly by popular vote, bypassing state governments altogether. Finally, through the European Court of Justice, whose rulings stand authoritative within member states, the union asserts judicial authority.

As for the second face of authority, the union's constitution prescribes definite criteria for membership, including a well-defined regimen for application. Under such criteria, the union has expanded from its original six members in 1950 to fifteen today.

Defining the third face of authority, the constitution also carefully apportions prerogatives over decision making in matters of trade, monetary policy, market regulation, and other matters among the member states and the various union institutions. The constitution, again, is sovereign not because it replaces the authority of the state, but because it is the root document that distributes prerogatives among the member states and the separate institutions of the union. Its sovereignty, though, is limited to the areas that it governs—trade, money, the market, and others, but not defense or education or health care. Both its sovereignty and the sovereignty of its member states are less than absolute.

The geographic extent and intrinsic significance of this constitution of international society are simpler matters. Its borders are its member states' borders, whoever and wherever these members are. Its intrinsic significance amounts to the amalgamated advantages and disadvantages of the amalgamation of governance. The economies of scale, the growth of the union's market, the resultant global clout in trade and foreign policy, any benefit of centralization—all are relevant, and all are controversial, as attested by the slim margins by which popular referenda on the Maastricht Treaty passed in France and Denmark. Less disputable is the significance of the innovation—the sweep of a revolution that revises all three faces of sovereignty, the novelty of a twentieth-century international organization that not only includes, but also transcends, its member states.

Internationally Sanctioned Intervention

Since the end of the Cold War, a new revolution has begun to take place, one that also crucially, historically revises Westphalia, in this case by abridging the most essential prerogative of states: nonintervention. Not envisioned or anticipated by the states that have cooperated to bring it about, the revolution has come piecemeal, through episodes. It is in several separate instances that the United Nations or another international organization has sanctioned what may broadly be called intervention: the dispatch of military troops to remedy an injustice within the boundaries of a state, or the administration of typically domestic matters from the outside. The military force has lacked the consent of the target state's government or of one of the parties in a civil war, thus departing from previous

UN peacekeeping operations, in Cyprus, Palestine, and elsewhere, where the consent of all warring parties was a prerequisite. What are the purposes of the new interventions? They vary, but have included the delivery of humanitarian supplies, the ending of civil war, the enforcement of democratic elections, the rebuilding of failed state institutions, and the arrest of war criminals. And where have they taken place? The venues have included Iraq, the former Yugoslavia, Bosnia, Kosovo, Somalia, Rwanda, Haiti, Cambodia, Liberia, and elsewhere.[19]

These interventions represent new conditions that the United Nations places on states' sovereignty, making them accountable to a higher authority for upholding certain standards of civilized behavior.[20] In this sense, the interventions revise the constitution of international relations. Through them, the United Nations and other international organizations—the North Atlantic Treaty Organization (NATO), the European Union, and others—have accrued the executive power to intervene in states' internal affairs under certain conditions. This is the first face revised. But it is only in a weak sense that these institutions are alternative polities to the state. Unlike the European Union, whose commission, court, and parliament all transcend the powers of the member states, the United Nations and NATO depend heavily on their member states for their decisions. The United Nations requires the unanimous assent of the permanent members of the Security Council for its decisions; NATO depends heavily on its most powerful members; in the foreign policy of the European Union, too, it is a handful of states that most influence intervention, an activity which the organization has only recently undertaken. In some cases—Haiti in 1993 and Rwanda in 1994, for instance—the international organization only authorized an intervention, leaving a single state to carry it out. But significantly, states have still acted through these institutions, at least to gain legitimacy, and often to elicit cooperation in sending troops and paying for them. It is in this sense that the institutions are notable new participants in intervention.

Much stronger is what intervention implies for the third face of authority. Certain states, under certain conditions, when they fail to uphold certain standards of justice—usually peace, order, basic human rights—are subject to the intervention of outside states that act in cooperation with an international authority. The target states are no longer absolute in their sovereignty. In the history of international constitutions, this trend is quite significant, for it departs from nonintervention, perhaps the most enduring and prominent tenet of the Westphalian settlement. Nonintervention's most recent historical articulation occurs in the UN Charter, which states the principle more than once, and in subsequent UN resolutions and declarations.[21] Throughout the Cold War, nonintervention remained robust as a norm, even if violated in practice. The United Nations consistently refrained from endorsing actual interventions, including unilateral interventions to end humanitarian disasters in Uganda, Cambodia, and Bangladesh.

It is not through an amendment to the United Nations Charter that the intervention now takes on legitimacy, but rather through successive UN resolutions and decisions by NATO and the European Union. The first major departure was Security Council Resolution 688 in April 1991, authorizing intervention against Iraq to stop its oppression of its Kurdish minority at the end of the Persian Gulf War. Although Resolution 688 fails to invoke Chapter VII, the portion of the UN Charter crucial for military enforcement, it authorized novelly intrusive actions, namely the delivery of humanitarian supplies without the consent of Saddam Hussein, Iraq's ruler.[22] A sharper cleft was Security Council Resolution 794 in December 1992, which authorized a multilateral force under Chapter VII to protect the delivery of supplies to relieve starvation in Somalia. For the first time, the United Nations sent a large military force on a humanitarian mission without obtaining the open consent of the target state's government; for the first time the Security Council counted a humanitarian crisis as the sort of threat for which Chapter VII could be invoked to justify force; and for the first time, the United Nations committed itself to rebuild a state's government without the approval of local warring parties or influential neighboring powers.[23] Further resolutions, toward Bosnia, Haiti, Rwanda, and other sites of calamity, have continued this precedent.

Intervention's significance as a transgression of Westphalia must be balanced by a recognition of its limits. First, although the entire globe is now potentially fair game for intervention—the norm is global in this sense—the intervention has been limited and selective. Depending on exactly how one interprets intervention, it has been practiced within somewhere between 5 and 15 states since the end of the Cold War, out of a total of over 190 states in the world. Intervention has failed to occur, too, in many states—Sudan, for instance—with injustices quite similar to those where it has occurred—Somalia, for example. Second, intervention is legitimate in the normative, constitutional sense only when authorized by the UN Security Council, or perhaps by NATO or some other international organization. Intervention is far from a unilateral prerogative. Third, the legitimacy of the intervention is not universal. Countries like China often dissent, although China has notably refrained from using its veto power as a Permanent Member of the Security Council to block any of the post–Cold War interventions.[24] Fourth, in most cases of intervention, the Security Council has justified its action as a response to a "threat to international peace and security," rather than explicitly citing an internal injustice, a signal of its refusal openly to label its actions intervention or to depart radically from its traditional interpretation of the charter. The justification is implausible, for the conflicts and injustices eliciting intervention were all primarily internal, but it does reveal the United Nations' reluctance to endorse a general doctrine of intervention.[25] Finally, it is not clear how robustly the post–Cold War precedent of intervention will continue. The interventions thus far have enjoyed mixed success; the practice is far from a durable fixture in a new world order. Despite these caveats, however, intervention—widely endorsed and significantly practiced—now seems well within the legitimate authority of the Security Council and other organizations.

Is Change in the International Constitution Really "Revolutionary"?

These are the revolutions that have created the constitution of international society as it exists today. Since they deal with sovereignty, first establishing it, then beginning to retract it, I have called them revolutions in sovereignty. They amount to a kind of history of international relations, one whose events and landmarks are changes in constitutional authority.

But might one question the events and landmarks, the revolutions, that I have chosen? Have I erroneously omitted any? Certainly, international constitutional history is far too neatly told as a story of these occasional revolutions, separated by perfect tranquillity, stability, and consistency of obedience. Most of the interim turbulence, though, we can account for as violations, exceptions, aberrations, and periods of contestation, as I explained in chapter 2. Yet there have been a few agreements that I have not mentioned whose establishment of basic authority, whose legitimacy and practice among a society of several states, make them constitutional norms. Often, though, their transferal of authority was too minor to merit discussion. An example is the European Convention on Human Rights, whose judicial powers originated in 1953 and expanded through subsequent protocols, but whose accomplishments extend little farther than banishing the spanking of British schoolchildren and a few other altered legal procedures in a handful of its member states.[26] Still others have proved more constitutionally significant, but were short-lived. The Concert of Europe of conservative great powers following the Napoleonic Wars, for instance, agreed to intervene jointly against domestic liberal revolutions, but it failed to practice this executive power beyond about seven years after it had agreed to exercise it.[27] Other constitutional revisions have achieved strong political support, but never the broad agreement among states to become constitutional provisions. Self-determination outside the colonial context is an example of this—a revolution that minorities around the globe have hoped for, but which has never been realized.[28] All such stories—of smaller revisions, of revisions that were not—would be included in a more comprehensive history of international constitutions.

Perhaps, though, the error is one of commission. That is, I have exaggerated in calling certain constitutional shifts "revolutionary" when they were in fact evolutionary. Westphalia's roots lay in the development of the state since medieval times and in the wars of the Protestant Reformation, which had raged for 130 years. The minority treaties as a constitutional revolution spread from 1878 to the 1920s. Colonial independence arose from decades of discontent and its organization. Can these long developments be revolutions? Now revolution and evolution are in fact hard to distinguish. The French Revolution, according to Tocqueville, was the result in part of two centuries of monarchical centralization; natural evolution, scientists now tell us, proceeded through short, intense periods of change, then stasis. The length of its historical roots, however, is not what makes a change revolutionary. Rather, it is a matter of how explosive, convulsive, and sharp the change is. Each of the above constitutional shifts indeed arose out of a crisis, often a major war, sometimes a major upheaval in the international system. This is their revolutionary nature. Westphalia came out of the Thirty Years' War, Europe's most destructive conflict prior to the twentieth century. Colonial independence came out of World War II and the intense fighting and protest in the colonies after the war. The European Coal and Steel Community was founded soon after World War II. Minority treaties came out of European great-power wars in the nineteenth century and after World War I. Finally, intervention has come out of the major changes wrought by the end of the Cold War. In most of these cases, too, the actual constitutional change, however far back lay its roots, occurred in a rather discrete moment—sovereign statehood at Westphalia, decolonization through a 1960 UN declaration and a decade of sweeping grants of independence, European integration through a founding moment, and intervention through a series of frequent instances beginning in 1990. Minority treaties were admittedly more staggered: 1878 and 1919–1920 were two important episodes. But concentration is still typical. Once a revolution has occurred, it may then unfold in stages; intervention continues episodically, the European Union evolves. But the initial revolutionary change typically happens in a crisis and in a moment, not through a long, gradual, incremental, corrosive evolution.

The episodes of constitutional changes that compose the story of sovereignty, then, are episodes of revolutions. I have described these revolutions as a double movement, the first toward sovereignty, the second away from it. It is with the first movement that the rest of this book is concerned. How did we come to have a sovereign states system, this pervasive, deeply structuring, ubiquitous organizing principle, one that covers virtually every inch of territory on the globe except the polar icecaps, amounting to the strongest candidate today for a principle that is actually agreed upon and practiced by the entire world? The system's subjection to challenge over the past century, leaving us to wonder how long it will last, how absolute it will remain, lends all the more urgency to the task of finding out how it came to be, and what historical forces lay beneath it. If we know how it arrived, we may know better how it might retreat. The question of its arrival is the one that I will attempt to answer in the following chapters. In chapter 4, I describe a central historical force behind the revolutions: potent, subversive ideas.

FOUR

HOW REVOLUTIONS IN IDEAS BRING REVOLUTIONS IN SOVEREIGNTY

IF REVOLUTIONS IN SOVEREIGNTY create new international constitutions, orders that empower or diminish princes, empires, colonies, nations, minorities, and intervening authorities, if they legitimate fresh ideologies and novel notions of justice, this hardly means that ideas or philosophies themselves bring the revolutions about. We cannot summarily dismiss ideas—at the scene of the revolution, they are usually loitering about in the writings and speeches of philosophers and publicists; we suspect them guilty of committing the act. But the evidence is at best circumstantial; the presence of ideas does not alone prove their influence. It could equally be true that princes earn their sovereignty only by marshaling enough troops and revenue to defeat a resistant emperor, or that colonies become free only when they become too costly, too restive, in the eyes of their metropoles. Armies and navies, territory, population, wealth, classes, factions, bureaucracies that can raise taxes and troops—these are the real phenomena behind international revolutions, while ideas are simply chroniclers or expressions of the movements of these forces. This is the view of skeptics who place their bets on the international distribution of military and economic power, the array of social classes, the character of political institutions. All of these structures constrain and enable people whose ends are economic gain and political advancement, and explain important historical events without referring to ideas, discourse, or reflection. Structural Realism is one of these theories; for international events, it is our principal skeptic. All forms of structural skepticism, though, are our leery interlocutors as we ask for international revolutions what scholars have thought entirely natural to ask about the French, American, Russian, and Chinese revolutions: Were ideas a central cause?

If ideas were a central cause, then how did they operate? How were they a mechanism of contradiction, creators of crises of pluralism? How it is that iconoclastic ideas move from the heads of intellectuals to international orders? To describe the effects of ideas, I offer a "framework of ideas" that models their workings. It consists of two "roles of ideas," each a different social dynamic by which ideas exert influence on politics. The first role of ideas is to convert people to new identities, leading them to want new political ends. Second, ideas wield social power, coaxing heads of state to pursue new courses. Converting to new identities, wielding social power—a sound account of revolutions in sovereignty must incorporate both roles. Such a framework echoes the commitments of international relations scholars who are now known as "constructivists." Like constructivism, it envisions the interests of states not as fixed or given, but as shaped from within the domestic realm and through diplomatic interaction; and it proposes that ideas, not just material forces, are the source of this shaping.

But ideas are not the only source of contradictions. Just as Marx, the materialist, stood Hegel, the idealist, on his head, what I will call "structural" theories offer alternatives to the two roles of ideas. Structural theories have old pedigrees, rooted in Realism, Marxism, and Durkheim's thought, and in modern variants, such as many works in the rational-choice school. Their insights cannot be ignored, and are indeed indispensable for explaining revolutions in sovereignty. But their sufficiency I dispute. Neither are ideas the sole cause of change, but they are crucial; ideas do not freely remake the world in their own image, but they are inestimably effectual. Ideas are a form of power, and are often a partner to other forms of power—and this, in intricate ways.

In this chapter, I describe the framework consisting of the two roles of ideas. I present first the claims and workings of the first role of ideas, then describe the reply of structural skepticism to these claims. Next, I do the same for the second role of ideas. I finally address the question, In the web of events leading to a revolution, how do we discern the skein of ideas' influence? Here, I take up matters of method and inference.

Interest and Power: What Any Account of International Revolutions Must Explain

The proximate cause of revolutions in sovereignty is the policies and pursuits of polities—states, empires, nations, or colonies, acting as collectivities, spoken for by their heads. It was states and semisovereign principalities and provinces that waged war and diplomacy for a European system of sovereign states; it was victorious states and a defeated empire that negotiated the Peace of Westphalia; it was states that relinquished their colonies; it was colonies that fought states to achieve relinquishment; it was states that agreed to the UN resolution on the freedom of colonies. Any account of revolutions in sovereignty must, then, explain how these polities come to have an interest in new constitutions of international society. By interest, I mean a general long-term goal that the polity actively pursues through diplomacy, war, and other means of statecraft. Here, the goal is realizing a new international constitution. The active pursuit is important; an interest is not merely a desideratum that leaders or their underlings express. To say that a polity has an interest in a constitution is to say that it intends and acts to bring it about.[1]

It is most importantly through explaining the interests of polities in revolutions in sovereignty that I will explain the actual revolutions. It is mainly these interests for which the two roles of ideas will account. It is true that the interests of polities do not explain revolutions entirely. The revolutions are, after all, international, meaning that once polities develop their interest in a new international constitution, they must still defeat other polities that oppose it and forge an agreement with those who support it. In the case of Westphalia, for instance, I will explain first, most importantly, how France, Sweden, the German states, and the Dutch provinces developed their interest in a system of sovereign states, but then how they went on to win this system through military victory over the Holy Roman Empire and its allies. The interest is most central. Here, an agent (a polity) takes on the crucial intention needed to bring about the crucial end (the revolution, the constitution). The interest of polities is the explanatory prize that any account covets.

That polities have interests, of course, says nothing about why they have interests. Their interests may be shaped by ideal or material forces, acting from within the polity, or in its international environment. Identifying these forces is also the charge of any explanation of revolutions in sovereignty. We ask of it, then, an account of power: What sort of power shapes these interests and enables polities to pursue them against opponents and achieve the revolution? Structural theories would claim relevance only for the international distribution of material power, or for economic, institutional, and technological forces. A theory of ideas holds that ideas themselves may be a form of power.

All of this I am about to describe in more detail. But I want to stress that my concepts of interest and power are open-ended. Interest cannot simply be equated with material interests, or power with material power—an equation Realists often make. Ideas are not opposed to something else called "interests," but instead are one force that may shape interests. Or may not, if the structural skeptics are right. Interests themselves may have any content. Similarly, power may include economic, military, and political power, but may also include ideas themselves.[2]

Two Roles of Ideas

My claim for the influence of ideas evokes old debates among sociologists, philosophers, political scientists, and psychologists. Karl Marx, for instance, argued that ideas about religion, politics, and philosophy are part of a contingent superstructure built by the real interests of humans, interests rooted in material activity and reflected in their class position.[3] Half a century later, Weber replied that no, it is not only our material interests that motivate us, but also other interests such as religious salvation, and that ideas, like railroad switchmen, can steer how we pursue these interests.[4] Traditions of theorists have since concocted eclectic treatments of ideas, some of them sharp and intuitive, like Weber's railroad switchman, others complexly charged with discourses, symbols, and construction. Over the past decade, ideas have experienced a revival in the field of political science. Within the international relations discipline, scholars have turned to ideas to account for trade and development policy, military doctrine, macroeconomic policy, foreign aid, intervention, the end of the Cold War, and sundry other events and phenomena. Constructivism is integral to the trend.[5]

My framework of ideas rests within the trend as well, drawing from it, continuing it. The framework consists of two roles of ideas. Each role is a manner in which ideas exert influence. First, *ideas shape identities*—mass identities across several societies—through the reasoned reflection of their holders. Skeptics of the first role hold that both ideas and identities are shaped by something else—one's class position, position in the division of labor, or a biologically based need for identity. To answer this skepticism, the first dynamic must show the *autonomy* of ideas—its cardinal criterion.

But to influence the interests of polities, ideas must also become *forms of social power.* This is the second role, which explains how converts to new identities mold political interests. Crucially, converts organize themselves—into parties, lobbies, cell groups, congregations, armies—to translate their commitments into costs and benefits for the head of the polity, the one who sets the polity's interest and pursues the policies that the ideas demand. These costs and benefits come in traditional political currencies—money, offices, votes, the prospect of violence. Skeptics of this role do not deny that ideas might shape ends, but they do deny the influence of those whose ends have been shaped by ideas. They question the *efficacy* of ideas—the criterion of the second role.

The two dynamics are distinct, but collaborative. Scholars of ideas often draw upon one or the other, but both are necessary to capture fully the rich road that ideas trod from minds to international orders. The first rests upon a conception of the person; the second is a claim about social power. The first is about influence and persuasion, the second about incentives. The first is discursive—ideas arrive through ethos and pathos, through suasion clothed in the pages of books, the spectacles of pedagogues, the robes of preachers, the rhetorical seductions of orators, the didactics of parents and grandparents. The second is mechanical—ideas push forward through the gears and levers of coercion, through the threats of lobbies to withhold support, through the threats of citizens and legislators to rebel

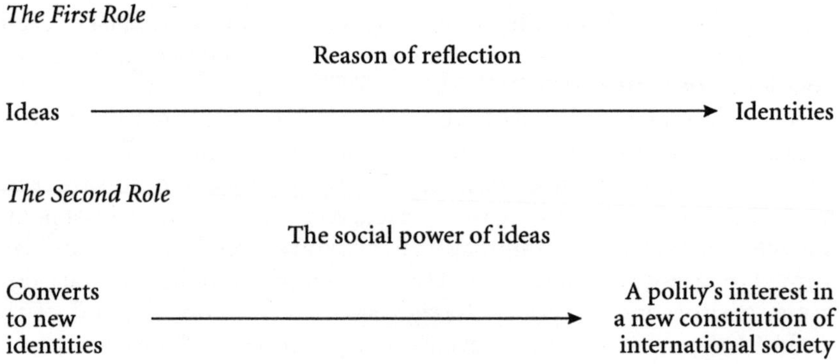

Fig. 4.1. The Two Roles of Ideas

or to withhold votes, taxes, or the willingness to be conscripted, through the potential of bureaucrats to stifle, hold up, and put aside. Absent both dynamics, an ideas account would be incomplete. Max Weber's famous thesis that Protestantism helped bring about capitalism would be greatly weakened if Protestantism itself were shown to be a passive offshoot of the rising bourgeoisie. And even if Luther's theology is the cause of Protestantism, this hardly means that religious ideas went on to influence politics or economics. I summarize the two roles in figure 4.1.

The two roles of ideas each echo the commitments of "constructivist" scholars. In explaining how interests are shaped, some constructivists match the first role of ideas in accounting for the very transformation of identities. Far more, though, stress how actors or institutions whose identities are defined by ideology and culture then exert social power to shape the interests of the state, as in the second role of ideas.[6] My own framework acknowledges and combines the two strands. Like constructivists, my account also takes issue with those rationalist theories–neorealism and neoliberalism–that assume that states have fixed identities and interests, usually material, and that they pursue these interests through rational end-means calculations. Rather, the identities and interests of states are shaped through their social environment.[7] But we should not draw too sharply the contrast with rationalist accounts, sophisticated versions of which take into account the role of identities, norms, and social contexts.[8] It is only those rationalist theories that take a structural materialist form which constructivism, and my own account, distinctly challenge. Most accounts of the formation of the state and the states system indeed express such a materialist rationalism.

In one respect, though, I propose to extend the constructivist agenda; that is, by explaining international constitutive normative structures, here, the structure of sovereign constitutional authority, as the result of the actions of agents, here, states. Constructivists, though they recognize the importance of sovereignty as a constitutive norm, typically treat it as a determinant and context, not a product, of state identities and behavior.[9] There are exceptions, most prominently Rodney Bruce Hall's *National Collective Identity*, which traces the relationship between national identity and the international system from early modern Europe through the First World War. Broadly sympathetic to Hall, my argument focuses in depth on what he calls "territorial sovereignty" and its origins in the Protestant Reformation, an event that he treats, but far more briefly.[10] Friendly commentators on constructivism call for just the sort of theoretical development that authors like Hall have begun, and which I seek to further: Jeffrey Checkel urges an explanation of how agents shape normative structures; Janice Thomson commends an account of the origins of norms of sovereignty.[11]

The First Role of Ideas: Shaping Identities

The first role of ideas is to convert people to new identities. There must first be an intellectual revolution for there to be a political revolution, a crisis of pluralism for there to be a revolution in sovereignty. In the intellectual revolutions discussed here, it is not just handfuls of individuals who convert, but wide social swaths—classes, regional sectors, intellectual strata. Before these swaths can wield the power of ideas over politics, they must arrive at the ideas in the first place. This arrival is what the first role describes.

The claim that ideas shape identities implies a conception of the person whose identity ideas can shape. It is a reflective conception, as I will describe. This parallels every structural theory's similar reliance, implicit or explicit, upon a notion of the person whom structure influences: Marx's material person, or rational choice theory's maximizer, with his fixed, ordered preferences. The first role also harbors a conception of power that contrasts with the traditional political science notion of coercion—the ability of *A* to get *B* to do what *B* would otherwise not do—and is more like the power of persuasion, the ability of people to bring others to revise their beliefs.[12] The power of ideas to persuade through reflection asserts, against structural theories, that ideas are autonomous.[13]

Reason of Reflection

Identity is what people value in accordance with their chosen role.[14] It is not necessarily their congenital traits. Religion, gender, nationality, class, and family are to some degree alterable, and do not alone determine how a person lives. Is a woman "traditional" or a "feminist"? If a man was born a Protestant, has he remained one, or has he converted to Catholicism or dropped religion altogether? I am concerned with political identity. Are we colonial nationalists? Opponents of the Holy Roman Empire? But if identity is alterable, neither is it ephemeral mental flirtation, casually and regularly assumed or discarded. To adopt an identity, to say I *am* a Jew, I *am* a conservative, is to commit to holding, and continuing to hold, this belief. And often it is not just a commitment to my own destiny, but also to the peers I choose—other Jews or conservatives—and to a view of myself as a part of a particular "we" that is distinct from a certain "they."[15]

That ideas form identities may seem like common sense. Or even true by definition: Do not ideas themselves compose identities? We can better see the meaningfulness of the causal claim, though, if we understand it as a claim about how people form their identities: That is, through reflection upon the very propositions of ideas. Put this way, it is much less obvious that ideas form identities, especially considering the manifold moderns who have sought scientifically to discover processes and influences, social, biological, and psychological, by which they could explain identities and even ideas themselves better than could those philosophers of the Enlightenment and earlier who still believed in an individual whose created nature is to act reflectively, deliberately, and rationally. Answering the challenge of the moderns returns us to this older conception of the person.[16]

This conception centers reflection. We are capable of reflecting upon ourselves, standing apart from any of our commitments, questioning their value, and revising them. We adopt identities into our identity, make them our own, because we find them more true, more just, more beautiful, a better account of empirical, moral, or spiritual reality, or a more effective means to one of our ends. We adopt ideas because of the intrinsic appeal of their propositions. I will call this "reason of reflection." Reason of reflection implies that we are autonomous, that we are agents, rational and free. It holds plausible that people adopt ideas into their identity upon reflection, deciding to value them over the long term. To accept reason of reflection is to trust the first-person standpoint: People may well adopt ideas for the reasons they think they do.

That we are capable of reason of reflection does not mean that we always engage in it or that it is the only way we form our identities. We may adopt an identity as an instrument to wealth, power, or social acceptance; we may be socialized into an identity quite passively. Reason of reflection, to the extent that we engage in it, also does not mean that we totally invent our identities or construct them de novo. We typically choose from a culturally bestowed menu of ideas, accepting, rejecting, and modifying them, but usually not inventing them.

This anthropology—stressing reason of reflection as a complex and partial cause of identity formation—reflects what I believe to be an accurate description of the person. But it says little about when or how often people reason reflectively. One could accept this description, yet still claim to explain historical identity shifts—the Protestant Reformation, colonial nationalism—by assuming that people act upon some other impulse: their desire for wealth, and so on. Reason of reflection is a hypothesis.

Though a mental process, reason of reflection brings about a social end, conversion of swaths of people. How it does this is complex and historically situational, but it involves two general stages. First, "entrepreneurs of ideas"—Martin Luther, John Calvin, colonial nationalist intellectuals—*create* new ideas, or new versions or applications of existing ideas. Their reflection is perhaps the purest; they change their identities through their own mental toil. In a second stage, these entrepreneurs persuade others, who then persuade still others, through discussion, writings, and speeches. If the first stage is "creation," we may call this one "diffusion." Its requisite feature is that the persuaded engage in reason of reflection. Only for a few, then—usually, intellectuals—does reflection approach invention. Others adopt ideas that others present to them.[17]

The Role of Circumstances

Now after meditating a bit on ideas in history, we may think the autonomy of ideas naive. Even if structures do not awe us, we still surmise that ideas do not arise out of nowhere, but always come out of some set of circumstances. Ideas about religion, the nation, and generally politics have varied strikingly, and we suspect that whether ideas are heard or ignored, whether they remain well tuned and vibrant or become rusty and dilapidated, has much to do with a society's commerce, industry, and production, its means of communication, its discourses and its literature, the state of its universities, and its history. The threat of circumstances to the first role of ideas is that they annul, act in lieu of, reason of reflection. But do they?

Circumstances are complex. The term is amorphous and encompassing; it denotes diverse phenomena with eclectic links to reason of reflection. I want to propose, though, a kind of circumstance that is an apprentice, not an alternative, to the autonomous energy of ideas. It not only leaves reason of reflection intact, but it can even be evidence for it. It is what I will call a "circumstance of reflection." I define it as *an event, institution, discourse, or practice that helps ideas to develop, lends appeal to ideas' intrinsic propositions, assists the transmission of ideas, and encourages the perpetuation of ideas, all without imposing ideas on the individual's identity, but instead leaving the ideas for the individual to adopt into one's own identity reflectively.*

One sort of circumstance of reflection is historical events. Happenings and experiences, often in the form of salient moral failures, are kindling for novel politics, philosophy and science.[18] World War II, for instance, galvanized both the human rights movement and colonial nationalism. The Great Depression bore Keynesianism; alleged late medieval Catholic decadence begot Protestantism. Historical events loosen orthodoxies, spur or shock minds, make plausible new hypotheses.

Institutions are also a circumstance of reflection. Universities, schools, churches, organizations, lobbies, international organizations, and government bureaucracies, through their literature, official documents, theology, curricula, and organizational cultures, act as "holding tanks," repositories that maintain ideas for people to reflect upon and adopt. Institutions may also foster fertile environments for new ideas. In these ways, institutions are conduits; through them ideas spread, are encouraged, and are perpetuated.

When enough people hold and repeat the ideas, they become a new shared cultural reality, or what Peter Berger and Thomas Luckmann called "social facts."[19] This very mutual acceptance, this embedment in a common culture, can then promote the further reflective spread of the ideas. That is, ideas as a social fact can themselves be a circumstance of reflection. A group is now a Protestant community, a colony with a national destiny that aspires to independence, or a state where human rights are a going concern. Now fixed, like a statue in a town square, ideas are available for further reflection.

Circumstances of reflection are evidence of reflection. Where there is a major shift in social identities, the presence of historical events, institutions, and social facts that are favorable to the ideas reveals that shifting identities were the work of reflection. These circumstances constitute such evidence because they are the kind of conditions that accompany and foster reason of reflection. When and where they occur, it is likely that reflection, too, occurs.[20] Now it may be unclear and debatable that any particular circumstance is a circumstance of reflection. An institution, for instance, might be a conduit of ideas, or might be the political structure that "imposes" ideas upon its members. This ambiguity is a problem for the analyst—a problem to be solved prior to investigation of actual historical phenomena—although it is not a unique problem for ideas-based explanations. It is equally incumbent upon the rational choice theorist or the Marxist to show why he thinks a particular structure operates by guiding the materially minded toward a particular idea. The burden of the analyst is that for any circumstance of reflection, prior to empirical explanation, one must explain how the circumstance indeed aids reflection and does not act as a material structure.

Structural Skepticism of Ideas' Influence upon Identities

If people did not act upon reason of reflection, ideas would not be free vehicles moving into identities on their own energy, but languid passengers aboard other kinds of forces. Marx is clear in *The German Ideology* that consciousness is shaped by material activity and class position, which flows from the forces of production. Emile Durkheim thought that the array of social groups was determining:

> I consider extremely fruitful this idea that social life should be explained, not by the notions of those who participate in it, but by more profound causes which are unperceived by consciousness, and I think also that these causes are to be sought mainly in the manner according to which individuals are grouped. Only in this way, it seems, can a history become a science and sociology itself exist.[21]

These are structural explanations, which explain identity formation entirely apart from reason of reflection, pointing instead to a very different kind of circumstance than one of reflection. I term it an *eclipsing circumstance;* it consists of *any structure that surrounds, eclipses, and circumvents, rather than assists or promotes, reason of reflection.* In this study, I focus particularly on material structures, by which I mean social constraints on the behavior of individuals and groups that do not consist of ideas themselves—technology, institutions of coercion and taxation, class, societal coalitions, the international distribution of power, and the like.[22] It is through such eclipsing circumstances that structural explanations will want to account for the Protestant Reformation and colonial nationalism, the revolutions in ideas behind revolutions in sovereignty.

Every structural theory identifies an eclipsing, structural circumstance that determines identities. Every such theory likewise posits a complementary conception of the person. Marx, Durkheim, Sigmund Freud, and B. F. Skinner—the structural giants—each attached a theory of human consciousness to his account of structure. Contemporary rational-choice theory also fits the structuralist description. Although only a few rational-choice theorists explicitly target identities, we often do hear loosely rationalist arguments that depict ideas as instrumentally adopted.[23] A rational-choice theory of identity would not remap the consciousness as the structural giants attempted, but would make simple assumptions about persons—that they have fixed, ordered preferences, usually for economic or political gain—and would then show how a certain structure leads them to adopt a certain identity in order to maximize this preference. The structure depends on the theory. It could be the nature of the political economy. For example, bourgeois merchants find that the Catholic

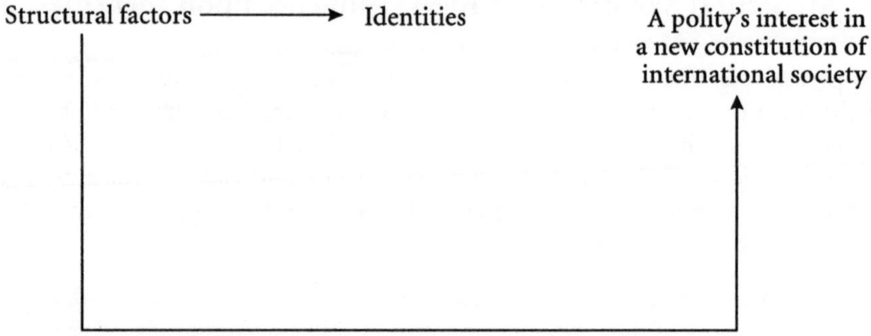

Fig. 4.2. Structural Skepticism of the First Role of Ideas

Church hinders commerce while the Protestant church allows it; the merchants become Protestants. Or it could be technology: New battle technology makes new ideas about military strategy more appealing; military commanders adopt them. Or it could be the shape of political institutions, the international distribution of power, and so on.[24]

Figure 4.2 depicts structural skepticism of the first role of ideas. It shows that structures cause not only identities themselves, but also the interest of the polity in a new constitution of international society. The identity change is fully explained by structures, and has no further effect of its own.

Ideas as Resolvers of Uncertainty: An Intermediate Version of the First Role of Ideas

Between reason of reflection and the diverse structural approaches that deny the autonomy of the ideas altogether is a middle way of explaining identity formation, the first role of ideas. In this third version, people do not alter their fundamental ends through ideas as they do in reason of reflection, but neither do they adopt ideas merely instrumentally. They have fixed "interests" such as wealth or power, as they do in rational-choice theory, but are uncertain how to pursue them—uncertain, that is, apart from ideas, which "function" as "resolvers of uncertainty."[25] The most famous version is still Max Weber's railroad switchman, a metaphor for the religious ideas that steer our pursuit of salvation.[26]

Framing ideas as resolvers of uncertainty does not challenge the autonomy of ideas as deeply as structural theories. People still reason reflectively that certain ideas are effective recipes. But this reflection is somewhat constricted. Fundamental ends are already there; what reflection helps to determine is the means. We must be careful here, for the line between what is a fundamental end and what is a means may be fuzzy. Do Weber's religions really "resolve uncertainty," or do they prescribe a fundamental value in the first place? I do not think we accomplish much in saying that religions "resolve uncertainty" about salvation. Not all people have some "need" for salvation that can be met equally well by any religion. Not all religions, for that matter, are salvific. Religions meet a "need" for certainty about salvation no more than a belief in God meets a "need" to know the truth about the universe or no more than ideas about racial equality meet a "need" for knowledge about justice. Needs, here, are wholly trivial. One can always invent an "need" that any idea meets, a "function" that any idea performs. Ideas are only significant as resolvers of uncertainty, then, if the fixed interest is concretely defined and can be discretely pursued in several ways—interests such as economic wealth, battlefield victory, or bureaucratic advancement will work.[27] In seeking to know how Protestant and nationalist identities were shaped, then, we must be open to the possibility that people adopted them as resolvers of uncertainty about how to pursue some prior end.

Ideas as resolvers of uncertainty and structures that eclipse ideas both cast doubt on the first role of ideas, as shapers of identity. This role, and also this doubt, I have sought to describe in this chapter. Most of the recent works on ideas in political science, ones that assert the influence of ideas, have little to say about this first role. They take believers in ideas as a given and show how they influence politics. But the first role is the transforming work of ideas. It is the fuel that provides initial energy to the causal pump, the essential precondition for social power, the set of gears that translates this energy into influence.

How Ideas Become Socially Empowered

It is not enough that ideas shape identities. Popular conversion alone does not account for how ideas bring leaders of states or principalities or empires to campaign or move troops on behalf of new constitutions of international society, or for how ideas hamper or overthrow obstructing leaders. Converts must bring polities to adopt an interest in new constitutions and back up their leaders with the power to achieve them. This means finding a way to defeat all of those forces, military, economic, political, and ideological, at home and abroad, that serve to uphold the old constitution. What is the link between changed identities and the interest of polities in new constitutions of international society? The second role of ideas—ideas as social power—explains how converts apply carrots and sticks upon their prince, parliament, president, or anyone who is in a position to deliver or hinder the new constitution, resulting in a transformation of the polity's interest, and eventually a revolution in sovereignty. It is through the second role of ideas that the crisis in pluralism becomes genuinely a political crisis, not merely an intellectual or religious one.[28]

The social power of ideas is *the ability of believers in ideas to alter the costs and benefits facing those who are in a position to promote or hinder the policies that the ideas demand*. Here, the policies are new constitutions of international society. The costs and benefits come in traditional political currency—votes, taxes, bureaucratic power, threats of war and rebellion—and, in a more complex version, reputation. Strictly speaking, it is not purely ideas that wield power; rather, converts use their economic and political sway to further the demands for which their ideas call. The social power of ideas, here, is broadly similar to rational-choice claims. We may conceive elite executors of policy as rational actors aiming to maximize their political power, the perquisites of office. What converts do is enhance the elites' milieu of incentives, their opportunity costs, so that they benefit (or avoid suffering) from promoting the demands of the converts. What is distinctive about the social power of ideas is that it is believers in ideas, motivated by ideas, who brandish these carrots and sticks in order to realize political results.[29] If the crucial criterion of the first role is the autonomy of ideas, that of the second role is the efficacy of ideas.

There is also a more complex, but commonly occurring, variant of the second role. It is what I call the *reputational social power of* ideas. Here, converts still alter the costs and benefits of elites, but more indirectly, in this case, by rhetorically damaging the reputation of elites for upholding their publicly professed ideals, thereby presenting elites with a political or economic cost. As I will describe in chapter 9, during the 1950s African and Asian colonial nationalists within the British Empire acutely criticized the British Cabinet for its slow progress toward colonial independence. The operative idea of the converts was nationalism, but they promoted it by appealing to the cabinet's generation-old official ideal of fostering colonial self-government. Arguably, the nationalists made the cabinet face a loss of its progressive reputation, a loss that the cabinet feared would result in a domestic political weakening and a strategic blow in the Cold War, as disaffected colonial powers aligned with the anticolonial Soviets. The cabinet responded by speeding up political progress, then granting independence. In this version of the social power of ideas, converts to new identities still alter the costs and benefits of elites, but in a more complex way.

Structural Skepticism of the Social Power of Ideas

The skeptic of the second role of ideas denies its central claim: that it is believers in ideas who wield the efficacious economic, military, political, and reputational power that transforms the interests of polities in revolutions in sovereignty. The skeptic assumes instead that maximizing these material kinds of power, not promoting ideas, is the sole end of those who influence political interests. It is then structure that determines how these seekers of economic, military, and political power proceed, and what kind of political ends they adopt to deliver this power. The central difference between the second role of ideas and structural skepticism of it, then, is the view of the ends of those who wield power. In the ideas account, it is the end prescribed by ideas; in the structural account, it is material power. The instruments that converts wield toward these ends are similar in both accounts. In the case of revolutions in sovereignty, it is changes in structures—economic, technological, institutional, the international balance of power—that lead polities to seek new constitutions of international society as the best way to promote their material interests. It is the contradiction evoked by this sort of change, not by crises of pluralism, that bring revolutions in sovereignty.

Structure, again, can take any form, depending on the commitments of the theorist. Class structure, the international distribution of power, and the structure of political institutions are the most familiar. But in any variant, the ends of the power seekers either defeat the ends of converts, or else the converts themselves drop their ideas under duress and pursue the ends of structure. Ideas are thus "socialized out."

Structure dominates politics, then, no matter what effect the first role of ideas plays. The deepest structuralists, like Marx or Durkheim, deny that ideas convert people to new identities in the first place. In these accounts, it only follows that the ideas of converts are not what shapes politics. But other structuralists are less demanding, allowing that ideas might fashion identities, but denying any effect of ideas beyond the edge of the mind—that is, on politics. Many rational-choice theories are structural; these ignore identity formation, simply assume that peoples' end is maximizing wealth or political advancement, and then show how structure leads them to pursue political outcomes. Many forms of Realism, the most enduring and influential tradition of international relations thought, also fall into this category. Realism's pedigree and, as I will show, its pertinence to revolutions in sovereignty, merit it a special look.

Realism, Ideas, and Revolutions in Sovereignty

The interest of the state is to preserve and rationally expand power. These interests are inescapably pursued, or at least ignored at great cost, because of an international milieu whose lack of a common superior makes attack a perpetual threat. Rarely do these interests include ideals of justice, which the same milieu will bring to defeat. Such are the tenets of the Realist school. They have generally been shared among Realists extending back to Thucydides in the ancient world, revived in early modern Europe by

Machiavelli and Hobbes, persisting through twentieth-century Realists Hans Morgenthau, E. H. Carr, and Henry Kissinger, and continuing all the way to contemporary Realists Kenneth Waltz and Robert Gilpin.[30]

Realism's skepticism toward the social power of ideas lies in these enduring commitments. Its own conception of social power is central to the tradition. Although some Realists like Thucydides and Rousseau allow that the character of the regime of a polity—aristocratic, monarchical, democratic—will affect how it pursues its interests—aggressively or moderately—they and all Realists agree that every polity has a common interest in pursuing power, by which Realists usually mean the resources for fighting war.[31] A central Realist insight is that the power to fight war is both an ends and a means. Land, wealth, access to natural resources, better technology, institutions that are stable and capable of supporting combat—these are the goals of all states, to be pursued at home and abroad. Wealth, strong armies, natural resources, technology, and so on—these are the universal means of attaining these goals. The interest of states is power; they pursue it with power.[32] They pursue it rationally, too, assessing their environment and calculating carefully the costs and benefits.[33]

To these enduring tenets about power, some Realists will append an important corollary. It begins with the notion that Realist power is both an end and a means, and asserts a linkage: The more Realist power a state possesses relative to other states, the more that state will expand its hunt for power abroad. Not all Realists openly articulate this insight, but it flows readily out of Realist thinking. Its upshot is that when the internal power resources of a state expand, so do its aims abroad. Industrialization in the United States after the Civil War, for instance, led to empire by the turn of the twentieth century. Economic growth, military reform, the development of natural resources, and the strengthening of government institutions lead states to strive more vigorously for colonies, the territory of other states, access to the resources of other states, zones of economic privilege—and new constitutions of international society.[34]

To a Realist, polities in an international system are clones, programmed identically, at least in the sense that they pursue material power, and do so as single entities. The most important difference between polities is their size. Some have greater means and thus more expansive ends. What is the iron die that molds polities into this conformity? Though many Realists point to human nature[35]—the *animus dominandi*, original sin—all Realists also believe that international politics has a logic of conflict unique to its structure, which explains the pursuit of power by polities. The key to this logic is the concept of anarchy.[36]

Anarchy, as I noted in chapter 2, is not by definition incorrigible rioting, but is the lack of a sovereign, the organizational predicament of Westphalian states. A Realist would accept this definition, but would still insist that anarchy unsettles; if it does not bring ceaseless war, it brings permanent precariousness. Hobbes first articulated the reasons for this, and his state of nature Realists continue to use as an analogy for relations between states.[37] Without a common sovereign, all peoples must remain preoccupied with their own security. They cannot relax vigilance or trust anyone enough to lay down their arms because someone else could kill them. But their efforts to defend themselves, in turn, provoke the fear of others, who also suspect that they are threatened. Frequently, conflict breaks out.

Hobbes's dilemma is not that people evilly intend to kill each other, but that they do not know one another's intentions and cannot trust one another's promises. Without respite, tranquil lulls, settled peace, a cushion of security, or a store of trust created by past harmony, a state cannot afford any interest but war-fighting power.

Hobbesian, Realist anarchy is a notion of how the social world is laid out and what the implications of this layout are: it is a structural theory. As long as people have arranged themselves into polities, and as long as these polities exist in a world with no common superior, these polities will competitively pursue power. Realists are less ambitious than Marx or Durkheim in that they do not expect their structure (anarchy) to explain ideas themselves or all of social life (domestic institutions, religion, and so on), but only international relations. But for Realists, too, it is the way social life is organized that counts.

Realism's View of Ideas

From the Realist's belief that anarchy is so pronounced, its effects so overriding, that war-fighting power is the inescapable end of polities, it is not hard to infer the Realist's view of ideas about justice and legitimate authority. Such ideas are manifestly not what polities aim to realize. E. H. Carr argues this most clearly, although the same contention is found in Machiavelli, Morgenthau, Thucydides, Waltz, and others.[38] Carr's *The Twenty Years Crisis* is a cutting commentary on the failure of Anglo-American internationalist ideals to overcome war through international law, free trade, and public opinion. In all realms of politics, ideas, especially ideas claiming universal validity, are inevitably the claims that dominant groups make on behalf of the whole. Britain and America proclaimed free trade, liberalism, and respect for law; free trade, liberalism, and respect for law benefited Britain and America most.[39]

This is Realism in its most brusque mood. Although this mood is generally characteristic, at times Realists' dismissal of ideas is not quite so gruff. Even Carr wants to avoid an overly consistent, determinist Realism: "Every realist, whatever his professions, is ultimately compelled to believe not only that there is something which man ought to think and do, but that there is something which he can think and do, and that his thought and action are neither mechanical nor meaningless."[40] Morgenthau, too, avers that although power is always the "immediate aim" in international politics, "statesmen and peoples" also have "ultimate aims" such as "freedom, security, prosperity, or power itself. They may define their goals in terms of a religious, philosophic, economic, or social ideal."[41] Realist Robert Gilpin allows that the prestige of the most powerful states in a system rests in part on "ideological, religious, or other common values," and that the most powerful states set the rules of the system partially according to "common values and interests."[42] Both Morgenthau and Henry Kissinger grant a role to legitimacy. Their ideal is the international society of European royal families, prior and subsequent to the Napoleonic Wars, whose aristocratic ideals for conduct moderated war and competition, contrasting strongly with the modern age of mass, totalistic politics. For modern Realists like George Kennan, it served as a model.[43]

Realists' ideas about ideas, though, are murky in the end. For Carr, ideas do not set interests in any fundamental way, but seem able only to provide course adjustments in the struggle for Realist power. For instance, England and France were free to appease Hitler's new order of power (which Carr at the time advocated), rather than oppose Hitler in the name of suspect universal ideals like self-determination. Nor is it clear in Carr's work exactly what relegates ideas to such a limited role; as one commentator points out, he has a thin sociology of knowledge.[44] As for Morgenthau, despite his acknowledgment of the diverse "ultimate" aims of states, it is difficult to see what role they play in his Realism. He seems to think it much more important that all states seek the "immediate aim" of power no matter what their "ultimate" aim; he refers often to ideologies as "masks" for interests; and one of his six fundamental principles of political realism is that states pursue interests defined in terms of power. The most coherent interpretation of Morgenthau's view of ideas, I believe, is that although actual states have diverse aspirations, their actual policies are close enough to the pursuit of Realist power that we may assume that Realist power is what they seek.[45] Nor are Morgenthau or Kissinger clear about legitimacy. For Kissinger, were the principles of the post–Napoleonic Concert of Europe shared ideas or merely shared means of promoting security? In Morgenthau's transnational aristocratic society of the eighteenth century, what discernible effect did the dynastic ideas have on states' decisions for war or their interests in general? The efficacy of ideas is profoundly ambiguous in Realism. Commonly expressed notions of legitimacy do not necessarily mean that ideas matter. Morgenthau and Kissinger give us little reason to believe that they do.[46]

What all Realists insist upon are the strong limitations upon the influence of ideas. Ideas will be impotent if they depart from the interest that polities have in power. Morgenthau, for instance, allows that ideas may at times limit the brutality of combat, but not the occurrence of war in the first place. He devotes several chapters to the paltry influence of international law and public opinion, and the failure of reformist projects.[47] That Realists commonly advise statespersons against pursuing ideals also reveals their skepticism. Stark description converts easily to considered prescription; what may seem like a misanthropic assessment, Realists present as wise counsel, as prophetic, tragic insight.

Most important, Realists only weakly allow that ideas might have social power—the ability to give a leader incentives to pursue what the ideas prescribe. Ideas are more likely manipulable. Carr, for instance, writes of the power to sway public opinion as one of the key tools of heads of state.[48] This view of ideas helps to answer a potential problem for Realists: If ideas have so little influence, why do the powerful even bother with legitimations? If there is no strong "demand" for ideas, then for whom must they be legitimated?[49] The best Realist answer, I think, is that some demand for ideas exists, but it is weak; that publics desire ideas to be promoted, but they are highly manipulable, not least because as members of the united state body they are already disposed to favor its interests in security and power.

The most systematic Realist reason for the pusillanimity of ideas is anarchy. Princes or presidents who want to pursue ideological or moral ideals, or who hear domestic calls to pursue them, look outward at the configuration of other states—the size of their populations and militaries, their geographical location—and think again. They revise, they adjust, they qualify. If, motivated by an idea of justice, they pursues a policy contrary to the interest of their state, they will be defeated, both by the resistance of other states, and by those within their own state who act in the name of the interest of the state. Ideas about justice and legitimate authority may be proposed, articulated, and advocated, in speeches, homilies, scholarship, and editorials, but they are rarely pursued; and when they are pursued, they rarely flourish—except when strictly compatible with interest defined in terms of power.

A Realist Account of Revolutions in Sovereignty

With Realism's canonical teachings about power, interests, anarchy, and ideas, we can sew together a Realist account of revolutions in sovereignty. I say sew together because constitutions of international society are not in the language of Machiavelli, Hobbes, or Carr. Morgenthau mentions sovereignty, but neither he nor any other Realist seeks the genesis of constitutions.[50] Are constitutions a matter in which Realists would even have an interest? In the case of each historical revolution, as I show in the following chapters, a Realist story is there to be told, and for each case there are historians and sociologists who in fact tell the story in strongly Realist terms. But why, then, do Realists rarely mention revolutions in sovereignty? There are two reasons for skepticism toward a Realist interest in constitutions, both of them, in the end, unconvincing.

The first ground for skepticism: Realists do not think constitutions of international society important enough to bother with. Recall again that norms are matters of both legitimacy and practice. It is the legitimacy part—the codification of norms, mutual recognition, lawlike character—whose importance Realists would doubt. What polities agree to at treaty tables, what they recognize as customary law or announce as legitimate, is a reflection of the strategic advantage of the powerful, a monument to the winner of the last war, not something to which polities are obedient or even cognizant of in deciding their interests.[51] But if constitutions of international society are impotent insofar as they are matters of legitimacy, Realists may be justified in ignoring them, but this does not mean they lack an explanation for them. Indeed, the Realist argument for the impotence of constitutions is also their explanation for them—constitutions are expressions of the interest of polities in power.

To the extent that constitutions of international society are practices, though, Realists should view them as more consequential. The definition of political authority, the criteria for becoming one of these authorities, and the prerogatives of these authorities—the three faces of sovereignty—involve strategic and economic stakes of the highest sort. If I am a seventeenth-century German prince, it matters a great deal to my military security whether there exists an emperor who claims control over my territory's religious affairs and regularly sends his troops to fight for it. If I am an imperial metropole, my colonies may provide me with riches and strategic outposts. Their independence is not a small affair. States and empires have indeed fought wars over such matters; to ignore an interest in them can only be arbitrary.

A second argument for skepticism toward the interest of Realism in constitutions of international society is more conceptual. It suggests circularity. Realism, this argument runs, assumes an anarchical system, one in which the polities are internally united and externally independent. But anarchy is itself a constitution of international relations, which means that I hold Realism to be interested in explaining what it already assumes. But we cannot logically assume what we are trying to explain; we ought not to put the Realist cart before the sovereignty horse. The alleged problem is especially acute in the case of Westphalia, in which the system of sovereign states first arose.[52]

The problem, though, is not as intractable as it sounds. Anarchy, for Realist purposes, need not exist between fully developed modern states, but only between polities who have developed enough control of their military affairs to put up a strong fight against anyone who would forcibly interfere in their borders (unlike medieval authorities, in whose realm outside authorities regularly interfered, and who often did not even govern a territorial "realm" with borders). Well before Westphalia in 1648—as early as 1300, as I will argue in chapter 5—the major polities of Europe fit the description of rough anarchy. England, France, and Sweden were fully sovereign states, and within the Holy Roman Empire, "proto-states" like Germany and the Netherlands governed many of their own affairs and would raise their own armies to win from the empire the Westphalian constitution. Until the empire's own medieval structure had disappeared, we cannot say that sovereign statehood was Europe's constitution—legitimate and practiced. But since all of these diverse pre-Westphalian polities had enough control over their internal affairs to fight, balance, ally, and make peace with one another, there is no good Realist reason to expect them to act differently than polities in rough anarchy always act.

A Realist explanation of revolutions in sovereignty, then, would be the following. Since polities have high stakes in constitutions of international society—in how the three faces of sovereignty are defined, at least insofar as norms are practices—then how these norms are defined will depend on the strategic power and interests of the economically and militarily strongest polities. In different eras, different polities have found different practices most conducive to their interest in power. *Revolutions in sovereignty, it follows, result from the rise in war-fighting power of polities whose interest in preserving (and rationally expanding) this power are served by the new constitutions, and from the decline of polities whose interests are served by the old ones.* The crucial piece of Realist logic is that when means expand, so do ends. When formerly weak polities grow relatively strong, they aspire to more ambitious ends, including new constitutions of international society, and when strong polities suffer relative atrophy, they become less able to uphold the old order.

At the center of the Realist case is the historical fact that revolutions in sovereignty have always followed general wars or sharp shifts in material power—events that consolidate generational power trends. Westphalia, then, resulted from the rise of states and the decline of the empire, culminating in the Thirty Years' War. Colonial independence was the product of the decline of Britain and France and the rise of the colonies and their superpower allies after the Second World War. Revolutions in sovereignty are the story of the rise and fall of great powers, of changes in the international distribution in power, the Realist version of the structure that overrides ideas.

Realism, then, is a strong structural skeptic of the social power of ideas. But it is not the only structural theory worth considering. Others, too,

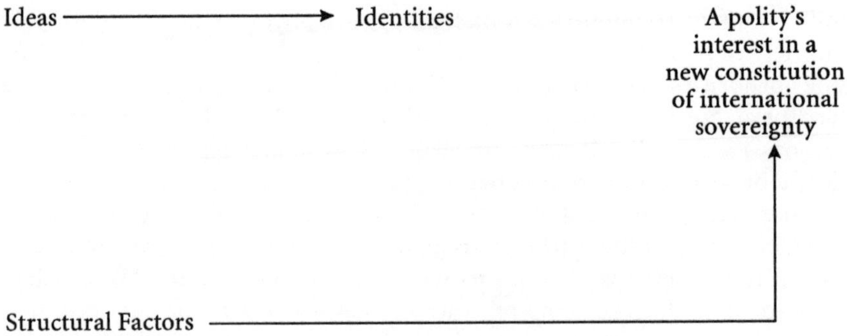

Fig. 4.3. Structural Skepticism of the Second Role of Ideas

have gained prominence in the literature of historical sociology and political science. Their relevance to Westphalia and colonial independence makes them worth considering. Barrington Moore's broadly Marxist account of the origins of modern democracy and dictatorship, Theda Skocpol's explanation of social revolutions, emphasizing class and the strength of state institutions, Brian Downing's argument that the paths of states to democracy and dictatorship originate in their experiences with the "military revolution" in the technology of warfare—works that find the origin of the state in developments in coercive power, economic changes, and military technology, and theories that explain the interests of states according to their constitution, their bureaucracy, the relationship between their executive and their legislature, their civil-military relations, their means of extracting taxes and troops, and other domestic structures—all yield structural hypotheses for explaining a system of sovereign states and the breakdown of colonial empires.[53] In the chapters ahead, I will identify such explanations, and pose them against arguments for ideas.

Figure 4.3 illustrates structural skepticism of the second role of ideas, showing that even if ideas cause identities, as the first role claims, converts to new identities have no further effect on a polity's interest in a new constitution of international society.

Ideas as Focal Points: An Intermediate Version of the Second Role

As with the first role—ideas as shapers of identities—there is an intermediate version of the ideas as social power thesis. On the social level, too, ideas may do the work of dispelling cloudiness for those who want to discover how they may pursue their ends of economic and political gain. This time the players are not individuals with economic and political ends, but coalitions seeking to influence polities and even polities themselves trying to influence international events. But here, ideas do not resolve uncertainty so much as they provide solutions to conflicts. They are "focal points" that provide solutions in bargaining, or "glue" that holds together coalitions whose constituents' interests are similar but not identical. The focal-points concept differs from the ideas-as social-power concept in that its agents already have fixed material goals—ideas only help them resolve conflicts. But it differs from structural skepticism in that ideas are efficacious; they influence political outcomes.

Geoffrey Garrett and Barry Weingast have argued that in the 1980s European Community member states found the principle of "mutual recognition," used by the European Court of Justice to settle disputes over certain economic conflicts, to be a mutually agreeable basis of an agreement that led to the notable Single European Act of 1986. The common preexistent end of states was economic growth; ideas helped them reach an agreement to achieve it.[54] Here, ideas matter not as ends, but as resolvers of conflicts. Constitutions of international society, in this view, are the compromises reached by polities with ends similar in nature (usually material power) but conflictual in substance (they may disagree on what sort of constitution best promotes this power).

Ideas as focal points, a version of the second role of ideas, completes our portfolio of mechanisms. Two roles of ideas, two kinds of skepticism, each posited in response to one of the roles, two intermediate roles—six sorts of theories are the result. For both revolutions in sovereignty, I will argue for the responsibility of the two roles of ideas, working together, but will also acknowledge the partial role of structural factors and the occurrence of intermediate mechanisms. Table 4.1 summarizes the possibilities.

Couriers of Ideas

In theory, shaping identities and becoming forms of social power are the labors of ideas. This is a claim about process, not players. But ideas do not perform their labors in the abstract, in an amorphous intellectual and political milieu. In the words of one scholar, "Ideas do not float freely."[55] In history, these labors are enacted by particular people in particular places, by townspeople, political organizers, theologians, professors, lobbyists, parliamentarians, generals, and heads of state, by people who discuss, persuade, preach, pressure, order, cajole, and shoot, who organize themselves into lobbies, armies, networks, and parties, who vie against all the same sorts of people, performing the same sorts of activities, on behalf of an opposing program, but who eventually win the international revolu-

TABLE 4.1
Summary: Three Versions of the Two Roles of Ideas

	Role of Ideas	
Theory about Ideas	First Role: Ideas as Shapers of Identities	Second Role: Ideas as Sources of Social Power
Ideas Account	Identities change through reflection upon the content of ideas (Important role of auxiliary circumstances)	Converts to ideas wield social power on ideas' behalf, altering the opportunity costs of heads of polities (Reputational social power is an important variant)
Intermediate Theory	Ideas as resolvers of uncertainty *Example: Weber's "switchmen"*	Ideas as focal points in bargaining *Example: Garrett and Weingast*
Structural Skepticism	Social structure explains the adoption of identities; in most versions, individuals advance their economic and/or political ends by adopting identities according to the logic of the structure (Eclipsing circumstances explain the adoption of ideas) *Examples: Marx, Durkheim, some rational-choice theories*	Social structure explains social outcomes sufficiently; it either overrides the influence of converts promoting ideas, or it causes converts to drop these ends in order to pursue economic or political advancement *Examples: Realism, Marx, Durkheim*

tion. I am committed to no single, general theory about who these persons are, how they are converted, and what form of social power they wield. Ideas in fact depend on diverse "couriers" to dispatch them to the doorstep of political change. In my arguments for the role of ideas in each revolution, I will seek to identify through what combinations of couriers and forms of power ideas shaped the interests of their polity. Together, these combinations constitute the "causal pathways" that ideas follow.

What are some of the couriers found along causal pathways? Recent works on ideas in international relations offer several examples. One is publics, meaning groups of peasants, merchants, voters, or anyone who is not in a government institution or activist organization, who, through their blessings or protest, expressed through pen, voice, vote, riot, or gun, convey the force of ideas.[56] A potent subset of publics is networks of committed believers, those who are intensely, usually vocationally, dedicated to spreading and empowering ideas. There are two sorts—intellectual communities and activist networks. Intellectual communities—Protestant theologians, colonial nationalists in European universities—are networks of people who create and organize ideas, and then seek their spread, either through their own efforts or by relying on others.[57] Activists, the other sort of network, are not special because of their dexterity and familiarity with complex theories, but because of their skill in presenting, spreading, and applying pressure on behalf of already developed ideas. Networks of activists are like-minded, actively cooperating, extending across borders, residing in both citizens' groups and sectors of government. Humans rights advocates, anticolonial lobbies in Britain, the preachers and town leaders who spread the Reformation—all are exemplary.[58]

Government institutions—bureaucracies, departments, committees, and agencies—are another purveyor of ideas. Institutions institutionalize. That is, they incorporate or "embed" ideas into their organization, an activity that involves shaping both identities and social power. Institutionalizing begins when ideas from outside the organization convert its members—its leaders or its functionaries. The more people persuaded, and the more powerful the people persuaded, the more social power the ideas will be able to exercise. In her work on American trade policy, for instance, Judith Goldstein similarly argues that ideas exercise influence by first persuading policymakers.[59]

But ideas also exercise social power in institutions, and they do so in two ways. First, powerful converts use their position to further the policies that stem from the ideas, both by shifting personnel within their organization—nonconformity means nonadvancement—and by exercising the power of their position on the government at large. The power of a cabinet officer is illustrative. Second, converts get ideas adopted into legal norms and routines that guide future members of the organization, who are then bound by the norms' regulative power (which alters their opportunity costs, acting as a form of social power), and who use the norms as "rules of appropriateness" to guide their activity (ideas act here like "resolvers of uncertainty").[60] Such norms can guide policy long after they are originally embedded. In Goldstein's work, liberal economic ideas were embedded in the laws governing the making of American trade policy.[61] Embedded, norms can then act as a "circumstance of reflection" for future generations. As new recruits come into the organization, they find themselves swimming in its milieu of ideas, and may come to adopt the ideas for themselves. In all of these ways, ideas shape identities and exert social power in institutions. As I will explain in the colonial independence case, established ideals of empire held sway in this way. They were institutionalized in the colonial bureaucracies of Britain and France, shaping the landscape that advocates of anticolonial ideas had to confront.

Another courier, a more amorphous one, I term broadly the "international context."[62] It consists of a loose cosmopolitan layer of diplomats, national government officials, and officials of international organizations, who transmit ideas across borders and knead ideas into policy. Distinct from activists and epistemic communities, this layer is restricted to agents of governments, both state and international, who negotiate, bargain, converse, and deal with one another. We find something like this international context, for instance, in the theories of sociologist John Meyer, who has proposed an efficacious "world polity" of culture and ideas shared among international elites.[63] In the activity of this courier, too, identities are shaped and social power is wielded; elites persuade and cajole one another. It is especially in the colonial independence case that this international context pertains. We will see there, for instance, how the context of the Cold War—interaction with the United States, the Soviet Union, and the United Nations—influenced the British and French cabinets in their decisions for independence. In the Westphalia case, it was not until the actual peace negotiations that an official layer of diplomats became influential.[64]

These are not the only couriers of ideas. Legislators, heads of states, and various members of "transnational society," such as business leaders, may all convert, be converted, wield social power, and be pressured to conform to the policy demands of ideas. I will note where they are relevant. Ideas, though, are not choosy about who sponsors them into politics. In bringing about any political result, they might employ any or all of these couriers. I aver only that we can better understand the work of these couriers by paying mind to the separate, but mutually necessary, roles of shaping identities and exerting social power.

The Nature of the Claim

Identifying couriers of ideas is a means of showing the precise mechanism behind the general claim: that ideas bring about revolutions in sovereignty. But how are we to know if the larger claim is true? First, just what sort of claim is it? Revolutions in ideas bring revolutions in sovereignty: This is a counterfactual assertion. Had there been no Reformation, there would have been no Westphalia. Without colonial nationalism, no revolution of colonial independence would have resulted around 1960. To be valid, a counterfactual claim of this sort must follow a "minimal-rewrite-of-history rule," posing an alternative world where the alleged cause is extracted yet other events and conditions remain intact. It must also meet a "cotenability" criterion, positing a theory of how, in this plausible alternative world, the remaining events and conditions might have brought about the same result.[65] Otherwise, the counterfactual is implausible, the imaginary world a straw man. In the revolutions that I will describe, it is not hard to envision such alternative worlds, one without the Reformation or without racial equality and colonial nationalism. These worlds are precisely the ones that the structural materialist accounts describe, a world where the state and the states system form completely apart from Protestantism, where colonial empires give up their colonies immune from the influence of anti-imperial ideas. But while such worlds meet the standard of plausibility, it is my central task to show that they are not compelling. Were it not for the Reformation, were it not for equality and nationalism held by the opponents of empire, history would have looked different.

How do we look for evidence for the two roles of ideas? By explaining revolutions in sovereignty through the separate polities that develop an interest in them, we can compare how ideas and their rival forces operate in these polities over time and place. If the ideas hypothesis has merit, then we will find the influence of ideas strongest in those polities that develop an interest in a new constitution of international society, weakest in those that do not. We will find, too, that polities which develop interests in new constitutions do so at roughly the same time that ideas exert their influence. Similar comparisons across time and place will support or diminish structural theories: Does the rise of interests correlate across time and place with economic, technological, military, institutional, and other sorts of change?[66] The evaluation of intermediate dynamics is more subtle. In each historical episode, we will ask, In what sense could it be the case that ideas steer the pursuit of some fixed prior end, and what sort of evidence would reveal this?

But if we are so to correlate causes and effects, how, then, do we discern them? For the two roles of ideas and for structural accounts, we look for "observable implications" of the causes and effects that they hypothesize.[67] For the first role of ideas, for instance, we need evidence that conversions to new identities took place. We can find referents in behavior: We know that people have become Protestants when they organize into new congregations, speak, worship, teach, and write like Protestants. Whether Protestants or nationalists are converted through reflection or under the influence of structural factors—a complex mental process—is more difficult to perceive. Here, though, we may turn to circumstances of reflection and eclipsing circumstances, proxy indicators of the intellect. Which correlate best in time and place with conversion? For the second role, too, we may find referents. A polity adopts an interest in a new constitution when it pronounces this interest and actively wages war or diplomacy for it; this we can perceive. We may discern the exercise of the social power of ideas upon this adoption through the activities of converts, their pleas and their protests, their organization into lobbies, parties, unions, and armies, and through the testimony of heads of polities as to the influence of ideas upon them. Changing structures—institutions, technology, economies—we can also discern through historical description and indices of power. Finally, once I have looked for correlations between cause and effect, I will then offer a story, a step-by-step account of the events through which the cause led to the effect.

Not Ideas Alone

Through these methods, this sort of evidence, I will attempt to substantiate my argument about revolutions in sovereignty. I must also be clear about what I am not claiming. Revolutions in ideas, though central, were not solely influential; in each case, I will recognize the role of structures and intermediate dynamics, showing their collaboration but not their sufficiency. Another qualification is perhaps more surprising: I do not claim the absolute necessity of having ideas. Constitutions of international society could, in fact, have developed without them. Even if Luther and Calvin had never penned their incendiary tracts, pamphlets, and hymns, it is thinkable that a sovereign states system might eventually have evolved through economic, military, technological, and organizational forces. Without colonial nationalism, imperial metropoles may yet have come to judge their colonies too costly to retain.

But if ideas did not have to matter, I will argue that they did matter, and with great historical consequences. In both cases, revolutions in ideas brought revolutions in sovereignty faster and in more sweeping fashion than they would otherwise have occurred. Without the Reformation, a sovereign states system would have appeared in a far later decade or century, piecemeal, and unaccompanied by the historical effects of the religious wars such as the Enlightenment, the eighteenth-century balance of power, the hegemony of France, and other consequences that proved monumentally important for subsequent history. Similarly, were it not for ideas, colonial independence would have come staggered and later, not virtually at once in the late 1950s and early 1960s, with important consequences for the history of Africa and elsewhere. This difference—between the actual history of international constitutions and their likely history in the absence of revolutions in ideas—is the causal weight of ideas.[68]

Demonstrating this causal weight on the revolutions in sovereignty that brought about a universal system of sovereign states is what I propose to accomplish over the next eight chapters. The framework of ideas developed in this chapter shows how ideas can bring revolutions in sovereignty, but not that ideas actually did bring such revolutions at Westphalia and through colonial independence. The evidence for ideas in these revolutions, I present in chapters 5 through 12. I begin with the revolution at Westphalia.

PART TWO

THE FOUNDING OF THE SOVEREIGN STATES SYSTEM AT WESTPHALIA

FIVE

WESTPHALIA AS ORIGIN

FORCED TO ABDICATE by his rival Bullingbrook, his divine royal aspect shattered, Shakespeare's King Richard II laments, "I find myself a traitor with the rest; / For I have given here my soul's consent / T'undeck the pompous body of a king, / Made glory base, and sovereignty a slave." In 1399, baronial ambitions continually threatened the English king, and when they prevailed he was denuded of his transcendent appointment, becoming a "traitor" to his calling.[1] To Henry V, ruling less than two decades later, such ambitions were not a threat. To conspirator nobles, he could say with poise, "But we our kingdom's safety must so tender, / Whose ruin you have sought, that to her laws / We do deliver you. Get therefore hence, / Poor miserable wretches, to your death."[2] By the reign of Henry VII at the end of the fifteenth century, actual, historical English kings could rule with the confidence of Henry V. Inside their realm, their authority was effectively supreme; their internal sovereignty established.[3] The English king was soon to realize external sovereignty, too. Centuries earlier, King Henry II had taken significant strides toward independence when he crushed the power and resistance of Thomas Becket, Archbishop of Canterbury, thus handicapping the political influence of the Roman Catholic Church in England. Henry VIII in the 1530s finally consolidated his ouster of Rome when he defied the pope's authority over his marriage, seized the Church's property, and created a national church whose bishops' temporal powers were under his own. By then, the English king was fully externally sovereign.

It was not until the Peace of Westphalia in 1648, I will argue, that virtually all of Europe's rulers enjoyed the sovereignty of Shakespeare's English kings and recognized this sovereignty in one another. In the generations after Westphalia, only the state would effectively command political loyalty in Europe. Not only the ideal, but any substantive reality, of united Christendom was gone. Europe was by then an assemblage of separate sovereign states—an anarchical "system" of states—fighting, allying, trading, negotiating, making peace, without yielding or genuflecting to any higher power.

A Europe of Henry VIII's was Machiavelli's Europe. Machiavelli had envisioned a new, secular politics in which princes held authority within their city-states and were free from papal and imperial interference, as well as from any moral restraint associated with the organism behind this interference.[4] The metaphor of the body by which medieval chroniclers described the political unity of Christendom now applied more aptly to the state. Princes and kings were no longer *primus inter pares* among many nobles, each with his own land and militia, but were now trustees or tyrants of a unitary state, a single body with corporate interests. It could now be taken for granted that with respect to the rest of the world, what happened inside this body was "private"; there was now such a thing as "internal affairs." From other states came not the threat of interfering with one's governance, but of capturing one's territory, defeating one's armies, sapping one's wealth. A new logic of necessity prevailed, by which the interests of states became preserving their territory, their armies, and their treasure. Together, such states formed a whole system of states, attacking, defending, and balancing, a system that found its most parsimonious expression in the writings of Emeric de Vattel, whose *Law of Nations*, written in 1758, portrayed a mechanical Enlightenment world where the only universally agreed upon law is that states have an equal right not to be hindered in their internal affairs.[5] This is a simpler, more familiar world, one for which the tradition of Realism provides an enduring portrait.

But the emergent Realist countenance of Europe was not necessarily the work of Realist or other structural forces. In chapters 6 and 7, I will argue that Westphalia was largely the outworking of the Protestant Reformation. First, though, I want to elaborate upon my premise, that Westphalia was in fact the origin of the sovereign states system. For although international relations scholars have long considered Westphalia's status as origin to be conventional wisdom, some have begun to attack it. Admittedly, the proposition that Westphalia founded modern international relations and closed the Middle Ages is not without its ambiguities. But a closer look at the Peace, its provisions and its surrounding historical circumstances, can sustain a defense of its traditional status. The present chapter gives that defense.

Westphalia's Significance

The most classic statement of Westphalia as the origin of modern international relations is a 1948 article by international lawyer Leo Gross, who calls the settlement "the majestic portal which leads from the old world into the new world." Hans Morgenthau and other top political scientists have echoed Gross, rendering Westphalia metonymy for the modern international system.[6] Recent iconoclasm, however, finds dubitable the "majesty" of Westphalia: Europe was substantially modern before Westphalia and persistently medieval thereafter; on the trek to modernity, Westphalia was not a continental divide, but just another hill.[7] The iconoclasm is thorough, not easily dismissed.

The prestige of Westphalia, I believe, can be rescued, but only with an updated defense, more subtle and qualified than the conventional wisdom, involving a close inspection of the history and provisions of the settlement. My contention: Before 1648, as long as the Thirty Years' War was still smoldering, significant features of political authority in Europe were incompatible with sovereign statehood; afterward, sovereignty prevailed. The careful historian naturally becomes suspicious. Change is never so stark. Indeed, I do not claim that Westphalia was an instant metamorphosis. Elements of sovereign statehood had been accumulating for three centuries, making Westphalia the consolidation, not the creation *ex nihilo*, of the modern system.[8] Even the victory of modernity after Westphalia we must slightly qualify, for some medieval anomalies persisted. But consummate fissures in history are rare; and I want to argue that Westphalia is as clean as historical faults come.

Absent Sovereignty: The Middle Ages

Politics after Westphalia appears sharpest in relief against the previous season at its peak—Europe during the High Middle Ages. The Pauline metaphor of the Body of Christ, which publicists, philosophers, theologians, and holders of power used to describe politics and society, renders the era well. All believers in the true faith were members of a single organism in which all individuals found their identity and purpose, where all lived under common laws and morals, where none were severed or independent in their authority or beliefs; yet in which not all were equal in purpose and role, but like the parts of the body were arrayed in an inclusive division of labor, a complex hierarchy with the pope and emperor at the head, with kings, barons, bishops, dukes, counts, and peasants all in their proper place, all connected by the most labyrinthine ligaments of privilege and prerogative. Society was united, just as the Church was united in the Body of Christ.[9]

In the *Respublica Christiana*, there was no supreme authority within a territory, manifestly no sovereignty. Some publicists and theologians claimed sovereignty for the pope and emperor, but neither figure approached the territorial supremacy that other historical emperors, Chinese and ancient Roman for instance, achieved. Both the pope and the emperor intervened regularly in the territorial affairs of kings, nobles, and, of course, bishops and other ecclesiastics, but these same authorities held prerogatives against the pope and the emperor, and against one another. Neither was any body of law sovereign. While natural law was a universal standard of morality to be enforced and interpreted by the Church, it did not prescribe offices or powers in the way that the United States Constitution, for instance, does. Nor was the requirement of territoriality met. The *Respublica Christiana* comprised all Christians, whether they lived in Europe or abroad in the Holy Land. Insofar as medieval politics can be summed up, it was simply a system that lacked sovereignty, what John Gerard Ruggie calls "heteronomy"[10]

Quintessentially medieval features marked this world without sovereignty. Political authorities possessed diverse roles and sets of obligations, unlike modern sovereign states, equal in their sovereign prerogatives. Politics and religion were commingled, too. Up and down the hierarchical ladder, the Church exercised authority that was, by any modern definition, civil. Bishops and archbishops held tracts of land, wielded the sword, and sat as the chancellors, regents, and officers of nobles, princes, and kings. The pope, a "spiritual leader," was also an executive, legislator, and judge. Finally, Christendom enjoyed moral and legal unity. Although natural law did not prescribe supreme authority, and thus was not sovereign, it was nevertheless a common law. Everybody was tied to somebody else by some sort of legal bond.

This portrait, brilliant in diverse authorities, sublime in harmonious ideals, is a self-portrait, one that theologians and philosophers etched most vividly at the apogee of the era, roughly between the eleventh and thirteenth centuries. What these descriptions often omitted, though, was the frequent violence of the period. If a web of obligations linked authorities together, the terms of these obligations were often unclear or perhaps just unsatisfactory, and were hardly always respected. Medieval authorities continually waged and avoided war through forming alliances, balancing against threats, and maintaining spheres of influence. As in any era, obligations did not enforce themselves solely through their normative force. This, virtually no latter-day medieval historian would dispute.[11]

War, violence, and strategizing hardly implied the absence of medieval links and obligations, only their contestation. Some recent skeptics, though, would cut more incisively into the philosophers' and theologians' portrait. Wielding Occam's razor—fittingly, a late medieval invention—they would slash through the very distinctiveness of the Middle Ages, revealing that behind the moral and legal embroidery of mutual, organic bonds was nothing more than the physics of knives, swords, and feudal armies, whose workings, when charted candidly, happened to match the workings of sovereignty. That is, however the laws and customs of Christendom may have limited the prerogatives of rulers, these rulers in reality exercised supremacy within their territories.[12]

Just how deeply does Occam's razor cut? The case of the skeptics rests on their ability to answer: If the Middle Ages was an era of de facto sovereignty, then who were the sovereigns? Possible candidates were the hundreds of feudal lords, a stratum of authority below the kings, the pope, and the emperor. In a classic study, historian Georges Duby shows that in the Mâconnais region of southern France during the twelfth century, lords were effectively free from royal, papist, or imperial rule—free to fight, ally with, and balance against one another.[13]

Twelfth-century France, however, was but a pocket of Europe during a pocket of the Middle Ages. Its typicality is far from clear. Even if this region were representative, it was not one of sovereignty, for its lords, if uncontrolled from above, still did not assert supreme authority over their vassals *below*. Typically, a vassal would pledge military service to a lord in exchange for a piece of land called a fief. But this exchange was reciprocal, more like an obligation between two independent parties than one between a minion and a sovereign, or between modern citizens and their government. Each set of obligations between lord and vassal had unique terms, determined by negotiations between them, not by a common law that prescribed obligations within a territory. Often a single vassal would have bonds with multiple lords, as well as with vassals further below him, who in turn had little meaningful relationship with the lord. It was rare that a lord could forcefully domesticate this dispersed loyalty. Feudal lines of obligation resembled a system of arteries in a body, not a pyramid with an apex.[14]

The pope and the emperor might also be candidates for sovereignty, the apex of a pyramid comprising the entire medieval world. But they did not qualify, either. In fact, contemporary struggles revealed them to be the chief checks on each other's authority. In 1073, Pope Gregory VII launched the investiture controversy, an attempt to widen his portion of the power to appoint bishops, a power that he shared with the emperor. During this struggle, engulfing half of Europe in half a century's wars, Gregory excommunicated the Holy Roman Emperor, Henry IV, and elicited the loyalty of the armies of the kings and nobles, who fought the armies of other kings and nobles equally loyal to the emperor. Yet never in this struggle did the pope claim theocratic rule, or the emperor claim sovereignty over the pope. During the twelfth century, Emperor Frederick Barbarossa strove for sovereignty within the Holy Roman Empire, but failed in his ambitions to conquer. Both the pope and the emperor also limited the territorial power of kings—witness the shared power of the pope and the emperor to appoint bishops, who had sizable civil prerogatives within the territories of kings. Certainly the terms of papal and imperial power were contested. But what sort of pope or emperor was it who, in these contests, could solicit the fealty of hundreds of nobles, kings, and their armies? For that matter, what sort of pope was it who could send thousands of troops on crusades to the Holy Land? Clearly, the authority of the pope and the emperor far exceeded whatever power they derived from controlling land and troops in sections of Italy or Germany. Plainly, this was not the age when Joseph Stalin would jeer, "How many divisions has the Pope?"[15] Even if the pope and emperor were not sovereign, they successfully kept kings from being sovereign. In the Middle Ages, virtually nobody was sovereign.

From the Middle Ages to Westphalia

This dispersed authority, of course, did not last forever. Following its apogee, the Middle Ages shed its diversity, leaf by leaf. Over the next three and a half centuries, this section, then that section, of the European landscape lost its eclecticism and became colored with sovereign states. By the eve of the Reformation in 1517, monarchs in Britain, France, and Sweden had established supremacy over the Church and other territorial rivals, while in Italy, a small system of sovereign states, sealed from Europe by alpine partitions, had survived for a century.[16]

But Europe's metamorphosis into modernity was far from finished. In the first decades of the sixteenth century, a great reversal in momentum occurred, one perhaps obscured by our retrospective sense of historical trajectory.[17] In 1527, the Italian states system imploded, and was swallowed and dismembered when Spain's army sacked Rome.[18] Even more jolting was the ascendancy of Charles V, who became king of Spain in 1517. This entitled him to rule Castile and Aragon, and also the Netherlands. Charles V was head of the Habsburg family. This gave him the inheritance of his four grandparents in Castile, Aragon, the Netherlands, part of Burgundy and Italy, and Austria; a decade later, he added the crowns of Bohemia, Croatia, and Hungary. Charles V became Holy Roman Emperor in 1519. By this title, he gained imperial prerogatives in Germany, in Switzerland, and in parts of the Netherlands and Italy. Imperial privileges were closely linked to another of his roles: Charles V was a Catholic. Although in Spain itself, the crown had already secured sovereign control over the Church, the Church still held many of its medieval prerogatives throughout the Holy Roman Empire, which Charles V would help to enforce. Its archbishops and bishops occupied temporal offices. It partially governed education, raised considerable revenues, and helped administer relief to the poor and carry out other public affairs, and most of all, often with the cooperation of temporal rulers, it monitored the religious allegiance of its members—their actions, their expressions of doctrine. Having sworn allegiance to the pope, to the upholding of the faith, Charles V served as the temporal enforcer of ecclesiastical orthodoxy, the commander of Catholic armies.[19]

But Charles V was not exactly sovereign over the empire, either. Only in Spain did this description fit his rule. The Dutch enjoyed rights and laws that predated, and limited, Spanish rule.[20] In Germany, the privileges of the emperor were significant, but many of them had become symbolic, too. The princes, nobles, and cities who made up the Imperial Diet (the legislative branch of the Holy Roman Empire), even those who held one of the seven positions of "elector" of the emperor, had become virtually independent in governing taxation, capital justice, trade, universities, internal order, economic regulation, and other matters. They consolidated their *Landeshoheit* (territorial lordship), and in place of the feudal law and parliamentary estates—old, conservative, and awkward—they imported the rational, precise, efficient system of Roman law, redolent of ancient Roman glory, and creating modern bureaucracies as tools for rule. Neither did imperial courts exercise significant influence.[21] Charles V, then, as emperor, king, Habsburg, and Catholic, stood at the center of a vast, eclectic, political conglomerate, yet was not a sovereign ruler in that realm; in this conglomerate, all political authorities were linked arcanely—medievally—over much of the surface of Europe, yet looked to no common ruler or law. This surface would eventually be refashioned as sovereign states, but not until 1648.

Later in the century, sovereignty made gains, but frail and reversible ones. When Charles V abdicated in 1555–1556, his successor as king of Spain, Philip II, failed to be elected emperor, thus severing his title over Austria and Germany. "Charles V's transcendental imperialism had deteriorated into a mere Spanish imperialism," writes historian H. G. Koenigsberger. Yet Spain still retained its other imperial possessions, remained a close dynastic ally with the emperor and the Habsburgs in Central Europe right up to Westphalia, and continued to be committed to Catholicism in Europe. For their part, the Habsburgs retained their universalistic aspiration to be prime rulers over a united Christian Europe.[22] In 1581, the northern provinces of the Netherlands declared independence from Spain, but they would contest it for seven decades, until 1648. And the efforts of Charles V, along with his Catholic German allies, to defeat Protestant heresy were defeated in the 1555 Peace of Augsburg. The terms of Augsburg revolved around the formula *cuius regio, euis religio* (whose the region, his the religion), allowing German princes to enforce their own faith, Catholic or Lutheran, within their own territory. For the princes, this meant sovereignty; it would complete their portfolio of powers.[23]

But Augsburg did not last. The settlement was packed with endless clauses and legal arcana, eliciting so much mutual dissatisfaction that Catholic and Protestant princes continually took up arms to dispute the succession of a neighboring prince of the rival religion. Over the following generations, religious war raged between a continually spreading Protestantism and the Counter Reformation, a revival of Catholicism across Europe whose most fervid participants fought for the eradication of the Protestant heresy and a restored Christendom.[24] Battles and skirmishes arose in the 1580s and continued on and off, expanding eventually into the holy cataclysm of the Thirty Years' War. Not until the close of this war did a proscription of such intervention become accepted and respected and practiced; not, indeed, until 1648.

The Novel Significance of Westphalia

What, then, was this Peace of Westphalia? Most literally, the settlement consisted of three treaties, ending three separate conflicts in the Thirty Years' War. On May 15, 1648, Spain and the Netherlands brought their war of eight decades to a close at a ceremony in the town hall at Münster. On August 6, at Osnabrück, the country of Sweden and Ferdinand III, the Holy Roman Emperor, made peace. Then, on October 24, representatives of the emperor and of Louis XIV, the young king of France, made peace in the name of their respective countries.[25] For many modern historians and political scientists, only the latter two treaties are the Peace of Westphalia. What is important is that in 1648, these key European disputes were settled—together, in the German region of Westphalia.[26]

Whatever principles Westphalia embodied, its designers meant for them to be comprehensive, governing all of Europe.[27] This very sweep is one of Westphalia's most significant novelties. In the words of historian Volker Gerhardt, the conference was "the first major political conference to be held by the European powers." Gerhardt goes on to explain, "This was not a Church Council, nor an Imperial Diet, but a meeting of independent territorial and political entities, where, for the first time, relevant alliances were taken into account. The Holy See was present only as an observer."[28] Participating in the negotiations were 109 delegations representing 16 European states, 66 imperial estates, and 27 other interest groups within the empire; 176 plenipotentiaries were involved in all. The negotiations were long and slow. It is not even clear when they began, or exactly when they ended, as envoys arrived in Münster and Osnabrück between 1643 and 1646 and departed between 1647 and 1649. Behind this puttering, sporadic rhythm was the absence of heads of state. Delegates were ambassadors, proxies, almost half of them lawyers.[29] A Venetian ambassador, Alvise Contarini, called the successful conclusion of the treaties a "wonder of the world."[30]

What is strange to modern observers is that such these diverse authorities conceived of themselves as members of a common society, Christendom. The delegates called themselves the "senate of the Christian world."[31] Such terms as "respublica christiana," "chrétienté," "orbis christianum," and "Christenheit" appeared in the treaties, as they did in other official documents of the period.[32] What is more familiar to moderns is that these members of Christendom negotiated not as members of a single political society, but as separate political entities. All of the negotiating partners with contractual capacity were legally organized and independent polities; even estates of the empire were partners to the settlement, alongside the emperor, monarchs, and republics. Only such independent powers were participants, unlike previous treaties, which involved members of royal families without ruling power. Every power involved was accorded legal equality, giving it freedom to sign or refuse all agreements—also a new development.[33]

Their appeals to Christendom reveal that delegates recognized themselves as a society; their independence and their separateness intimate that this society was a system of sovereign states. But was it a system of sovereign states that the parties themselves actually agreed upon? That is the crucial question. At first glance, the text of the settlement seems to lack any sort of general, founding principle at all. The treaties amount, rather, to a congeries of particulars, to settlements of myriad indemnity disputes and territorial squabbles from the Thirty Years' War. Nowhere, certainly, do they declare sovereignty or a system of sovereign states.[34] Although I will argue that crucial elements of sovereignty do appear in the treaties, these are admittedly woven in, not obvious. But a strict, literal, textual analysis only partially reveals the meaning of Westphalia. Just as courts often look not only at the literal text of law but also at the intentions of its framers in order to discern its intelligibility, meaning, and purpose, so we cannot understand Westphalia without asking what principles its signers understood it to embody. Finally, since constitutions of international society are matters of practice, not just legitimacy, we also find Westphalia's significance in the discernible behavioral changes that followed the settlement.

Text, intentions, and practice—these, then, are three tools for judging Westphalia as turning point. They answer our crucial question with respect to sovereignty: How did Westphalia render the authority of the polities of Europe? We may, in turn, apply these tools and answer this question in two contexts: first, the respective status of states and imperial institutions, and, second, the matter of religion. We will see that although Westphalia's standing as a historical breakpoint must be more qualified than the conventional wisdom suggests, the peace yet warrants recognition as a fulcrum, not just an incremental milemarker, in the evolution of a sovereign states system.

In 1998, an international symposium of scholars gathered in Münster to commemorate the 350th anniversary of Westphalia. Seeking to plumb the meaning of the peace, several historians confirmed precisely the conclusion of the turning point. Heinz Schilling, for instance, wrote, "As a religious peace treaty, which unlike that of 1555 was to be lasting, and as a peace treaty both within and between states, the Peace of Westphalia put an end to an epoch marked by 'belligerence,' Reformations and endemic religious warfare." He then averred that "we can speak of 1648 as a turning-point of universal historical significance."[35] Heinz Duchardt concluded similarly: "There can be no doubt that the Peace of Westphalia . . . brought about not inconsiderable territorial alterations, ended an eighty-year process of emancipation for one new republic, formally recognised the unrestricted sovereignty of another new political entity, and thus represents a crucial turning point in European history."[36] Heinhard Steiger echoed the judgment, specifying that sovereignty "became the fundamental principle of the European order."[37] Volker Gerhardt addressed sovereignty, too: "[The year] 1648 saw the emergence of a concept of sovereign statehood more modern than that of the nineteenth-century nation-state."[38] Clearly, the conclusion is neither outdated nor mythic. What is the substance behind it?

The Triumph of the State System over the Empire

In the wake of Westphalia, states were the chief form of constitutional authority in Europe, and their authority faced no serious rival in the Holy Roman Empire. This is the heart of my claim about historical change. Again, the treaties never announce the general constitutional authority of states.[39] Only in the eighteenth and nineteenth centuries did lawyers, princes, and philosophers—Vattel, most prominently—widely pronounce sovereignty, the equality of states, and nonintervention as principles of international society.[40] Westphalia, especially the Treaty of Osnabrück, was officially a new set of laws for the Holy Roman Empire—seemingly far from an abolition of this last medieval entity, which lasted until 1806. The empire was a major signatory to both treaties, thus legitimating the ongoing authority of its institutions. Several German bishops retained temporal authority; Sweden gained control of imperial bishoprics in Germany, thus allowing it representation at the Imperial Reichstag and in the assemblies of imperial circles.[41] There would continue to be an emperor, an Imperial Diet, and imperial judicial institutions. Some theorists of the time even concluded, drawing upon the writings of Jean Bodin, that the imperial institutions were themselves sovereign. Johannes Althusius, a seventeenth-century philosopher, argued more subtly that sovereignty lay in a constitution that spread power between imperial institutions and estates. Dieter Wyduckel, one of the historians at the commemorative gathering of 1998, concludes that in the Treaty of Osnabrück, it was the imperial estates whose rights advanced toward sovereignty, but also that "the threshold of the contemporary understanding of sovereignty is neither reached nor crossed."[42] Even less willing to be categorical was Samuel Pufendorf, who described the empire as an *irregulare aliquod corpus et monstro simile* (irregular and monsterlike body).[43]

Yet, for all of this imperial persistence, in momentous respects the treaties moved the sovereign authority of states into modernity. Again, the basic protocol of the negotiations posited equality among the parties, a truncation of imperial authority. The Spanish-Dutch treaty signed in Münster in May 1648 gave the United Provinces sovereign independence; the Swiss confederation gained effective independence, too. The bequeathing of this political status reveals its contemporary prestige. Major sections of both treaties (Article 8 of Osnabrück, paragraphs 62 to 66 of Münster) reestablished the "ancient rights" or even the "free exercise of territorial rights" of the German states against the Holy Roman Empire. Article 64 of Münster, although only a single article in the settlement, is remarkable in its sweep:

> To prevent for the future any Differences arising in the Politick States, all and every one of the Electors, Princes and States of the Roman Empire, are so establish'd and confirm'd in their antient Rights, Prerogatives, Libertys, Privileges, free exercise of Territorial Right . . . that they never can or ought to be molested therein by any whomsoever upon any manner of pretence.[44]

Article 65 then incorporates into these rights another fundamental characteristic of sovereignty—the right to ally outside the empire, a vital perquisite that princes had long enjoyed, but which the empire had contested during the Thirty Years' War. True, this right was qualified: no alliance could be directed against the empire. But in conferring the freedom to conduct foreign policy, the article recognized a crucial prerogative of independent, sovereign states.[45]

These conclusions, though, arise only from the literal text of the treaties. State authority shone much less diluted in diplomatic communications, statements that point us to the underlying notions of their authors. In his careful study, Andreas Osiander shows these communications to be laced with principles that buttress the authority of the state. A "leitmotiv" in the negotiations was state autonomy, a principle that was to be extended to states within the empire, and was to replace the old medieval, imperial notion of obedience and subordination. Equality—the equality of European states, the rejection of universal papal and imperial authority, the logical complement to autonomy—also made frequent appearances.[46]

Evidence that the diplomats viewed the Westphalia settlement in terms of new, modern notions of international politics also comes from what we know of their home countries' contemporary outlooks on foreign policy. Over the previous generation, the two victor states in the Thirty Years' War, France and Sweden, had both developed new foreign policy goals and visions for the international system. Most definitive for the time was the vision of Cardinal Richelieu, chief minister to the French king Louis XIII. In his writings and in his policy, Richelieu worked out *raison d'état*, a secularized notion of politics in which the interests of European Christendom were identical with the power and prosperity of the French state. Internationally, Richelieu envisioned an equilibrium, a balance between the major powers of Europe, and even a rudimentary system of collective security, notions only intelligible if they assumed independent action among independent states. He was willing to allow confessional pluralism, too. Although he did not call for the abolition of the Holy Roman Empire, he desired the defeat of its universalistic aspirations, which meant, above all, its deference to the "liberties" of the German princes. These liberties, once untied from imperial enforcement of religion and the involvement of the Church in temporal affairs, amounted in substance to sovereignty. Richelieu died in 1642. But his ideals were carried forth in French diplomacy by his successor, Mazarin, who adopted nearly wholesale Richelieu's political philosophy. It was he who brought the spirit of Richelieu to the table at Westphalia.[47]

Swedish diplomats thought similarly. Their inspiration, one who had also adopted a new vision of international politics into Swedish foreign policy, was Gustavus Adolphus, the great Swedish king who brought Sweden into the Thirty Years' War in 1630. Gustavus had not developed a theory of politics like Richelieu's *raison d'état*, and, as a Lutheran king, his sympathies for the German princes were more openly partisan, but his substantive goals were largely the same: the defeat of the empire and the Habsburgs, and the autonomy of the German princes. It was with these aims that he justified the intervention of Sweden in the Thirty Years' War:

> It will be sufficient to say that the Spaniards and the House of Austria [Holy Roman Empire] have been always intent upon a Universal Monarchy, or at least designed the conquest of the Christian states and provinces in the West. . . . That House has made such progress, that if this brave and generous northern prince [Gustavus Adolphus] had not bestirred himself, and opposed that torrent, she had pushed her ambition and arms to the most distant kingdoms and provinces, which have hitherto preserved and maintained their liberty. . . . This is what has given occasion to His Majesty of Sweden to put fleets to sea and bring armies into the field, in order to preserve his friends; being thereto invited by several princes and states of the Empire, before they were entirely reduced to servitude and misery, wherein they now find themselves shackled.[48]

Like Richelieu, Gustavus died before the Westphalia negotiations, he in 1632. But also like Richelieu, the policies of Gustavus were carried on by his successors. In 1633, the Swedish chancellor, Count Axel Gustafsson

Oxtenstierna, announced Sweden's reason for entering the war: "to preserve the *aequilibrium* in all Europe."[49] Such was the vision that Sweden, like France, eventually sought to realize at Westphalia.

The German and Dutch states at Westphalia did not possess the grand vision of Sweden and France, but what they desired for themselves—freedom from imperial rule in their territorial affairs—was the set of powers that would make Europe a system of sovereign states. After Westphalia, the Dutch public began to look back to 1648 as the crucial year in which they had won their coveted independence.[50] It was the defeated states, too, that viewed Westphalia as the upset of universalism and the victory of separate rule. Generally, the Holy Roman Emperor Ferdinand harbored "substantial misgivings with regard to the confessional and dynastic concessions made during the peace negotiations."[51] But these were mild in comparison to the reaction of Pope Innocent X. During the negotiations, the pope's nuncio, Fabio Chigi, warned the members of the empire that they should agree to nothing that would contravene the ecclesiastical councils and orders of the Church. Once the settlement was signed, the pope found in it precisely such a contravention. Sensing the defeat of universal Catholic temporal authority, he issued a bull, *Zel Domus*, condemning the treaties as "null, void, invalid, iniquitous, unjust, damnable, reprobate, inane, empty of meaning and effect for all time." A clause in the settlement, though, had already declared preemptively that papal protests would not nullify the treaties.[52]

It was in the practice of politics immediately following Westphalia that sovereignty emerged most saliently of all. Though provisions of the settlement continued to uphold imperial prerogatives, in fact states became virtually uninhibited in their authority over internal matters. Imperial institutions were not totally defunct, for they encouraged peace, solidarity, and military cooperation among the many German states.[53] But they did not abridge sovereignty, as they exercised no control over the territorial affairs of German princes. Nor did they even prevent breaches in German solidarity. Despite the inoculatory clause in Article 65 of Münster, German states allied freely outside the empire, sometimes even contrary to the empire's interests. The emperor himself retained significant power only because he and his successors were Habsburgs, a family with sizable royal holdings and prerogatives. But the prerogatives of the Habsburgs were effectively contained within their central European lands—they were just another sovereign. They no longer even enjoyed dynastic solidarity with their kinsmen in Madrid.[54] John Gagliardo, a leading historian of the empire, observes, "The empire after 1648 was never again to function to any significant extent as a real supraterritorial government."[55]

There is an exception to the empire's general deference to state sovereignty—the Imperial Circles, regional organizations of princely states that were revived in the late seventeenth century, whose members would at times combine their military forces under a single command. But this exception was limited. The strong form of military cooperation was limited largely to the Franconia and Swabish circles, which were composed only of small German states, and which lasted only from 1697 to 1714, when they defended themselves against the invasions of Louis XIV.[56] There were other exceptions, too. For instance, a few imperial knighthoods remained after Westphalia, although they were a quickly declining institution. Together, these exceptions proved to be anomalies, imperfections in a historical fissure. Other vestiges of imperial authority that appeared in the treaties turned out to be unimportant in practice. For instance, Sweden's control of bishoprics in Germany, and France's control of bishoprics in Toul, Metz, and Verdun, amounted to sovereign control, displacing meaningful imperial control, replicating the general pattern of states monopolizing authority within their territories. There was little, then, to detract from the conclusion of historian Heinhard Steiger:

> The external legal relations between the powers were formed on the basis of the principle of "side-by-side" order and mutual independence. The medieval principles of a hierarchical *ordo* with Emperor and pope at its summit had been controversial since the fourteenth century. They finally lost their acceptance in the sixteenth and seventeenth centuries with the strengthening of the kings, the growing weakness of the Empire and the religious schism. Sovereignty—as a form of complete external and internal independence and self-determination in relation to every other power—became the fundamental principle of the European order. Thus, a horizontally conceived order of powers developed, in which all powers, including Emperor and pope, were legally placed side by side. To a certain extent, the treaties of Münster and Osnabrück provided the confirming conclusion to this development, thus at the same time marking the beginning of a new era.[57]

Religion and Sovereignty

Aside from the its elevation of the state and diminishment of the empire, the other major context in which Westphalia effectively ushered in a system of sovereign states was its prescriptions for politics and religion. Here, too, the text of the treaties does not explicitly establish sovereignty—at least not in the exact form of Augsburg in 1555, which granted German princes authority over religion in their land and allowed them to establish uniformity. Instead, princes consented to internal pluralism, agreeing to allow enumerated proportions of Catholic, Lutherans, and Calvinists to remain in their territories (taking the proportions existing in 1624 as their benchmark), to respect the rights of specified dissenters to worship, and to refrain from converting one another's subjects.[58]

But the crucial question for sovereignty is not whether princes signed agreements that simply affected their internal affairs. After all, modern states frequently agree to regulate prices or pollution within their borders without compromising their sovereignty. Rather, the question for sovereignty is whether any institution outside the state was vested with the constitutional authority to execute, legislate upon, or judge these agreements about religion. Here, the text of the treaties calls for arbitration of religious disputes, but through compromise, not majority decision, leaving the sovereign right of assent (and veto) virtually intact.[59] But given the outlooks of contemporary statespersons and diplomats, and considering subsequent practice, even these procedures would mean little. Historians of the period commonly agree that even in the late stages of the Thirty Years' War, political leaders had lost their religious zeal and ceased to contest religion as a political affair.[60] There is little record of any religious matter being contested or adjudicated through imperial institutions, either. Finally, unlike after Augsburg, neither princes nor the emperor would intervene to contest religion within another prince's territory. In general, religion ceased to be a casus belli. Whereas before Westphalia, religion was a constant cause of war and the cause of the gargantuan Thirty Years' War, during the period 1648–1713, Kalevi Holsti notes, religion caused only three wars, all between Europeans and Muslims. The trend continued in subsequent periods, too.[61]

Like the curtailment of imperial authority, this denominational neutrality, this willingness of political leaders to allow religious dissent, was also a novel departure. Augsburg was a failed attempt; this new scheme would last. The parties to Westphalia still conceived the agreement as a *christlicher Friede* and concluded it in the name of the Holy Trinity. Seventeenth-century poet Paul Gerhardt commemorated the peace in a spirit that virtually all of its signers could accept: "The peace that he gives / is all that is Good. / And he spreads the word— / the end is nigh; / be now with God / in eternal peace and calm."[62] But this was a Christian peace for a disunited Christendom. Catholics, Lutherans, and Calvinists sat together at the tables; the Treaty of Osnabrück even included the Russian Orthodox Church, represented by the grand prince of Moscow.[63] But none of them was to sustain a claim to a political order of a uniform faith.

The Formative Legacy of Westphalia

Together, text, context, and practice combine in a strong case for Westphalia as origin of a European system of sovereign states. The claim must be qualified by the absence of an explicit enunciation of sovereign statehood, by imperial persistence in the text of the treaties, and by a few anomalies in practice. But weighed against all those respects in which the new system advanced at Westphalia, such historical impurities fail to dethrone the conventional wisdom of historians and political scientists about the event in 1648. Westphalia has achieved its revolutionary constitutional significance, though, not only through its innovation, which guarantees it as nothing more than an interesting but episodic set of victory terms, but through its robustness, the endurance of its provisions even to today. Recall again what a constitution of international society is. Most important, it is constitutive, defining the holders of sovereignty and their most fundamental prerogatives. It does this according to the three faces of sovereignty. Its constitutive norms are both legitimate and practiced. These norms may be violated; there are exceptions to them; there are aberrations. But the constitution remains the substantive entity that is violated, and to which there are exceptions and aberrations.

After Westphalia, of course, subsequent revolutions in sovereignty have revised the Westphalian constitution. In chapter 3, I described the last half millennium of international constitutions as a double movement, the second movement composed of revolutions that have circumscribed sovereignty, beginning to erode Westphalia. Even these emendations of Westphalia, though, have far from nullified the enduring states system. The European Union, though a "supranational" entity that partially transcends the sovereign state, is still governed most forcefully by a Council of Ministers composed of states. The revolution of colonial independence revised the requirements for becoming a state, yet extended the sovereign states system to the entire globe. The minority treaty system created a domestic justice requirement for statehood, but left intact the requirement that a would-be state exhibit the fundamental attributes of statehood. Internationally sanctioned intervention after the Cold War violates the absolute sovereignty of the state, but does not create a permanent restriction on the state's authority, and often, indeed, leaves behind an ever more robust set of state institutions. These revolutions, then, are revisions of the state system, changes in the attributes of a substance, and are not creations of a wholly different kind of political system, emanations of a wholly new substance. Westphalia has experienced restrictions, truncations, modifications, and limitations, but Westphalia remains the thing restricted, truncated, modified, and limited.

The Durability of the First Face

Westphalia refashioned each of the three faces of sovereignty; its legacy is the persistence of this refashioning over the following three centuries. At Westphalia, the state became the legitimate polity within Europe, while the Holy Roman Empire virtually lost its sovereign prerogatives. Thus did the

Westphalian constitution determine the first face of sovereignty. States deepened the legitimacy of this determination by rearticulating it in subsequent treaties and law. They practiced it by crowding out the effective authority of alternative polities and by replicating themselves all across the globe.

What the 1713 Peace of Utrecht made clear, what this settlement of the War of Spanish Succession, the first major European diplomatic conference after Westphalia confirmed, was that states were the only significant European entity to declare and fight war, and that they fought war for their interests, above all else, their territorial might and integrity. The key objective of the settlement was to create a balance of power in Europe—one between states. At the Peace of Utrecht, the Holy Roman Emperor, refusing to desert the defiant spirit of Pope Innocent X, first claimed precedence over, and second, sought to represent, the estates of the empire rather than allow them to speak fully for themselves as sovereign states. Osiander notes the result: "On the latter point, he was defeated. On the former point, the congress eventually made a concession by awarding him a place of honour in front of a large mirror."[64] This world—one of states dealing with states, absent an effective Holy Roman Empire—had been present throughout the wars of the second half of the seventeenth century.

Equally impotent after Westphalia was another contemporary principle that might at first seem a challenge to sovereignty: dynastic ties. The monarchs of Europe remained richly connected by marriage and family ties, which often governed succession within their realm, shaped their alliance commitments, and even acted as a cause of war, though never a sufficient one, as Holsti points out.[65] But sovereignty, once again, is a matter of authority, not of what forces determine the conduct of international relations. Clearly in this period, no monarch, by virtue of his dynastic affiliation, exercised legal, constitutional authority within the territorial affairs of another monarch. Dynasties may have defined the holders of sovereignty within states, but they did not compromise sovereignty. Holsti describes how, indeed, dynastic claims faded even as an influence upon relations between states:

> In the eighteenth century, as territory took on increasing importance for state-building, defense, and general foreign policy purposes, concerns for succession began to relate less to the right to rule (who has the better claim to succeed in a particular jurisdiction; who is the true king, queen, or prince?) than to other values derived from territorial possession. . . . [T]erritory no longer resulted from a claim; the claim resulted from the demand for territory. Dynastic rights were systematically violated in the numerous territorial exchanges of the period. Even the selection of monarchs became a matter of strategic and diplomatic calculation, for the convenience and interests of the powers, and not a matter of discovering the correctness or priority of compet-

> ing claims. Matters of succession, in other words, had become fully internationalized, and the means for selection were either negotiated agreements among all parties concerned or the verdicts of the battlefield.[66]

More and more, dynasty was a legitimation, not a source of legitimacy; long before dynastic ties had ceased to be a restriction on sovereignty.[67]

Subsequent comprehensive diplomatic settlements—1815, 1856, the two world wars, the end of the Cold War in Europe—were likewise ones between sovereign states and often created rules for the conduct of these states. In the late nineteenth century, positive international law emerged, creating common explicit rules to govern war, recognition practices, commerce, the treatment of foreign nationals, and other matters—again, between states. The trend burgeoned in the League of Nations at the end of the First World War and culminated in the United Nations at the end of the Second World War, both settlements aspiring to unite every sovereign state into a common organization with common laws. The United Nations system more deeply than ever institutionalized what Westphalia began.

The robustness of the Westphalian state system has also emerged through its global replication. One of the grand themes of the twentieth century has been the decline of empires. Remarkably, the ubiquitous polity into which the British, French, German, Japanese, Dutch, Spanish, Portuguese, American, Belgian, Soviet, Ottoman, and Austro-Hungarian empires have been resolved, the polity into which Yugoslavia and Ethiopia have broken down, even in the 1990s, has been not a fiefdom, an empire, a barony, or a tribal society, but the sovereign state. Such a universal outcome testifies to the obduracy of the Westphalian die.

That obduracy in turn explains the defeat of most aspirants to a polity that transcends the sovereign state; Hitler and Napoleon, for example. The chief, striking exception, of course, is the European Union, the yield of a formidable revolution in sovereignty, as I described it in chapter 3. What this union proves is that although the Westphalian system has endured the industrial revolution, the rise of mass politics, other enormous changes in economic and political systems, and revolutions in technology, culture, and communication, there is yet no iron logic by which it must last. Westphalia is persistent, not permanent. All that I have wanted to show is the remarkableness of this persistence.

The Durability of the Second Face

It was only natural that as the Westphalian system expanded, its members would develop criteria for determining who could join—the second face of sovereignty. The skeletal core of these criteria has remained intact over the centuries since Westphalia, revised in important ways to be sure, but persisting recognizably. They came to be explicitly articulated in nineteenth-century international law, eventually formulated most famously in Article I of the Montevideo Convention of 1933: "The state as a person of international law should possess the following qualifications: (a) a permanent population; (b) a defined territory; (c) government; and (d) capacity to enter into relations with other states." Some scholars would add further criteria; the application and practice of all these criteria involve complexities that constitute an entire branch of international law.[68] In their essentials, though, the criteria amount to nothing much more than a description of a functional, independent state. To be recognized as a state, a polity must look like a state. The criteria grow out of, reflect, and help to expand the very constitutional authority structure established at Westphalia.

For an aspirant state, what is at stake in the criteria is what Stephen Krasner calls "international legal sovereignty"—the recognition of its sovereignty and its claim to independence that other states confer.[69] This general recognition is itself a trait of an international constitution, which is, after all, a mutually shared, commonly affirmed set of rules of authority. For polities that achieve statehood, recognition confers resultant boons—the possibility of official diplomatic relations with other states, membership in international organizations, and all associated benefits. Another consequence of recognition norms vivifies the contrast between politics before and after Westphalia. By providing procedures, channels, and standard expectations for becoming a state, the criteria make it possible for a polity to accede to statehood peacefully, without having to fight for the status. Possible, but far from automatic, of course. Where a norm of self-determination does not apply—that is, with the prominent exception of colonial cases after 1960, virtually always and everywhere in the Westphalian system—state-seeking polities within empires or larger states have enjoyed no general right to their desired status. They must achieve statehood either by negotiating it or extracting it through military struggle from their mother state. But when there exists a set of norms awaiting and assisting polities who have brought their captors to agree to independence, peaceful transition is a more likely possibility.

Prior to Westphalia, by contrast, achieving the recognition of one's independence from outsiders only meant war. The Dutch fought Spain for eighty years; the German states fought the Holy Roman Empire for 130 years, for their "liberties." To be sure, following Westphalia, there are also plenty of examples of long wars for independence. The United States, many of the South American countries who won independence from Spain in the early nineteenth century, some Eastern European states who became independent in the late nineteenth century, Ireland, Algeria, Indochina, Angola, Croatia, Bosnia, and others all come to mind. But far more numerous, in fact, have been peaceful accessions. Brazil, Canada, New Zealand, Australia, and the vast majority of the African and Asian states who gained independence after World War II, to which those states who fought long wars for independence were prominent exceptions, all fit this description. Still other polities, ones that were never colonies but had remained separate from international society, also came to be fully recognized in a manner that was both peaceful and norm governed—Russia in the early eighteenth century, the Ottoman Empire in the nineteenth century, and Siam, Japan, and China in the twentieth century.[70] Of course, it is difficult to say, apart from looking closely at any of these instances, what sort of factors, material and ideal, led imperial states and recognizing states to accord recognition to new members. At the very least, though, criteria for recognition provided normative channels by which the transition could occur and a standardized status into which a new member could arrive.

Over the centuries since Westphalia, the standards themselves have undergone some degree of revision. In the decades after Westphalia, European states recognized only Christian states as members of their system. In the nineteenth century, they secularized the standards as they recognized the Ottoman Empire. Toward outsiders, they still applied a "standard of civilization" requiring that a state protect the basic rights of its citizens as well as foreigners, that it maintain a domestic legal system that guarantees legal justice for all under its jurisdiction, and that it avoid certain "uncivilized" practices such as suttee, polygamy, and slavery.[71] By the twentieth century, though, even these standards were dropped. The Montevideo Convention demands nothing regarding the internal characteristics of an applicant to statehood. Neither do the League of Nations Covenant or the United Nations Charter. Both documents demand mainly a willingness to abide by the terms of the organization and acceptance by the organization's members.[72]

Larger revisions, departing more starkly from the Westphalian norm, have occurred, too. These are the revolutions in the second face that I described in chapter 3—the minority treaty system and the revolution of colonial independence. The minority system, though, is now defunct, and the colonial revolution is virtually consummated. There are few remaining peoples who fit the international legal definition of a colony—separated from their ruling state by a body of saltwater—who desire independence from their larger state. As is true for all norms, there are also individual exceptions to rules for recognition. States at times withhold diplomatic recognition of other states, of whose actions or internal character they disapprove.[73] The United States, for instance, withheld recognition from the Soviet Union for the first decade and a half of its existence, and from Communist China for the first two decades of its existence. Yet, the fact that withholding recognition even constitutes a violation of international norms makes little sense were norms of recognition not generally practiced in the first place. What these norms uphold is little other than the Westphalian system that has existed all along. If a polity has arrived at effective independence and will agree to the rules of the system of sovereign states—that is, if it looks and acts like the sort of polity that populated Europe at the Peace of Westphalia—then it is generally entitled to be recognized as a state.

The Durability of the Third Face

Constituted states that are recognized members of international society relate to each other according to rules—the third face of sovereignty. The most essential features of this face also have persisted largely intact since Westphalia. The most fundamental rule of all is *pact sunt servanda*, the principle that states ought to keep their treaty commitments. Upon it, the entire body of international law, the very possibility for the thousands of current legal agreements between states, is built. States consider the rule no less valid today than they did over three hundred years ago.

Nearly as crucial is nonintervention, the principle that states should refrain from seeking to alter the constitutions, regimes, or internal policies of other states. In the decades prior to Westphalia, religion was the last, though hideously potent, remaining rationale for intervention. The wane of this rationale solidified nonintervention. By the eighteenth century, Vattel identified nonintervention as a constituent principle of the international order. The principle has remained central ever since, and is now articulated in Articles 2(4) and 2(7) of the United Nations Charter.

Like rules of recognition, nonintervention has experienced exceptions, but none of which efface the constitutive centrality. Following the Congress of Vienna of 1815, Europe's conservative monarchs agreed that intervention could be conducted to quell revolution. In scattered historical stretches, some states have practiced regular intervention, sometimes justifying it by appealing to provisions of international law, such as the right to protect their endangered nationals. The intervention of Great Britain on the European Continent during the nineteenth century, the intervention of the United States in Latin America in the twentieth century, the intervention of both the United States and the Soviet Union around the world during the Cold War—these are all exceptions. Even the UN prohibition on intervention today is not absolute. In prohibiting intervention "in matters which are essentially within the domestic jurisdiction of any state," and in holding that nonintervention "shall not prejudice the application of enforcement measures under Chapter VII," Article 2(7) leaves room for intervention under some circumstances. Finally, as I described in chapter 3, the current revolution of internationally sanctioned intervention, in which UN-authorized interventions have become sharply more frequent, is a revolution in sovereignty, a significant revision of the third face of Westphalia.

But this revolution, like all of the exceptions and qualifications, fails to efface the general presumption of nonintervention that governs the system. The Congress of Vienna consensus on intervention lasted no longer than seven years. The practice of intervention by individual states never attained even close to the sort of general consensus that constitutes a revision in the constitution of international society. During the UN period prior to the end of the Cold War, few interventions ever attained UN Security Council approval, including humanitarian interventions aimed at stopping massive suffering in East Pakistan (now Bangladesh), Uganda, and Cambodia during the 1970s. Current interventions, though a significant development, must still attain the approval of the United Nations Security Council, and are still exceptional in the affairs of the world's states. Nonintervention is still a broadly constitutive principle, as it was in the wake of Westphalia.[74]

With respect to all three faces of sovereignty, then, a distinct contrast exists between the world prior to Westphalia and the world that arose out of Westphalia and has persisted ever since. It is indeed in the political history of the century prior to Westphalia that we best discern the tremendous historical significance of state sovereignty. States' invasions of other states to alter their religious practices, the empire's military assertions of religious uniformity—this religious war and its attendant abridgments of sovereignty were the chief sources of contention in European politics for over a century, the sources of internal struggles in France, Sweden, England, the Netherlands, and Germany, and the central cause of the Thirty Years' War, a war that involved most European powers, wiped out perhaps a quarter of Germany's population, and proved the most destructive and protracted European war prior to the twentieth century. "The houses have been burned down / the churches destroyed / The villages have been ransacked / all provisions eaten / One sees the cities, the country's hope, ablaze / The splendour of the country can no longer be seen," lamented an anonymous poet of the seventeenth century.[75] Large-scale religious conflict in Europe ceased after Westphalia; such change is what made it revolutionary. Westphalia was a firebreak, the firebreak that halted a raging world. In chapter 6, I will argue that the source of the rage is a central source of modern international relations.

SIX

THE ORIGIN OF WESTPHALIA

ALL THAT I HAVE ARGUED so far is that after 1648, Europe was no longer just as it was before. People less and less saw themselves as existing in a great chain of being, extending from the lowest peasant, plants, and animals even, up through the local lord, then perhaps to a prince or king, then through to the emperor, the pope, and finally God. And more and more, they were inhabitants of a local entity, where a single ruler was their ultimate temporal superior. It was becoming an age in which religion was private, the glory of monarchs public, while on the continental scale, the internal affairs of states were private, while the only publicly agreed upon value was noninterference. Europe was Machiavelli's world, Vattel's world.

Of a world in which sovereign statehood is the constitution of international society, this is a portrait, a description. I have said nothing at all about how it came to be. If sovereign statehood was a new practice among states, a new way for rulers to pursue their interests, I have said nothing about why rulers took an interest in this practice. If a system of sovereign states was codified into legitimacy, this does not mean that it was notions of legitimacy, ideas, and worldviews, rather than changes in technology, militaries, economies, or institutions of government that over centuries brought rulers to give it legitimacy. So this is the issue. If Westphalia was an origin, what was the origin of Westphalia?

The proximate cause of Westphalia was the Thirty Years' War and the coalition of powers that won it. The Protestant German principalities, the Dutch provinces, France, and Sweden each aspired to a Europe of sovereign states, and together they amassed the armies and wealth to defeat the emperor, the Catholic German principalities, Spain, and the Habsburgs of Central Europe, the sentries of a unified Catholic Christendom. Both the aspirations and the power of the victors were absent in 1517, when Martin Luther allegedly posted his 95 theses on the door of the Castle Church in Wittenberg to protest the corruptions of the Catholic Church. To explain Westphalia, we must explain what sort of dissonance arose in the interim.

That dissonance, I argue, was the Protestant Reformation. Through its conversions and its social power, Protestantism brought polities to conceive and pursue an interest in Westphalia that they did not possess previously. The domestic turmoil that brought them to adopt this interest and the international war caused by their pursuit of it together added up to a centurylong, continental crisis in pluralism, fueled by the Reformation, and finally settled by the establishment of a system of sovereign states.

No Reformation, No Westphalia: The Logic of the Counterfactual

That much of Europe was still politically medieval in 1517, even ebbing away from a system of sovereign states as Charles V consolidated his lands, intimates that between 1517 and 1648, some novel source of gravity arose to reverse the tide of history back toward Westphalia. We can even locate the reversal: At strewn points during these 130 years, several European political entities acquired for the first time an interest in a system of states. An ideas account notices that in many of these cases, this interest appeared roughly at the same time that Protestantism did. Structural accounts cannot deny this coincidence, but would portray it as little more than coincidence. Believing structures inexorable, they would minimize the reversal toward modernity. Charles V was but the final paroxysm of a dying Middle Ages; interests in sovereign statehood, even if they arose amidst Reformation furor, were the culmination of economic and institutional change that had germinated centuries earlier.

Ideas versus material interests: The Reformation has been classically implicated in such imbroglios, ever since it got tangled up in Max Weber's claim in *The Protestant Ethic* that it caused capitalism, in R. H. Tawney's rejoinder that capitalism caused it, and in so many sequels, epigones, and updated syntheses.[1] My thesis is an analogue to Weber's: The Reformation was a central cause of the international system. I am not the first to suggest the Reformation's influence upon Westphalia; social scientists and historians have already pointed it out.[2] But no historian or social scientist has described systematically the mechanisms of this influence—persuasion, social power, their sites and dates—nor demonstrated the independence of these mechanisms from structural forces. Indeed, virtually every account of the state and the states system rendered by sociologists and political scientists over the past couple of decades stresses structures almost exclusively. Faced with this skepticism, without a systematic demonstration, the influence of the Reformation can only remain a hypothesis.

Like Weber, I will argue for a multiplicity of causes. The Reformation was a partner to other forms of power. At the time of Luther's theses (1517), the European system had already begun to calcify through the formation of separate state institutions in England, France, and Sweden, and even a small system of states in Renaissance Italy—all prior to and independent of the Reformation and its social convulsion. Structural forces may well be largely responsible for this formation; if they are, then we must concede them this piece of the explanation. But if the potency of the Reformation is not exclusive, neither is it quotidian. Protestantism was not just one in a host of causes, but a central cause. Its early sixteenth-century injection into European history was crucial for bringing about the Westphalian system of sovereign states.

If I assert the centrality of the Reformation, I do not claim its absolute necessity. I cannot deny that had the Reformation not intervened in history, structural forces might still have brought about the states system. But the Reformation did intervene in history, and because it did, the state system came far sooner, in a far different manner, and with far different historical consequences, than it might otherwise have come. Were it not for the Reformation, medieval impediments to a sovereign state system would not have disappeared when they did, but at a much later time. Nor would they have receded as sweepingly, as simultaneously. Protestant ideas were continental in geography and encompassing in their content. They challenged all temporal powers of the Church and the empire. Sweeping causes produced sweeping effects. Were it not for the Reformation, the recession of the Middle Ages would likely have been staggered, this feature disappearing at one time, that feature disappearing decades, or a century, later. Material accounts themselves support this claim, for they show different states developing at different times.[3] With Hendrik Spruyt, I argue that "competitor" institutional forms persistently challenged the sovereign state long after the High Middle Ages, right up to the consolidation of the state. Spruyt places the time of this consolidation roughly at the time of Westphalia, but he does not treat the Reformation as an important explanatory cause.[4] My argument is that without the Reformation, institutional eclecticism would have continued long after Westphalia.

A different route to a system of sovereign states would in turn have yielded a very different subsequent history. For out of the religious wars, caused by the Reformation and settled at Westphalia, came the hollowing of the Holy Roman Empire, the hegemony of France under Louis XIV, the rise of the eighteenth-century balance of power, the Enlightenment, and the increased separation of religion and politics. Had these events not occurred, much else would have been different, too, with the trajectory of each historical branch becoming ever more speculative. The Reformation, then, was not a sole cause, but a central cause; although it was not absolutely necessary for the establishment of a system of sovereign states, it was indeed effectual in bringing it about. If a European sovereign states system had been fashioned solely by changing structures, we would not call it Westphalian, but would instead associate it with some later century, and some different—unimaginably different—combination of memorable wars and slowly acting historical forces.

How can we judge this counterfactual claim? We can best explain Westphalia, I propose, by explaining its proximate cause: the interest in the settlement that separate polities came to adopt and fight for—the adoption of a European system of sovereign states as their goal and their active pursuit of this goal through diplomacy and war. As the causes of Westphalia are colossally complex, this narrowing will simplify our story and will also enable us to compare polities' interest in Westphalia and their experience with the Reformation. Finally, the interests of polities in Westphalia were a centrally important cause of the settlement itself. An interest in having a system of sovereign states was the crucial precondition for a polity's pursuit of it; it was the key result of the Reformation crisis in pluralism; and the interests of several such polities were the vital turning points in the journey to Westphalia. Now, explaining these interests does not wholly explain Westphalia. Once I have accounted for how polities adopted their interests, I will then note how they won victory over other, opposed polities through international war. But the new interests are paramount; they are the crucial change, the point at which Westphalia became the intention of powerful leaders.

The German states, France, Sweden, and the northern provinces of the Netherlands were the main polities that developed an interest in Westphalia—all at some point between the beginning of the Reformation and the first decade of the seventeenth century. Some polities, the German states and the northern provinces of the Netherlands, were "proto-states," partially independent—for them, this interest meant independence for themselves and all those similarly situated. Others, who were already independent—France and Sweden—came to define their interest as achieving sovereign statehood for the rest of Europe. But the interests were essentially the same: the victory of a system of sovereign states against any political body that would deny it. We can identify within a decade precisely when each polity arrived at this interest. This date, I will seek to show, corresponds tightly with the onset of a polity's Reformation crisis. I will stress, too, a strong geographic correspondence. Those polities that were influenced by the Reformation adopted an interest in sovereign statehood; those who did not experience it did not. That these correspondences—across time and place—were tight is what it means for the Reformation to be a central cause.

Beyond these correspondences, it is necessary to know how the subversive ideas led to the political interest. The details vary, just as the effects and course of the Reformation varied from France to Germany to Sweden, but every version shares some constants. In all cases, ideas exercised influence by creating a crisis of pluralism, a miniature of the crisis of pluralism that spread to the Continent in the Thirty Years' War. In all cases, too, the eventual solution to this crisis was a secularized conception of politics, a new wide separation of temporal and spiritual authority. Incorporated in this conception was the notion of a system of states free from the constitutional powers of the empire and the papacy. Perhaps surprisingly, these effects of Protestant ideas—a crisis of pluralism, secularized politics—did not always achieve what might have been expected: a popular victory for the Reformation and officially Protestant states. Although a Protestant triumph did take place in Germany, the Netherlands, and Sweden, it was not a necessary condition for a polity to have an interest in sovereign statehood. The evidence for the alternative lies in France. There, Protestantism became only a minority sect, was never the official religion, and was eventually wiped out. But what the French Reformation did bring was thirty years of religious war—a crisis of pluralism. Destructive of France's political order, this crisis in turn evoked the *politiques*, a party of Catholics that advocated secularized politics: tolerance at home, in order to achieve social peace, and *raison d'état* abroad, pursued by sovereign states within a system of sovereign states. Though the French story is more circuitous than the others, its bears the same essentials. A Reformation crisis led to a secular conception of politics that included an interest in having a system of sovereign states.

In all instances, interests in sovereign statehood arose from social crises. But not just any sort of social crises. They were ones whose causes, character, and results were linked to the intrinsic propositions of Protestantism. The solution to these crises was not lower taxes, a weakening of the nobility, democratic politics, a people's republic, an end to monarchy, or a cession of land, but a new separation between temporal and ecclesial realms, resulting from the effect of the spiritually subversive ideas.

It was through their two roles and various couriers that Protestant ideas brought such a crisis of pluralism. Protestant ideas originated with theologians and spread through transnational networks of monasteries, universities, and churches, shaping the identities first of clergy, then the laity, including town leaders, merchants, nobles, artisans, the urban poor, sometimes peasants, and at times princes and other rulers. Converts then exercised social power through worshiping, organizing, and congregating separately from the Roman Catholic church, through allying with the local prince, and through forming armies to fight Catholic rulers. Against a recalcitrant prince, this social power acted as pressure; on behalf of a cooperative prince, it provided support against opponents of the change. The Reformation did not always come from "below"; in England and Sweden, it was monarchs who introduced it, although these monarchs took up the Reformation only after it had spread widely and popularly elsewhere, and they relied on the readiness of their populations to adopt it in spreading it further. Everywhere, both conversion and social power were the tools through which Protestantism shaped the interests of the polities that fought the long struggle for Westphalia.

Structural Skepticism of the Reformation's Efficacy

Structural skeptics are wary of these alleged workings of ideas, their nuanced and detailed social crafting. These skeptics come at two levels. The boldest doubt even the Reformation's first role of shaping identities. Protestantism was capitalism's pliant veneer of holiness, the early modern state's softening coloration. The other skeptics, less ambitious, allow that ideas might have shaped identities, and that the Reformation might have remodeled souls, but they deny the second role of ideas—that they exerted social power or had any real influence upon the interests of early modern polities in a Westphalian international constitution. Instead, metamorphoses of state institutions, of technological, economic, or class structures, rendered the Reformation redundant.

Skepticism about the social power of ideas is found among most of the social scientists who have sought out the early modern origins of the European state. Their skepticism is usually not explicit; they do not openly doubt the role of the Reformation, but rather they have little to say about it, or about ideas, at all. They believe that the unfolding of capitalism and monarchy, new military technologies, the rise of trade, or some combination of impersonal forces all made the state a more competitive, survivable form of institution than the cities of the Hanseatic League, the Italian city-states, or the Holy Roman Empire. In some cases, the state prevailed because it could best fight war. War is central in the work of Charles Tilly, as it is among theorists of the "military revolution," the early modern transformation of military technology and organization that expanded the cost and scale of warfare. States, the theory runs, were better able to adapt than any other institution.[5] In other versions, the state won because the state could best produce wealth. A state had the strength, scale, and ability to provide such advantages as the power to establish property rights in order to create markets, extract taxes, and credibly commit to trade agreements with other states.[6] In still other versions, changes in the early modern class structure resulted in the state.[7] Any of these theories of the state may be extrapolated to the modern states system. The same forces that created individual states created a whole continent of states, and when these new states became states, they began to act like states. They extended their territory and wealth as they rationally could, sought to eradicate threats, and, when the number of states in the world made it possible, they used the classic tool of states—war—to defeat the Holy Roman Empire, the last medieval holdout.

The most recent version of these theories, this one focusing on the modern states system, is in the work of Hendrik Spruyt, who seeks to challenge the traditional view of social scientists—Weberian, Durkheimian, Marxist—that the states system developed along a direct path away from the medieval system of feudal, papal, and imperial authority. He shows that not only states, but also city-states (as in Italy) and city-leagues (as in Germany), grew out of medieval soil. The state system triumphed only after defeating these rival successors to the Middle Ages. Spruyt's task is twofold: to show first the reasons for the initial diversity of postmedieval institutions, and then to show why the state system eventually proved the most robust. Economic changes such as the growth of trade, the response of nobles, kings, and urban merchants to this change, and the importance of the beliefs of these actors are all crucial for Spruyt. His claims for these influences are insightful, as are his claims about the indirect evolution of the modern states system. Spruyt, however, hardly mentions the Reformation. Although he notes the importance of ideas about modernity, he stresses the efficiency of the state in creating markets, preventing free riding, and coordinating its actions with other states—all structural causes.[8]

Finally, there are Realist versions of the triumph of the state system. A Realist account may at first seem misleading. Does not Realism assume that a sovereign states system already exists? Strictly, yes, but we can still find accounts, closely resembling Realism, of how the European balance of power shifted away from the Habsburgs and toward an alliance of France and the partially independent German and Dutch "proto-states." The Thirty Years' War was the hegemonic war that consolidated this power shift; the Westphalian system of sovereign states was the set of terms that sanctioned it. For Realists, this reconfiguring of relative power, not the Reformation, was the crucial change of the century prior to 1648.[9]

If my account can meet such skepticism, establishing that new ideas, not changing structures alone, wrought Westphalia, it must then face the more grasping skepticism of the Reformation's very autonomy, according to which Europeans took up Protestantism because their advantaged position in changing economic and political structures made the ideas fit like a well-tailored suit. This skepticism challenges the first role of ideas, their shaping of identities. Most often, the argument is that Protestantism was the religion of the rising bourgeoisie. Over the past generation, scholarship on Reformation history has generally favored such social history, emphasizing class and social predicament, departing from previous purely theological and doctrinal accounts. Recently, though, historians have offered more complex syntheses, granting ideas more independence. These are in the spirit of my claims. Like ideas as forms of social power, ideas as shapers of Protestant identities were a central influence, not a sole cause.[10]

We must grant structures their due. Alone, they played a strong role in creating separate states and even a small Italian system of states. I will seek to identify specifically what part they play in the Westphalian story—and what part they do not play. In the end, I claim, their evolution fails to correspond to the interests of polities well enough to explain them. As structural skepticism lies in the tradition of historical sociology, so, in making the case for Protestant ideas, I seek to argue in the same tradition, using broad comparisons over time and place to show the influence of ideas.

In the rest of this chapter and in chapter 7, I will seek to demonstrate the Reformation's causal centrality. First, I will describe Reformation political theology and how it translated into a desire for sovereign statehood. The crucial comparative evidence follows—that is, the geographic and temporal correspondences between the outbreaks of Reformation crises and polities' adoption of an interest in a system of sovereign states. In chapter 7, I show how, through conversion and social power, Protestantism elicited these interests. Then, I describe briefly how, once polities adopted their interest, they attained Westphalia through struggle. The ensuing sections take up structural skepticism. I address arguments that the Reformation was merely an instrument of the power of princes, or that interests in sovereign statehood can be explained entirely as a result of the growth of state institutions. Finally, I treat skepticism of the very autonomy of the Reformation, reducing Protestantism to class or political interests.

The Political Theology of the Reformation

Everything began with the Fall. Not in the road to Westphalia, but in the theology of Martin Luther, which begins with the "corrupt tree" of humanity: "bound, captive, wretched, sick and dead."[11] It was this bleak fallenness and Luther's hopeful solution to it that thousands of Europeans understood and accepted, adopting Protestant teachings into their identity. What exactly were these teachings? And how did this stark description of humanity's spiritual predicament ever translate into politics? Into an interest in sovereign statehood?

A reader of John Calvin's *Institutes* today, one who had been only casually informed of its historical context, might be surprised to find Calvin prosecuting his vituperative case not only against the Roman Catholic "whore of Babylon," but also against perhaps a dozen other rival reform movements, all of which proposed their own conflicting interpretations of baptism, confession, worship, the Eucharist, the Virgin Mary, the saints, the liturgy, the structure of the Church, and the relationship between the Church and the state. The Reformation was not simply a single social uprising, but a whole litter of movements, Lutheran, Calvinist and other, each begetting further splinter movements, an incessant mitosis that continues through this day. Protestantism was a spate of protests, the Reformation a plethora of reforms.

What virtually all Protestants agreed upon, though, was what they protested against. That was the Catholic Church, or as many of them called it, the Roman Church, a label meant to particularize its claim to catholicity, or universality. The basic fault of this Church was accretion. During the Middle Ages, it had added to the pure simple gospel of the early Christian church a worldly, wealthy, powerful papacy and hierarchy; beliefs about Mary, purgatory, indulgences, and the saints that far exceeded Scripture; classical Aristotelian learning; bishops who held political office; and other corrupting, allegedly human inventions. Against such encrustations, the Reformers sought to preach the mere essentials of the Christian gospel, that which was alone, solely important. It is through the four *Solas* of the Reformation that we may thus summarize the commonality of this revolution in ideas. Most important was *Sola Fide*, or justification by faith alone, the doctrine that salvation comes solely through the faith of the believer, and is not merited through good works or penance. Closely related were *Sola Gratia*—by grace alone the believer is saved; *Sola Scriptura*—Scripture alone is the source of revealed truth; and *Soli Deo Gloria*—to God alone belongs glory. In these *Solas* lay the "mere Christianity" of the Gospels.[12]

The most memorable leaders of the Reformation, Luther, Calvin, Luther's cohort Philip Melanchthon, and others, understood the *Solas* first as theological propositions, ones they had arrived at through careful reading of Scripture, studious retrieval of early church teachings, and engagement with late medieval philosophical movements.[13] The same theologians, though, along with their allied preachers and propagandists, skillfully presented the same doctrines to merchants, artisans, and crowds through sermons excoriating priests as fleshy, indulgent, licentious, drunken, hoarding thieves, through tracts and pamphlets depicting the Church as a dragon or a devil, through woodcuts that etched the Harlot Rome, through satires of the Mass, hangings in effigy, and mock processions. It was typically tropes that led Protestants to their new identities. But as colorful, roughshod, rhetorical, screeching, and mocking as such symbols were, what they advocated were quite the same reforms as the theologians, in all their reflection, urged.

For the contemporary social and political structure, the weightiest implication of all of this iconoclasm was the stripping of the Catholic Church of its powers, and of its claim to be the seat of visible unity in the Body of Christ. This aim, too, was rooted in Reformation theology. The "universal" church, as Luther now defined it, was not a single visible institution under a single, fallible, human head, but was simply the aggregate of doctrinally authentic local churches. How was one to know which churches were authentic? Here, the reformers proposed a set of "marks" or "signs" that would reveal the true church. Exactly which marks mattered depended on the reformer. In the Augsburg Confession of 1530, for instance, Melanchthon declared the church present wherever "the Gospel is rightly preached and the sacraments are rightly administered."[14] Luther himself revised his doctrine of the "signs" over the course of his career.[15]

But whatever the precise marks were, they amounted to a spare definition of the church when contrasted with the church that permeated the social structure of Christendom, stretching into matters that we now consider squarely temporal. A major source of the vast wealth and power of the Catholic Church was its holdings of land, which it taxed and defended, and where it administered government and justice. Within the Holy Roman Empire alone, the Church held one-third of the land in general and one-fourth of the property in the cities.[16] It was quite common for a bishop or other prelate to hold a powerful temporal office under a prince or a king. The pope himself was head of an Italian state, and engaged in defense and diplomacy. He could excommunicate any secular ruler, a source of considerable power. Throughout Europe, the Church exercised deep control over the universities and poor relief. Most pervasively of all, it enjoyed the cooperation of secular rulers, from the Holy Roman Emperor down to princes and nobles, in enforcing its authority over its priests and the orthodox religious practice of its parishioners. The Church thus sharply limited the powers of secular rulers within their territories. The military power of the emperor also came from outside the state, and princes who cooperated with the Church acted on behalf of an authority outside their territorial realm. All of this, the reformers disputed. Not only did they challenge the involvement of the Church in secular affairs, but even its very universal hierarchical authority within its most proper matters—the status and functions of priests, the role of monasteries, and practices of confession, penance, and liturgy. In such things, the reformers thought they could act without the consent of Rome or Rome's bishops.[17]

But such relinquished powers, at least the political and economic ones, could not be left adrift, and it was the secular authorities who took them up—in Germany, princes; in the Netherlands, the States-General; in Sweden and England, the king. This, too, was prescribed in Protestant theology. Denuding the Church of its temporal powers meant creating a greater separation between spiritual and temporal realms, an idea articulated strongest in Luther's "Doctrine of the Two Kingdoms and the Two Governments"—his political theology. God created two earthly orders with two forms of government, Luther's reasoning ran. One order was the "realm of the spirit," the site of the relationship between Christ and the soul of the believer. Animating this realm was the Word, not visible institutions. The other order was the "realm of the world," the order of secular society, of visible institutions, governed through civil magistrates, laws, and coercion. All believers were to submit to both realms; each realm would promote their good in a different sense. In the realm of the spirit, they would encounter the Word and the Sacraments, vital to their salvation. The realm of the world was one where public order was ensured through the restraint of sinful human beings. The demand of the reformers was that the two realms be separately organized. The pastors and leaders in the Church, the realm of the spirit, were not to perform the duties of public order, just as magistrates, princes, and kings would not preach or perform the sacraments.[18]

We must avoid anachronistically labeling Luther's doctrine a "separation of church and state." The reformers admonished princes to be godly rulers; after all, in his Letter to the Romans, St. Paul had taught Christians that rulers are ordained "for your good."[19] Churches could appropriately instruct and guide rulers in their conduct. Much more intrusive, at least to the twentieth-century liberal democrat, was the role of the state that the reformers envisioned. Luther, Calvin, John Knox in Scotland, and many others called for the state directly to support church authority, a principle known as "Erastianism." This might mean suppressing dissenters; a Lutheran prince might prevent Calvinists and Catholics from worshiping in his realm, for instance. The state might also play a strong role in selecting the leaders of the church within his realm. "[U]ltimately," writes Reformation historian Euan Cameron, "the Lutheran churches became very largely departments of state in their respective territories."[20] Not all reformers were Erastians. Anabaptists such as the Mennonites, for instance, argued that Christians were to participate as little as possible in secular government, and that government ought to have as little as possible to do with them. But the major reform movements became national churches—German Lutherans, Swedish Lutherans, Scottish Presbyterians, the Anglican Church, and so on, organized within a territorial realm, dependent upon a territorial government, but not as entangled with this government as the Catholic Church was with temporal authorities in Christendom. The Protestant arrangement was a direct reflection of Luther's Two Kingdoms Doctrine and its close cousins.[21]

A territorial state free from the temporal power of the pope, the emperor, and the entire Catholic Church, a territorial state whose ruler had appropriated Catholic Church lands and powers within its realm, assisted splinter churches in freeing themselves from Catholic authority, and defended these churches against the emperor—this was a state whose ruler would now be sovereign. In none of Luther's tracts, nor in Calvin's *Insti-*

tutes, do we explicitly find mention of sovereignty, or still less, a Westphalian system of sovereign states. But what their political theology prescribed was the substance of sovereignty. If the Catholic Church's formidable remaining temporal powers were transferred to secular rulers, the temporal powers of these rulers would then be complete and supreme. Rulers would be absolutely sovereign. The point is crucial: sovereignty, in substance if not in name, comes directly out of the very propositions of Protestant theology, in all of its variants. The secularized conception of politics entailed in the political writings of leading Protestants contained all the content of sovereignty. It was entirely fitting that those who came to hold these propositions as their own beliefs would seek to pressure the ruler of their polity to seek sovereignty, in his own state and elsewhere, as a political end.

The emperor Charles V, speaking for the Catholic Church, condemned Luther in the famous showdown at the Diet of Worms of 1521. A decade later, Charles V sent his troops to quell the heresy in Germany. Later in the century, he similarly sought to stamp out the Calvinist reformation in the Netherlands. Over virtually the entire period between 1530 and 1648, the emperor and some combination of Catholic princes, drawing upon the surge of Counter Reformation energy, sought the military erasure of Protestantism. Facing armed eradication—of their practices and their persons—reformers now found even more reason to ally with, and give full sovereignty to, secular rulers, whose armies could protect them. This pursuit of protection was a second, more indirect, route through which the theological propositions of the Reformation led their adherents to sovereign statehood. Although physical protection considered in isolation is hardly a theologically laden desideratum, the need of the reformers for it is scarcely intelligible apart from their heretical beliefs, propositions that alone elicited the armed response of the emperor and, in turn, their need for defense. The dynamic is cyclical: Protestant propositions provoked the hostile reaction of Catholic authority, leading the holders of the propositions to seek goals that reinforced their content. Sovereign statehood was the carapace that would stanch the Counter Reformation.

Direct propositions and the pursuit of protection, then, are both features of the intrinsic efficacy of Protestant ideas. In their very content lay the prescription for the new Westphalian order. This connection between content and political result is the first element in the argument "no Reformation, no Westphalia." But if the argument is about the potency of propositions, a certain objection might here arise. It notices that the Reformation was not the first "heresy" to challenge Catholic authority and doctrine. If it was heretical ideas that led to Westphalia, then why did not previous heresies, also iconoclastic in their content, have the same political effect?

The answer, true to the argument, lies in the very conte
ous heresies. Quite simply, they were not the same ideas. W
other heresies? The three strongest movements were the L
gland, the Waldenses in parts of southern France, Italy, and G
most prominently, the Hussites in Bohemia. Each was a netw
who held and spread beliefs contrary to those of the official c
ally they were a minority within a local population, always claiming to be against its dominant culture, often internally divided, constantly debating among themselves whether certain factions were "selling" out to the culture and the Catholic Church. Continually persecuted by Rome, such movements remained weak. The Lollards in England were inspired by the dissenting theologian John Wycliffe, and continued to preach from the late fourteenth century up to the eve of the Reformation. The Waldenses on the Continent sustained a community of traveling preachers from at least as far back as the middle fourteenth century and continued up to and through the Reformation. The Hussites, followers of the Bohemian preacher Jan Hus, became the strongest of all, succeeding in organizing a separate church, the "Brotherly Unity," by the second half of the fifteenth century.[22]

The preponderance of the grievances of each group was with this or that abuse within the Church. The right of sinful priests to hold authority and power in the Church, the denial of the chalice to the laity, the wealth and status of the Church within society, and some Church dogmas such as the reality of purgatory or the value of prayer for the dead all came under question in one movement or another. But what none of these movements developed was a systematic theology of the church or anything approaching the ideas in Calvin's *Institutes*, which set forth key Christian doctrines of faith, works, grace, scripture, and ecclesiology in opposition to the Catholic Church. Most importantly for the question of sovereignty, none of them set forth, like Luther, a Doctrine of the Two Kingdoms or any set of ideas about where temporal and spiritual authority should appropriately rest. The Hussites came closest to developing an actual Reformation state. They formed a church, denied that the Roman hierarchy was necessarily the seat of the unified earthly Christian church, and were supported in their schism by the secular rulers in Prague. But even the Hussites developed no extensive theology about the "signs" of an authentic church or about the proper powers of secular authorities. Their schismatic urges were motivated mostly by their reaction to abuses in the Catholic Church, not to the essence of the Church. No previous heresy, then, contained propositions that enunciated the substance of temporal sovereignty, whereas the theology of Luther, Calvin, Knox, and other leading reformers contained just such propositions. It is not my claim that these propositions alone account for the efficacy of the Reformation in producing interests in sovereign statehood. Favorable "circumstances of reflection" were also influential, as I shall argue. But it is the political theology of the Reformation that finds an affinity with the continental revolution in sovereignty, while the complaints of the earlier heretical movements envisioned little more than underground movements or a small established church on a small piece of Czech land.[23]

The Correlation between the Reformation and Polities' Interests in Westphalia

That sovereignty springs from the very words of the Reformation begins to suggest the power of Protestantism. But if Reformation theology and interests in sovereignty are connected intrinsically, conceptually, we now need evidence that they are connected historically and causally. Notice, then, a very impressive historical correlation: every polity that came to have an interest in a system of sovereign states had experienced a strong Reformation crisis, whereas in every polity that had fought to prevent a sovereign states system, the Reformation won few converts. The correlation is also one of timing: Most of the polities that acquired an interest in a system of sovereign states did so soon after, usually within a generation of, the day when Protestantism arrived in their land; most of them had shown little inclination toward a sovereign states system before Protestantism arrived. These correlations anchor the argument. The first three columns of table 6.1 show this correlation in simplified form. The table shows that the presence and timing of a Reformation crisis corresponds strongly with a political interest in Westphalia. In the four chief polities (or region of polities, in the case of Germany) that fought for Westphalia—Germany, the Netherlands, Sweden, and France—an interest in a system of sovereign states arose within a generation of its Reformation crisis. England, Denmark, and Transylvania were not integrally and powerfully involved in the armed conflict for Westphalia, but they too experienced a Reformation crisis and supported the anti-imperial powers diplomatically. Important, too, is the fact that none of the Catholic polities, the Catholic German principalities, Spain, Italy, or Poland developed an interest in a system of sovereign states at all. Through the century of the Reformation conflict, they remain allied with the Holy Roman Empire.

Table 6.1 is a summary. When the mutineers against the Middle Ages adopted their seditious interest in sovereign statehood, what exactly it meant for various polities to have an interest in Westphalia, and when they experienced the Reformation beg more careful description.

TABLE 6.1
The Correlation Summarized

Policy	*Interest in Westphalian System of Sovereign States*	*Reformation Crisis*	*Growth in State Institutions*
German Protestant States*	1520–1545	1520–1540s	Gradual in sixteenth century; sharp after 1650
German Catholic States*	None	Weak, remaining minority status	Gradual in sixteenth century; sharp after 1650
Netherlands (United Provinces)	1581	1560s	Sharp, beginning in 1590's
Sweden	1540s	1520s	Gradual after 1600; sharp between 1672 and 1718
France	1620s	1560s–1598	Gradual after 1600; sharp after 1650
Spain	None	None	Sharp from 1470s to 1550s
Italy	None	None	1400s, growth of city-states, approximation of sovereign states system until 1527
Poland	None	Moderate spread of Protestantism, but no significant crisis	Little significant growth
Habsburg Hungary	None	Mild spread of Protestantism, but no significant crisis	Little significant growth
Transylvania	1618	1550	Little significant growth
Denmark	1538	1520s and 1530s	Little significant growth
England	Support for European Protestants short of all-out war 1560s–1648	1530s	Significant growth through sixteenth century

* Some German states switched between official Catholic and Protestant status as a result of war and political bargaining between the 1555 Peace of Augsburg and 1648. I label the states here according to the status which they first assumed during the Reformation crisis of 1520–1545.

Germany

In Germany, the Reformation began; in Germany, it first had political effects. In the German-speaking territories, including Swiss and Austrian regions, princes and city magistrates in the early sixteenth century came to desire a full portfolio of sovereign powers, much like those that kings in England and France already enjoyed. Although they could hardly conceive of a Westphalian Europe, one in which German, Swiss, and Dutch principalities were all independent of the Holy Roman Empire, German rulers' pursuit of their own independence was a crucial piece of the Westphalia puzzle.

German princes, nobles, and city leaders began to wrest away remaining imperial prerogatives not long after Luther's public dissent in 1517. In Luther's own region of Saxony, the Elector John, once he took his position in 1525, placed Church lands under state control, replaced the bishops who governed the Church with a "Visitation" committee of electoral councilors and theologians, and began to enforce devotional uniformity, improve the standards and conduct of the clergy, and oversee the moral and spiritual affairs of the laity.[24] Much the same occurred in dozens of cities and principalities across Germany between 1523 and the late 1540s, when the German Lutheran Reformation finally ceased to expand. The princes often took greater control over the splinter churches than Luther had intended, although he was generally supportive of their appropriation. He actively assisted Elector John of Saxony, for instance, in placing church governance in secular hands. During the rest of the sixteenth century, the reliance of Protestant churches on the prince only grew stronger.[25]

Emperor Charles V and the stalwart Catholic princes then had to respond. The Imperial Diet of Speyer in 1526 agreed to a vague conciliatory resolution, but the absence of the emperor at the Diet left it without force. Archduke Ferdinand, Charles V's brother, then decreed that Protestantism be abandoned and the bishops restored. The Lutherans answered with a "protestation" (hence the term "Protestant") in 1529, and a showdown ensued in 1530 at the Diet of Augsburg, for which Charles V returned from his war with the Turks. Despite Protestant Philip Melanchthon's moderately stated Augsburg Confession, and despite Charles V's desire for a unified German front against the Turks, discord over papal supremacy prevented agreement. As Luther quipped to Melanchthon, "Agreement on doctrine is plainly impossible, unless the pope will abolish his popedom."[26] The Protestants organized into the Schmalkaldic League for defense, Charles V became determined to end the schism, and from this point on, both sides would fight and the possibility of a unified empire was doomed.[27]

Not all princes and magistrates went along with this thinking. Hesse, Brandenburg, Electoral Palatinate, Saxony, and tens of other principalities and cities became officially Protestant; rulers in Bavaria, Austria, and elsewhere remained Catholic; and some regions switched back and forth during the sixteenth century. Victory, sovereignty, the Protestant principalities won formally at the Peace of Augsburg in 1555, whose principle *cuius regio, euis religio* granted temporal executives *jus reformandi*, the right to determine the religion of their territory. Yet this simple formula disguised restless revisionism on both sides; and because it posited not tolerance for dissent, but a "winner take all" religious solution in each region, it created strong casuistic quandaries, the most difficult being whether Catholic authorities who became Protestant would retain their offices and privileges. The arcane provisions of the settlement on this matter became the cause or pretext of melee and war, of conversion in this region, counterconversion in that. All of these difficulties intensified after Catholicism received new energy for the Counter Reformation from the decrees of the Council of Trent in the 1560s. After a Catholic triumph in Cologne in 1585, more and more conflicts broke out over religious succession, rights, and property, not only in Germany but now in the Netherlands and Habsburg Austria and Bohemia, until in 1618 a dispute in Bohemia ignited thirty years of continual war, ending in Westphalia. Historian John Gagliardo writes, "Since conversions and reconversions continued to occur after 1555, Germany's confessional map resembled a periodically changing checkerboard into the time of the Thirty Years' War." Only after Westphalia would the sovereignty of German states rest unchallenged.[28]

German assertions of sovereignty during the 1520s, 1530s, and 1540s corresponded remarkably well with the furious advance of the German Lutheran Reformation during this same period. Prior to Luther's defiance of 1517, German rulers, though they had long appealed to German nationalism and brought hostile grievances against the Church and empire before Imperial Diets, had not threatened or hinted at a takeover of the temporal powers of the Church. It was not until after Luther rebelled that the first German ruler took up the cause; and no ruler took up the cause until his own subjects had first taken up reformed teachings. In Germany, the coincidence in timing, between the Reformation and interests in sovereign statehood, was virtually exact.[29]

The geographic coincidence between the Reformation and these interests arises in comparisons between German polities. In Germany, the diffusion of the Reformation was incomplete. Some regions became mostly Lutheran; some remained mostly Catholic; some ended up quite divided. The political outcomes—the faith that the prince adopted for himself and officially for his region—thus varied, too, and were often unstable, as Germany after the Augsburg peace reveals. With very few exceptions, though, polities that were officially Protestant fought for sovereign statehood and independence from the Holy Roman Empire, while officially Catholic polities remained loyal to the empire, fighting for its powers. In two periods of German war—the first between the 1530s and the 1550s, the second from the 1580s through Westphalia in 1648—alliances between Protestant polities fought alliances of Catholic polities and the empire. With strong consistency, alliance patterns followed confessional lines. Thus was true even when a polity changed religious hands. Typically, it would then change its alignment, too.[30]

The Netherlands

For the Dutch Provinces, as for Germany, sovereignty meant independence from the Holy Roman Empire. Although they enjoyed a long history of parliaments and liberties up through the middle of the sixteenth century, the provinces were still subjects of a governor-general appointed by the Spanish king. Though the king dominated all areas of policy except fiscal ones, few of the leading nobility in the Dutch States-General desired independence.[31] In the 1560s, when the Dutch Revolt began, the provinces appeared weak, divided by language, by parochial loyalties, and now by Protestant missionaries, who had arrived shortly after Luther's revolt in Germany and had benefited from the humanist legacy of Erasmus of Rotterdam, but who thus far had been silenced, stunted, beheaded.[32]

Provinces with local loyalties and an imperial administration—this was a brittle arrangement, brittle and strained by the end of the 1550s. The local nobility and King Philip II of Spain began to dispute over taxation, church reform, and the presence of the Spanish troops. While the nobility protested and maneuvered over dioceses and property and rank, less subtly discontented were the lower classes, the unemployed, and the throngs of urban laborers given the moniker "beggars," who gathered regularly and illegally in "open-air" meetings to hear Calvinist preachers and often riot afterward. Toward this fervor, the ruling nobles were ambivalent. Few sympathized, even those who themselves had converted to Calvinism; most were contemptuous. But neither could they alienate the Calvinists, whom they needed as allies against Spanish encroachment, and whose rebellion they feared. The solution put forth by the most prominent of the nobility, William of Orange, was religious toleration, a compromise inspired by the Treaty of Augsburg in Germany. In 1565, Catholic and Protestant aristocrats agreed upon toleration and appealed to Philip II for acquiescence.[33]

Philip II refused. In 1566, an opposition coalition in which Calvinists played a crucial part then revolted against Philip once again. In 1575, after a decade of fighting, William of Orange, the Dutch leader, could agree to recognize Philip II's royal authority, but religious freedom divided them irrevocably and ensured continued fighting. Even then, though, Orange did not demand sovereign statehood for his territories. It was only in a third revolt that the leaders of the Protestant united provinces came to pursue independent statehood. At the Pacification of Ghent in 1576, the governing States-General of the entire Netherlands agreed to allow religious toleration and continuation of Spanish rule—*cuius regio, euis religio*—but again encountered the intransigence of the Spanish king. Only on July 26, 1581 did a States-General of several northern Protestant provinces sign the Edict of Abjuration, renouncing entirely the authority of Philip II and asserting an interest in sovereignty. They would come to govern themselves as a loose confederation under the leadership of a common "stadholder." Their interest, then, was taken up less than two decades after the Dutch Reformation crisis began, and while it was still raging. Over the next seven decades, the provinces pursued this interest through war with the Spanish, pausing for a twelve-year truce between 1609 and 1621, ending finally in Spain's recognition of the sovereignty of the United Provinces at Westphalia.[34]

France

France defined its interest in sovereign statehood from a very different standpoint than Germany or the Netherlands did. France did not seek its own independence from the empire or the Catholic Church, which it had already effectively enjoyed since perhaps 1300, but rather it desired sovereign statehood for the rest of Europe, meaning the defeat of the powers of the Holy Roman Empire over its princes, cities, and estates.[35] Even more dissonant, though, was France's retention of its official Catholicism, a status that may appear quite at odds with my argument about the Reformation and Westphalia. Again, though, the argument is not that a polity had to adopt Protestantism as its official religion in order to be interested in Westphalia, but rather that the Reformation had produced a secularized conception of politics that entailed a system of sovereign states. This is precisely what happened in France.

How could a Catholic ruler embrace such secularism? Consider only Catherine de Medici, Catholic regent to the French king in the 1560s. Ruling at a time when French Calvinists, the Huguenots, were multiplying rapidly and threatening the stability of the French state, she was one of the first French leaders to advocate toleration of Protestant worship. She recommended toleration pragmatically, not out of deep principle but to strengthen the French crown, for which she would sacrifice the purity of Christendom. For the state, she could also compromise toleration, as she did in acquiescing to the St. Bartholomew's Day massacre of Huguenots in Paris in 1572. Catherine de Medici did not innovate a new foreign policy, for her country was plundered in its internal fracture during her reign. But she introduced the possibility of allowing toleration, for the state. Is it not entirely fitting that she was the granddaughter of the man to whom Machiavelli dedicated *The Prince*?

Catherine de Medici is iconic for the thesis at hand. It was Cardinal Richelieu, chief minister to the French king beginning in 1624, who first led France to take up a clear interest in Westphalia, a tolerationist solution for Europe. It was he who developed the new doctrine of *raison d'état*, privileging the state's security and power over any fealty to Christendom or its putative imperial and Habsburg representatives. France had never clearly pursued such a policy before. True, since 1519, its central policy goal had been to avoid Habsburg "encirclement." Between 1521 and the Peace of Cateau-Cambrésis of 1559, France's chief foreign pursuit was the Habsburg-Valois Wars, its chief venue Italy, where King Francis I fought Emperor Charles V for land. Francis I's chief goal was defensive, thwarting Charles V from completely surrounding France, and preventing the intervention of this emperor, whose publicists frequently wrote of a restored, unified Christendom. In pursuit of French security, Francis I was willing to ally with Protestant German princes and even the Turks, drawing the revulsion of orthodox Catholics. Henry II, who succeeded Francis in 1547, allied with German Protestants in order to gain for France the imperial bishoprics of Metz, Toulouse, and Verdun. No French king, however, sought a system of sovereign states or the general defeat of the Habsburgs. Despite its alliances with German princes, which had been designed to protect French borders, the crown never aimed to guarantee these princes sovereignty against Charles V. In signing a truce with Charles V at Crépy in 1544, Francis I agreed to support Charles V against the Turks, and against the Protestants should they refuse the decisions of the contemporary Council of Trent. Henry II, allying with German Protestants in the early 1550s, refused to wage a general war for the Reformation, as such a war would have weakened the Habsburgs, but he fought the armies of Charles V only insofar as it was necessary to secure Metz, Toulouse, and Verdun for France. It was in important part the need to fight heresy that led France to settle for peace at Cateau-Cambrésis in 1559.

Between 1560 and 1598, the French state was imploding, torn apart by civil wars between Calvinist Huguenots and defenders of the Catholic order. Then, it had scarcely a foreign policy at all, except for a brief defensive war against Spain during the 1590s. In May 1598, France entered a new phase of its political history as it officially adopted a policy that it had never before allowed: domestic toleration. Then, Henry of Navarre ascended to the throne as King Henry IV, made peace with the Spaniards, and signed the Edict of Nantes, a tolerationist compromise that permitted some Huguenot worship in some regions. Henry IV was a member of the *politique* party, a faction that advocated religious toleration at home in order to secure social peace and the acceptance of religious diversity abroad to preserve French security. Until his assassination in 1610, Henry IV pursued an anti-Habsburg foreign policy through small military forays against surrounding Habsburg lands, although it was unclear whether a general dismantling of Habsburg power was his aim. Between 1610 and 1624, under King Louis XIII, French foreign policy was in the hands of orthodox Catholics, and took a very different direction. France remained at peace with the Habsburgs in order to favor the restoration of Christendom. The contrast here is sharp. When a new approach to religion became empowered, foreign policy changed.[36]

It was not until the age of Richelieu, who became chief royal adviser in 1624, that France adopted an offensive policy of weakening, then destroying, the Holy Roman Empire and the Habsburgs by fighting for the permanent sovereign rights of German princes—that is, showing an interest in European sovereign statehood. He led France into wars against Catholic principalities in Italy during the 1620s, and into the Thirty Years' War against the Habsburgs and the empire in 1635. For the first time in its history, France fought for the dismantling, not merely the containment, of the Habsburg empire.

Like Henry IV, Richelieu was a *politique*—quintessentially so. The *politiques* were Catholics, and sanctioned the official Catholicism of France. But they could allow Protestants to remain within the realm. Toleration was pragmatic, reversible. Huguenots, still a threat to the Catholic crown, were to be contained, their expansion bottled. Richelieu himself fought the Huguenots, defeating them in battle in the late 1620s. But in the *politique* conception, it was at least possible for truces to be signed, a policy of eradication to be shelved. Abroad, the *politiques* advocated a counterpart policy, one that allowed the toleration of Protestantism within Christendom. This meant respecting the sovereignty of the Dutch and German Protestants within the Holy Roman Empire, and a corresponding defeat of the constitutional powers of the Holy Roman Empire over these realms.

What tied together the two strands of toleration—domestic and foreign—was the *politique* interest in the stability and security of the French state. The *politique* call for religious toleration was clearly motivated by a desire for the restoration of social peace following a generation of civil wars with the Huguenots. The *politiques* indeed proposed a new doctrine of the state, a secular, modern doctrine, one criticized for being heretical and Machiavellian. It held that the state was a collective personality with its own interests, separate from the interests of any particular rulers or the Church. Bodin proposed that the monarch should enjoy absolute sovereignty, that his will was above even the civil law. Such a doctrine could tolerate dissent. Even though the *politiques* preferred a world without the Protestant menace to social peace, they thought it better to attain order through a *modus vivendi* than to have constant violence and an impotent state.[37]

The external face of *politique* ideology was *raison d'état*, the idea that foreign affairs were to be conducted solely according to the rational interests of the state collective, without regard for international Catholicism or any separate ideal of justice. *Raison d'état* was Realism, a doctrine uniquely suited for a world of states. "Raison d'état," writes Friedrich Meinecke, "is the fundamental principle of national conduct, the State's first Law of Motion."[38] It made possible a foreign policy that showed no deference or restraint toward the Habsburgs. Of course, *raison d'état* was to be pursued rationally, cognizant of the opposing armies of other states. But as long as it was feasible, there was no reason why France should not stop short of vanquishing the whole Habsburg empire, dividing it into smaller, less threatening, sovereign states. This was precisely the aim of Cardinal Richelieu. But Richelieu envisioned far more than a Habsburg defeat. In place of Habsburg universalism, he would institute a European equilibrium, a balance of power between independent, sovereign entities that would prevent Habsburg hegemony and preserve the stability of Christendom and the stability of France. Dutch and German rights to autonomy were a centerpiece of this vision; sovereignty was entailed in it. Richelieu was not only profoundly influenced by *politique* thought, but authored one of its classic statements.[39] And he was one of its classic practitioners.

The security interests of France vis-à-vis the Habsburgs had long been central to its foreign policy. But prior to the *politiques*, this interest was shaped and tempered by its deference to Christian unity. With the *politiques*, France's security interests could be entirely prioritized above the welfare of Christendom. Unlike its partner pursuers of Westphalia, France did not arrive at its interest in a system of sovereign states through becoming Protestant. It arrived at its interest through becoming *politique*. But this, too, was a secularized conception of politics that grew out of a Reformation crisis. The *politiques* did not demand the sort of separation of temporal and universal ecclesiastical powers that Protestants in Germany, the Netherlands, and Sweden did; in France, the emperor and the pope had long ceased to challenge royal sovereignty. But in a different sense, the *politiques* did call for a separation. They no longer thought it imperative for the crown to enforce religious uniformity; they no longer thought that a legitimate public order had to be confessionally unified. This *politique* approach, seeking to abolish religion as a source of contention in politics both inside and outside the borders of France, originated during France's sundering civil wars between around 1560 and 1598. These wars were themselves brought on by the Calvinist Reformation, which first roiled France in the 1550s. The French state adopted an interest in sovereignty, then, within less than a generation of its religious wars, and out of a viewpoint whose genesis coincided exactly with its Reformation crisis.[40]

Sweden

Sweden's interest in sovereign statehood combined elements of France's, as well as that of Germany and the Netherlands. Like France, but unlike Germany and the Netherlands, Sweden was independent of the Holy Roman Empire prior to its Reformation, although it was only liberated from Denmark in 1523. It was in the 1540s that Sweden took up its active interest in European sovereign statehood. Then, King Gustavus Adolphus brought Sweden into the Protestant Schmalkaldic League, supporting the German prince's drive for sovereignty. Sweden's strongest pursuit of its interest came in 1630, during the Thirty Years' War, when its invasion of the Continent at Peenemünde, on behalf of the German Protestant princes, proved to be the turning point in the demise of the empire. Between the 1540s and 1620s, Sweden had showed little interest in the affairs of the empire, instead attending to disputes over territory and dynastic claims with Russia, Poland, and Denmark.

But unlike France, and like Germany and the Netherlands, Sweden fought for Westphalia as a Protestant polity. The Lutheran Reformation had arrived in the 1520s under the leadership of King Gustavus Vasa, and virtually every Swedish king thereafter was a Lutheran, right up through the reign of the devout Gustavus Adolphus, who ruled between 1611 and 1632. Sweden's crucial intervention was doubtless dependent upon geostrategic factors, not simply commitment to its religious allies. For most of the sixteenth century and the beginning of the seventeenth, Sweden was preoccupied with war and posturing for war with Denmark. It was not until a peaceful lull arrived in 1614 that Sweden was free to pursue the defense of the German Protestants. It was also not until the acme of Habsburg military gains that Sweden would intervene on the Continent. In 1629, the Holy Roman emperor Ferdinand II declared the Edict of Restitution, calling for a restoration of Catholicism to all lands that had become Protestant since the 1555 Peace of Augsburg, convincing the Swedes of Protestantism's mortal danger. But if Sweden did not pursue Westphalia actively until the 1630s, it had expressed rhetorical and diplomatic sympathy with the cause of the German Protestants ever since its own Reformation. Taking up an active interest was a departure from passivity, not from any Habsburg, imperial, or Catholic sympathy.[41]

Other Reformation Polities

Interests in a system of sovereign states correspond well with Reformation crises in the four major regions of polities that defeated the Holy Roman Empire in the Thirty Years' War. Reformation crises spread to other European polities, too. Although these did not act as forcefully for Westphalia, they yet favored it and opposed the Catholic empire, adding strength to the correlation. England, whose own civil wars kept it mostly out of the Thirty Years' War, was reformed in the 1530s by King Henry VIII, who seized church property and clipped the island from papal authority. Over the following century, as long as its monarchs were Protestant, England generally gave economic aid, arms, and assistance in dynastic intrigue to its Protestant brethren in the Netherlands and Germany, while opposing the empire, even defeating the Spanish Armada in 1588. The sharp contrast of England's foreign policy during its brief restoration to Catholicism under Queen Mary between 1553 and 1558 accents religion's importance. Then, England allied closely with Spain as Henry VIII's daughter Mary married Philip of Spain and entered into the Habsburg family; afterward, Protestant queen Elizabeth I made England Spain's enemy.

Denmark followed a path similar to Sweden. Its bishops and nobility took sides and fought over the Reformation in the 1520s and early 1530s until Lutheranism was finally made official in 1536. In 1538, it allied with the German Protestant princes in the Schmalkaldic League to fight for their effective independence from the Holy Roman Empire. Hungary fits the pattern, too, but more peculiarly, due to what happened at the Battle of Mohacs in 1526—there, Hungary's armies were routed by invading Ottoman Turks. After another defeat in 1541, Hungary was divided triply between western and northern Hungary, which came under Habsburg rule, central Hungary, which came under direct Ottoman rule, and Transylvania, which became a Turkish vassal state ruled by a Hungarian prince. It was in Transylvania that the Reformation spread widest. Here Lutheranism spread through the cities, and became established by 1550. By contrast, the Habsburg regions remained officially Catholic. Eventually, during the Thirty Years' War, religious loyalties would correspond with foreign policy. The Habsburg regions, of course, remained loyal, while Transylvania allied with the anti-imperial forces.[42]

Enduringly Catholic Polities

The obverse of the Reformation thesis ought to hold true as well. Those polities in which the Reformation never managed to chink Catholic piety, practice, and authority, we ought to discover, were those that aligned with, and perhaps fought to preserve, the Catholic empire. This pattern, too, early modern European history corroborates. I have already noted that in Germany, officially Catholic polities aligned with the empire from the inception of the Reformation up through Westphalia. Most obviously fitting is Spain, whose dynastic links with the empire and zealous advocacy of Catholic uniformity in Europe made it the most pro-Catholic polity on the Continent. It was also the European polity that the Reformation least penetrated.

The Reformation also did not notably penetrate the Italian city-states. Several theologians and church leaders, "Italian evangelicals," as today's historians now call them, demanded many of the same reforms that Luther and Calvin did, but none challenged directly the Church's authority or led a popular splinter movement. Nor did Italian city-states advocate a European system of sovereign states or oppose the empire in their foreign policy during the sixteenth and seventeenth centuries. Savoy even fought in the Thirty Years' War on the side of the empire between 1629 and 1632.[43] The Italian link between persistent Catholicism and foreign policy is no less significant for the fact that the Italian city-states themselves constituted an effective system of sovereign states during the fifteenth century and up through the sack of Rome in 1527, the very system that inspired Machiavelli's writings. My argument, again, is not for the necessity of the Reformation in eliciting any system of sovereign states—one might very well have developed without it. Rather, my argument is for the role of the Reformation in bringing about the system of sovereign states, the victorious and enduring continental system of Westphalia. This system, the post-Renaissance Italian city-states—these Catholic states—did nothing to bring about.

The other major enduringly Catholic power during this period was Poland. True to its identity, it also remained loyal to the Holy Roman Empire, coming to intervene on the imperial side several times during the Thirty Years' War.[44] Poland was not immune to the Reformation. Lutheran congregations arose in several Polish towns in the 1520s; Calvinism spread into the land in the late 1540s. But compared to the upheaval in France, Germany, the Netherlands, and Sweden, the Polish Reformation was a failure. Protestant uprisings in Polish towns during the 1520s were forcibly suppressed by the nobility. A small minority of gentry or otherwise powerful members of society converted, but only a small portion of the peasantry adopted the new teachings. This was not a Reformation crisis. There was no civil war to fashion a *politique* ideology, no threat to Poland's status as an officially Catholic state. It was true that an official policy of toleration was adopted at the Confederation of Warsaw in 1573, but this was little more than a tactic of the nobility to limit the power of the Church, not a general secularization of politics or still less part of a doctrine that included *raison d'état* or a system of sovereign states. Poland's Catholicism, and Poland's loyalty to the Holy Roman Empire, complete the continental correlation between Reformation crises and interests in Westphalia.

From the looks of things, princes, kings, and magistrates came to pursue an interest in a system of sovereign states not long after, and in those same locales in which preachers and pamphlets spread religious reform among the populace. This strong correlation is important evidence for the Reformation's influence. But it is not enough alone. We need to see the links, the cogs and pinions, through which Protestants were first converted to their new identities, then went on to exercise the social power of ideas, altering the costs and benefits for heads of polities to pursue an interest in Westphalia on their behalf. An account of the two roles of ideas provides narrative, the stories behind the correlation. It is the subject of chapter 7.

SEVEN

THE POWER OF PROTESTANT PROPOSITIONS

A MAP OF EUROPE shaded according to Reformation crises would lay neatly onto a map of Europe shaded according to polities interested in Westphalia. But neither map would tell us the stories of the cities and the rural areas where theological propositions put forth by preachers were accepted by hearers, translating into religious tumult, protest, and war, finally bringing a crisis of authority, one abating and intensifying, in and out, over a century. How did the two roles of ideas bring leaders to pursue a sovereign states system?[1]

The Two Roles of Protestant Ideas

First, how did conversions to the new Protestant identity take place? Who spread the ideas? Who became converted? These questions inquire into the first role of ideas. It was the theology of Martin Luther that led immediately to the Reformation crisis. Luther himself, of course, did not create his ideas de novo, but was influenced by the milieu of late medieval theology, especially nominalism, which emphasized God's inscrutability and fallen man's distance from Him. Luther's own spiritual crisis, borne of excessive monastic discipline, and his revulsion against Church corruption—most saliently the sale of indulgences for the remission of temporal punishment due to sin—served also as precipitants. It was first through the monasteries—Luther himself was a member of the Augustinian order—and then through the clergy that Luther's ideas quickly and alarmingly circulated. Through the clergy, Luther's ideas then spread to congregations. Elsewhere, the Reformation proceeded similarly, beginning with theologians, spreading through missionaries and church pastors, then outward.

Two main conduits aided this dissemination, both of them fairly novel to the era—the sermon and the pamphlet. Protestant theology and worship placed new importance on the sermon, the pastor's conveyance of the Word, a remedy for the excess zeal and superstition that had allegedly infected ritual. The sermon's imprimatur of authority attracted its hearers to its injunctions.[2] In the same period, the print media burgeoned. Between 1517 and 1520, Luther's followers printed thirty of his writings in more than one-third of a million copies, in pamphlets read most vigorously in the universities and among clerics, who then spread their ideas through word of mouth to larger audiences. Pamphlets proliferated in other venues of the Reformation as well.[3] Both modes of communication, sermon and pamphlet, were received by peasants, proletariat, nobles, magistrates, and princes, but most widely and predominantly by the middle classes, that is, by merchants and artisans, who made up the majority of Protestants. All of these features of conversion, though varying in emphasis, can be found all across the Reformation. They are the couriers and contexts involved in the shaping of identities, the first role of ideas.

The evidence of conversion, of identity formation, lies in the new religious practices of those who adopted the Reformation. Protestants attended churches where preachers taught Protestant theology; they conducted mass, confession, and the other sacraments as the new teaching prescribed; the more unruly of them smashed icons and rioted against Catholic churches; and they refused to obey the sanctioning authority of Rome. All of these activities were outward signs of inward conviction.

The couriers of ideas brandished diverse carrots and sticks—the social power of ideas, ideas' second role. The Catholic Church's authority over the believer depended most directly on the believer's practice, not only upon his deference to Rome and the hierarchy, but on his faithful participation in the Eucharist and the Mass, practices replicated everywhere and through time. When believers simply practiced otherwise, this authority was most directly snubbed. Heterodox religious practice alone, then, was itself a form of social power. Defiant practice had many moods. Rambunctious urban crowds channeled through streets, smashing statues on cobblestones and burning images; more irenic and pious parishioners—merchants, artisans, laborers—refused the old rites and practiced the new mass; recalcitrant priests and monks preached new doctrines, left their cloisters, married, and disobeyed their bishop and the pope.[4] All such practices left the Church fractured, weakened.

Practical dissent ultimately required a coarser power, too: Protestants took up arms. They fought against the emperor on behalf of the prince who would ally with them; they rebelled against the resistant prince. Merchants, laborers, artisans, peasants, and nobles of all ranks offered their military service in one of these ways. This familiar form of social power almost always proved necessary.

In every case, any form of social power had to provide the prince, king, or magistrate with the incentive and means to seize the Church's lands and temporal powers and perhaps also to fight the emperor. If the head of a polity himself converted, then he could exercise the social power of ideas by virtue of his position. He could enforce doctrinal uniformity within his territory, appoint new church leaders, nullify the authority of the Roman hierarchy, disband the monasteries, seize Catholic Church property, and raise troops to fight the empire. But even if he did not convert, out of either obstinacy or indifference, he might still further the Reformation in these ways, either because he feared the rebellion of converts or because he saw an opportunity to gain wealth and power through allying with them. Whether he was pious, rapacious, opportunistic, or afraid, it was only because of the array of Protestant social power around him that a leader could successfully defy the Church.[5]

This broad story is of "Reformation from below." In England and Sweden, social power was exercised somewhat differently, better described as "Reformation from above." Here, monarchs acted with far less prompting, seizing church lands, wealth, and leadership, and declaring new doctrines for their national church, without strong pressure from the middle class or other sectors. Here, too, though, Protestant ideas had spread into the land before the monarch proclaimed reformation, creating fertile ground for the changes. Nor did monarchs proclaim the Reformation before the ideas had been made available by the Reformation theologians, also evidence for the ideas' efficacy. Reformation from above is a matter of emphasis, not of diametric difference. The French route, which I call "the politique solution," is a third one. Here, the monarch never proclaimed the Reformation as official, but rather declared tolerance for Protestantism as a way of providing social peace.

"Reformation from below," "reformation from above," and "the politique solution" constitute three causal pathways through which conversion and social power operated. In figure 7.1, I summarize each of the pathways schematically, showing the chain of events through which the two roles of ideas unfolded. Then, I discuss Germany and the Netherlands as examples of Reformation from below, Sweden as an example of Reformation from above, and France as the site of the *politique* solution.

Germany

In Germany, the course of conversion was paradigmatic, involving virtually all of the elements I have just described. The pattern of social power differed somewhat from region to region. In virtually every German city or principality that became Protestant, the Reformation first spread popularly before the town councils or princes allied with and abetted reformers. In many northern cities, merchants and craftsmen who were excluded from political privilege converted and then attempted coups, often winning the acquiescence of city leaders. The Reformation also reached the rural proletariat, who rose up in the peasant rebellions of the mid-1520s, only to be cruelly and summarily defeated. In other cities, in central and southern Germany and northern Switzerland, a "civic reformation" took place in which conversion occurred across several layers of society, but most cru-

Reformation from Below: (Germany, the Netherlands, Transylvania)

Pathway of Conversion:

Reflection of theologians → monasteries and universities → ordinary clergy → Conversions in a broad array of sectors, including ruling elites

Pathway of Social Power:

Broad array of Protestant social sectors especially urban middle classes, exercising social power of defiant religious practice, resistance, and participation in armed forces (social crisis) → elites → the polity's interest in Westphalia

Reformation from Above: (Sweden, England, Denmark)

Pathway of Conversion:

Reflection of theologians → monasteries and universities → missionaries → ordinary clergy → Conversions in a broad array of sectors, including ruling elites

Pathway of Social Power:

Protestant ruling elites exercising the social power of their position (social crisis) → the polity's interest in Westphalia

↕

broad array of Protestant social sectors, empowering and empowered by ruling elites (social crisis)

Fig. 7.1. The Causal Pathways of the Influence of Protestantism

The *Politique* Solution: (France)

Pathway of Conversion:

Reflection of theologians → monasteries and universities → missionaries → ordinary clergy → Conversions in a broad array of sectors, including nobility

Pathway of Social Power:

Protestants in a broad array of sectors exercising social power of armed resistance (social crisis) → Interest in secular *politique* solution among powerful Protestant and Catholic elites → *Politique* compromise whose foreign policy includes an interest in Westphalia

Fig. 7.1 *(continued)*

cially among literate and influential elites who were able to defeat other elites opposing the movement. In most German principalities that became Protestant and supportive of Westphalia, monarchs converted only after vast swaths of their publics had first converted. By contrast, in those German polities such as Bavaria, which remained steadily Catholic and allied with the empire throughout the sixteenth century, the Reformation spread comparatively little among the populace, evincing further the link between popular conversion and political outcomes. Apart from the spread of Protestantism, there appears to be no geographical pattern by which polities became Catholic or Protestant. There is no pattern, for instance, that corroborates a proximity-of-threat hypothesis drawn from Realist international relations scholarship, one that would predict lands on the border of Habsburg Austria would remain Catholic in order to attain safety from the Holy Roman Empire, and that more distant, buffered lands would become Protestant. In fact, both Protestant and Catholic lands bordered Austria, and were scattered throughout Germany without apparent pattern.[6]

Netherlands

In the Netherlands, conversion was first the work of missionaries, trained in Geneva and at the University of Heidelberg, who brought Calvinism to the country in the late 1550s. They produced cadres of committed converts, disciplined and knit together tightly in local congregations—a regimentation, a potential for political impact that Lutherans and Anabaptists in the Netherlands lacked. Calvinists during this time, both in the Netherlands and in France, were also more radical in their political theology than the Lutherans of the German Reformation. Theologians began to emphasize the idea of a covenant between rulers and citizens that would allow magistrates and sometimes even bodies of citizens lawfully to resist a tyrannical or idolatrous government.[7] Calvinist converts were rebellious converts, and it is not surprising that open-air meetings at which preachers urged conversion were followed by rioting against Catholic churches, or that by 1565 the Spanish administration dreaded rebellion, or that in 1566 Calvinist consistories in Antwerp tried to create a military general staff. The most committed of the rebels crusaded for no less than a theocratic state where non-Calvinists would be tolerated as little as Calvinists were then. Such defiance could be found among all classes. Its commanders were often the lower nobility, its troops were "anti-clerical merchants, . . . artisans and small shopkeepers labouring under war taxation and rising prices, sailors and shipbuilders affected by rebellion and privateering, weavers and labourers hit by unemployment and repressive guild-controls, small squires lacking regular military employment and faced by the effect of inflation on their static landed incomes."[8]

If Calvinism was potent, it was not necessarily widespread. In 1560, roughly 5 percent of the Netherlands was Calvinist; in 1587, roughly 10 percent; and by 1600, only 50 percent of Holland and New Zealand, the strongholds of the United Provinces, had converted.[9] Yet both anticlerical sentiment and support for toleration were common, and many who did not support the Calvinists were not enthusiastic about the Spanish regime and its violation of local privileges, either. Favorable still more was the weakness of popular allegiance to Catholicism at the time.[10]

How did this array of Dutch converts exercise social power? In the Netherlands, the ruling nobility was profoundly reluctant to align with the Reformation; it was rebellious Calvinists who began the Dutch Revolt and forced it to become an independence movement, not merely a quest for constitutional and tax privileges from imperial Spain. The desire for the sovereignty of William of Orange and his noble allies in fact came well after the revolt was under way. As late as the Pacification of Ghent in 1576, a united and tolerant but still obedient Netherlands was the vision of most of the nobles in the States-General. Historian Jonathan Israel confirms the judgment. He asserts that widespread resentment over royal prerogatives was the first major cause of the revolt. But then: "What prevented . . . [compromise] being negotiated was [a] second factor: the escalating strife over religion which had held the Low Countries in its grip since the 1520s."[11]

The ideas of the Spanish, the Counter Reformation inspired by the Council of Trent, also contributed to the Dutch revolt, and to the Dutch interest in independence. It was in reaction to Calvinist unrest rather than the long-standing recalcitrance of the States-General on taxation and bishopric reform that King Philip II of Spain sent his troops to the Netherlands in 1567. He sent the inquisitorial Duke of Alba not merely to impose constitutional authority, but to eradicate religious dissent. Israel describes the campaign:

> Alba arrived with 10,000 Spanish and Italian troops, having marched overland from Genoa and Milan, in August 1567. His severity in the Low Countries certainly had a spectacular impact, and by no means only in the Low Countries. Altogether 8,950 people, from all social strata, were accused and convicted of treason or heresy, or both, during the years 1567–72, and over one thousand of these were publicly executed, in many cases burnt to the stake.[12]

It was to pursue his campaign for Catholic uniformity that Alba also imposed the "tenth penny" tax, a 10 percent sales tax that was despised by the middle class, forced upon the States-General, radicalizing moderate critics of the Spanish and further broadening opposition. Alba was successful in temporarily squelching Protestantism, but his efforts created in the process an exile community of Calvinists who prepared to invade the country. Of course, the tenth-penny tax was not a mere religious issue, nor was the desire of nobles in the States-General to preserve their powers, nor was an economic trough in the mid-1560s, all of which also motivated dissent. But without Calvinism, the revolt would not have begun, elicited the Spanish response, or resulted in an interest in sovereignty. Absent Calvinism, both sides could quite conceivably have found a mutual compromise on the terms of Spanish rule.[13]

France

As in the Netherlands, Protestantism came to France through Calvinist missionaries. By the mid-1550s, conversion in France was epidemic. Calvinism spread through an international network, just as it had in the Netherlands: Missionaries emerged from Geneva and converted their hearers, who then formed congregations. At the onset of the civil wars, 10 percent of the French people and 40 percent of the nobility were Calvinist.[14] Unlike in the Netherlands, however, the nobility allied immediately with the congregations, some out of conviction, some out of desire for Church property, some out of both. Like the Protestant German princes, they confiscated Church lands, gained control over local and provincial governments, and then fought off Catholic princes and armies supplied by the congregations. By 1569, the Huguenot armies numbered 25,000, and they strode into battle singing psalms.[15]

But the exercise of Calvinist social power in France was more indirect than elsewhere. As I have described, it did not achieve official Protestantism, but instead set off a conflict that in turn evoked a new way of thinking about politics—the *politique* approach—which prioritized the stability of the state, its political and material power, over its Catholic unity. *Politique* thinking called for the pragmatic toleration of Protestantism both at home and abroad, even at the expense of the uniformity of Christendom sought by the Holy Roman Empire, the Habsburgs, and the Catholic Church. It was through challenging the official Catholicism of the French political order and miring France in deep religious conflict that Calvinism brought the *politique* solution. It was the desire for civil peace, after all, that motivated the *politiques* more than anything else. A policy of toleration was not endemic to the ideals of either side of the conflict. Although some Calvinists, in both France and the Netherlands, called for religious toleration, many others, including Calvin himself, sought a uniformly reformed state. In opposition, orthodox Catholics fought to preserve pre–civil war France, where heresy was outlawed and the realm ruled according to the creed "*un roi, une loi, une foi* (one king, one law, one faith)." But during the civil war, distressed by the civil destruction, a new movement of more moderate Catholics began to speak of toleration. The chief *politique* voices, including administrator and philosopher Michel L'Hôpital and Jean Bodin, still desired religious uniformity, still considered Protestantism befuddled apostasy, and rejected religious liberty as a deep principle. Yet, they believed that when the commonwealth was being riven apart by unresolvable religious conflict, toleration might be permitted—for social peace, to avoid ruin. Just such a solution was embodied in the 1598 Edict of Nantes, signed by *politique* King Henry IV.[16]

Behind Nantes were echoes of one version of the second role of ideas, ideas as focal points in bargaining. The civil wars of France were settled around an idea—*politique* toleration—that was not equivalent to the ideas of either side in the conflict. It was a compromise solution that became more and more attractive as both sides realized the futility of attaining a complete victory for their ideals. Despite this important role for bargaining, though, it would be a mistake to see toleration as a solution to the mere, bald dilemma of instability. Apart from Calvinism, France's civil wars are inexplicable; the conflict was a deeply religious one. Apart from the clash between Calvinism and Catholicism at its deepest, the *politique* solution would make little sense. The settlement, too, had everything to do with religion. Though the social power of Calvinism was indirect, though the French interest in Westphalia arose as a solution to a conflict, both conflict and solution resulted from converts' direct exercise of the social power of ideas.

The secularized *politique* approach was the chief route by which Protestantism evoked a French interest in a sovereign states system. There was also a secondary route—Calvinism's power of resistance. Even when French kings permitted some Calvinism, they still opposed its wider spread. Such was the pragmatic, provisional character of *politique* toleration. After Nantes, the crown continued to view the Huguenots as a threat and often sought militarily to quell them. As this required resources needed to fight abroad, the ability of kings to make war against the Habsburgs depended inversely on Huguenot strength. When the Huguenot threat was strongest, the king had to divert his armies inward, attenuating pressure on the Habsburgs; when Huguenots were defeated (by royal force) or contented (with an edict of toleration), the king could fight the Habsburgs more vigorously.

France's pursuit of an interest in a system of sovereign states, then, required that two conditions obtain: foreign policy had to be in the control of the *politiques*, and the Huguenots had to be in abeyance. Shifts in French foreign policy over successive periods between the early sixteenth century and Westphalia yield evidence for the importance of these conditions.

Up until the very end of the Habsburg-Valois Wars of 1521–1559, Calvinism had made little impact in France; there were no *politiques.* The foreign policy of France was generally Realist, aiming to prevent Habsburg encirclement, contracting alliances with non-Catholic polities, and yet avoiding the guarantee of the sovereignty of Protestant polities and refraining from pursuing general Habsburg defeat. How much the restraint of the French crown was based upon strategic motives, how much it rested in a Catholic unwillingness to see the defeat of Christian uniformity, is difficult to say. Francis I's 1544 agreement with Charles V to guarantee the Council of Trent, the French crown's internal suppression of growing Calvinism during the 1550s, this based on its perception of Calvinism as a threat to the stability of the state. Such factors suggest the influence of orthodox Catholic ideas on the most vital matters of security, but it is only in contrast to subsequent periods that the power of ideas is crisply apparent.[17]

Between 1562 and 1598, Calvinism spread, Huguenots revolted, and the nobility, the king, and their troops waged a succession of eight civil wars. Protestant nobles captured forts and towns, and formed a league; Catholics formed a league to fight them. During the 1560s, under the influence of L'Hôpital, regent Catherine de Medici attempted to reconcile the two sides and proclaimed limited toleration of the terms of the Edict of Amboise of 1563. But in 1572, under pressure from the Catholic Guise family, Catherine became convinced that the Huguenots were planning an attack, and she acquiesced to the massacre of St. Bartholomew's Day, killing much of the Huguenot leadership. The Huguenots persisted in fighting, though, and did so steadily until the 1590s. They would win more territory, agree to truces that permitted some degree of toleration, and then return to battle when such truces collapsed.[18]

The advance of Calvinist conversion radically altered the milieu of costs and incentives facing nobles and kings. Nobles could ally with Huguenots or fight them off. If they allied, they could gain wealth, office, and armies, but they would then have to war against Catholic nobles and their armies. Kings, almost all of them Catholic, now had to choose between fighting Protestants or tolerating them. Fighting would mean raising armies and using them internally, not abroad; toleration would mean losing the crucial political support of Catholic nobles. After the St. Bartholomew's Massacre, kings typically issued edicts of toleration only when their resources had been stretched too thin from battling Protestants. Vulnerable paucity, though, was fairly frequent. Kings relied heavily upon the nobility, to whom they sold offices for revenues and armies, and enjoyed the support of only that faction whose favor they could curry at any one time. Ideas created conflict, and conflict sapped the resources of the king. The result for foreign policy was that France was unable to expand its territory or promote foreign clients against the Habsburgs. During much of this period, a unitary foreign policy did not exist at all; in fact, French Huguenot princes often made military alliances with Dutch Calvinists.

But the same conflict gave rise to the *politique* idea, which proved its solution. When Spanish troops aiding the French Catholic League infiltrated Brittany and Languedoc, and even established a garrison in Paris in 1590 and 1591, the French king was ever more burdened. Only through order in the commonwealth, and social peace among the warring faiths, would France be unified enough to fight Spain. The *politique* option, advocated through pamphlets of sympathetic members of the Catholic League, gained in stature and made possible the accession of Henry of Navarre. Navarre was heir to the throne, a quintessential *politique* who had once led troops of Huguenots, but had converted to Catholicism, yet promised toleration. With the help of the English, the Dutch, and both Catholic and Huguenot armies within France, Henry IV staved off the Spaniards and mollified the Protestants; that is, until 1597, when Huguenots again threatened revolt because their demands for toleration had not yet been met. In May 1598, Henry IV both made peace with the Spaniards on terms that left French territory intact and signed the Edict of Nantes, granting Huguenots liberty of worship in specified regions and fifty-one garrisoned towns. True to *politique* premises, the Edict of Nantes did not provide universal toleration, but only a compromise that permitted some Protestantism in some places.

During the next half-century, no French king attempted to deny toleration completely. They continued their struggles with the Huguenots, but avoided sustained civil war. Aside from the Huguenots, among the powerful Catholic nobles who influenced policy, the debate over toleration continued. One faction was the papist preservers of orthodoxy, who would not tolerate dissent; the other was the legatees of the *politiques*, who would pragmatically allow that amount of dissent necessary to preserve order. Attitudes toward toleration squared with foreign policy. Until Henry of Navarre was assassinated in 1610, he tolerated Huguenots at home and pursued an anti-Habsburg policy abroad through several small-scale wars. In the mid 1610s, as Catholics and Protestants within the empire squared off into opposing leagues and prepared to fight, the Catholic-Protestant cleavage within France was extended to foreign policy. The pro-papists, by this time known as the *dévots*, generally favored at least a peace settlement that favored the Habsburgs, and some desired Habsburgs to take back Catholic lands. The heirs of the *politiques*, now called *bons français*, were aggressively anti-Habsburg, for they viewed the Habsburgs as a threat to the security of France and were willing to see any remaining Catholic unity in Europe destroyed. For the first half-decade or so of the Thirty Years' War, the *dévots* held sway. France did not become militarily involved in the conflict; it mediated at most.[19]

In 1624, this would change. Cardinal Richelieu was arguably the culmination of the *politique* tradition. Well before he became Louis XIII's First Minister in 1624, he had been influenced profoundly by *politique* thought, and had come to espouse the *raison d'état* that he eventually wrote about in his *Testament Politique*. Although he was evidently sincere in his own religious convictions—he was a cardinal of the Church, after all—he also saw France as the main champion of the Catholic faith, and perceived little difference between the welfare of the French state and the welfare of Christendom. One Catholic critic said of him, "You make use of your religion as your preceptor Machiavelli showed the ancient Romans doing, shaping it, turning it about one way after another, explaining it and applying it as far as it aids in the advancement of your designs. Your head is as ready to wear the turban as the red hat, provided the Janissaries and the Pashas find you sufficiently upright to elect you their emperor."[20]

The first condition of an anti-Habsburg foreign policy, having a *politique* in office, was now met. Upon taking office, Richelieu departed from an earlier *dévot* policy and supported strongly a French military campaign on behalf of Protestants and against the Habsburgs in the Valtelline, a region between Italy and Austria. Yet, in the mid-1620s, a Huguenot revolt occupied Richelieu, preventing him from committing France's resources irrevocably against the Habsburgs. Like previous *politiques*, Richelieu did not believe toleration to be an enduring value, and as part of his general attempt to crush noble resistance to the crown, he conquered Huguenot strongholds in La Rochelle and Languedoc in 1627 and 1628, respectively. He acted not out of a passion for the Counter Reformation, but out of his desire to strengthen the French state and weaken those he thought its enemies. After defeating the Huguenots, he turned around to support the Protestant Duke of Rohan, also of *politique* sympathies, in a campaign to thwart Habsburg claims in Italy.

Having established himself as firmly anti-Habsburg, in the 1630s, Richelieu formed alliances with German princes and provided funds to Sweden and to Dutch Protestants, who were both already at war against the Habsburgs. After Habsburg forces defeated Swedish armies at Nördlingen in 1634, he decided to enter the war in Germany, which would culminate in 1648. His aims were not limited to extending French territory, or to rolling back the Habsburg armies, but included a comprehensive design for a community of sovereign states under a system of collective security, bound together by law, led by France. Like Francis I, he viewed alliances with Protestants and defeat of the Habsburgs as part of French interests, but he defined these interests much more expansively, with none of Francis I's Catholic restraint, none of the concerns for halting the Protestant heresy that pre-civil wars kings showed. Against the eternal Habsburg threat, a system of sovereign states based on collective security, allowing France to guarantee the German integrity of princes, would best serve the interests of the French state. This was the *politique* foreign policy, which might (or might not) allow internal dissent, depending on the needs of the state, and which might allow the breakup of the Catholic empire, depending on the interests of states abroad. At Westphalia, this breakup would be realized.

Sweden

Sweden's adoption of an interest in sovereign statehood for the rest of Europe also depended upon the social power of Protestantism, but in a pattern very different from those of France, Germany, and the Netherlands. When Gustavus Adolphus led Sweden into the Thirty Years' War in 1630, he was not acting under the armed threats of Swedish Protestants; nor was he protecting Swedish Protestants against imperial attack in exchange for his taking control of church property. Sweden had become a Protestant land a century earlier, much as England had become Protestant around the same time under Henry VIII: The king imposed reformation from above. With comparatively little violent struggle, an earlier king, Gustavus Vasa, succeeded in establishing the Lutheran Church in Sweden, indeed so pervasively that Sweden became, in the words of historian Michael Roberts, a "Lutheran Spain."[21] Certainly, the success of Vasa depended upon theologians and clergy. Inspired by Luther, they were already espousing reform. It depended upon a cooperative urban populace as well. But society exercised scant pressure upon Vasa to establish Lutheranism or adopt any foreign policy on its behalf. Nor were Swedish Protestants ever threatened with attack by the Holy Roman Emperor, thanks to Sweden's buffered geography.[22]

Protestantism empowered Swedish foreign policy largely through the office of its king, who remained Lutheran and who could easily command the foreign policy of the state. In the 1540s, the Lutheran king Gustavus Vasa brought Sweden into the Protestant Schmalkaldic League; subsequent kings continued to support the Protestant cause diplomatically. Sweden's most active interest in sovereign statehood—its intervention in the Thirty Years' War—came through one very important and devout Lutheran: King Gustavus Adolphus himself. Gustavus was deeply committed to his Protestant faith, and the collective mind of the Swedish aristocracy with whom he ruled was also strongly Lutheran. Gustavus linked Protestantism with sovereignty, too. He is rumored to have carried in his saddlebag the writings of Hugo Grotius, a philosopher who also joined the two concepts. With the social power of his position as king and with the cooperation of the aristocracy, Gustavus defined Sweden's national interest as European sovereign statehood.[23]

Apart from the Protestantism of Gustavus and the Swedish leadership, it is difficult to explain Sweden's interest in intervening on the Continent. Never before had Sweden taken a strong strategic interest in Germany or the empire. But by the late 1620s, when the Habsburgs took virtually all of Germany under their control, Sweden saw fit to intervene. Why? Germany was hardly vital to Sweden's security. There was little chance that the Habsburgs would ever be able to invade Sweden itself; in fact, a Germany controlled by Habsburgs could counterbalance Sweden's traditional rival, Denmark. Strategic factors are at best indeterminate. What threatened Sweden's interest far more saliently was the empire's threat to Protestantism. In 1629, the Emperor Ferdinand issued the Edict of Restitution, calling for the return to the Holy Roman Empire of all Catholic lands secularized since 1555, threatening to eradicate Protestantism throughout the empire. But this action is only intelligible as a threat if Sweden included Protestantism in its security interests. Historian Michael Roberts describes the position:

> The motives which prompted the invasion of Germany are not in doubt. Gustav Adolph sought the security of his country; and that could be achieved only if the Imperialist forces were evicted from the Baltic shore, and the nascent Habsburg naval base at Wismar wrested from their hands. But political security included as one of its main elements security from the danger of resurgent Catholicism, since in the idea of national freedom no constituent could be more important than that of religious freedom: as Oxenstierna observed to the *råd* in 1636, "it was thus a question not so much of religion, as of *status publicus*, in which religion is comprehended."[24]

Gustavus and the nobility themselves claimed Protestantism as the reason for war, and employed legions of clergy to rouse their congregations to fight for the cause.[25] In the negotiations at Westphalia, Sweden sought the protection of Protestant estates in the empire as one of its most central goals.[26] It was the social power of all of these Protestants, most importantly the monarch, that led Sweden to fight for sovereign statehood.

The Reformation and the Thirty Years' War

The social power of Protestantism was coincident with, and plausibly connected to, the crucial interest in a system of sovereign states that led German polities, the Netherlands, France, and Sweden to join together to defeat the empire during the Thirty Years' War. But the interests of these countries in Westphalia does not entirely explain the settlement, which arrived well after any state adopted an interest in it. In order for the aims of Westphalia to be achieved, German polities had to wage over a century of war after they had arrived at their interests; the Dutch provinces, eighty years of war; France and Sweden, over a decade of war. The defeat of the empire required the social power of arms, applied through international conflict. But we should not divorce this conflict itself from the power of religious ideas. The struggle culminated in the Thirty Years' War, a war involving virtually every power on the Continent, and one whose original cause, virtually every major historian of the conflict agrees, was the continued disputes between Catholics and Protestants in Germany and Bohemia. Certainly, as the war progressed, it became intertwined with other stakes: the ambitions of the military entrepreneur Wallenstein, who amassed immense wealth and lands fighting for the Habsburgs; the fate of Spain as a great power; the sea power of the Netherlands; and the strategic position of Sweden. Most historians would agree, too, that by the last decade of the war, religious passions were spent, and rulers fought on for wealth and territory, presaging European politics after Westphalia. It is in this final stretch that the concept of "focal points" applies best: Westphalia was a mutually acceptable bargaining solution for powers that wanted to end the war, but with the best possible strategic apportionment. The complex religious clauses of the settlement were a modus vivendi that enabled Protestants and Catholics to coexist in an age in which they cared less and less about the uniform establishment of their faith. But how states came into the conflict in the first place, how they developed the interests that led them into this war that produced this solution, is inexplicable apart from the social power of Protestant converts.[27]

Skepticism toward the Social Power of Protestant Ideas

Despite these correspondences and these narratives of the two roles of ideas, many scholars have described the rise of modern states and the modern states system with hardly a reference to the Reformation. What alternative story do such skeptics tell? Focusing first on the second role of ideas, how is it that structural forms of social power supplant the Reformation's social power in explaining Westphalia? One version of skepticism rests on the motives of secular rulers. It claims that they used the Reformation instrumentally to garner the popular support that would enable them to seize the Catholic Church's remaining powers and wealth, the final roadblock to their sovereignty. Ideas, here, were nothing more than "hooks."[28] Now, some rulers doubtless carried such motives, and the realized material gains of sovereign statehood partially explain their pursuit of it.[29] But for four reasons, such motives remain unpersuasive as a substitute explanation for ideas.

First, Reformation historians reveal the rapacity of some princes and rulers, but also assert the veritable devotion of others, such as Frederick the Wise of Saxony, who protected Martin Luther. Their motives varied. But even if we assume that every prince was motivated by familiar material desiderata, the argument encounters a second objection of historians: It is unclear that ecclesial booty was even a rational desideratum at all. Most reforming princes failed to acquire great wealth from seizing Church lands; some risked their power, even their lives, for their stand. That the benefits outweighed the costs was hardly clear.[30] But even if we assume, further, the instrumental rationality of siding with the Reformation, there is a third problem with the argument: It does not explain what sort of social power enabled princes to seize the powers and wealth of the Church. Who fought in their armies? Who occupied the churches and disobeyed the bishops? The argument about the motives of rulers alone fails to explain this, and requires an additional argument about the sources of a prince's popular support. The fourth—and most debilitating—problem with the argument is that it fails to explain why, if secular powers stood to gain from Church goods, it was not until this time, and only in certain places, that the princes seized sovereignty. Why did some European princes and nobles rebel against the emperor, while others, similarly rich and empowered, remained loyal? And why did the rebellious rulers not pursue sovereignty one hundred years earlier? Late medieval theology, after all, was full of ideas that challenged traditional authority, and which might well have served as "hooks."[31] The argument from motives alone possesses little capacity to explain the historical specificity of the interests that rulers found in Westphalia.

A more compelling alternative explanation to ideas would focus not on motives, but would pose a different sort of social power that explains better the timing and geography of interests in sovereign statehood. It would look instead toward the centuries-long accrual of the coercive and economic power of princes. In this version of things, the story of Westphalia is the story of the state, how it grew, and how it triumphed over its rival institutions—the Holy Roman Empire, the Hanseatic League, or Italian city-states.[32] When the state evolved from the estate of the most exalted noble of a realm into an impersonal body politic that outlived and transcended the body of any of its rulers; when it established a permanent bureaucracy, a standing army, and a standing treasury to raise troops and taxes in "ordinary" times, not just in "extraordinary" times of war; when it regulated and standardized commerce, coinage, education, and justice, unifying its legal code under Roman law, creating new symbols of office and rank, curtailing the influence of parliaments and courts and constitutional restraints—when enough of these states developed, and when the like powers of the empire and other institutional forms atrophied or failed to develop, secular rulers naturally enough seized the prerogatives to legitimate their powers, the prerogatives of Westphalia sovereign statehood. From the state flows the system.

The story of the state, as I have mentioned, many social scientists have told, most of them finding its origins in changes in economics, organization, military technology, the international distribution of power, and the very activity of war. Here, I do not assess the relative merits of these accounts, but rather treat them as a common skepticism, an alternative to the social power of ideas. If the growth of the state turns out wholly to explain the system of sovereign states, then we can debate exactly what caused this growth. But for now, I take the statist account to hold that through some combination of material forces, in a grand historical trajectory running from the High Middle Ages to the eighteenth century, France, England, Sweden, Prussia, other German states, and the Netherlands grew into statehood and adopted an interest in a system of sovereign states for Europe. The substantial truth in this epic, I do not deny. State growth began well before the Reformation. In their invaluable contribution to our understanding of this growth, state-building theorists explain a good portion of this growth with scant reference to the Reformation. But the question is whether the rise of the state alone is the source of interests in a Westphalia state system. To establish this, the state-building account must render state growth as a locomotive. Materially fueled, this growth steams ahead constantly and inexorably, right up to the day when polities adopted their interests in the Westphalian system that would ensconce and legitimate their powers. The Reformation, meanwhile, occurred on the side, its social power redundant or irrelevant.[33]

If a structural explanation is correct, then, we ought to see a growth in the state institutions and general material power of those polities that adopted an interest in Westphalia; a growth occurring before, and leading up to, the interest. The explanation is strengthened if we witness a decline in the institutions of those polities that did not favor a system of sovereign states. Rather than the presence or lack of a Reformation crisis, it would be the presence or absence of state growth that explains the interest of polities in Westphalia.

Admittedly, over the course of the fifteenth century, state institutions across Europe secured stable powers over their citizens and notable autonomy from the Church, following civil war and conciliar controversy. But the momentum abated. The period between 1500 and the end of the Thirty Years' War is one that several leading early modern historians characterize as one of crisis, war, and monarchical trepidation.[34] Certainly, monarchs asserted a new divine right and festooned themselves, godlike, with crowns and courts, claiming, and seeking to expand, powers of bureaucracy, taxation, and military command. But aristocrats fought back, often with even greater force, containing the swelling of the Renaissance courts, and demanding patronage and prerogatives from the monarchy in a contentious sort of bargaining that yielded a litany of revolts, bankruptcies, and civil wars, of intrigue, spies, and murder, between families and factions. In the first half of the seventeenth century, the central state apparatus did expand somewhat in France and Sweden, but revolts and calamity also continued, especially in France. It was not until after the Thirty Years' War that "bureaucratic-military absolutism," epitomized by France's Louis XIV, finally developed. It was then that the military revolution—itself evoked by the Thirty Years' War—elicited the sharp expansion of the state in France and Prussia, and when monarchs came to enjoy the stability and state apparatus that their fathers and grandfathers had desired.

But contrast this timing of state development with the development of an interest in a system of European sovereign states. As table 6.1 shows (see chapter 6), in polities that adopted this interest, this adoption precedes—sometimes far precedes—the sharp distention of state institutions. When princes, nobles, and free cities in Germany seized control over religion, coming to desire sovereignty, in the 1520s and 1530s, they were numerous, totaling over 300, or even over 2,000 if one counts the extant, declining, imperial knights. As monarchs, they were also weak. Although by the fifteenth century, most of these authorities had come to govern capital justice, taxation, internal order, trade, production, education, and agriculture independent of the empire, aspirants to executive, royal authority still remained legislatively and constitutionally constrained by their own estates, the *Landtage*. It was not until the later seventeenth century—after the Thirty Years' War, and, as many scholars have argued, in response to the destruction caused by this war and the military revolution that it created—that the elector in one of these states combined with the military caste to build the absolute monarchy of Brandenburg-Prussia, of Frederick the Great. By this time, though, German rulers had long sought, and had recently won, a system of sovereign states.[35]

The Netherlands also grew into a great sea power in the seventeenth century, its Golden Age of global commercial dominance. But its spurt, too, did not begin until the United Provinces had already declared, and begun to fight for, independence. "By the late 1580's, the Republic resembled a compressed spring taut with pent-up impetus," writes historian Jonathan Israel.[36] Its exceptional explosion came in the 1590s. Then, the commerce of the next century began to blossom. During the previous part of the century, the Netherlands had grown in prosperity, especially through the rise of Amsterdam and other commercial cities, but such growth was gradual and piecemeal compared to the Golden Age that was to follow. It also failed to translate directly into independence. The nobility, those who most benefited from the commercial expansion, also most strongly opposed liberty for the provinces. In the 1590s, the Spanish enemy was diverted by the civil wars in France, offering the Dutch a strategic respite. The Dutch army and navy dramatically expanded then, too. The military was prototypical in experiencing and adapting to the technological revolution, which led it to grow from 20,000 troops in 1588, to 32,000 in 1595, to 50,000 in the 1630s, and become the most technically proficient and second-strongest armed force in Europe. It was also during this decade that seven United Provinces consolidated into a federal government under the sovereignty of a States-General, a central source of revenue and military command. But all of this followed the 1581 Edict of Abjuration and its claim of sovereignty.[37]

In France, the *politique* vision of *raison d'état* that emerged at the turn of the seventeenth century not only provided the inspiration for contribution of France to Westphalia, but also called for building up the powers of the crown within the realm. But this actual attempt to build the state was preceded by the ideology, and it did not finally succeed until half a century later. After a generation of civil war that had debilitated the crown, the Duke of Sully, minister to Henry IV, dramatically paid off massive state debts, reorganized the state financial machinery, and increased state expenditures by over 60 percent. After he gained power in 1625, Richelieu, too, would seek to build the state. He increased the size of the army from 12,000 men in 1629 to 200,000 during the French intervention in the Thirty Years' War, and began tax collections that would quadruple revenues within a decade. Whatever growth did occur was primarily the project of political ministers, whose vision of the French state and its role in Europe was an essential *politique* tenet. Yet even during this period, the crown remained weak. Its total peak revenue during finance minister Sully's administration was less than the royal revenue prior to the civil wars, taking inflation into account. For revenue and arms, the French king remained deeply dependent on the nobility, whose hereditary offices made them powerful and independent. Noble opposition prevented Richelieu from succeeding in most of his attempts at reforming the state. His efforts to reorganize the royal councils, reduce royal household expenses, enforce the counter-reforming Tridentine decrees in the Church, do away with venality of office, and increase the number of royal offices and *intendants* all failed. The efforts of the crown to extract revenue, recruit armies, and centralize power resulted in three uprisings between 1635 and 1643 and four years of civil war during the Fronde uprising, beginning in 1648. The continual struggle against Huguenot uprisings also hampered the crown. It was not until after the Thirty Years' War, after Westphalia, during the reign of Louis XIV and his minister Colbert, that France experienced its military revolution. It was only then that the crown created a massive state apparatus to support a standing army, and succeeded in raising revenues from the nobility to carry out its wars throughout Europe.[38]

Sweden never achieved the absolutism that Brandenburg-Prussia or France did, although between 1672 and 1718, its kings, Charles XI and Charles XII, approximated the control that the kings of those other countries wielded over their military and taxation system. Prior to the Thirty Years' War, King Gustavus Adolphus had succeeded in strengthening the Swedish treasury through reform and the building up of a standing army through conscription, but he had failed in his designs to increase revenue at home, due in good part to the resistance of the nobility. During the war, Sweden built its forces up from 42,000 to 150,000 troops, but it did so by acquiring foreign loans and mercenaries, thus avoiding heavy taxation and conscription, the sparks of the absolutist state. But this military buildup and subsequent zenith of monarchy followed the intervention of Sweden in the Thirty Years' War, where it fought with France and the German Protestant princes to achieve the interest in a Westphalian victory that it had already developed a century earlier.[39]

That Westphalia is a mere corollary of the Leviathan's bursting forth is a theorem that stumbles upon history's timing. Bodies politic were interested in Westphalia before their heads—the crowns—and their limbs, that is, their bureaucracies, ministries, military commands, and tax-collecting powers, experienced their dramatic adolescent growth. But the problem of timing goes beyond sequence, and is also one of suddenness. In each case where rulers came to advocate Westphalia, little such talk had been heard even a generation earlier. If the gradual growth of states over centuries explains Westphalia, then why did not their interests also grow gradually, right along with their institutions? This abruptness suggests another form of social power entering upon the scene.

Even more damning than timing was Spain. The Spanish state, like other European states, gained strength in the fifteenth century, unifying its territory through the marriage of Ferdinand of Aragon and Isabella of Castile. It then experienced, by some measures, the earliest and rapidest growth of any contemporary European state. It expanded its military from 20,000 troops in the 1470s (smaller than England's or France's) to 150,000 in the 1550s (three times that of France), established an overseas empire that fed it hordes of silver and gold, and enlarged its treasury and royal bureaucracy.[40] Like other European monarchs, the Spanish king was also multiply beleaguered, by a powerful Castilian nobility, and by mutinies, bankruptcies, and indebtedness, but Spain's relative might was unquestioned. Yet, the Spanish colossus never sought or fought for a Westphalian system of states, and was indeed its archopponent, regarding it as heresy. If state growth led to an interest in Westphalia, then why did not the strongest state of early modern Europe develop such an interest? The reasons I hardly need repeat. The Spanish state—pervasively Catholic, the imperial ruler of the Netherlands, its king the Holy Roman Emperor for the first half of the sixteenth century and afterward still closely tied to the imperially linked Habsburg dynasty—saw itself as the defender of what remained of medieval Europe.

Other Catholic states experienced no similar state growth, at least not the dramatic sort that would disconfirm the link between this growth and an interest in Westphalia. In Poland, the most important political trend during the sixteenth century was the growth in the political power of the nobility, and their ability to limit the power of the king through legislative prerogatives. Noble power certainly did not increase the extractive capacities of the state, and may well have hampered it, leading to Poland's eventual partition in the eighteenth century. In Hungary, itself partitioned in the early sixteenth century, nobles in the Habsburg region also held, and increased, strong power over the king. The institutions of post-Renaissance Italian city-states changed little in substance following the sack of Rome. But all of these cases offer only mild support for the negative side of the link between growth in state power and in interest in Westphalia. The strong correlation in time and place between Reformation crises and this interest remains, as does the problem of Spain, which was the most powerful state institution of the century and the most important supporter of the empire and Catholic Christendom. Generally, a geographic comparison supplements the temporal comparison in challenging the story of Westphalia as a mere spin-off of the state's coming of age.[41]

A final version of structuralism, a Realist version, looks not simply at individual polities, but at the balance of power between them. The change in this balance, against Spain, the Habsburgs, and the empire and in favor of the polities that desired Westphalia, is the key to explanation. Although Spain remained dominant in military size throughout the Thirty Years' War—fielding 300,000 troops in 1635, compared to only 150,000 for France—in the years following the Peace of Cateau-Cambrésis, its military commitments increased dramatically, leading it into "imperial overstretch," its ends far outdistancing its means. It became involved not only in the Dutch conflict, to which it would send over 50,000 troops at a time, but also aided Austria in Germany, fought repeated wars against the Turks, and put down several revolts, as late as 1640 in Catalonia and Portugal, and 1647 in Italy. It declared bankruptcy in 1607, 1627, 1647, 1652, 1656, and 1662, and generally failed in its efforts to centralize its administration over regions and reform its financial system.[42]

Meanwhile, both France and Sweden grew gradually in their state capacities in the first half of the seventeenth century, while the economy and military of the Dutch Provinces grew dramatically during the same period. The Dutch military struggle and France's alliance with Sweden, who contributed an official 150,000 troops by 1632, proved essential to reversing the Habsburg conquest of Germany of 1629, and eventually to achieving Westphalia.

The shift of the military balance and the alliance of anti-Habsburg powers were vital conditions for Westphalia. But these strategic factors were permissive, not sufficient. What they do not explain are how polities arrived at their interest in Westphalia in the first place and why they made the alliance choices that they did. I have tried to show that these interests are products of the ideas of the Reformation. It is only once the interests were in place that the pro-Westphalia powers threw their might into the international conflict that finally brought the settlement about. Realism, in the end, is an apprentice to our account, but not the central story.

Not only does the growth of the state and the shift in the international balance fail to replace Reformation ideas, but, as the embattled politics of this period of crisis reveal, it was deeply shaped by these ideas. From 1530 to 1648, armed conflict raged continuously in at least some part of Europe. The vast majority of these conflicts was caused in large part by the conflict between Protestants and Catholics—the biggest crisis of the period. In most European polities that experienced it, the crisis itself was the chief brake on state growth. In the Netherlands, Prussia, and France, it even wrought civil war. And it was in response to this chaos that the most politically powerful in these polities echoed the period's most innovative philosophers—Hobbes, Bodin, Spinoza, Bacon, and Grotius—in prescribing as a solution the establishment of a strong secular state, firmly in command within, free from ecclesial influence from without. The international version of this crisis was the Thirty Years'

War, the international version of the solution, the Peace of Westphalia. The Thirty Years' War mirrored, extrapolated, and intensified the religious conflicts in Germany, the Netherlands, and France. In each venue, stalwart devotees of one faith or the other fought to the death, and a middle ground of tolerance was adopted as the solution. Westphalia was the *politique* solution in France, the toleration espoused by William of Orange in the Netherlands, the Augsburg solution in Germany—applied internationally. Finally, it was amidst the religious wars of the seventeenth century that technological developments led states to organize their militaries on a much larger scale, necessitating in turn that the state institutions raise the money and the troops to support their militaries. The military revolution was also in part a product of the Reformation, and an imminent source of absolutism.

Trends besides the Reformation also helped to bring about Westphalia. During the first half of the seventeenth century, Spain suffered bankruptcies and decline, Sweden rose, the Netherlands flourished economically, and the empire became overextended, fighting not only Protestants but also Turks, all reflections and results of factors other than the Reformation. Again, I do not deny that a system of sovereign states could have arisen solely from the rise of new states and the decline of the empire, militarily and economically. But in the absence of the Reformation, the chaos it sparked, the secular political solution it evoked, and the institutional development it spurred, it is very difficult to say when the sovereign states system would have arisen and what this alternative historical universe would have looked like.

The Autonomy of the Reformation

What if, after all of these arguments for the Reformation's efficacy, the Reformation itself turns out to be the precipitate of other forces, say the rise of the bourgeoisie? So claim skeptics of the first role of ideas, of the autonomous shaping of identities. These skeptics must be answered, for if the Reformation is not substantially autonomous, then it cannot be efficacious. Debates about the causes of the Reformation are old and still continuing among historians and sociologists, and are ones to which I cannot freshly contribute here. Similar to my argument about the causes of sovereign statehood, I do not assert a single influence. Cultural and theological factors combined with economic and political ones to bring the Reformation. It is rather the irreducibility of the Reformation that I assert.

The strongest positive case for the autonomy of Reformation ideas lies in several "circumstances of reflection." These are theological and cultural factors that are compatible with the autonomy of Protestant ideas. They help to explain the historical circumstances that brought the Reformation while respecting the reflection of its converts. Most obvious and familiar is the perceived corruption of the medieval Church, its demands of penance and devotion, and its priests and orders, who used their offices, and even the sacraments, for financial gain and influence, not for spiritual service. In Germany, where the Reformation began, this perception was indeed stronger than anywhere else in Europe, and had grown steadily over the decades prior to the Reformation.[43] Intellectual, theological movements also correspond well. Christian humanism, espoused most famously by Erasmus, nominalist challenges to medieval scholastic theology such as that of William of Ockham, and the lay piety of the *devotio moderna*—all precursors and influences upon Reformation theology—were most widespread in Germany, Switzerland, and the Low Countries, where the Reformation occurred earliest and most intense, and had been steadily building influence over the previous two centuries.[44]

Other circumstances of reflection that favored the Reformation are associated with towns. In the urban centers were most commonly found the printing press, which produced propaganda pamphlets upon which the Reformation depended for its success. In the towns, too, was the largest literate population, able to read the pamphlets, and receptive to a faith that called the layperson to read the Scripture, hear the vernacular, and consider the meaning of the doctrines. It was also the towns that possessed the administrative autonomy that fomented in their inhabitants resentment of centralized papal and imperial control and sympathy for a faith whose practice centered upon the local church and community. Finally, the towns were the site of deep social dislocation at the time, the destination for dislocated peasants, and the site of struggling journeymen and artisans. At the time of the Reformation, Germany was one of the most urbanized regions of Europe. It was thus endowed with all of the factors that helped to make Reformation ideas more appealing. Throughout the rest of Europe, too, it was in urbanized regions that the Reformation converted most strongly, and in the strongholds of the rural nobility that it took root the least.[45]

But in acknowledging all these circumstances, we should not forget the very content of Reformation theology itself, which was far more radical in its content, its radical ideas far more widely espoused, than any previous notion of reform. Hus in Bohemia and Wycliffe in England had preached somewhat similar ideas in the previous two centuries, but did not develop them nearly as systematically as Luther and Calvin did, while no major medieval theologian had departed as far from Catholic orthodoxy as Luther or Calvin had. This, too, helps to explain why the Reformation happened when it did.[46]

Skeptics of the autonomy of the Reformation point to circumstances of a different sort. They appeal to circumstances that "eclipse" reason of reflection—overriding it rather than assisting it, eviscerating autonomy rather than acting as an apprentice to it. Most frequently cited is the rise of capitalism. Now, few Reformation historians will assert that the Reformation completely reduces to capitalism, such that we need not even mention reflection upon its ideas. Such an assertion would indeed encounter the problem of correspondence. Say we emphasize the rapid growth in trade, commerce, and population during the first half of the sixteenth century, arguing that trade and profit making undermined the authority of the Church. The difficulty here is that economic growth occurred all across Europe, in urban and rural areas, in places where the Reformation spread and in places where it did not. A more focused version of the explanation might look to the towns, particularly to the rising bourgeoisie, the commercial class, whose independent activity, whose simple, austere, and cerebral values made them find Protestantism attractive. While this explanation corresponds to the urban character of the Reformation, it fails to explain the many commercial towns and centers where Protestantism did not arise—in Italy, for instance. It also neglects to explain the crucial support for the Reformation found among nonbourgeois Europeans. Virtually every class took up the Reformation to some degree—artisans and proletarians in Germany and the Netherlands, the rural nobility in France, others elsewhere—and all provided impetus to its social power.[47]

A modification to the thesis might add that not only did the Reformation require prosperous towns, but also a state that would protect it against armed suppression: One without the other was not enough. This helps to explain the persistent Catholicism of Italy and Spain, where a "Counter Reformation state" suppressed Reformed ideas while allowing commerce.[48] But difficulties remain. Still unaccounted for are regions where Protestantism developed even in the absence of strongly commercial towns—Scotland, Switzerland, much of Sweden, and Hungary.[49] Unexplained, too, is how strong states chose their religious allegiances: Why did Spain and France not choose Protestantism?

There still remains a strong correlation between the towns and the Reformation. But this alone fails to show that the Reformation "reduced" to economic factors. At most, we can assert what Weber called an "elective affinity" between the commercial class and Protestantism. The productive mindset was well disposed toward the new ideas. We can assert that capitalism was one factor—in addition to the other important urban factors I have mentioned—that helped evoke the Reformation. To say more, to say that capitalism wholly determined the Reformation, would require abundant evidence of the personal experience of converts, showing that they were unreflectively socialized by capitalism or that Protestantism was merely instrumental to capitalism. Not only is such evidence unavailable, but its very interpretation would be controversial, rooted in difficultly discerned psychology and motivations. But in the absence of such evidence, there is no good reason to doubt reflection, and no good reason to doubt the independence of Reformation ideas in their fashioning of a sovereign states system.

Westphalia, Pluralism, and Hugo Grotius

Over the last chapter, I have been arguing for the appearance of novelty in early modern Europe, culminating in 1648. The claim for novelty should not be surprising; it is implicit in the notion "revolution in sovereignty." Westphalia, I have argued, was the origin of modern international relations. Emergent here was a Europe where virtually every political authority practiced sovereignty. Virtually every political ruler was now supreme within the territory of a polity whose affairs he regarded paramount over all others. Less familiar to today's conventional wisdom about Westphalia, yet equally novel, was the continental acceptance of a new political arrangement: religious pluralism. This did not yet amount to individual religious freedom. Nor was it even the victory of Augsburg, for princes did not simply declare a single religion within their borders; rather, many agreed to tolerate dissenting faiths within specified regions. But it did mean that authorities across Europe—many but not all—were now prepared to accept Augsburg's underlying commitment to (limited) toleration, to live with public expressions of Christian beliefs other than their own. Prior to Westphalia, there were enough authorities who did not accept such a state of affairs to keep Europe at war. At the height of Emperor Ferdinand's conquests in 1629, many Catholics had hoped, even realistically, for the restoration of Catholic uniformity within the Holy Roman Empire. After Westphalia, at least within the Christian world, wars to spread religious orthodoxy to other states became all but extinct. Westphalia was Augsburg, the *politique* solution, writ continental.

International relations, a system of sovereign states, religious toleration across borders, religious toleration within borders, Machiavellianism—all of these new notions rose together and were linked. Their ascent, though, required a prior theological shift, which was to Protestantism. The Reformation created religious pluralism, which led to the crisis that was eventually resolved through Westphalia's toleration, the abjuration of international enforcement of religion. The Reformation also yielded the idea that the authority of territorial kings and princes could be separated from the temporal powers of the universal Church. Both of these prongs of Protestantism—toleration and separation of powers—led to a system of sovereign states at Westphalia, a solution of pluralism to a crisis of pluralism.

International relations scholars often locate Hugo Grotius's *Law of War and Peace* (1625) as the first systematic description of a system of sovereign states, of European polities bound by no higher authority, although at this time still obligated by the common law of Christendom. What these scholars usually overlook is that Grotius was not just a jurist, but also a theologian. His theology is integral, for in it he asserts the virtual impossibility of reaching certainty or social agreement upon Christian doctrines that extend beyond the natural law—the organization of the Church, the Trinity, baptism. On these matters—what Catholics and Protestants fought over—Grotius advocated freedom of conscience.

Grotius set forth such views in his *Truth of the Christian Religion* (1627), a work for which seventeenth-century Europe knew him better than it knew him for his *Law of War and Peace*. That is because the seventeenth century was a time when the knowability, indeed correctness, of doctrines was a matter of enormous gravity. Of course, not everyone agreed with Grotius's view. Certainly the pope did not; neither did strict Calvinists, the Gomarists who jailed Grotius when they took power in the Netherlands. These disputants fought the most destructive European war prior to the twentieth century.

Grotius's theological stance fit well the terms of Westphalia, the agreement that ended the Thirty Years' War. To be sure, at the moment of Westphalia, many European Christians had not reached Grotius's view. They could not accept Grotius's assertion of irresolvability, which departed not only from classical Christian philosophers such as Aquinas and Augustine, but also from Luther and Calvin. The war finally ended for pragmatic reasons, out of exhaustion, its settlement at Westphalia coming not as an agreement on principle, but as a modus vivendi, a truce, an abeyance in the destruction of at least a quarter of Germany's population. Over time, though, Grotius's view came to be shared by more and more Europeans. Still others continued to think theological doctrines knowable, but came to repudiate the public enforcement of their expression, a considerable move toward Grotius's position. If Westphalia did not enjoy universal philosophical assent, it initiated practices that eventually came to enjoy wider assent, and ended the struggle for practices rooted in older, universalistic conceptions of politics.[50]

The settlement was a Protestant victory in that it allowed wide swaths of Europe to remain Protestant; the device that protected Protestants was sovereign statehood. This world of sovereign states was also one that Realism would so enduringly describe, one in which the crusades of states to alter religious practice and belief within the borders of other states came to appear strange, even difficult to imagine. Perhaps this strangeness helps to account for the materialist cast of contemporary social scientific accounts of how this world came to be. But if what I have argued is correct, the Realist world did not itself evolve solely from Realist factors, inexorably, by its own logic. It was the result of much more: a new conception of humanity's relationship with God.

PART THREE

THE REVOLUTION OF COLONIAL INDEPENDENCE: THE GLOBAL EXPANSION OF WESTPHALIA

EIGHT

IDEAS AND THE END OF EMPIRE

A CLOSE RELATIVE of Westphalia's litter of causes—a sovereign states system, toleration, Protestantism, the proscription of intervention for religion—was the more familiarly modern end of self-determination, the political autonomy of a people. Threaded through the visions of Richelieu, Gustavus Adolphus, the early modern German princes, Dutch patriots, and Hugo Grotius was the liberation of states, the freedom of states from the more universal form of authority in the Holy Roman Empire.

Outside Europe, though, most of the world was still organized imperially. Sovereign European states were themselves at the center of some of the largest empires of the world, their constitutional powers extending to the Americas, Africa, and Asia. Under the Westphalian constitution of international society, such control was legitimate. As it evolved, the second face of sovereignty prescribed that only those polities that exercised control of their territory and could enter into international agreements would be recognized as sovereign. Colonies, by definition, did not practice such de facto sovereign powers. Over the three centuries following Westphalia, European powers continued to swell, rendering the rest of the globe in one manner or another less than sovereign: partitioned, divided into spheres of influence, colonized, or otherwise restricted in authority. Some colonies—the United States, Canada—did become respected as full sovereign states, but these were exceptions. Even freed Latin American states found their authority restricted by European intervention.[1]

The victory of self-determination for the rest of the globe, like its victory at Westphalia, required a reversal of momentum, the disintegration, and finally, the defeat, of empires—here, colonial empires—British, French, Dutch, Belgian, German, Spanish, American, Portuguese, and Japanese. The global expansion of the Westphalian constitution of international society was consummated through the 1960 UN Declaration on colonial independence, and through the contemporaneous sweeping secession of colonies in Africa, Asia, and Latin America from Britain and France, the largest remaining colonial powers. In this new constitution of international society—global sovereign statehood—the second face of authority prescribed that all colonies were now entitled to sovereign independence. This universalizing provision was the terminus of the long campaign of the state to capture the territory of the globe.

Like the revolution in sovereignty at Westphalia, this revolution was the result of a crisis of pluralism sparked by a revolution in ideas. The central ideas were colonial nationalism and racial equality, both of which challenged the justice of empires. For imperial constitutional prerogatives to be overthrown, couriers of these ideas had to erode, crack, and undermine the legitimacy of the constitutions. These couriers, acting out of different locales and circumstances, wielding different forms of social power, were colonial nationalists, anticolonial superpowers, anticolonial United Nations members, and parties and lobbies within the metropolitan powers, all of which became convinced that colonies were unjust. Structural forces were important, too. That imperial implosion was the result of relative economic and military decline, the economic drain of the Second World War, the cost of maintaining colonies, the changing nature of economic markets, and shifting strategic realities is indubitably, partially, true. But like the effect of Reformation ideas upon Westphalia, the influence of ideas upon colonial independence was, I will argue, central. In this chapter, I first describe in greater detail the nature and historical significance of this revolution in sovereignty, then outline my argument for ideas as a cause of it. Then, in chapters 9, 10, and 11, I argue for the role of ideas in bringing the British to abrogate empire and support a institution of colonial independence. In chapter 12, I argue the same for the French.

The Revolution of Colonial Independence

How was colonial independence a revolution in sovereignty? Revolutions scrap old orders. In this case, the old order was the Westphalian constitution as it existed between 1648 and 1960. This constitution was entirely consistent with the holding of colonies. With respect to the second face of the constitution, its rules for membership, colonies were never allowed a claim to statehood. Colonial rule did not go unprotested—philosophers and jurists from the sixteenth century onward, including Victoria, Gentili, Bodin, Grotius, and Pufendorf, objected that natural law denied Christian states legitimate title over the inhabitants of non-Christian lands. But European practitioners of statecraft regarded colonial rule as legitimate.[2] Nor should we overlook the different manners of colonial rule—the imperial rule of Spain and Portugal, organized centrally in the bureaucracies of Madrid and Lisbon, contrasted with that of Britain, which allowed much more self-government.[3] But in all cases, with regard to sovereignty, colonies were extensions of European metropoles; they were territories for whose inhabitants the European authority was supreme, the authority to which all authority in the colonies was answerable. The British Viceroy of India in 1926 stated it baldly: "The sovereignty of the British Crown is supreme in India and therefore no ruler of an Indian State can justifiably claim to negotiate with the British Government on an equal footing. Its supremacy is not based only upon treaties and engagements, but exists independently of them."[4]

Despite the constitution that allowed colonial rule, some colonies indeed achieved their independence during these centuries. Having defeated their colonial master in war or benefited from the defeat of their master at the hands of a separate European power, some of these freed colonies became full international citizens, accorded all of the privileges of sovereign states. But they did not attain this citizenship, or any kind of legitimate claim to it, until their colonial masters had freed them.[5] That is, some states changed their status under the constitution, but the constitution itself remained the same.

In altering this status quo of three centuries, in bringing colonies the right to independent statehood, the first half of the 1960s was truly revolutionary. The second face of authority was redrawn: colonies became full members of the community of sovereign states, without regard to their "standard of civilization" or readiness for self-government. As for the first and third faces of Westphalia, colonial independence was not a revision but a reinforcement. Once independent, colonies came to practice all of the prerogatives of a state, most importantly, nonintervention. The legitimacy of the state as a form of polity became strengthened, too, through its very replication across the globe. With respect to all three faces of authority, colonial independence extended globally the formula of 1648.

But how exactly did the norm of anticolonialism become both legitimate and practiced in the 1960s? In practice, the two largest colonial empires—Britain and France—quite simply relinquished the lion's share of their remaining colonies. Belgium followed suit, and since the United States, Spain, the Netherlands, and Germany had at least a decade before given up their empires, any remaining colonies—a few minor British ones, and those of Portugal—were anomalies. In 1955, the British and French flags together flew around the globe; in 1970, they flew only in the Ascension Islands and a few other rocky outposts, in what the French called "*les confetti de l'Empire*."[6] Between 1957 and 1967 (and especially between 1960 and 1966), the rate of decolonization far exceeded any previous or subsequent period. Then, imperial powers granted independence to a total of 66 colonies.[7]

If the legitimacy of a constitution lies in polities' public pronouncements and agreements, ratifications and protocols, the central exhibit for colonial independence is the United Nations "Declaration on the granting of independence to colonial countries and peoples," General Assembly Resolution 1514, adopted on December 14, 1960. The United Nations, of course, had been the foundational international organization since

1945, its charter the primary source of international law. Its imprimatur lent special legitimacy to any declaration. The declaration on colonial independence has indeed been called "the Magna Carta of decolonization."[8] Originally proposed by the Soviet Union, finally adopted in a version authorized by a coalition of African and Asian states, and supported by the vast majority of UN members, the resolution maintained that "all peoples have the right to self-determination" and that "any attempt at the total or partial disruption of the national unity and the territorial integrity of a country is incompatible with the purposes and the principles of the United Nations." What action did it demand? The transfer of "all powers to the peoples . . . without any conditions or reservations." "Inadequacy of political, economic, social, or educational preparedness," it declared, "should never serve as a pretext for delaying independence."[9]

Self-determination is central here. But the exact meaning of this malleable, contested concept, required the interpretation of UN Resolution 1541, adopted the following day. Resolution 1541 asserts that Chapter XI of the UN Charter, the portion dealing with "non-self-governing territories," is applicable only to "territories which were then known to be of the colonial type." Self-determination was to apply only to colonies, not to nations or regions within existing states or within the territory of colonies once they became independent.[10] What was a colony? Here, international lawyers applied the "saltwater rule," holding that a colony is a secessionist land separated from a larger state by a body of saltwater. The declaration, it followed, proscribed only what international lawyers have called "saltwater imperialism"—rule of overseas territory—but not any other sort of imperialism.

International lawyers have vigorously debated whether the 1960 declaration and subsequent similar declarations amount to a legal "right" to colonial self-determination. I will not try to settle the issue here.[11] What is important for the legitimacy of a norm is that states publicly assent to it. That the 1960 declaration passed by a vote of 89 in favor, none against, and nine abstentions, and that subsequent declarations on colonial self-determination also passed by large majorities, is evidence that most of the world regarded colonial independence as legitimate. The abstentions in 1960, though, cannot be overlooked. They are the votes of, among others, Great Britain, France, the United States, Belgium, Portugal, and South Africa—the remaining colonial powers plus their Cold War ally, the United States. Is the legitimacy of colonial independence thereby nullified? Such a conclusion is too hasty. It is notable that these powers abstained, whereas they had voted "no" to previous anticolonial resolutions. From 1960 onward, they never—with the exceptions of Portugal and South Africa—explicitly opposed the general norm of colonial independence. The abstention of the United States, which had spoken against colonialism since its own revolution, can be explained by its desire not to snub Britain rather than any reluctance about favoring colonial independence.[12] As for Britain and France, as long as they still held significant colonies, they were unwilling to assent to any resolution that seemed to allow the United Nations to direct their internal affairs. Once they had actually given up the bulk of their colonies, however, they came to support many anticolonial resolutions, including ones against South Africa and Rhodesia. Although they were wary of UN efforts to tell them when and how to dispense with their colonies, they dispensed anyway—at their own pace, without protesting the substance of this new constitution. The major European powers, then, practiced the norm; international law gave it legitimacy; and no major power (except Portugal) detracted from its legitimacy by explicitly opposing it.

Colonial independence was revolutionary not only because of its scope, but also because of its suddenness. Previously, European powers had agreed to only scant approximations of it. At the 1885 Berlin Conference, these powers explicitly had legitimized colonial rule. Gathering to settle the terms and boundaries of the just-completed partition of Africa, they sanctioned the principle of acquisition by occupation: a state could validly hold a colony as long as it occupied and governed it.[13] The powers only hinted at a commitment toward colonial progress, agreeing to the "preservation of the native tribes, and to care for the improvement of their moral and material well-being," along with the extinguishing of slavery and the slave trade.[14]

At the close of the two World Wars, this ideal of trusteeship—that imperial powers were stewards of the progress of their colonies—was expanded. Acting upon the principle of self-determination, under the impetus of Woodrow Wilson and to a lesser extent the British, the victors of World War I created a "mandate system" to administer the colonies that they had acquired from the defeated empires, German and Ottoman. The mandates were classified into "A," "B," and "C," depending on their readiness for self-government: "A" mandates, such as Palestine and Iraq, could become independent relatively soon; "B" mandates, including tribal African peoples, would need an unspecified period of European economic and political guidance before governing themselves; and "C" mandates, the most primitive peoples of the Pacific and the Hottentots of South-West Africa, would remain European-ruled indefinitely, possibly forever.[15]

At the end of the Second World War, the victors found themselves with the task of realizing the right of all peoples "to choose the form of government under which they will live," a principle that they had announced as a war aim in the Atlantic Charter, and which President Franklin D. Roosevelt and segments of the British left wing had declared global, not just European, in its reach. In constructing the United Nations Charter, they accordingly centered self-determination—though as a principle, not a right—in Articles 1, 55, and 56, and prescribed obligations toward administered territories, dividing them into "non-self-governing territories"—consisting of the colonies of the victors—and "trust" territories, comprising former League of Nations mandates and territories taken from the defeated states. Toward the "non-self-governing territories," the victors acknowledged a "sacred trust" to promote the "well-being" of the ruled and agreed to submit reports to the UN Secretary-General concerning "economic, social, and educational conditions in the territories."[16] For the trust territories, there was more. The goal for them was "progressive development towards self-government or independence"—an aim that was largely fulfilled during the 1950s.[17]

The settlements of both wars, then, recognized a commitment to progress in European-ruled regions; the United Nations Charter made a commitment to self-government for the trust territories. But compared to the sweep of the 1960 declaration, these were limited aims. The United Nations Charter's commitment to self-determination, far from a right to which colonies were entitled, was a principle open to wide interpretation; the trust territories were only a fraction of the territories that Europeans governed; and the victors had made no commitment whatsoever to the independence or some other form of self-government for their other colonies.

Like Westphalia in 1648, the constitution of colonial independence of 1960 was the consolidation of a trend, not the creation of a new order *ex nihilo*. Throughout the nineteenth century, and at an increasing pace after World War I, states here, then there, attained their independence. The American, Dutch, German, Spanish, and Japanese empires had all been dissolved, resolved into sovereign states, earlier in the twentieth century. Britain, too, had unloaded important portions of its empire, most notably India in 1947. But it was not until 1960 that anything resembling a new constitution arose. It was only in 1960 that a universal international body declared all colonies illegitimate, and it was only in the early 1960s that the massive release of most remaining colonies took place. Legitimacy and practice—these were the conditions of a true constitution.

An Argument about the End of Colonial Rule

Opposed to the optimistic and paternal notion that colonies are apprentices, the charges of stewarding wards, that they are adolescents being groomed for their eventual independence or for incorporation into a greater empire as equals, is the claim that colonies are slaves. Slaves, simply for being colonies. For a colonial nation or collection of tribes to live under another power's tutelage—even one that claims benevolence—is unjust, and not simply because imperialists prostitute laborers in mines and fields, deny local inhabitants rights and representation, and sometimes kill dissenters, but more so because the colonial arrangement is intrinsically flawed: It subordinates, it chains, it suppresses the separate fate that the colony has come to envision for itself.

That slavery most appositely described the political plight of African, Asian, and Central American peoples was the conviction that socially empowered people had to adopt into their identity if they were ever to place their moral explosives at the very foundation of colonial empires. Beginning in the early twentieth century and continuing through the 1950s, this conviction was indeed adopted by young colonial intellectuals in European universities, later to be nationalist leaders, as well as by key sectors of the British Labour Party, the French Socialist and Communist parties, of portions of elites and the public in the United States, and, finally, by small citizens groups, in pockets, corners, nooks, interstices. Like the ideas of the Protestant Reformation, anticolonial ideas then spread outward, infusing wider nationalist movements, lobbies, and parties, in colonies, metropoles, the United States, the Soviet Union, and the United Nations. Becoming socially empowered, this dissent created dialectical dissonance with imperial ideas, contradictions with the colonial order, a crisis of pluralism.

My argument, here again, is that this crisis in pluralism brought the revolution in sovereignty, the new constitution that legitimized statehood for colonies. This revolution, this constitution, arrived through the very decision of heads of states to make it the interest of their state to lower their imperial flag. This interest entailed the very relinquishment of their colonies; and this relinquishment was at the very heart of the constitution of colonial independence. In contrast to the revolution at Westphalia, then, once key states adopted an interest in the new constitution, the revolution was simultaneously accomplished. There was no work left to be done, no defenders of the old order left to defeat. These key states, the ones that I will investigate, were Great Britain and France. In these two empires lay the vast preponderance of the remaining colonies in the world at the time of the revolution. It was these two empires that made the decision to relinquish, or soon relinquish, the vast preponderance of their remaining colonies, roughly around 1960—the date of their interest. What ever brought them to resolutions of such colossal consequence?[18]

Here again, I argue for a counterfactual claim. Were it not for the rise and spread of anticolonial ideas, Britain and France would not have come to their interest in colonial independence around 1960. Again, too, I deny the sole influence of ideas. Structural forces—the relative military and economic weakening of Britain and France, and the increased cost of holding colonies—conspired to bring the revolution. But they were far from sufficient. I again deny the necessity of ideas as well. We can imagine a scenario in which structural forces alone brought the imperial abrogation of Britain and France. But this is a scenario of an imaginary later generation, and of a different, imaginary, set of circumstances. Because of influential ideas, the revolution came far sooner than it would otherwise have come—far sooner, indeed, than British and French statesmen themselves had expected it to come only a few years earlier. That the revolution arrived around 1960 had important historical consequences, too. Certainly for the new states, attaining independence then meant that they faced the challenges of political and economic development at a far earlier time then they otherwise would have. In the eyes of many colonial officials, the birth of new states was even premature, auguring future crises. To other officials, the rejection of further delay was wisdom, for it averted the far more violent struggle for independence that might well have otherwise resulted. Where freedom did come through war—in Indochina, Algeria—the granting of independence meant avoiding a far more prolonged conflict. But whatever one's view, the timing mattered. The timing also had important consequences for the international system. Over the next thirty years, many of these newly independent states became battlegrounds in the Cold War, the fate of their regimes viewed by superpowers as important strategic stakes. All of these fates, realized and averted, were the causal consequence of the timing of the revolution.

At the close of the Second World War, neither Britain nor France remotely intended a general relinquishment of their colonies or a constitution of colonial independence. In granting independence to India, Britain admittedly gave up its largest colony, but it intended no universal policy. Under the postwar Labour Government, the British Colonial Office developed long-range plans for the development of its colonies; France proudly reasserted its commitment to its empire; both Britain and France sought to minimize the oversight and influence of the United Nations upon their colonial affairs. Our focus, then, will be on the period between the end of World War II and the interest in general colonial independence, which these states adopted a decade and a half later. What forces brought the change? An ideas explanation expects to see anticolonial ideas refashioning identities, increasing in their social power, exercising influence upon heads of state.[19] The most common form of structural skepticism about colonial independence doubts the social power of ideas, their second role, and proposes instead the importance of relative military and economic power. World War II left the metropoles weakened, unable to sustain their empires, and their colonies restive, more willing and able to challenge empires. Some structural skeptics go even deeper, challenging the first role of ideas, holding anticolonial identities were themselves the product of class or political position.

How Anticolonial Ideas Brought Change

If ideas were behind the revolution, what exactly were these ideas? Just as Reformation theology was in fact a set of theologies, dissent against empire was not just one simple notion. Nationalism within the colonies, the position of the British Labour Party, the anticolonialism of the United States or the Soviet Union, the views of intellectuals like Frantz Fanon or Jean-Paul Sartre, were all variations on a wide theme. Two major strands of dissent motivated these critics. They are conceptually separate, though often articulated together, even by the same person. One strand was anticolonial nationalism, the idea that a colony is a nation, a group of people that has a common identity and history and is entitled to a state of its own.[20] The other strand was racial equality, holding that colonialism by its very nature subordinated Asian, African, and Central American peoples to European rulers, implying their inferiority and perpetuating their domination. Only the end of colonial rule itself could restore equality. The two strands were related. Their common proposition was that that colonial rule was fundamentally illegitimate and that colonies had a right to self-determination, by which critics meant acquiring the legal status of an independent state. They rejected the ideals of stewardship, trusteeship, "responsible gradualism," a "civilizing mission," or any other notion that, in their eyes, denied the equality of cultures and races. Some versions also rejected capitalism, but not all of them did. The entire set of such ideas, I will call "anticolonial ideas." Directly contradicting the existing constitution of international society, anticolonial ideas were revolutionary ideas.[21]

Anticolonial ideas came to exert social power on British and French cabinets and heads of state. True to the nature of the second role, they gave these leaders incentives to define and pursue colonial independence as the interest of their state. I do not hold that heads of states alter their own identities so as to become anticolonialists; rather they had to be convinced of the political and economic benefits of releasing colonies, and the similar costs of keeping them. Responsible for reconfiguring the incentives of leaders were the couriers of ideas, who included anti-imperialist publics, intellectuals, activists, and opposition parties in colonies and metropoles, as well as in the United States, the Soviet Union, and the United Nations. All of these couriers, I will argue, were converts to anticolonial ideas, and effected a portion of the decisive social power of these ideas.

In the revolution of colonial independence, the social power of ideas was more complex than it was in the revolution at Westphalia. In this revolution, couriers of ideas also exercised a more indirect version of the social power of ideas, one that I described in chapter 4, and that I want to apply here. I call it the reputational social power of ideas. It operated in Britain, but not in France. It was Britain, as I will explain, whose official ideology of empire allowed it to operate. Here, it was the causal pathway by which ideas brought the end of empire.

Central to reputational social power is the interaction between two kinds of ideas—revolutionary ideas and established ideas. Revolutionary ideas, I have been discussing all along. They are the agents of change, the ideas that challenge existing international constitutional orders. Here, revolutionary ideas are simply anticolonial ideas. Established ideas, by contrast, are official ideologies that uphold existing constitutional orders. They are institutionalized, meaning that they are widely accepted among a polity's official elites, and are ensconced as "norms of appropriateness" in bureaucracies and official agencies.[22] Officials do not necessarily hold them with deep conviction or as a part of their identities. The official ideology may instead be better described as a "resolver of uncertainty" about how to pursue the state's strategic and economic interests. Most importantly for reputational social power, established ideas are justificatory—elites draw upon them in order to justify their policies to their publics. In pronouncing established ideas, elites later become constrained by them.

Here, established ideas are the ideals by which Britain and France justified their empires. To generalize, Britain justified its empire during the twentieth century with the claim that it was gradually preparing its colonies for self-government and, one day, independence. France's ideal was assimilationist, planning to incorporate its colonies eventually into a Greater France, ruling its colonies from central bureaucracies in Paris, and aiming to teach its colonists the French language and way of government. These established ideas were not agents of change, but acted as a structure that hindered, channeled, or empowered transforming revolutionary ideas.

In all forms of the social power of ideas, couriers of ideas impose costs and benefits on heads of state. In wielding reputational social power, these couriers impose such costs and benefits through threatening to undermine the reputation of heads of state for upholding their established, justificatory ideals. Reputational social power has several features. First, it only works when leaders have developed a reputation for upholding an established idea—in this case, the British ideal of gradual self-government. They become associated with the idea, perceived as advocates of it. Second, the heads of state with this reputation must perceive the revolutionary ideas as calling them to account for not living up to their established ideal. They worry that they will lose their reputation if they fail to answer the criticism. Such pressure can only work if the two ideals are relatively close in content. For the members of the British Cabinet, anticolonial ideas challenged their reputation for bringing about gradual self-government, and since gradual self-government also shared the general end of colonial progress, the Cabinet felt that it had to answer this criticism in order not to lose its reputation. The revolutionary ideas suggested that the Cabinet was not living up to its own promises. Third, the costs of losing one's reputation may be measured in conventional forms of power. We do not need to assume that leaders are concerned with reputation for its own sake; it may not be the loss of reputation itself that leaders fear. Rather, they may fear that losing their reputation will result in costs imposed by certain audiences who care about their reputation. In this case, the Cabinet feared that its loss of reputation might mean, first, a strategic setback in the Cold War as its colonies withdrew their allegiance and threw it to the Soviet bloc, and, second, the loss of votes from British citizens who expected the Cabinet to uphold the state's professed ideals. But fourth, even if the costs are conventional, ideas have still created the structure of influence that results in the costs being borne. If leaders were not concerned about their reputation for certain established ideas, and if revolutionary ideas were not able to call this reputation into question, then the leaders would not fear the consequences of losing their reputation. It was only because Britain was concerned about its reputation, and because anticolonial ideas could strain its reputation, that it would pay a cost for losing its reputation. Reputational social power is thus more complex than the forms of the social power of ideas that I have discussed so far. Describing a normative environment that creates a new array of costs and benefits, it weaves together ideas and material power.

In France, the conditions for reputational power did not obtain, thwarting its possibilities. France's leaders had developed a reputation for upholding a very different established ideal, an assimilationist ideal, whose very content prevented these leaders from being called to account by anticolonial ideas. As there was a wide public consensus that an assimilationist empire, Greater France, was essential to France's national identity and greatness, politicians would in fact pay a high price for concessions to anticolonial demands—exactly the opposite of British leaders' incentives. In France, then, revolutionary and established ideas were widely distant, not similar. Because French politicians were not concerned about upholding any reputation for progress to which anticolonial ideas could appeal, there was no cost to be paid in losing such a reputation. In fact, the very suppression of anticolonial ideas could even bolster a leader's reputation for defending Greater France. For the opponents of French empire, reputational social power was simply not available. Without the preconditions for its exercise, couriers of revolutionary ideas were forced to convert the price of colonies into the currency of war—a conventional, direct form of social power and a different causal pathway. In fact, colonial nationalists first appealed to Paris for gradual advances in self-government of the British sort, and only turned to arms when rebuffed.

Different established ideals meant that different forms of the social power of ideas brought about colonial independence in the British and French empires. Alongside the central argument, that ideas explain the occurrence of interests in colonial independence, I want also to offer a supporting companion argument: that ideas explain the pattern of decolonization, namely whether it was relatively peaceful or violent. Pattern and occurrence are different kinds of outcomes to explain, but the two are corroborative. If ideas did nothing to bring about colonial independence, then they were impotent and could not possibly affect its pattern. Evidence for their influence on pattern is evidence for their influence on occurrence. The pattern indeed differed in the two cases: Britain's transition was relatively peaceful; France fought long, foul wars in Algeria and Indochina and briefer wars in Tunisia, Morocco, and Madagascar. The comparison is not perfect, for France never fought insurrection in West or Equatorial Africa, while Britain fought small ones in Kenya and Malaya. But relative to each other, Britain's end of empire was peaceful, France's violent.

What explains the contrast is the different forms of interaction between revolutionary and established ideals. Britain's gradualist established ideal allowed the ideas to act through reputational social power—generally, a peaceful kind of social power. The social power of arms, by contrast, is violent by definition. France's assimilationist established ideal made arms the only sort of social power available. Figure 8.1 seeks to capture this logic. It shows how established imperial ideals mediate the social power of anticolonial ideals to produce different patterns of decolonization.

Evidence for two arguments—my central claim, that ideas caused the revolution in colonial independence, and the companion claim that they explain its varying pattern in Britain and France—I necessarily present together. To show that ideas caused colonial independence, I will show their correspondence in time with the revolution and describe how they caused it. Doing this means describing how they exerted social power, which in turn means describing how they exerted reputational social power in Britain and conventional social power in France. Though distinct, the arguments draw upon the same evidence.

Competing Explanations

Other social scientists, too, have argued that the end of empire resulted from new notions, not just new material circumstances. These notions, many of these scholars render as "norms," by which they mean ideas about

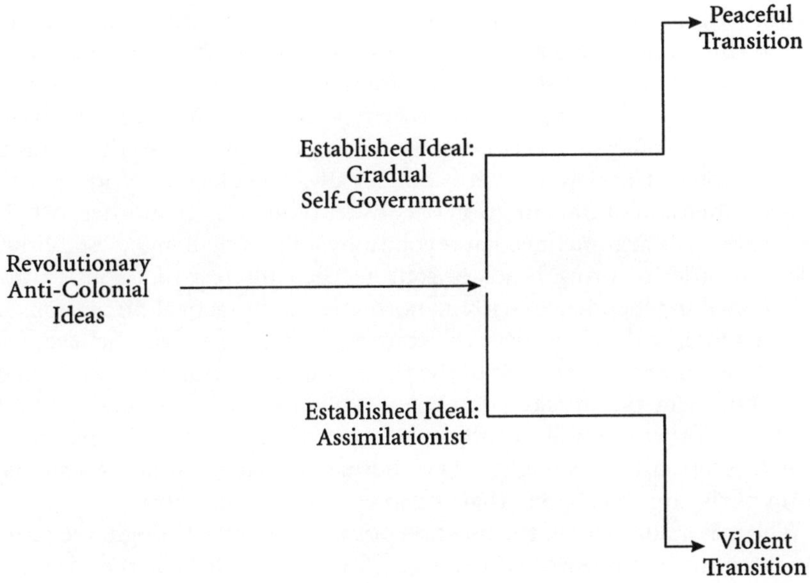

Fig. 8.1. Explaining the Pattern of Colonial Independence

the illegitimacy of colonialism that are held by a network of international elites—influential politicians and officials in the United Nations, the superpowers, the colonies, and the metropolitan states. Sometimes with sophisticated quantitative methods, they demonstrate the influence of norms on decolonization. On its occurrence: The global growth of norms made colonies illegitimate and brought independence itself. On its timing: A metropolitan state's previous grants of independence made the practice more legitimate and future grants more likely. And on its pattern: States whose previous grants had legitimized colonial independence were more likely to continue to grant independence peacefully. All of these effects of norms, these studies have convincingly established.[23]

I am sympathetic to these studies. But my own argument is importantly different. It is qualitative and comparative, focusing upon two imperial collapses within a short time, detailing the complexity of historical decision. It is not quantitative and does not encompass several empires over several centuries across hundreds of decisions for independence. An important difference, too, is my treatment of ideas. Whereas these studies focus on one force, which they call "norms," mine recognizes the distinctiveness and vital importance of three separate kinds of ideas, which play separate but synergistic parts in the drama of colonial independence. One idea, closest to what I have called a norm in chapter 2, is the legitimacy component of the international constitution of colonial independence—the official, mutual recognition that Britain, France, and other members of the United Nations gave to decolonization. A component of the constitution of international society, this idea is a part of the outcome that the other forms of ideas explain. Another type is what I have called "established ideas," official ideals of empire. It is one of the causes that leads to the outcome, the new constitution. Finally, "revolutionary ideas," another dimension of the causation of constitutions, are yet another sort. All are crucial. My argument is that revolutionary ideas challenged established ideas in order to bring heads of state to their interest in a constitution of colonial independence, with its normative and practical dimensions. A focused look at decisions over the course of a decade or so, I believe, will reveal the importance of each of the three kinds of notional forces. Including all of them amounts to complexity, but a necessary complexity. Omitting any of them inhibits a full explanation of the timing and manner of this revolution in sovereignty. The alternative that I dispute is a simpler form of the argument, one that collapses or elides the three.

The major alternative, the most skeptical alternative, though, are structural arguments, most of which argue for World War II as the dizzying, weakening economic and strategic blow that sapped Britain and France of the resources and will to sustain empire. In some versions, it was the diminished wealth and military might of Britain and France that left them unable to support their globally flung possessions. In other versions, colonies became costlier to run and provided fewer economic benefits, while Britain's and France's financial and trade interests shifted away from their empires and toward the European Community and the rest of the industrial world.[24] It was such trends that brought imperial cabinets to their interest in colonial independence.

Indisputably, there is truth to these trends. After the war, Britain and France fell markedly in their power rankings, while their colonies became costlier in some respects. But these indices alone, I will argue, point to no distinct conclusion about keeping empire. Does diminished rank mean that a power should shed empire so as to preserve resources, or that it should retain and develop its empire in order to increase its revenues? If colonies have become more costly, might they become more beneficial through development? Is an empire essential to bolstering the prestige of a bruised great power? These questions, objective power trends alone do not answer. Cabinets had to answer them for themselves; and answering them involved interpreting, not simply observing, their state's new position. That is, we cannot argue that material factors led to imperial abjuration unless we see that imperialists perceived their power position, its present and its future, in a way that convinced them to release their empires.

So the question for a structural account will be, Is there evidence that cabinets saw the net material costs and benefits as declining after World War II and up to the time of colonial independence?[25]

An ideas account also relies upon the perceptions of cabinets. It offers evidence that it was the challenge in ideas, not changes in their material power position, that led cabinets to their interest in a revolution in sovereignty. Over the next four chapters, I will assess the evidence for both kinds of explanations in the cases of Britain and France. In chapter 9, I will argue for the reputational power of ideas in bringing Britain to give up its empire. In chapter 10, I show the role of ideas in forming colonial nationalists, one of the key sources of anticolonial criticism that pressured Britain's reputation. In chapter 11, I will seek to show it was not primarily its concern for its material power position that led the British Cabinet to colonial independence. Chapter 12 then looks at France, where the ideas of colonial nationalists led them to take up arms against the French empire, evoking its demise.

NINE

THE END OF THE BRITISH EMPIRE: CASHING OUT THE PROMISE OF SELF-GOVERNMENT

IN 1940, the British Parliament legislated a new imperial audacity. For the past two centuries, the Colonial Office in London had entrusted governance to its colonial officials in India, in the Gold Coast, in Malaya, all across its empire. The Colonial Office had been a small department. Now, the Colonial Development and Welfare Act charged the office with a modernizing mission: to construct harbors, roads, agricultural projects, and dams for electricity and irrigation, and to develop the colonies, spurring their economic, perhaps even their political advancement, and, also extracting revenue for an empire strained by world war. After World War II, committed and competent leaders took up the mission: Arthur Creech Jones of the Labour Cabinet and Oliver Lyttleton under the Conservative government of Winston Churchill, which took power in 1951. For Britain, developing its colonies meant keeping its colonies. At least until that faraway day when they would be ready for independence.

The edifice that the colonies would become was to be symbolized by the edifice that the Colonial Office would be. Churchill and Lyttleton commissioned architects to design a grand headquarters, one to sit across Parliament Square from Westminster Palace. Churchill made sure that the building would include an impressive audience chamber, where prime ministers and the cabinet would meet governors, chiefs, emirs, and pashas from throughout the British Empire.[1]

By the early 1960s, though, the Colonial Office continued to rent rooms. The government never built the edifice it had envisioned only a few years earlier. In the late 1960s, the government demoted the office even further, now moving it into an obscure nook of the Commonwealth section of the Foreign Office. The Colonial Office was never to realize its prestige, architectural or political. By this time, there were few British colonies left.

What is most interesting and puzzling about Britain's forfeiture of empire is its suddenness. Until late 1959, no Cabinet official intimated, either publicly or behind closed doors, that Britain was about to begin the negotiations and concessions that would lead it to grant independence to its remaining colonies in eastern and central Africa, in Central America, and in Malta and Cyprus, all within a few short years. It was not the first time that Britain had released colonies, to be sure. But this quittance was wholesale, far exceeding previous piecemeal releases, and accompanied by Britain's acquiescence to the 1960 United Nations resolution condemning colonialism. The revolution was hardly premeditated; neither was it an inevitable choice. The flurry of protests, strikes, and riots that spread through Britain's colonies in 1959 certainly helped to precipitate Britain's decision. Yet the government had reacted to similar unrest in the early 1950s by suppressing uprisings in Kenya and Malaya, toppling a hostile regime in British Guiana, and jailing nationalist leaders throughout the colonies. Britain's solution—to concede independence, to avoid prolonged wars—was also quite different from that of other empires such as France or, for that matter, the Netherlands or Portugal. The burden of any account of Britain's change in course—the occurrence of decolonization—is to show what conditions had changed by the late 1950s, and why Britain responded to them by negotiating, compromising, then ceding independence—the pattern of decolonization.

The centrally important cause: During the 1950s, criticism of Britain's entire colonial project, its aspirations for development and all, grew stronger and wider than ever before. The criticism gestated in three forums, through three different couriers: nationalists in the colonies themselves, domestic quarters of opposition within Britain, and something vaguer that I will call the "international context," consisting of the United States, the Soviet Union, and nonaligned states within the United Nations who were formerly colonies. Behind all this criticism were people who had come to anticolonial identities—the first role of ideas. Their social power—the second role of ideas—depended upon the established ideal of empire according to which the British Cabinet reacted to criticism. We may summarize the ideal as "gradual self-government." The purpose of empire was to prepare colonies to rule themselves and perhaps eventually become independent, a policy that Britain would pursue slowly, over time, by extending political privileges gradually and only when it thought the colonists ready for them. The ideal of gradual self-government was a justification for empire—an established idea. Challenging it were anticolonial ideas—revolutionary ideas—that held that empire, any empire at all, was altogether unjust and ought to be disbanded at once.

British Cabinet officials and Colonial Office officials had voiced their established ideal over decades, so repeatedly that it had become an official ideal, a public justification for empire and a socializing influence within colonial bureaucracies, where it became "institutionalized." Britain took on a reputation for the ideal, one that both Labour and Conservative Cabinet officials thought important to uphold. The ideal, the reputation, provided a ready response to the public questioning of empire. Whenever confronted with criticism of the slowness of colonial progress, the use of arms against dissenters, or the very retention of empire, officials would draw from the ideal. Too much haste would be unwise and would leave the colonists unprepared for governing themselves; the purpose of empire was precisely to prepare them. Throughout the twentieth century, in small crisis after small crisis, the Cabinet mustered this reply successfully, at least politically speaking. That is, it avoided a widespread reactionary reputation through its colonies, within British public opinion, and among other world powers. As anticolonial ideas spread and converted, though, the reply carried less and less efficacy. By the later 1950s, Britain's defense sounded strained against the din of calumny from the combined sources of criticism.

Couriers of anticolonial ideas from diverse quarters together drew up the British government's statements about self-government and presented these statements back to the government as a promissory note, demanding to have it cashed out. As reputational power exerts itself through imposing different kinds of cost, so each courier confronted Britain with a different form of price for failing to cash out. Domestic critics presented the Conservative Cabinet with the loss of popular electoral support were it to appear reactionary. International criticism created the risk of losing the colonies' sympathy to the Soviets amidst the heat of the Cold War. Finally, nationalist criticism from the colonies, which had so far resulted in riots, protests, and strikes but seemed likely to swell into something more, cornered Britain into a choice between looking reactionary by sending troops or moving forward toward independence. These anticolonialist ideas worked together. The riots, protests, and strikes in the colonies forced Britain into a choice between repression and rapid, perhaps wanton, political progress, but it was the domestic and international critics who would indeed be sure to create a reputation for Britain as a reactionary power. None of these ideas would have been socially powerful, though, had not British officials established and sought to uphold a reputation for gradual self-government. Britain's reputation was a necessary chemical ingredient for yielding the reaction of colonial independence. It would so react when combined with the right combination and proportions of active agents, which were anticolonial ideas.[2]

This is what I expect ideas to explain: Britain's interest in a new constitution of international society, and its relatively peaceful pursuit of that interest. What I do not expect them to explain is the timing and occurrence of Britain's many historic decisions to release colonies, scattered over the previous two centuries. I do not offer a general theory of decolonization. In fact, at least three waves of colonial secessions had occurred earlier in the twentieth century. The first was the independence of the Anglo settler colonies, South Africa, Australia, New Zealand, and Ireland, all as of 1922; the second was that of four Asian countries, India, Pakistan, Burma, and Ceylon, all in 1947 and 1948; the third was that of the Gold Coast, granted independence in 1957, and Nigeria, which received it in 1960, both of which Britain began to negotiate rapid constitutional changes with in the late 1940s. Now ideas may well help to explain these waves, but I do not want to defend the proposition here. Rather, I am concerned with the new constitution of international society that arrived around 1960. Why did it arrive? Why did it arrive when it did? Why did it arrive in the way that it did? Two features of anticolonial ideas—both pertaining to their width—will help to explain why they brought a new constitution and not simply the independence of a few more colonies. First, the couriers of the ideas were more widespread than ever before, both within the colonies and in domestic and international quarters, all forums where couriers had been scant prior to World War II. Second, the content of the criticism was wider than ever before. Earlier, colonial nationalists advocated their colony's independence; now nationalists, and even more so, domestic and international critics, took on the very institution of colonialism. Wider ideas, in both senses, produced a wider result.

Toward this entire argument about ideas, structuralists are skeptical. It was material challenges, also marked after World War II, that led the British Cabinet to colonial independence, not changes in ideas. Having been deposed from its global hegemony by the end of World War II, Britain did not have the same military and economic power to maintain its empire. If it turns out that the cost of maintaining colonies, too, had increased, the argument is fortified. Its strands combined, the material argument is the central challenge that an argument for reputational power must meet.[3]

How do we sort out these competing claims? Much will depend on perceptions. What sort of influences did the British Cabinet perceive as pressuring it toward adopting an interest in colonial independence? Threats to its reputation posed by anticolonial criticism? Or its relative decline? The crucial evidence is that which answers these questions. In the rest of this chapter, I present the case for ideas. First, I describe Britain's established imperial ideal, its development and its strength. I then seek to show that in deciding for general colonial independence, the Cabinet acted upon this ideal in responding to anticolonial criticism, both from abroad and at home. In chapter 10, I document the growth of protest and dissenting ideas in the colonies, seeking to show their roots in reflection. In chapter 11, I will consider the case for structural skepticism.

Britain's Imperial Ideal and Its Custodians

Britain's ideal of gradual self-government meant that colonists would come to govern themselves more and more fully until they could one day be independent. The intended path of their progress resembled suspiciously Britain's path from the Magna Carta to the modern Parliament. The first stage was typically the establishment of a legislature or at least a house of a legislature for the colonists, along with a franchise, usually limited by property. Next, native colonists might be incorporated into administrative or even cabinet posts in the colonial government, although the central executive power would remain firmly in metropolitan hands. Then, gradually, the colonists' legislature, franchise, and share in offices would be expanded, until they reached the penultimate stage before independence: full control over colonial affairs except for defense, foreign policy, and trade. Eventually, independence itself might come. Even as independent states, the colonies would hopefully remain within the British Commonwealth, an arrangement fully compatible with sovereign statehood, but involving close cooperation in military, commercial, and monetary affairs. Never, however, was it Britain's official policy to make its colonists British citizens, Anglophones, or culturally British. Great Britain was never to become Greater Britain. Rather, colonists would learn and practice self-government one step at a time. Official vocabulary was often parental: words like "trusteeship," "stewardship," "responsibility," "sacred trust," "grooming," and "civilizing mission" were common in the memoranda and speeches of colonial officials.

If boorish domination was to be avoided, though, so was undue haste. Gradual self-government contained a promise, but also a refusal; an intention of progress, but also a rejection of too speedy progress. This duality made the ideal compatible with policies other than progressive political reform. Dispatching troops to end revolt or riot, for instance, could be justified as a check on rash progress. Gradual self-government was also consistent with other unprogressive ideas. Along with it, officials often espoused a notion of racial hierarchy by which Anglo-Saxon peoples were more civilized than Asians, and still more than Africans. British rulers spoke of the empire, too, as a source of prestige and national greatness. Self-government was, after all, an *imperial* ideal. Both parties' cabinet ministers continually praised empire—it constituted Britain's greatness, and was revered by a good portion of the voting public.[4]

We read and hear about gradual self-government in white papers, declarations, treaties, policy speeches, cabinet discussions, and even memoirs and private communications, all of which officials wrote or uttered in order to explain policy decisions.[5] Officials first began repeating the ideal at the close of World War I; by the end of the World War II, they had been stating it consistently for a generation—it was an "official policy." An established idea, unlike revolutionary ideas, is not necessarily one in which officials deeply believe. I thus make no claim that gradual self-government was a part of the identity of British officials, or that they had "converted" to it out of reflection. Rather, it was a norm of appropriateness, one institutionalized in the British Cabinet, Foreign Office, and Colonial Office. Many officials, particularly ones in the Colonial Office, may in fact have believed the ideal. The historic British notion of parliamentary, representative government doubtless left its legacy in many official minds. But other Cabinet officials may have seen the ideal more like a rule of thumb—a "resolver of uncertainty"—for preserving Britain's economic and strategic interests. Allowing self-government would best minimize costly local challenges to imperial rule. This belief, too, had a pedigree in British foreign policy; it was what historians Ronald Robinson and John Gallagher have notably called "the imperialism of free trade."[6] In fact, several motivations for the ideal most likely coexisted, both among different officials and within single officials' heads. But in the logic of reputational power, what is important for an established ideal is not the sincerity by which officials hold it, but the publicity they give to it. Using it for public justification, officials gain a reputation for defending it. It is this reputation that lends the ideal potency for anticolonial critics. That officials widely and repeatedly made the argument of gradual self-government, then, would later have consequences.

The Development of the Ideal

Prior to the twentieth century the British government had rarely announced publicly an intention to grant greater autonomy or independence peacefully to a colony, except, perhaps, for Canada. Then, in conceding independence to South Africa, Australia, New Zealand, and Ireland during the first couple of decades of the twentieth century, Britain developed a strategy for keeping these former colonies closely allied. It granted them "dominion status," and later, in the 1920s, Commonwealth membership. The former colonies would remain in an imperial customs union and persist as strategic allies. In fact, the trading bloc materialized, and Australians and South Africans fought at Gallipoli and the Somme, just as other Africans did. Although some British officials wanted to retain control of the members' defense policy, foreign policy, and even some economic affairs—former colonial secretary Joseph Chamberlain had envisioned a more highly integrated federated union—the Commonwealth members were never more than close allies, and remained fully sovereign, supremely authoritative within their territories.[7] In granting dominion or Commonwealth status, the British government began to speak quite directly of self-government. The colonial period had been a time of gradual preparation for self-maintenance; the new status was the next stage. By such a rationale, giving up empire was planned, wise, and magnanimous.

It was after World War I that Britain made gradual self-government a general policy across its colonies. The mandate system was Britain's response to another type of restless colony—the defeated European states' territories. To the mandate system's schedule of tiered development, the British attached the rhetoric of self-determination: The trust territories were to be groomed for eventual self-government. It was not only in the trust territories, though, that the ideal was to be applied. Toward all of its colonies, the government applied the concept of "Indirect Rule," administration through local elite middlemen. It was a former colonial governor, Lord Lugard, who articulated the concept most fully in his widely read book of 1922, *The Dual Mandate in British Tropical Africa.* As Lugard explained it, Indirect Rule was not only a practical, efficient way to govern, but was a means of civilizing the colonies as well. Part of the British mission was the

> training of native rulers; the delegation to them of such responsibility as they are fit to exercise; the constitution of courts of justice free from corruption and accessible to all; the adoption of a system of education which will assist progress without creating false ideals; the institution of free labour and of a just system of taxation; the protection of the peasantry from oppression, and the preservation of their rights in land, etc.[8]

"Responsibility," "fit to exercise," "progress," "a just system," "protection"—this was the language of stewardship, of a colonial power proposing to lift up its colonies.

Britain carried out this ideal by establishing limited measures of self-government in Africa and Asia. Its most dramatic initiatives were in India. The Government of India Act of 1935, London defended strongly in the language of self-government. It intended the measure to be an iteration in a series of reforms that advanced autonomy but fell short of independence.[9] During World War II, Britain publicly endorsed the same language in signing the Atlantic Charter, which gave "peoples" the unqualified right to choose their own form of government—a statement heard widely throughout the colonial world. True, Churchill denied that the charter applied to the colonies (although his deputy prime minister Clement Attlee openly disagreed), much as Britain qualified its other declarations for self-government. Commonwealth status applied only to a handful of advanced states; mandate status was only for trust territories, and provisions for India were only for India. But the ring of such statements was not easily dampened. For those tasting independence, the qualifiers are overlooked, the pith remembered.

By the end of World War II, we also find British officials beginning to countenance more speedy progress toward self-government in the colonies in general, and even independence in India. Officials had rarely mentioned either as late as 1939.[10] But we also find them consigning these prospects to the long run: India's independence was to be well into the future, and Africa's and the rest of Asia's decades away. Nothing resembling a norm of colonial independence was remotely in the offing. We should remember, too, that there persisted a substantial faction of Conservative "Die Hards" who continued resolutely to oppose any retreat from empire.[11] Nor still should we forget that Britain was not above using its imperial military and its police to slow down change in India and elsewhere when it perceived the pace going too fast. By this point, only this much was clear: A wide swath of officials was speaking the language of self-government, using it widely enough to ensconce it in its accumulated pattern of rationales. Gradual self-government was an established idea, part of the structure in which revolutionary ideas would have to operate.

Colonial Development: The Postwar Shift in the Ideal

After World War II, Britain came to advocate developing its colonies economically, a concept to accompany progressive political development and gradualness in its imperial ideal. Cabinet officials—prime ministers, foreign secretaries, colonial secretaries, and defense ministers—espoused this combination with remarkable continuity, from the Labour government of Clement Attlee (1945–1951), through to the Conservative governments of Winston Churchill (1951–1955), Anthony Eden (1955–1957), and Harold Macmillan (1957–1963).[12] Colonial development became institutionalized in several bureaus, a policy that officials adopted, espoused, and promoted. In initiating the policy, the Labour cabinet was strongly influenced by the Colonial Fabian Bureau, an independent socialist lobby growing out of the previous generation's Fabian movement of Sidney and Beatrice Webb. Though socialist, the bureau was not strongly anti-imperialist. It espoused an ideology of "modernising imperialism," calling for the economic improvement and gradual political development of the colonies while maintaining them under imperial rule for the foreseeable future.[13]

This ideal applied mostly to Africa, but also to those parts of Asia outside India, Pakistan, Palestine, Burma, and Ceylon, which were nowhere close to independence. The epicenter of developmental imperialism was the Labour Colonial Office, the ministry charged with overseeing colonial policy. The Secretary and his close subordinates proclaimed it enthusiastically, charging it to the officials of the office. In a 1948 memo written by H. T.

Bourdillon, the head of the Malayan Department, we find heady words about colonial development. He calls it a "gigantic experiment, surpassing in importance any of the much publicised experiments indulged in by the Soviet Russians or by anybody else. . . . In this concept of the evolving Commonwealth I see the boldest stroke of political idealism which the world has yet witnessed, and on by far the grandest scale."[14] From early 1946 on, there were calls for a "redefinition, redirection and broadening of the goals of African administration," a rethinking that was carried out under the direction of the Colonial Secretary, Arthur Creech Jones. Colonial Office memos of the period show a massive policy review, the organization of an African Colonial Governors' conference to promote ideas for development, the bureaucratic reorganization of the Colonial Office to include an African division and an African Studies Branch, and a widespread commitment to colonial development.[15] The goal of the reorganization was, as one official wrote in a July 1948 memorandum on the "reorientation of the Colonial Office," to make the office more of a "thinking and planning department on a worldwide scale," becoming "far less Auditor-General, Home Office, Agriculture, Town and Country Planning," and "far more the Foreign Office, Ministry of Defense, M15 and Economic Policy Committee."[16]

These were inspired ideas, urgent and ambitious. They led to economic development schemes, designed to bring colonies "to the point where they are able economically to sustain the financial burdens of self-government and to stand on their own in the world economy."[17] The phrasing points to an important Colonial Office tenet: economic and political development would go together. Again, though, the watchword was gradualness. Step by step, the British government would lead colonies through the stages of constitutional development toward self-government, beginning by incorporating Africans into the rudimentary tasks of government, expanding their participation once they had mastered a stage, always hoping that the demands for speedy progress would not outpace the controlled schedule.[18] Local government and administration was the emphasis; here, African leaders would be trained for higher responsibilities.[19] The test cases would be the Gold Coast and Nigeria, which Colonial Office officials thought to be the most developed in their progress.[20]

As for independence, though, Labour colonial officials viewed even Nigeria and the Gold Coast as far from ready. In a 1947 report on the African Governors' Conference, Deputy Under-Secretary of State Sydney Caine expressed the general opinion of the Colonial Office:

> It is clear that in Africa the period before self-government can be granted will be longer than in most other parts of the Colonial Empire. Prophecy as to the length of this period is idle, but it may be said that in the Gold Coast, the

territory where Africans are advanced most politically, internal self-government is unlikely to be achieved in much less than a generation. In the other territories the process is likely to be considerably slower.[21]

Self-government meant reform—reform that would allow more Africans to vote, hold office in the legislature, and eventually serve in cabinets. Independence was only something to speculate about; planning it or setting a date for it, officials thought, would be foolish. In general, Labour ministers thought Africa to be uncivilized, backward, far behind the progress of the more backward parts of colonial Asia, and much further behind India, Pakistan, Burma, and Ceylon. Attlee said as much in 1942; foreign minister Ernest Bevin and even Creech Jones made several comments to this effect; and H. S. Morrison captured the sentiment when he remarked in 1943 that allowing "self-government" to colonies would be like giving a ten-year-old "a latch key, a bank account, and a shot gun."[22] The colonies first had to gain experience in government, expertise in agriculture and economic administration, and ethnic peace. To force the pace would undermine the ideal. In Cabinet members' minds, the principle giving the colonial system legitimacy required its very perpetuation.

Gradual Self-Government and the Cession of Empire

Under the Conservative government, right up until the shift to sweeping grants of independence initiated by Prime Minister Harold Macmillan and Colonial Secretary Iain Macleod, the Cabinet held to the essentials of colonial policy set forth by Labour. It maintained the dual goals of economic and political progress; it saw political change as gradual and in most cases independence as distant; it continued to encourage the political progress of the exceptionally advanced Gold Coast and Nigeria; and the Colonial Office continued vigorously to argue for progress.[23] When the Cabinet finally and sweepingly negotiated the colonies' independence beginning in late 1959, its policy and its rationale conformed to the ideal of gradual self-government. As parties formed, and riots, strikes, and protests broke out all over Britain's colonies, London responded by first agreeing to negotiations on a particular colony's constitution, hoping to quell dissent by partially meeting colonists' demands short of independence, then finding that once negotiations were under way, the colonists would expand their demands wider and wider, forcing Britain into a more and more difficult choice between independence and a refusal to compromise that would surely appear reactionary. London tried to maintain its commitment to political progress while doing all it could to slow it down. It had taken the same approach toward India, Burma, and Ceylon between 1945 and 1947. It did not at first adopt the pattern in East and Central

Africa, where Britain reacted to the 1953 Mau Mau rebellion in Kenya by sending its troops to suppress it, jail its leaders, and quell its energy. But by the mid-1950s, it began to consider constitutional conventions and political concessions for these regions, although still hoping to proceed gradually. It was also Britain's approach in the Gold Coast and Nigeria, the two African colonies whose independence Britain granted—again after trying to brake progress with negotiations—in the mid-1950s, before the others. Each of these policies, Britain defended by expressing its interest in the colonies' development.

Britain advocated its ideal of self-government right up until the end, and succeeded in carrying it out relatively smoothly. But it had to abjure gradualness. In almost every case, the negotiations proceeded much faster than the Cabinet desired. Even while conceding independence to a colony, the Cabinet typically lamented its unpreparedness. Right up until the eve of negotiations for independence, Cabinet officials thought the prospect distant. In an important 1954 Cabinet memorandum, Commonwealth Secretary Lord Swinton assessed that during the "next ten to twenty years," the Gold Coast, Nigeria, the Central African Federation, a Malayan Federation, and a West Indian Federation would be ready for full independence (hopefully within the Commonwealth), that twenty-two other territories "are never likely to achieve independence," and that "there remains an intermediate group where the future course of political development is uncertain": Kenya, Tanganyika, Uganda, and Sierra Leone.[24] Even as late as May 1959, a major report of an interdepartmental Africa Committee, "Africa in the Next Ten Years," judged the pace of progress toward colonial self-government and concluded that by 1970, East African colonies might be ready for "responsible self-government," a status leaving Britain control over defense and foreign policy, and that Central Africa was nowhere near ready for independence.[25] In my search of the official archives, I have found no document that augurs or advocates the wholesale release of empire, nor evidence that Prime Minister Harold Macmillan or Colonial Secretary Iain Macleod—the chief advocates of independence—planned or foresaw such events. Indeed, in a 1965 article in the *Weekend Telegraph* Macleod himself denied that the Cabinet ever passed a formal resolution to end empire.[26] There is evidence, though, that by late 1959, Macmillan and Macleod had consciously decided upon a new approach, if not one of attempting to free the British Empire, certainly one of entering negotiations and considering concessions at a faster rate than ever before. In 1964, Macleod wrote, "It has been said that after I became Colonial Secretary there was a deliberate speeding-up of the movement towards independence. I agree. There was. And in my view any other policy would have led to terrible bloodshed."[27] Macmillan's and Macleod's concerted efforts in 1959 and 1960 to convince Die Hard Conservative backbenchers to accept colonial independence also reveals deliberation. General decolonization was not planned in advance, but it was not unintended, either. Our question is what brought Macmillan and Macleod to accelerate progress toward self-government so suddenly and sweepingly.

Anticolonial Ideas: Their Action, the Cabinet's Reaction

To the imperial ideal of gradual self-government, revolutionary anticolonial ideas posed both a condemnation and an appeal. Because they rejected colonialism—all of it, everywhere—they condemned the failure to grant immediate independence. But because both anticolonial ideas and the established ideal of gradual self-government advocated independence at some future date, the anticolonial ideas could appeal to the established ideal to live up to its own commitments. The two were similar enough for reputational power to work. As anticolonialist ideas won more converts and grew in social power, they became more difficult for the established ideal to live with, and eventually forced the British Cabinet into a choice: Either suppress anticolonialism directly through arms, rejecting the condemnation by abandoning the ideal, or succumb to anticolonialism's appeal by relinquishing empire. The stronger anticolonial ideas became, the more difficult and stark the choice for Britain. Below, looking at the three contexts of international criticism, domestic criticism, and colonial criticism, I seek to show that between World War II and the early 1960s, anticolonial criticism—the numbers and the ardor of those whose identities were shaped by anticolonial ideas—steadily increased. I seek to show, too, that the Cabinet responded to this criticism in its cluster of decisions to cede its colonies. That anticolonial criticism grew, and that the Cabinet responded to it, is evidence that ideas caused the occurrence of general colonial independence. That it was the Cabinet's concern for this criticism that led it to accelerate political progress is evidence for reputational social power, the kind of social power that entailed a relatively smooth transition.

The International Context

Beginning in World War II and to a steadily increasing degree throughout the 1950s, Britain encountered foreign criticism of its empire. Who voiced it is simple. It was most shrill from the Soviet Union and from formerly colonial states—Latin American states and, more fiercely, Nasser's Egypt and Nehru's India, which prided themselves on being "nonaligned." It was gentler, but still quite influential, from the United States. Each of these states had developed an anticolonial identity. Either its leaders were anticolonialists or it spoke in the name of strong anticolonialist constituencies. Why the British took the criticism so seriously is more complex. It involves two contexts: the Cold War and the United Nations.

The Cold War was a struggle between two superpowers inordinately preponderant in military might, but it was also an ideological struggle, fought between the liberal democratic capitalist West and the Communist bloc. It is the ideological dimension that I want now to consider. Both superpowers, precisely because of their ideologies, possessed an anticolonial identity; both worried deeply about the colonies (as well as nonaligned states) going over to the other side; and both criticized extant colonialism.

The United States had publicly opposed colonialism since its own rebellion against Britain in 1775, a tradition that continued through Woodrow Wilson's advocacy of self-determination in World War I, and which grew stronger and more focused through President Roosevelt's wartime diplomacy and his liberal interpretation of the Atlantic Charter. During the Cold War, the United States persisted in its criticism, but muted it somewhat, for it now faced competing imperatives. Its overriding preoccupation became the struggle against communism, which demanded that it refrain from weakening the prestige of Britain, its most important European ally, and that it support the struggles of both Britain and France against Communist insurgencies in their colonies, but also that it maintain its reputation as a liberal power, one that was on the side of history's momentum toward self-determination. To achieve this balance, American Presidents and Cabinet members refrained from publicly criticizing Britain, but gently prodded it behind closed doors. In private diplomatic meetings and correspondence, we find evidence only of the United States nudging Britain, never telling it face-to-face to free its colonies, and only sometimes telling it to speed up colonial progress. William Roger Louis, in his study of American policy toward the British Empire during World War II, determines that from about 1943 onward, the United States President generally supported, rather than sought to undermine, the British Empire.[28] Members of Congress, by contrast, criticized Britain publicly. Both kinds of criticism were important. In exchanges between government officials behind the scenes, America used its status as a crucial ally to pressure Britain. The public criticism was important in a different sense: as the world's most powerful democracy, the United States lent great momentum to ideas like self-government and self-determination. Concerned about maintaining its reputation for self-government, Britain could not allow itself to be criticized too strongly by the United States.[29]

Combining with U.S. anticolonial criticism, completing the Cold War context, was the constant readiness of the Soviet Union—whose Communist ideals were also deeply anticolonialist—to take rhetorical advantage of anything smelling reactionary. This other pincer pressured Britain all the more, for it raised the cost of losing its reputation for colonial progressivism. The Cabinet's fear was that the colonies and the nonaligned world might throw their allegiance to the Communist bloc, resulting in inestimable strategic, economic, and moral costs. Anticolonial ideas, operating through the destruction of Britain's imperial ideal, thus converted their energy into the currency of threatened Cold War losses, in this way exerting social power. In responding to this pressure, Britain's strategy was to stay closely enough in step with colonial demands that it could appease the United States and avoid lending credibility to the Soviet Union, while also urging the United States to temper its censure. As both colonial demands and international (and domestic) criticism surged, this balancing act of avoiding both criticism and concessions of independence became increasingly difficult.

It was in the United Nations that opponents of colonialism spoke loudest. The closest thing to an embodiment of world order and opinion, its Charter the foundation of international law, the United Nations rendered unique legitimacy to anticolonial criticisms.[30] As a member of the Security Council, the most powerful body of the United Nations, Britain could hardly ignore this criticism. The United Nations challenged colonialism in several ways. Its Charter proclaimed the principles of self-determination and the imperial duty of a "sacred trust" toward colonies, a duty that anticolonial critics could always claim unfulfilled. The Charter also set forth provisions for exercising colonial oversight, including a Trusteeship Council for trust territories and procedures obligating colonial powers to report to the Secretary General regularly on the progress of "Non-Self-Governing Territories." Both ensured that the issue of colonialism would remain constantly public. The greatest pressure against Britain came in the General Assembly, where opponents of colonialism pressured the Trusteeship Council to exercise more oversight, and took up colonial matters that the Security Council would not.[31] Between World War II and the early 1960s, the ferment in the General Assembly increased as more former colonies joined the United Nations. The addition of India and other Southeast Asia states in the late 1940s added to the rancor, as did the accession to membership of seventeen former colonies, mostly those of France, in 1960.

The United Nations's effect augmented and complemented that of the Cold War. It added to the pressure on Britain's ideal of gradual self-government and made more imminent the costs of losing colonial sympathy. In reaction to the UN criticism, Britain's strategy was also both to cooperate with the United Nations, avoiding rejecting it openly, while attempting to use its Security Council influence to dilute the UN's bile. Britain generally complied with its Charter obligations to provide information to the Trusteeship Council and the Secretary General, but protested any further oversight of its colonial policy as an unlawful interference in its internal affairs.

The best evidence of growing Cold War and United Nations pressure and its influence upon British colonial policy resides in the memoranda, minutes, and correspondence of British Cabinet members and their subordinates. It was ultimately the Cabinet's decision to free the colonies. It is the Cabinet's perceptions—their worries about U.S. criticism, their anxiety about the Cold War, their irritation at the United Nations, their assessments of colonial loyalties—that matter most in the case for reputational social power..

During the Labour years, the Cabinet sensed increased international criticism. The combined role of the Communist threat, the United Nations, and the United States is apparent in a major Colonial Office policy survey:

> [O]ur colonial policy now rests upon . . . a growing consciousness among the colonial peoples that they are moving steadily to a stage where they can stand by themselves. This realisation is fundamentally a political concept, and in the colonial peoples, no less than in the Europe and America of the 18th and 19th centuries, nationalism is an emotion requiring to be harnessed for constructive purposes if it is not to become extremist, destructive and the instrument of Communist incitement. Whether in fact it is to become a constructive force is now one of the major issues at stake. Generally speaking the Colonial Empire has now reached an extremely important stage in its development. The next few years are likely to be critical for the success or failure of our colonial policy; and at this stage more than any other in the history of the Colonial Empire ignorant or prejudiced outside interference would do incalculable harm. It is for this reason that we could not accept United Nations supervision over the affairs of the Colonial Empire (save in the limited field of trusteeship). Such supervision is, however, the aim of many members of the United Nations; and the principle that Metropolitan Powers should, in their conduct of colonial affairs, be accountable to the United Nations is implicit in an increasing number of Assembly Resolutions.[32]

It was fear of these encroaching demands for accountability in the United Nations that Colonial Office and Foreign Ministry officials expressed again and again in memos and letters about UN strategy. The same memo noted that it was "the anti-colonial countries . . . normally led by India, the Philippines, Egypt, and Cuba" that attempted to exercise constant pressure on Britain in the Assembly.[33] In the eyes of the Colonial Office, such countries, like the United Nations, were ignorant of colonial affairs and unqualified to manage Britain's affairs.

Britain hoped that the United States would help to counter this criticism, or at least refrain from voting negatively in resolutions concerning colonies. The same Colonial Office memo worried that "the U.S. attitude in the U.N. is conditioned, first, by their reluctance to go against the will of the majority . . . and, second, by their desire to show themselves sympathetic to what they (as we think, sometimes erroneously) judge to be the aspirations of the colonial peoples, largely for fear that otherwise these peoples will turn to Communism." Britain's strategy in response was as follows: "The U.S. will never support us when we, as they put it, 'go negative,' and are likely always to urge compromises on us on the grounds that otherwise something worse will result. If, however, we can avoid a negative line and certain of the other members of the U.N. can be persuaded that our attitude is a reasonable one, we have a better chance of securing the support of the U.S. and moderate members of the U.N."[34] Numerous memos from the same period evince the same concerns, and by 1951 the Labour Cabinet even felt that it had achieved progress in softening the United States.[35]

During the first five years of the Conservative government, the United States again reminded Britain regularly of its anticolonialist preferences, but refrained from opposing Britain too directly in the United Nations, where criticism from the Soviet bloc and the former colonies continued unabated.[36] Under the Eisenhower administration, U.S. criticism became more vituperative in the hands of Secretary of State John Foster Dulles, who saw colonialism as a weakness for the West in the battle against the Soviets.[37] A pivotal moment was the 1956 Suez Canal crisis, when Britain was forced to abandon its threat to loosen Egyptian President Nasser's hold on the canal. During the crisis, both Dulles and Eisenhower, as well as several UN members, openly attacked British and French colonialism.[38] After the crisis, the Conservative Cabinet acquired several new dogmas, including the importance of not diverging too widely from U.S. policy, the imperative not to become isolated again at the United Nations, and the folly of using military force to protect colonial interests.[39] Britain's concern about U.S. and UN pressure had grown stronger than ever.

When the Conservative Cabinet entered the negotiations that would lead to independence, it again and again expressed concern about the Cold War, the United Nations, and general international criticism. The quite important "Africa: The Next Ten Years" report opines, "The position and influence of the United Kingdom in the world depend to a large extent on what other countries think of us."[40] Looking to the future, a 1960 Cabinet memorandum predicted, "There seems little doubt that international pressures will in the future have a greater influence on the internal policies of our territory."[41] Amidst these pressures, most British officials considered it vital to remain on the side of Western ideas. Poignant evidence of Britain's concern for its reputation, we find in a letter written by the Foreign Secretary, the Earl of Home, in 1962: "The prestige of the United Kingdom in the past has depended in no small measure upon a long (though occasionally chequered) record of championing freedom and human rights." He goes on to argue that the East-West struggle existed largely "in the minds of people" and was conducted "by means of propaganda in the widest sense of that word." Britain, the secretary insisted, had to stand on the side of individual freedom and democracy, but above all, national independence.[42]

Central to the Cabinet's concerns of this time was its perception of a Soviet effort to penetrate the colonies, a fear that was a key purpose behind "Africa: The Next Ten Years."[43] The report concludes, "The strategic objective of the Soviet Union is to remove Western influence from Africa and ultimately to bring the peoples of the continent within the Communist system." The Soviets had not yet succeeded in this penetration, the report went on, for there was evidence of African suspicion toward them, but they nevertheless had the advantage of anticolonial credibility: "The less sophisticated areas of Africa will be increasingly exposed to the efforts of the Soviet Government to identify themselves with all the different manifestations of 'anti-colonialism.' "[44] The Cabinet also thought the Soviets menacing in their UN rhetoric. A 1960 memorandum expressed concern that the swelling African and Asian membership of the United Nations would increase Soviet influence.[45] Macmillan, too, feared the Soviets, concluding by November 1958 that refusing colonial independence would only advantage Marxism.[46] How did the Cabinet propose to act upon its fear? The "Africa in the Next Ten Years" report concludes that if

> we are too intransigent in opposing African aspirations or, where European minorities are dominant, are too ready to appease them, we run the risk of being identified with the extreme racial doctrines of the Union of South Africa, of exacerbating African hostility towards the European and of provoking the African states, when they finally achieve independence—as in the end they must—to turn more readily towards the Soviet Union.[47]

The report notes that proceeding too rapidly would also be unwise, for it would leave ill-prepared governments exposed to communism. It thus advocates a moderate pace.[48]

During the final days of empire, Britain also felt strong pressure from the United States. In the diplomatic flurry surrounding Britain's spring 1957 Bermuda Conference with the United States, British officials expressed frustration that the "Americans are still somewhat reluctant to accept the thesis that our colonial policy is the best means of keeping the Communists out of Africa."[49] One official thought that American "misinterpretation" of "so-called British 'colonialism' has colored the official attitude toward such vital matters as the Suez problem and the Baghdad Pact, and has encouraged a spirit of neutralism on these and other issues (e.g., Cyprus) which has already been highly deleterious to our joint interests and could be disastrous to them in the future."[50] It was even thought that American anticolonial pronouncements contributed significantly to criticism of Britain in the United Nations, and therefore to weakness in the general struggle against communism.[51] A Foreign Office steering committee observed in 1959 that "[t]he fact that the pressure for independence is now so powerful and that resistance to it evokes condemnation from the United Nations and from sections of opinion in the United Kingdom itself, is due in no small measure to the United States attitude over the last decades."[52]

Again, the British responded not by summarily rejecting anticolonialist arguments, but by insisting upon their policy's progressiveness. A major objective at the Bermuda Conference was to urge the United States government to revise its attitude on British colonialism, for "the objectives of British policy are the antithesis of 'colonialism' as commonly represented," namely, to promote "human advancement," which is the best barrier to communism.[53] The British policy of nation-building "has no relation to [the Americans'] out-of-date conception of 'Colonialism' "[54] The best way to counter the Soviets was to lead the colonies toward "self-government or independence" so that they might remain allied with the West.[55]

Around the time that Britain decided for colonial independence, the British Cabinet perceived stronger criticism than ever before from the United Nations. The addition of new members in 1960—nearly all former colonies, with strong anticolonial identities—was a chief worry. A Colonial Office memorandum of early 1961 predicted a more aggressive United Nations: "It is very likely that when the General Assembly resumes its session in March, there will be attempts to follow up the resolution on Colonialism, possibly by means of attempting to fix target dates for the independence of all territories."[56] Target dates were indeed a major issue for the Foreign Office following the momentous UN Declaration of 1960. UN members tried to impose them on Britain through several resolutions; British diplomats, fearing too rapid a pace, tried to moderate these resolutions if not prevent them altogether.[57] Generally, Britain expressed reservations toward the UN's anticolonial measures, but refrained from openly obstructing them. Again, it abstained from, rather than opposed, the 1960 Declaration. A long memorandum by the Foreign Secretary in 1962 reluctantly advocated participating in the UN "Committee of Seventeen," created to oversee the Declaration's implementation. His reasons? If Britain refused to participate, it would nevertheless encounter criticism from the United Nations—so why not try to moderate it?—and would also be criticized by the United States, domestic opinion, and Parliament, along with having its "general standing and influence" at the United Nations undermined. "This would leave the United States, broadly speaking, alone to face the uncommitted and the Soviet *bloc* with consequent damage to the Western position as a whole."[58] Finally, in several decisions to grant independence to specific colonies, top foreign policy officials gave UN criticism as a reason for pushing ahead with self-determination.[59] This was especially true in the case of Tanganyika, which was a UN trust territory.[60] To UN criticism, as to other international criticism, Britain responded by insisting rhetorically on its ideal of gradual self-government and exceeding it in practice. Again and again, it fretted about its reputation, irritated and surprised that it should be so challenged.

The Domestic Context

References to domestic criticism in the Cabinet papers are fewer than references to international criticism, but are still frequent. During the last days of imperial unburdening, the Conservative Cabinet fussed about one sort of criticism in particular: that of the Labour Party. It mentioned Labour's criticism right along with international criticism and likewise feared its corrosion of the imperial ideal. Labour's social power, of course, was not the threat of Cold War losses, but the threat of lost votes.

Like international censure, Labour's dissent grew stronger during the 1950s. I have noted the substantial continuity between the Labour and Conservative governments' imperial ideal of gradual self-government. But these are only the Labour and Conservative *governments*. In Parliament and beyond, the parties debated colonialism vigorously. During Labour's years in power, the party contained two schools of empire. One was the liberal humanitarian tradition, represented by the Fabian Colonial Bureau, which provided the party with most of its official views. Its stance was nearly identical to the developmental ideal of Creech Jones and the Colonial Office. The other was a more radical internationalist school, led by the activist Fenner Brockway and composed of members of the Independent Labour Party and Christian socialists, opponents of empire whose views had formed during the 1930s. This was the anti-imperialist tradition of J. A. Hobson, and the tradition whose participants we can safely call converts to anticolonial identities. As early as the 1930s, they held racial equality as a central belief, rejected racial hierarchy, and announced political independence for the colonies as a central plank. "For Brockway, national self-determination was a first-order good, and there could be no morally acceptable case for its being delayed or compromised in pursuit of other goods," writes one historian.[61] What about Communists? Never during British decolonization did they exercise significant influence.[62]

During Labour's years in opposition, this more radical wing not only grew in its activist following and its number of supporters in Parliament, but eventually saw the Labour leadership adopt its stance as official policy. This leftward shift may seem natural for an opposition party—a response to the lack of governing responsibility and the need to differentiate—but there are better reasons, I think, for Labour's move. Labour did not begin seriously to oppose the Conservative Government policy until 1953, two years after it had left the government. At this point it did not call for an alternative to the gradual self-government ideal so much as it protested Conservative colonial repression, which stretched the ideal's boundaries. When the Conservatives bloodlessly toppled a regime in British Guiana that had Communist ties, Labour divided itself into supporters and opponents; when the Conservatives sent troops to put down uprisings in Kenya and Malaya and proposed to unite Southern Rhodesia, Northern Rhodesia, and Nyasaland into a white-dominated Central African Federation, Labour united itself in opposition.[63]

It was these events that contributed exigency and appeal to anticolonial ideas, and increased the ranks of those who held them. Meanwhile, in 1954, Fenner Brockway organized anticolonial forces in the Movement for Colonial Freedom, which began to criticize the moderate Labour leadership and Colonial Fabian Bureau. By 1956, the Labour leadership had appointed a Commonwealth Subcommittee, which united the party around an African policy "scarcely distinguishable from that of indigenous nationalists in the plural societies."[64] From the mid-1950s, this view drove House of Commons debates on colonial matters during a time when a greater percentage of parliamentary time and members' energy was devoted to colonial issues.[65]

The Conservative Party also divided into two schools. A moderate, pragmatic faction, which for most of the 1950s included the Cabinet, was flexible toward empire. Influential for them was the dominion model, by which colonies could be given independence but would remain members of the Commonwealth, just as India had. The moderates were still committed to a broad, gradual self-government ideal, though, and winced at Labour's increasing itchiness toward colonies. To the right were the "Die Hards," who persisted in seeing empire as a source of prestige and economic benefit, who were especially sympathetic to the interests of white settlers, and who formed themselves into tight-knit lobbying groups, such as the Suez Group and the Monday Club. During the 1950s, the Die Hards declined in parliamentary numbers and strength. Most significant was the 1959 election, in which a wave of younger, more liberal Conservatives, devoid of the old sentiment for empire or settlers, was elected. For Macmillan and Macleod, this eased considerably the granting of independence.[66]

As is always the case with ideas, however, the existence of favorable anticolonial trends—the rise of Labour criticism and decline of Conservative stalwart support—does not necessarily prove the influence of these trends upon those who decided for colonial independence. We need testimony. The most powerful evidence lies in Prime Minister Harold Macmillan's appointment of two independent commissions of experts in 1959, both responding to domestic outcries over acts of violence committed by white-settler governments against Africans. The Devlin Commission investigated the behavior of the Central African Federation government in putting down African unrest in Nyasaland; the Monckton Commission looked into the fatal beatings of Africans at the hands of prison guards in a detention camp in Kenya. It is hardly to be expected that such commissions would be appointed. These were not the first instances of white-settler cruelty. Such commissions are politically dangerous for a metropolitan government, too. The very act of appointing them, not to mention their ultimate findings, calls further attention to the injustice of empire and strengthens empire's opponents. It is difficult, then, to explain Macmillan's creation of the commissions apart from the intense attention that the newspapers, the House of Commons, and antiimperial lobbies gave to the incidents. Records of Cabinet meetings concur: Cabinet members argue continually for the commissions as an answer to domestic criticism, especially from Labour in Parliament.[67] Macmillan's own concern is apparent in his wrangling over the terms of the Monckton Commission with Hugh Gaitskell, the Labour leader. Beyond the Monckton and Devlin commissions Cabinet records show Conservative officials generally stewing during the late 1950s and early 1960s over domestic efforts to speed up the pace of independence.[68]

The opposite sort of opposition—that of the Die Hard Conservatives—also concerned the Cabinet, particularly Prime Minister Macmillan and Colonial Secretary Macleod. A faction of about eighty well-organized Conservative Members of Parliament were determined to resist vigorously the appointment of the Devlin and Monckton commissions and the pursuit of constitutional negotiations over Kenya and the Central African Federation. Through reassurances that the negotiations would not sell out the interests of white settlers, Macleod was able to contain, and even diminish the size of, this opposition. The results of the 1959 election, a defeat of the Conservative right wing, helped Macleod, too.[69] It was after the election of October 1959 that Macmillan and Macleod began to engage in negotiations.

Mention of public opinion and the 1959 election, however, should not mislead us into thinking that colonial issues were of major concern to the voter. Candidates, in fact, hardly discussed them in the campaign.[70] This is not to deny the voter's influence, for the Cabinet may have feared that domestic elite criticism would eventually become mass criticism, electorally costly, or that it would enhance the harm of international criticism if it were left unanswered. Domestic elite critics wield the social power of ideas through their ability to make top officials pay a price that is higher than the critics' own disapproval. In the end, we do not know definitively how much of an electoral cost the loss of Britain's progressive reputation would have meant, for the Conservatives' accommodation of colonial response made the issue moot. But it is clear that the Cabinet was quite concerned about domestic criticism, whose swelling it feared should its colonial policy come to involve large-scale armed suppression. This fear, in turn, is hard to account for apart from an attendant fear of political consequences. As historian David Goldsworthy remarks:

> The Macmillan-Macleod approach brought the Government to a position barely distinguishable from that which sections of the Opposition had been advocating since at least the early fifties. "I have not been conscious of any gulf [between Macleod and myself] over the last eighteen months", remarked [Labour Leader] Callaghan in 1961.[71]

The Conservative and Labour party positions came to be "barely distinguishable," though, at least in part because the Conservative Party perceived a threat from the Labour Party's position.

Official memoranda, letters, papers, reports, and the like demonstrate this. They demonstrate a similar logic for the international context. These are important conclusions for reputational power: heads of state respond to criticism that pressures their reputation for their ideas, presenting them with political costs for losing their reputation. The records show, too, that British officials held the established ideal that I have described: gradual self-government. But we have not yet considered another crucial source of anticolonial criticism, the creators of the precipitating events to which the Cabinet had to respond. This source is nationalists in the colonies themselves, the subject of chapter 10.

TEN

REVOLUTIONARY IDEAS IN THE BRITISH COLONIES

INTERNATIONAL AND DOMESTIC criticism raised the ante for British gradual self-government. Suppressing riots and demonstrations with troops and police, jailing nationalist leaders, rejecting nationalist demands to accelerate self government, all policies that Britain could once justify as necessary to keep progress salubriously moderate, would now be met with a swarm of criticism, undermining Britain's reputation, possibly eliciting the feared costs of the loss: a strategic setback in the Cold War, a political weakening at home. The Cabinet could not appear to move backward or reject anticolonial demands too brusquely. But international and domestic criticism alone did not translate to immediate colonial independence. Absent robust protest and clamor in the colonies, Britain need not repress baldly and scandalously, and could continue to claim a policy of attentive nursing. Something had to force the pace. Independence required a precipitating pressure, one that would compel Britain to choose between proceeding faster with political progress or looking reactionary, losing its reputation.

This precipitate was social protest in the colonies. The formation of political parties that would advocate independence, the speeches and campaigns of these parties' leaders, newspaper editorials, strikes, the occasional riot, and intermittent outcries over scattered cruelties—all of this was protest. In the British colonies, it was through communicating discontent that protest exercised social power. Unlike a military insurrection, which forces the metropole to fight back, paying military and economic costs, protest forced Britain to answer, that is, to deny, repress, or respond.

Protest grew slowly and steadily during the 1950s, mostly in Africa, until right around 1959, when a spate of incidents and movements broke out. In Kenya, two African parties formed in 1960, and Africans in the legislature demanded progress more vociferously. In Tanganyika, the Tanganyikan African National Union demonstrated that African Tanganyikans were united behind it as it organized demonstrations, boycotts, and strikes. In Nyasaland, the government of the Central African Federation declared a state of emergency in 1959. Its police beat and killed Africans, while the government outlawed the Nyasaland African Congress, just as it had outlawed the Zambian African Congress of Kenneth Kaunda. In the West Indies, opposition to colonial rule was organizing as well. The Devlin Report and Monckton Commission of the same year revealed to the Cabinet that African discontent with white rule was far more widespread than it had thought. And outside of the British colonies, shootings of Africans in Commonwealth South Africa, the repression of a secessionist war in the Congo by Western powers, and the resultant condemnation of colonial powers in the United Nations reminded the Cabinet of the price of using violence.[1] In Cabinet papers, we find that it is in response to these events of 1959 that officials fretted most intensely about international and domestic criticism and its consequences. It was right around this time, too, that Prime Minister Macmillan decided to lead Britain down the road to general independence. But what was behind the protest?

Revolutionary ideas, I argue—ideas playing their two roles. For protesting colonists, the ideas were nationalism and equality, which they translated into the demand for political independence, Westphalian statehood, for their colony. It was through their reflection upon these ideas that a small stratum of educated, elite Africans, Asians, and Latin Americans came to desire this statehood—the first role of ideas. It was then these converts to revolutionary ideas who exercised the social power of protest—the second role of ideas. Aside from their efforts, the parties never would have formed, the campaigns never would have taken place, and so on. Together, both roles explain the protest.

Toward both roles, structural theories would be skeptical. They question the autonomy of nationalists' reflection. They assume that nationalist leaders aimed at economic or political gain as their end, and then point out shifts in economic or political structure—eclipsing circumstances—that led them to seek national independence as the best means of advancing this end. What were these shifts? Changes in economic growth, changes in class or social structure, an increase in the oppression of the colonial government, and the like. These theories also doubt the centrality of converts in wielding the social power of protest. Rather, discontented peasants, workers, and merchants, those whose aims were economic and political, were enough to mobilize dissent. Nationalists may have indeed converted, but the revolution could have happened without them. These structural arguments, I take up in chapter 10. Here, I ask, What is the case for the two roles of ideas?

The Conversion of Nationalists

It was far from plain to the inhabitants of colonies that nationalism was the solution to their subordination. That a colony ought to aspire to become a Westphalian state was a European idea; indeed, as I have argued, a Protestant idea. Other responses to oppression also commanded large followings all the way through independence. One was tribalism. Identification with tribal authority, rather than any larger, wider entity such as a nation, attracted many colonists, and often posed no challenge to colonial rule. It was rather simply an assertion of local prerogatives. Another was Christian millenarianism, which substituted the colonists' spiritual destiny for political change as an object of their devotion. Far from all Christian churches and sects held such views, but some did.[2] Another response was simply economic and political change—improved wages, opportunities, property laws, and so on, but no change in the political status of the colony. It was hardly obvious that nationalism was the rational solution to the condition of colonial domination.[3]

We can find evidence that colonists came to have nationalist identities through their writings in newspaper and pamphlets, in their speeches, in their pronouncements. But this leaves open the question of *how* they came to have these identities. Was it the product of reflection or structural change? As I argued for Protestant ideas, one quite misleading key to conversion is the political or economic benefit that colonists derived from nationalist views; that is, did they attain position or wealth? Many nationalist leaders, like leaders of most successful movements, eventually benefited in both respects, some becoming presidents or high officials of independent states. Of course, some nationalists, Jomo Kenyatta or Nelson Mandela, were imprisoned by colonial powers, others were imprisoned by rival nationalists even when their state attained independence, and some were put to death. But whether or not they risked or gained says little about how or why nationalists came to their beliefs. All nationalists, even Mahatma Gandhi, were doubtless motivated to some degree by the desire for political and economic influence, but this hardly establishes that they did not adopt their beliefs upon reflection; it only means that their motives were mixed. The question for explanation is whether there existed structural circumstances that corresponded with the timing of ideas' adoption and that plausibly explain their adoption. Or must one also take into account experiences that, by their very nature, could not have been eclipsing, but instead promoted reflection upon the ideas? These experiences are circumstances of reflection. They give exposure to, and lend plausibility and attractiveness to, nationalist ideas. What sort of experiences were relevant to colonial nationalism? We find them first in the last couple of decades of the nineteenth century. By then, colonial structures of governance were being solidified, non-European colonial peoples were becoming decisively excluded from government, and tribal structures were breaking down.[4] Amidst this rapid change, three circumstances shaped nationalism: education, religion, and war.

Only a small elite of colonists became nationalists. Almost all of them were professionals of some sort—doctors, lawyers, teachers, journalists, ministers, managers in firms—who held occupations for which there were few opportunities. Almost all of them possessed an advanced modern education, meaning a university education in England or the United States, or in the upper reaches of European schools within the colonies. In the Gold Coast, perhaps the colony in Africa in which Africans were the most advanced, this elite numbered about 1,000 in a society of 4.5 million.[5]

These elites brought back their national identities from abroad, offering them to colonial peoples who had little sense of national identity. During the late nineteenth and early twentieth centuries, nationalism and equality arrived through two portals: Western education and Christianity. The first importers of the European model were former slaves from America and the West Indies, part of a "back to Africa" movement, who became "creoles" in African societies. They desired to impart Christianity and Western political teachings to native Africans, whom they saw as savage and backward. Many future African nationalist leaders, for instance John Chilembwe and Hastings Banda of Nyasaland (Malawi), were educated at American Negro colleges. There, they were exposed to the "Pan-Africanist" ideas of African-Americans W.E.B. DuBois and Marcus Garvey, both of whom preached liberation for Africans along Western lines. Colonists in Asia and elsewhere were also educated in European universities, both in Europe and in their own colonies, where they became acquainted with Western political ideas.[6]

Christian churches and sects in Africa were another major forum in which Africans came to hold European ideas. By the turn of the twentieth century, Africans were almost universally excluded in these churches, from leadership positions, which a few Africans had actually been allowed to hold during the nineteenth century. In the first couple of decades of the twentieth century, then, African breakaway churches arose, for instance the Ethiopian movement, which originated in South Africa, and which gave Africa a special place in a divine plan. A more radical trend was Christian millenarian movements, which viewed Africans as a chosen people and looked forward to a Day of Judgment in which colonial rule would end and a happier era would begin. Although neither Christian movement carried with it a political program—some actively discouraged one—both developed new forms of African community and solidarity that created awareness of an alternative to European rule and proved fertile ground from which nationalist ideas arose and African political leaders emerged.[7]

It was through these influences that elite non-European colonists came to write, teach, and generally advocate European ideas, or more precisely, an application of European ideas to their own contexts. In many parts of Africa, there developed an idea of "négritude," which combined European ideas with African traditions, leading Africans to seek European political forms for themselves, including the nation. Elsewhere, similar trends took place. By the 1920s and 1930s, a stratum of professionals and intellectuals in almost every colony had come to seek the European political model. These professionals and intellectuals were the same people who had been exposed to missionaries, received Western education, or participated in Christian churches. Each of these influences was a discursive forum, a mode of transmitting ideas through persuasion, making ideas more attractive through teaching them, preaching them, and writing them, presenting them to the recipient for reflection and acceptance.[8]

Besides education and religion, one other crucial experience formed nationalists: war. I mean primarily World War II, although World War I was also important in some colonies, especially India. In several ways, war lent nationalism appeal. It exposed non-European soldiers to European ideas. In both world wars, European metropoles conscripted thousands of Africans and Asians to fight on European fronts. Recruitment in British West Africa alone numbered 160,000 by 1943.[9] In some cases, Africans and Asians fought side by side with white European soldiers, in one of the few forums where such equality was practiced, although many colonial soldiers also suffered discrimination. But most colonial troops were exposed to Western ideas of freedom and equality, a war aim that pervaded Western armies. Basil Davidson quotes a letter from a Nigerian volunteer, who writes, "We all overseas soldiers are coming back home with new ideas. . . . We have been told what we fought for. That is 'freedom.' We want nothing but freedom."[10] It was not just colonial soldiers who were so exposed, either: Colonial societies came into contact with these ideas via white soldiers who passed through their lands.[11]

War served not only to expose metropolitan political ideals to more colonists, but the metropolitan powers themselves heightened the legitimacy of the ideals by proclaiming them as war aims. The Atlantic Charter was pivotal. Despite Churchill's disclaimer that it did not apply to colonies, the Charter, announcing "the right of all peoples to choose the form of government under which they will live," had resonated deeply throughout the colonies. It found its way into the resolutions of nationalist congresses; nascent political parties formed societies of literate colonists to consider its ideas; and it created wide expectations that after the war, more rapid progress toward independence would ensue.[12] But while war committed Britain rhetorically to these ideals, it also sapped Britain's prestige. Denunciations of imperialism by the United States and Soviet Union, the predicament of having to appeal to the colonies for support, Britain's limited consultation of the colonies to whom it appealed—all heightened colonial skepticism toward Britain as an upholder of its own ideals. Together, these effects of war created new nationalists and radicalized old ones. This we can see in the attitudes of soldiers returning home from war, and in the written and oral reactions to war of nationalist activists.[13]

Colonists' thinking changed over time. Those colonists who first began to look toward a European model of progress in the late nineteenth and early twentieth centuries were relatively conservative. They advocated reform, greater access to colonial civil service and high positions in universities and churches, and, increasingly, an extended franchise and parliamentary representation. Only in the 1930s did a few begin to speak publicly of national independence; only after World War II did most nationalists speak of independence regularly. Strictly speaking, "nationalism" was not nationalism at all until this late stage. This was the timetable in most of Africa; on the Asian subcontinent it was chronologically advanced. But in all cases, despite their evolution, the ideas had in common, first, that they were European political ideas, and, second, that they were almost solely political ideas; elite nationalists would have little do with communism, socialism, or other social change. In holding these ideas, nationalists were a unique sector of colonial societies, self-consciously and willfully separated from the "masses" of these societies.[14]

Education, religion, and war made converts, and made converts more zealous in somewhat different patterns in different parts of the British empire. In British West Africa, the "back to Africa" movement was especially prominent in the nineteenth century. Liberia and Sierra Leone became regions for liberated slaves and their children, creoles who spread throughout British West Africa with the Western ideas that they had acquired in America and the West Indies. In Sierra Leone, Liberia, the Gold Coast, and Nigeria, many prominent former slaves and Africans who had been educated in America became involved in sundry civic organizations, and frequently expressed their aspiration to Western ways in newspapers, in universities, in churches, and in other public forums. By the early twentieth century, they began to complain about colonial rule, but mainly about the discrimination it imposed and the lack of access it provided to Africans, not about the fundamental arrangement of the system itself. These Africans wanted to realize the European civilizing mission, and began to criticize the Europeans for being poor stewards of it.[15] It was in West Africa where Africans in the Christian churches originally broke with colonial elites in the late nineteenth century, and where the American ideas about Pan-Africanism of Marcus Garvey and W.E.B. DuBois influenced many eventual nationalists.[16] Other African leaders, tribal chieftains, dissented, advocating a return to tribal customs—these leaders collaborated most closely with the British.[17]

In British West Africa, the evolution of nationalism proceeded roughly according to the timetable I have described. In the 1930s, younger nationalists began to look toward an independent state. Most ardent were former activists in youth movements, who had become more radical than their parents through the influence of Western-run universities. Kwame Nkrumah, future president of Ghana (formerly the Gold Coast), was just such a nationalist, a man who had spent many years in universities in the United States and in London, where he came under the influence of West Indian radicals.[18] In British West Africa, World War II also had the effect I described above. African participation, European pledges, and colonial disillusionment with Europe led to a rise in the number of Africans writing about and demanding nationalist ideas.

In East and Central Africa, Kenya, Tanganyika, and Northern and Southern Rhodesia, the sources and timing of nationalism were quite similar to those in British West Africa; the chief difference was that Western-educated Africans were far fewer. In these regions, nationalism was also more strongly influenced by Christian millenarianism. The widespread Watchtower fundamentalists, for instance, were a crucial forum for future nationalists.[19] Nationalist movements that sprang up here after World War II indeed found one of their central appeals in the memory of Christian Africans who had resisted the original British conquest in the nineteenth century.[20] In other respects—the timing of the idea's evolution, the role of World War II, and so on—though, East and Central Africa were quite similar.

In India and the other Asian colonies, nationalism appeared and evolved similarly, although on an earlier timetable. Asian protest, of course, far predated the clamor that led the British Cabinet to its sweeping decisions for independence around 1960, and does not, then, explain directly the new international constitution. But its history does strengthen the evidence for the pattern and causes of nationalist ideas for which I have been arguing. The elite stratum of Indians who formed the Congress Party in the mid 1880s had been educated in European-run universities, aspired to European careers and political goals, and found itself being denied entrance to the Indian Civil Service a decade or two earlier than Africans experienced the same circumstances. Out of this generation came Mahatma Gandhi, Jawaharlal Nehru, and Mohammed Ali Jinnah. Since Christianity had not spread into India as it had into Africa, it was left to European universities and British-run schools in India to form nationalists (although we should not overlook the important influence of Christianity on the thought and methods of Gandhi). In India, it was prior to World War I, rather than during the 1930s or after World War II, that nationalism, as opposed to mere political reform, developed. In India, it was World War I in which Indians fought and came to expect political progress as their reward, resembling the effect of World War II upon Africans. During the interwar period, Indians, led by Gandhi, carried out massive protests and boycott campaigns against British rule. By the 1930s, most nationalists had come to desire political independence.[21]

In India, education and war were the crucial circumstances of reflection; compared to Africa, they influenced events earlier. British rule in India, British schools in India, and Indian participation in British schools began decades earlier than the same sort of experiences in Africa. And whereas Africans also fought in World War I, nationalism was much further developed among Indians by the time they fought in the war than it was among Africans; war could thus further nationalism along even more. That the experiences of education and war were available much earlier in India than in Africa, and that nationalism also developed there much earlier, is evidence for a link between the experiences and the formation of the identities.

The Social Power of Nationalists

Nationalists converted to nationalism in the context of education, religion, and war. But was it they who wielded the social power of protest? One level of structural skepticism, after all, allows that ideas may fashion identities but fail to exercise social power. What evidence is there for the social power of colonial ideas in the revolution of colonial independence?

When significant social protest appeared, when large political parties formed and agitated, when newspaper campaigns and boycotts and public protests took place, nationalists were teamed up with allies, coalition partners whose own aims were mostly more limited and material: "cocoa farmers, coffee growers, chiefs, cultivators, traders and lorry owners," who demanded higher wages, better working conditions, and reformed property laws.[22] But it was nationalists who found these allies, forming coalitions, piecing together enough protest to tip the balance against British rule. British rule indeed relied upon a balance. In general, it did not operate through massive armies and bureaucracies in the colonies, but through collaborators, local leaders who would support or even participate in the colonial government, and contain their more recalcitrant countrymen. When collaborators began to dwindle and opponents amass, Britain was in trouble, and was forced either to firm up its rule through the use of troops and police or to make rapid concessions toward independence.

But what anticolonial ideas rarely did, at least in the British colonies, was bring about a massive popular rebellion or an armed resistance movement, one fired by the injustice of European political dominance. There was no "revolt of the masses." Only episodically and sporadically did crowds of proletarians, peasants, or tribespeople participate directly or enthusiastically in the social protest. Speaking on behalf of the "nation," in the name of the European ideal of the "state," nationalists sought independence—the "national struggle." But they showed little zeal for the "social struggle," for the fight against unjust wages, land laws that kept the vast majority of fertile and productive land in the hands of a few, or many other structures of domination.[23] In fact, in almost every case of nationalist protest, British or French, African or Asian, the leaders wanted to avoid allying with enthusiasts of the social struggle for fear of being drowned out by their numbers, disempowered by their mass strength. To some extent, they had to make such alliances in order to mobilize the strikes or boycotts that would bring independence. But proletarians or peasants rarely became members of the parties or part of the protest leadership. Nationalists succeeded in minimizing this collaboration, so much so that when independence finally did arrive, proletarians and peasants, and later, neocolonialist and dependency theorists, complained that statehood brought none of the social transformation for which they had hoped.

In each case of protest, nationalists—converts to nationalist beliefs—were crucial. Before they allied with any collaborators outside their stratum, they had already formed nascent party organizations. Once the protest did occur, nationalists were essential in organizing and leading it. In British West Africa, the key public voices of protest during the 1930s were heard through youth movements led by the most prominent of the Gold Coast intelligentsia, J. B. Danquah, and other leaders in the Gold Coast and Nigeria. But these movements were only tiny coteries of intellectuals. After World War II, when the British government conceded only a meager constitution to the Gold Coast, Danquah formed a political party, the United Gold Coast Convention (UGCC), to demand faster political progress, and eventually independence. The party leadership was almost entirely composed of university graduates and conservative nationalist elites, fearful of mass involvement. Sensing the need for a broader mobilization of protest, the UGCC leadership brought home from London the radical intellectual and political organizer, Kwame Nkrumah, at the end of 1947. Under Nkrumah's leadership, the character of Gold Coast political activity changed as he sought to mobilize broader sections of the public. Widespread and constant protest ensued, involving trade unions, ex-serviceman organizations, and other networks, carrying on strikes, boycotts, riots, and newspaper agitation, culminating in a march of ex-servicemen in February 1948 in which one ex-serviceman was shot by the police and days of rioting followed. Those who favored this social dimension of the protest broke off from the UGCC in 1949 and formed the Convention People's Party (CPP), which attracted commoners in its organization and its following. In the 1951 general election of a legislature to which the British had conceded a new measure of power, the CPP won a majority. Subsequently, it was the party leadership who carried on the negotiations that culminated in independence in 1957.[24]

Although the social protest took on, and benefited from, support outside the nationalist elite, the nationalist elite remained in the top leadership roles, even of the CPP, coordinated most of the resistance, and carried on negotiations for independence once the popular agitation had died down after around 1950. Although the nationalists had collaborators, the role of nationalists was indispensable. Alone, the unions, or the teachers, or even the ex-servicemen showed no initiative to press for more rapid political reform or independence, but only for better economic conditions. In Nigeria, protest had even less of a popular character. Most of the nationalist leaders had studied abroad and returned home to become doctors, lawyers, and journalists. The trade union movement there was deeply divided and unwilling to join left-wing parties. It was rather newspaper grousing and the petitions and verbal threats of parties that carried on the struggle.[25]

In British East and Central Africa, the nationalist struggle was more closely linked with the social struggle. There were fewer elite nationalists than in West Africa. The colonial government's strong suppression of resistance movements made it difficult for nationalists to develop organizations and parties. Nevertheless, during the interwar period in Kenya, Tanzania, Uganda, and Rhodesia, nationalists whose identities had been formed in European universities or religious movements—Jomo Kenyatta, Julius Nyerere, and Hastings Banda—led cultural associations and sometimes political associations that formed the basis for postwar parties. In Kenya, such organizations, most prominently the Kikuyu Central Association, were outlawed in 1940, their nationalist leaders thrown into prison. Cautious reforms allowed Jomo Kenyatta to form the Kenya African Union during the 1940s, and he associated closely with peasant and worker movements. In the early 1950s, thousands of workers and peasants took up arms in the Mau Mau rebellion, a sustained armed confrontation with Britain. With its nationalist leaders again imprisoned, the rebellion continued until 1956, when British armies crushed it. In the late 1950s, Britain opened up negotiations for independence, but this time with nationalist leaders, who formed new parties at the end of the decade.[26]

The protest that moved the British to negotiate in the end was, in part, armed resistance, which gathered much of its strength from those with social and economic demands. But again, it is difficult to imagine this resistance without the leadership of nationalists whose identities were formed through Western education and churches and war. Well before independence, Britain defeated the troops of economic and social change, and it was with nationalists that it negotiated in the end. These nationalists, it could trust more easily to safeguard the interests of British settlers in Kenya. In the era of independence, these nationalists were indeed little disposed to bring about social change. Nationalists also formed the prewar organizations that became broader protest movements after the war, imbuing them with European politics. It was from this model that the social protest movements in Kenya grew. In Tanganyika, Uganda, and Rhodesia, parties also allied more closely with peasants and workers than they did in West Africa, but again they were led by, and originated from the organizations of, nationalists.[27]

In India, Congress Party leadership and membership was restricted to Western-educated elites well before peasants and workers took part in the mass demonstrations of the interwar period. Throughout this period, too, the leadership remained elite, and was always reluctant to extend party membership beyond its own stratum. To be sure, Gandhi's campaigns of *satyagraha*, or nonviolent resistance, drew their strength from the involvement of masses of commoners who would march and boycott under the direction of Gandhi and his disciples. But they were led and organized entirely by nationalist elites.[28] As India's social protest happened a couple of decades before African protest, we may again draw a comparison on behalf of ideas: In that region in which colonists first converted to nationalists, social protest occurred earlier as well. As elsewhere, nationalists were a crucial force behind this protest.

Ideas and British Colonial Independence

Behind colonial protest were ideas, converting and motivating social power. Protest provided the clamor at the end of the 1950s to which the British Cabinet was forced to respond: repress or concede progress. It was steadily growing international and domestic criticism of colonialism that ensured that repression would destroy the government's reputation for gradual self-government and that the government would pay concrete political costs for appearing reactionary. The sources of anticolonialism, then, cooperated in a division of labor. As archival records show, the Cabinet perceived this clamor, this criticism, and this potential reputational loss, and responded by granting independence more quickly and more widely than it had ever previously thought it would. Granting independence, rather than fighting costly wars to keep colonies—the general but not universal British pattern after World War II—amounted to a peaceful dismantling of empire, at least relative to the French experience.

Alternatively, perhaps ideas were influential, but in a different manner than I have described. What of the intermediate versions of the two roles? Might they better capture the workings of ideas in the colonies? As an alternative to the social power of ideas, the concept of focal points holds that ideas assist bargaining between opponents whose ends are material, or at least different from the ideas themselves. Ideas' role here is to "suggest" a workable compromise. In a focal point account, we should see that colonists, international and domestic critics, and imperial officials alike were concerned with advancing political and economic power, that they engaged in intense conflict over the issue, but then resolved the dispute when the idea of colonial independence entered into their deliberations. But focal points are implausible here. In fact, the ends of anticolonial critics were not something other than nationalist ideas themselves. I have argued that purveyors of revolutionary ideas were converts to nationalist and egalitarian ideas, holding colonial independence as their end, and motivated by this end in their struggle. As for colonial officials, they may have regarded empire as an enterprise for wealth, but they bargained as upholders of the established ideal of gradual self-government. Nor did ideas suggest a compromise between positions, either. Colonial independence was the very outcome that the revolutionary ideas demanded, and which colonial officials resisted, not a settlement that bridged the difference between competing pursuers of material ends.

There is also an intermediate version of the first role of ideas, an alternative way of explaining nationalism. That is, ideas could have been resolvers of uncertainty. Here, rather than fundamentally shaping identities, ideas propose to people a way to pursue an end other than the idea itself—the acquisition of wealth, for instance. But it is not clear what end the idea of colonial independence advanced other than the intrinsic value of colonial independence. Colonial independence certainly empowered nationalist leaders in many cases, but power itself does not explain why they sought this form of power rather than some other position, within either a tribe or the colonial government. Prior to the experiences that formed their nationalist identities, few of them had even conceived of independence. These experiences created this end for them in the first place. Unless nationalists sought some form of political power in the first place, and then seized upon colonial independence as the best of forms, then it is difficult to see what ideas as resolvers of uncertainty explain. There is little evidence that nationalists reasoned in this way.

Ideas as resolvers of uncertainty are more plausible in the case of colonial officials, with respect to their established ideas. The idea of gradual self-government may have helped many of them solve the problem of how to pursue empire in a way that would advance Britain's economic and strategic interests, yet attain public justification. It was after World War I, when colonial empire was coming under increased public moral scrutiny, that the government began regularly, assertively, to proclaim gradual self-government. After World War II, this ideal took the form of colonial development, arguably a way to solve the problem of how to gain economic benefit from the empire. Gradual self-government, then, provided a way to pursue empire, but was not a deep conviction of imperial officials. Some officials, of course, may have either believed deeply in the ideal of spreading British self-government, having reflectively incorporated it into their identities. Others may have viewed it as entirely instrumental, a covering for empire as a mere source of wealth. But for many officials, Britain's established ideal of gradual self-government was quite plausibly a resolver of uncertainty, providing an answer to the riddle of how to pursue and justify empire so as to maintain stability in the colonies and approval at home. It is with respect to established ideals, in fact, that we would expect the concept of resolvers of uncertainty to work best. The issue of public justification indeed takes the form of solving a problem: How to pursue empire most stably, successfully, and popularly? If ideas acted as resolvers of uncertainty, though, this does not detract from the reputational power of ideas. It is only revolutionary ideas that we expect play the strong version of the two roles of ideas, shaping identities and exercising social power. Revolutionary ideas may well interact with established ideas that have not made their way deeply into personal identities.

Another alternative to my argument is that ideas are important, but that the reputational social power is too complex. Perhaps a single form of ideas—revolutionary or established—or fewer couriers of ideas would explain colonial independence just as well. I have tried to argue, though, for the importance of every element—both forms of ideas, international and domestic critics, colonial nationalists. Colonial officials did not themselves become converts to new ideas; nor were they simply, directly, forced into colonial independence by a rebellion or looming electoral loss. Only their commitment to their reputation for gradual self-government and its complex relationship to strategic and political stakes can explain why officials feared appearing reactionary and why they sought to avoid this fate through promoting colonial independence. Only the combined forces of international and domestic criticism and protest from the colonies, each playing its own role, can in turn explain why the officials' reputations came under stress. To omit any of these elements would leave the explanation incomplete.

The final alternative is that ideas were not influential at all. It is structural forces that explain nationalist identities, the social power that brought the British Cabinet to decide for independence, or both, depending on how deep the skeptic envisions their influence. It is a much more challenging alternative, one that enjoys scholarly prestige, and that requires more extensive consideration. I consider it in chapter 11.

ELEVEN

BRITAIN'S BURDEN OF EMPIRE

DEEP DOUBTERS of the claim that anticolonial ideas lassoed and felled the British Empire would likely argue that Britain's decision arose entirely from the decimation of its army and economy after World War II, its decline relative to the United States and the Soviet Union, the shift of its trade away from the empire and Commonwealth and toward Europe, the declining value of its colonies, and the expense of maintaining them. The colonies grew onerous; Britain let them go. The most common structural explanation of Britain's demise is broadly Realist. It was Britain's relative economic and strategic decline in the global power balance—changes in material social power—that led it to relinquish empire. Such structuralism supplants the social power of revolutionary ideas. Cabinets may have declaimed an official ideal of self-government, colonists and critics may have asserted their criticism out of their formed identities, but such communications were impotent. For this structural skepticism, there is circumstantial evidence. Britain's decline was indisputable. I will argue, though, that the evidence is little more than circumstantial. The crucial question is whether the Cabinet itself perceived a link between Britain's relative decline and the merits of colonial independence. This link, I contend, is missing. There is a more penetrating skepticism, too, one that doubts even the first role of ideas, the autonomy of colonists' and other critics' reflection. Their identities were rather the product of class and political position, it holds. Neither are these eclipsing circumstances, though, successful in their skepticism. Behind the social power that ended empire, I contend, was authentic conversion. Both sorts of skepticism, each aimed at one of the two roles of ideas, I take up in this chapter.

The Decline of Armed Forces and Wealth, Not the Rise of Ideas

"The good old rule, / Sufficeth them, the simple plan , / That they should take, who have the power, / And they should keep who can," ran an imperial ditty.[1] Its obverse: They who took and have now lost power can no longer keep. This is the structural argument for Britain's embrace of colonial independence. The crucial event is World War II. After the war,

Britain had clearly lost the global hegemony that it had held at the turn of the century.[2] It was now in a world of superpowers, one where it no longer needed far-flung defense commitments, where its trade was being diverted away from its empire to Western Europe, where its colonies had become less valuable for Britain's trade and monetary balances. The argument takes a Realist form: As Britain suffered a decline relative to other powers, so it also came to scale back its ambition for dominance. Its interest in a constitution of colonial independence, its sweeping release of colonies, were but a ratification of retreat.

There are three versions of the argument.[3] The first is that Britain gave up its colonies because its economic and military resources for maintaining its possessions became enfeebled, ebbing independently of any colonial influence, due to the war, a relatively declining industrial base, and so on. The second is that Britain gave up its colonies because changing global markets made them less valuable. Complementary, these two versions may work together in a structural explanation.[4] A third version contradicts the second, but is compatible with the first. It holds that in, fact, the economic value of the colonies did not plummet, but that Britain chose independence so as not to alienate nationalist elites, whose cooperation it needed to secure the economic interests that it still valued.[5] This version leaves open the issue of how there came to be nationalist elites in the first place. Unless it can explain their conversion through structural forces as well, then it remains only a moderate critique of ideas. The Cabinet acted on behalf of its economic interests, but it was still nationalist ideas that placed these interests under duress.

What is the evidence for these alternatives? Few historians would dispute that World War II diminished Britain's economic and military rank to a level from which it would never recover. Although by the early 1950s, Britain was still the world's third-largest power, its production outpacing Germany's by 50 percent and France's by 250 percent, it was handicapped. Again and again the Cabinet recognized that it could no longer maintain its strategic commitments.[6] Britain devoted a far greater proportion of its spending to defense, and far less to developing industry, than its rivals in Europe and Japan. Its effort to maintain its currency, sterling, often brought on growth-stifling deflation.[7] After the war, Britain was the world's largest debtor.[8] Its military forces had been ravaged. By 1952, it still had not rebounded from capital losses from the war, which added up to one-fourth of the nation's wealth.[9] Although Britain share of world export markets increased from 21.3 percent in 1937 to 25.4 percent in 1950, it then decreased to 16.2 percent in 1961.[10] Britain suffered dangerously low sterling balances and strained to maintain sterling's value, most acutely in a convertibility crisis in 1947 and a major devaluation of 30.5 percent in 1949.[11] In the early 1950s, the balance-of-payments deficit was expanding rapidly. Chancellor of the Exchequer Richard Butler reported its growth at £700 per year.[12] The colonies in fact held much of Britain's sterling assets. Between 1945 and 1955, the level of Britain's sterling liabilities to its colonies grew from £454 million to £1281 million.[13] Finally, during the fifteen years after World War II, Britain's exports to and imports from Western Europe expanded proportionately to its trade within the empire and Commonwealth, a notable redirection of its economic interests.[14]

During the same period, Britain both expanded its social welfare provisions and increased its defense budget. As the Cold War began, countering Soviet expansion required committing troops to NATO on the Continent, which added to Britain's existing imperial commitments in the Middle East, Asia, and Africa. The outbreak of the Korean War led the Cabinet to the largest peacetime military buildup in British history. It expanded military spending by £1555 million over three years (estimated 1951 amount).[15] In response to this plight, key Cabinet memoranda warned frequently and starkly of overcommitment: the mismatch of means with goals. Most prominent was a 1957 Defence White Paper, a major Cabinet policy review that had been initiated the previous year by Harold Macmillan. The report stressed that Britain's economy was incapable of continuing to support its worldwide military presence: "Britain's influence in the world depends first and foremost on the health of her internal economy and the success of her export trade. Without these, military power cannot in the long run be supported."[16] Constantly throughout this period, Cabinet officials stressed this tension between commitments and resources.[17]

Imperial Britain, stretched and strained, was doubtless reevaluating its commitments. But did the Cabinet conclude from its recognition of the country's weakness that liquidating the empire was a way to save costs? I can find no evidence that it ever made such a determination, either generally, or for the most part, toward a particular colony. The one exception was perhaps its decision to free India in 1947. The empire's largest colony and by far the most costly to administer, India more than any other possession brought the Cabinet to reflect upon the war's toll and its resulting inability to hold colonies in the face of nationalist resistance.[18] But freeing India did not entail general colonial independence. There is little to suggest that Britain extended this reasoning to the rest of its empire.

The Labour Cabinet's policy of colonial development brightly reveals that Britain still valued its colonies after the war. Development was partly a response to international moral criticism, but was even more importantly Britain's effort to revive its economic fortunes through 'its colonies. In the 1930s, Britain had set up an "imperial preference union," along with a "sterling area," a system of trade preferences and a common currency that was supposed to retain investment capital and sterling balances within

Britain and its empire. From these measures, Britain hoped to reap benefits in two ways. First, as part of the sterling area, colonies could sell commodities for dollars, which would increase the sterling-area dollar pool.[19] Second, the colonies could supply Britain with much needed raw materials at a low price, a provision the sterling area made possible. "The demand for most colonial products was bigger and stronger than it had ever been; cocoa, fats and oilseeds were in short supply, where previously they had been in surplus," writes historian Ronald Hyam.[20] The colonies could also contribute strategic war materials for the defense buildup.[21] To increase the colonies' production, the Colonial Office attempted several development projects, including the Overseas Development Corporation and a quickly aborted "Columbo Plan," most of which were failures, but which illustrate the economic stake that Britain perceived in its colonies.[22]

Although the Conservatives shied away from Labour's more ambitious schemes and favored private investment, they encouraged the development of the colonial infrastructure and small-scale projects in agriculture, education, health, transportation, and communication, all in the hopes of increasing production. The Conservative Colonial Office also lobbied actively and successfully to have Parliament renew the Colonial Development and Welfare Act, the key colonial-development funding legislation, in 1955.[23] As late as 1959, we still find a Cabinet Committee extolling the value of the sterling area to the British economy.[24] During the 1950s, expenditures on colonial development as a percentage of GDP fell 27.8 percent between 1950 and 1958, but then actually rose again 34 percent between 1958 and 1960.[25] Although Cabinet papers, especially those of the Treasury, do at times reveal arguments for cutting back development resources, no document during this period concluded generally that the colonies were an economic liability.[26] Right up until the end of empire, the Cabinet saw them as a net asset. In requesting a balance sheet of colonial costs and benefits for 1957, Harold Macmillan concluded that "the economic considerations were fairly evenly matched. Consequently, it was felt that the economic interests of the United Kingdom were unlikely in themselves to be decisive in determining whether or not a territory should become independent."[27] And in fact, measured in terms of exports and dollar earnings for the empire, the colonies did contribute to Britain's economic recovery.[28]

White Papers and memoranda show that the Cabinet was aware of Britain's general overcommitment, but also in favor of solutions other than getting rid of colonies. The cost of maintaining colonies, after all, was minuscule compared to defense or social service budgets, which were far more common targets for proposed reductions.[29] Another major proposed remedy was burden sharing, the assumption of a portion of Britain's defense commitments in the Middle East and Asia by the United States and Commonwealth countries.[30]

At the time when Britain did begin to negotiate independence, its desire to keep its former colonies in the Commonwealth, with its common currency and sundry economic agreements, shows that even at the last hour it still thought its colonies economically valuable. Britain did not value the colonies any less because its trade was shifting toward Europe, either. Even as it began to consider joining the European Economic Community in the mid-1950s, the Cabinet rejected any plan that would compromise its privileges in the Commonwealth and colonial empire.[31] It was not until the mid-1960s, after the Cabinet had already made most of the decisions for independence, that its trade with the Commonwealth sharply declined, a drop whose magnitude would lead Britain to disassociate from its former imperial bloc.[32]

If Britain did not release its colonies because it perceived them as less valuable, then perhaps, as neocolonialist arguments claim, it gave them up in order to win the favor of colonial nationalists and thus preserve its economic interests. It is clear that Britain indeed wanted to preserve its economic ties with independent former colonies—hence, its ubiquitous effort to negotiate for Commonwealth status with sterling benefits, trade benefits, and so on. The records reveal little evidence, however, that this benefit was a central motive, rather than an attendant desideratum, in the decisions for independence.

But economic forces do not exhaust potential structures. Britain had another central motive in holding colonies: a strategic one. Colonies were crucial for guarding trade routes, sea-lanes, and military bases. One might argue that it was only when Britain's global strategic burdens shifted to America, making its colonial expenditures redundant, that it decided to give up its colonies. Strategic structuralism, though, overlooks one sense in which the Cabinet came to estimate its African colonies as even more valuable during the 1950s: it saw them as vulnerable to communist encroachment. Providing adequate defenses in fact became a higher priority.[33]

As for their traditional strategic value, as guardians for trade routes and turf for military bases, only a few colonies in the empire were worth defending in the first place—Aden, Singapore, Cyprus, and Malta. It is true that Britain perceived their worth as declining, but not as disappearing. In each case, Britain sought to negotiate an arrangement to retain bases or maintain defenses as part of the independence agreement. Exceptionally, Kenya grew even more valuable after Britain left Suez in 1956.[34] The rest of the colonies held little strategic value at all, no value whose decline would lead Britain to give them independence. In the end, Britain did not systematically delay or obstinately negotiate the independence of its strategically valuable colonies any more than it did that of its other colonies, a difference that we would expect if strategic value was important. Britain may have stalled a bit more vigorously in Malta and Aden, delaying their freedom to the tail end of the independence cluster (1964 and 1967, respectively), but it freed Malaya (including Singapore) and Cyprus at roughly the time that it freed the others (1957 and 1960).

The forms of social power stressed by structural skepticism—economic, strategic—then, do not correspond well with what the Cabinet did or with what it perceived itself to be doing. It is impossible to say that such power did not make a difference: Might the Cabinet have been more inclined to keep its colonies had Britain never been weakened by World War II? We do know that the Cabinet perceived net value in its colonies right up until colonial independence, and that it did not perceive them as the source of Britain's overcommitment or their relinquishment as the solution. Neither do strategic factors explain well the timing or sweeping pattern of colonial independence. Clearly, the Cabinet deliberated constantly over these issues during the 1950s—its global military commitments, economic competition, the Cold War, its alliance with the United States, the prospect of joining the European Community. But these influences did not lead it to give up its colonies; they fail to supplant the second role of ideas.

Suspicion of Anticolonial Ideas Themselves

It still stands, then, that it was nationalists, British leftists, Americans, Soviets, and voices in the United Nations, their moral outrage and their measured censure, that moved the officials who sat in Cabinet rooms to cede colonies in the complex way that reputational social power describes. Deep skeptics, though, ones who doubt even the first role of ideas, may suspect the outrage and censure themselves. They suspect that critics of colonialism were those who were most economically and politically interested in its demise. They suspect that critics arrived at their criticism through changes in economic and political structures that led them to see colonial independence as the most rational route to their economic and political advancement. Anticolonial identities only legitimated material interests. What is the case for such deep skepticism?

International and Domestic Criticism

Behind the ideas of those critics who instilled in Britain its fear of a reactionary reputation—the United States, the Soviets, Third World members of the United Nations, and British domestic voices—sponsors of suspicion promise to find strategic and economic interests. Consider the United

States, who had preached a global mission of national independence since its own revolution.[35] Perhaps its preaching followed its purse. Or its position in the global balance of power. Perhaps it only actively, practically favored colonial independence when it furthered these economic and strategic interests. Major schools of thought on American foreign policy express exactly such skepticism. Revisionist historians of the Cold War have long thought American foreign policy to be at the service of capitalist interests. Behind America's criticism of colonialism was the prospect of abolishing the British imperial preference system, creating a free market for U.S. trade with Africa and Asia. For American Realists, it was the global balance of power that drove U.S. interests. U.S. anticolonial rhetoric was only packaging for its goal of preventing Asian and African states from becoming aligned with the Soviets in the Cold War. In both schools, liberal rhetoric disguises underlying interests that can better be described by Realism or revisionism.

American liberalism and American interests are difficult to disentangle. American liberalism, after all, is an ideology that prescribes the rational pursuit of material interests. Free markets, capitalism, liberalism, self-determination, peace, prosperity, security—liberalism links them all together. Yet there are flaws in a simple revisionism or Realism, one that discounts the independent force of liberal ideas. An interest in free markets does not account well for what U.S. officials prodded Britain to do, both privately and publicly—dismantle its empire. If only markets mattered, then why did not the United States simply seek an end to Britain's imperial preference system rather than its entire empire? The United States may well have pressured Britain along free-market lines, especially in the first couple of years after the Cold War, but the British Cabinet papers that record the complaints of British officials about U.S. pressure show nary a concern about the U.S. stance on trade. In private discussions, the United States did not even push for a complete end to empire, but instead for more rapid colonial progress to avoid anticolonial criticism, a result that would do little to open up markets. It was not even clear that an end to empire would bring an end to imperial preferences, for Britain might still seek a Commonwealth customs union. If markets drove American criticism, then should not the records show direct American efforts to promote free trade?

But perhaps it was the global balance of power that motivated America's anticolonial criticism. The alignment of colonies was the stake. America's worry, in this Realist explanation, was that colonies would become part of the Soviet bloc, one by one, rapidly, like dominoes. Undeniably, America did harbor such a worry. The United States perceived a strategic interest in the alignment of colonies as it did in the alignment of all African, Asian, and Latin American states during the Cold War. Clearly, America's overriding foreign policy concern during the forties and fifties was its overall war against communism. It is this concern that explains, for instance, why, in French Indochina during the forties and fifties, the United States was interested not merely in ending French rule, but even more so, in ensuring that communism would not replace colonialism.[36] American anticolonial rhetoric could well have been subordinate to, and at the service of, America's global strategy.

But the strategic argument also fails to account for anticolonial criticism. It is flawed in part because it does not explain why America did not choose a very different, but also plausible, stratagem for prosecuting the Cold War. It might have altogether avoided criticizing Britain, taking care not to threaten its empire, in order not to weaken this critical strategic ally. Since Europe was the central theater of the Cold War, prioritizing Britain's strength made rational sense. American Presidents did acknowledge the danger of weakening Britain, after all, through muting their public criticism of British colonialism, confining their concerns to gentle, private prodding. But for the Realist, America could have, should have, abjured moralistic criticism altogether and regarded Britain solely as a strategic, military, ally. But America did not choose this course, either.

The largest problem with any structural, Realist, balance-of-power explanation is its failure to explain why America criticized British colonialism at all. If the future alignment of colonies was America's concern, then it must have conceived the Cold War as an ideological, not just a material, struggle, one on whose winning side it wanted to be numbered. American officials must have thought that colonists cared deeply about the ideology and progressive reputation of superpowers and European powers, so deeply that colonists would make it a factor in their alignment decision. Otherwise, why take seriously the project of winning the colonists over with anticolonial rhetoric? Neither the colonists' definition of interests, nor the U.S. perception of this definition, nor the U.S. desire to shape this perception, make sense in a purely strategic, Realist world. In this world, the colonists would align with whomever threatened them the least, could best guarantee their security, or provide them with aid; and the United States would be chiefly concerned with convincing them that it could provide these goods, not with convincing them of its anticolonialist sympathies.[37] Similarly, if Britain's strategic power was America's concern, then it is hard to explain why America prodded Britain to release its colonies—unless America also thought that a reactionary reputation would have brought colonies to rebel and become more of a liability than an asset for Britain. But if this were the case, then again, the United States must have thought that reputation mattered.

U.S. officials, it cannot be denied, were concerned about the global alignment of the colonies in the larger power struggle against the Soviets, considered British power crucial, and were occupied above all with the Cold War. But colonial alignment and British power, they also thought, were not mere matters of strategic power, but were closely linked with the ideological struggle. Only if they thought that the Cold War had a consequential ideological context, and only if they thought that America's liberal identity could help shape this context, would U.S. statesmen assert America's historical ideological commitment to national independence.

The argument runs little different for the Soviets or for nonaligned colonial critics like Egypt and postindependence India. The Soviets, like the Americans, were concerned about the alignment of colonies in the Cold War struggle. But here, too, their rhetorical strategy of winning colonies over to their side made little sense if it did not conceive of the Cold War as ideological struggle, and of themselves as a state whose identity could hold appeal in this struggle. National liberation was important to Communist ideology, as it was to liberal ideology, although in the service of the class struggle rather than liberal freedom. Nonaligned states, which desired not to be in the service of either side, had a strategic interest in increasing their own ranks, but also brandished anticolonial criticism in order to chink Britain's reputation. These states, too, pursued strategic interests, but did not consider them detached from the social power of ideas.

Structural explanations for anticolonialism within Britain are the least plausible. The most likely alternative structure, here, is class, especially the working class, whose interests would most supposably have been advanced by the end of empire. Resources spent defending the colonies, the working class might have believed, did little to advance its interests, and could better be spent at home on domestic welfare. The anticolonial activists who publicly criticized empire, creating the greatest threat to Britain's progressive reputation, were themselves members of lobbies and tightly organized groups, not a class, and not systematically composed of any particular class. It was these activists who were most influential in convincing the Labour Party to adopt an anticolonial platform. But maybe class power does help explain Labour's decision. The working class, after all, grew more powerful after the war, and its interest in welfare programs expanded. But there is little actual evidence that working-class voters perceived a tradeoff between welfare and empire, nor even that they thought empire an important issue. Leading politicians themselves rarely focused on empire in their campaigns or in their speeches. If the power of class is to be measured electorally, there is little evidence of its efficacy toward ending empire.[38]

Anticolonialism from the Colonies: The Product of Structural Change?

Colonists were also a crucial source of criticism, indeed the precipitate of the end of empire. But their criticism, too, skeptics may suspect, is the product of class and political position. Protest of empire was led by African and Asian lawyers, doctors, teachers, engineers, and professors, who were educated, wealthy, and advanced enough to resist colonial rule and think themselves capable of ruling themselves, and willing and able to ally with farm laborers, urban workers, miners, servants, peddlers, and drifting poor, everyone anticipating a far better living and far better status in an independent state. Economic and political motives, structured by class and colonial rule, made middle-class colonists into nationalists, led nationalists to protest, and led other classes to protest with them.

These structures challenge both roles of ideas in the colonies—the social power of colonists' protest, the second role of ideas, and the formation of nationalist identities, the first role of ideas. In the last chapter, I sought to show the centrality of converts to nationalism in mounting protest, and the roots of their conversion in circumstances that foster reflection—education, war, and religion. But how strongly do class and position correspond to both conversion and the social power of protest? Are they eclipsing circumstances? Alternative forms of social power? As I argued for the Reformation, I claim that these causes explain nationalism and protest in part, but do not override the social power of ideas.

Behind all gathering clamor for national liberation is a growing bourgeoisie, the sector of society that most favors independence. The argument is as plausible here as it was in the Europe of the Reformation. A member of the bourgeoisie—that is, one who holds a "bourgeois" occupation such as a trader, a civil servant, a doctor, a professor, or a lawyer—might see in colonial independence, in the removal of color barriers to education, political office, and company management, the opportunity to advance economically, professionally, and politically. This interest, this motive, was not only an element in an alloy of motives, but was the circumstance, the eclipsing circumstance, in which colonists developed nationalist ideas and protested colonial rule. What kind of evidence supports such skepticism?

One compelling sort would be an expansion of a colony's middle class prior to a swell in its ranks of nationalists and in its protest.[39] Although it is difficult to find data on colonial middle classes during the seventy or so years when nationalism gestated, the descriptions of most colonial historians confirm that these classes expanded little. As colonial administrative institutions took form in Africa around the turn of the century and a generation earlier in India, access to the civil service and to top positions in companies, churches, and other organizations become more restricted, not less. Nor did the proportion of colonists engaged in trade or other bourgeois occupations, either in Africa or Asia, change substantially, either. During the depression of the 1930s and World War II, social structures rigidified even more as the British became even less willing to open up their organizations in a time of austerity. Across the British colonies, bourgeois Africans or Asians in the colonies failed to multiply.[40]

Comparisons across colonies might also reveal middle-class strength. Where middle classes were largest, we should find more nationalists and more social protest. Colonial middle classes were generally tiny, but some were larger than others in proportion to their colony's population. Contrasting most crisply are East and Central Africa, where large throngs of white British settlers resided and dominated the social structure, and other British colonies, where few settlers lived. In the settler colonies, indigenous middle classes were far smaller. Indeed, in these colonies there were also fewer converted nationalists, and a smaller proportion of nationalists involved in social-protest movements—a positive piece of evidence for class.[41] But the contrast is limited. It shows only that a larger middle class nurtures, not that it solely causes, nationalism. It is not even clear whether a middle class is truly an eclipsing circumstance. Classes are complex, their members united not merely by common economic plights, but also by common ideas, idioms, songs, stories, sports, and memories.[42] As members of the middle class, colonial nationalists were not only of similar professions and wealth, but also often shared a Western education, a circumstance of reflection. It is very difficult to separate the influence of economics and education, surely a necessary task for the advocate of the sufficiency of economic structures. There is even evidence that education exercised independent influence. Historians' descriptions show that in the Gold Coast, Nigeria, and East and Central Africa, it was those middle-class colonists with a Western education or a religious or wartime experience who espoused nationalism and led protest on behalf of nationalist ideas; other middle-class colonists, who had not encountered these circumstances of reflection, might have protested in one way or another, but did not possess a nationalist identity or act upon it in protest.[43]

But perhaps I have been wrongly describing the influence of the middle class. Perhaps it is not a strong middle class, but the failure of the middle class to advance, that produced nationalism—through frustration, in this account. The real cause of nationalism, in this argument, is political and social structures, the ones that inhibited middle-class progress. As the African and Asian bourgeoisie were continually denied passage into the highest positions in their societies from the turn of the century through the aftermath of World War II, they adopted ideas that captured their frustrations and favored this advancement; and as younger colonists witnessed the failures of their elders, they adopted increasingly radical versions of these ideas. Finally, they organized the protest that actually changed the inhibiting structures. As such failure to advance was a constant across all colonies, at least prior to World War II, was it a structural cause of the nationalism that also arose in all colonies?

It is hard to judge such an argument. Failure to advance was constant, not only across colonies but also over the relevant decades. We cannot identify a date when failure to advance began, one that might be correlated with the onset of nationalism. Doubtless accumulating frustration contributed to colonists' desire for political progress and, eventually, independence. William Quandt, in his study of Algerian political socialization, illustrates how successive generations of young Algerians during the twentieth century became increasingly radical after being convinced of their parents' failures. Algeria, of course, was a French colony, but we can hypothesize similar experiences elsewhere.[44]

But if young colonists were convinced of their failure to advance, how did they become so convinced? It might be true, after all, that nationalists came to their nationalism through an experience that not only converted them to the idea of European statehood, but which also convinced them that their forebears' reformist version of the European idea had borne no fruit. Failure to advance alone says nothing about the reasons for desiring advance. The argument tells us little that we have not already learned from education, religion, war, and class.

Comparisons among colonies might also reveal the importance of the middle classes' failure to advance. Some colonies prevented this advancement more oppressively than others. Although advancement was slight everywhere, color bars, parliamentary membership restrictions, and exclusive economic practices were most repressive, again, in the settler colonies. A handful of West Africans or Indians might become business leaders, professors, or members of the colonial parliament, but practically no Africans could in East or Central Africa. Were nationalists most common where structures were most oppressive? In fact, the opposite was truer: there were fewer nationalists in the most exclusive structures. Not only did oppressive structures fail to breed nationalism—on their own, independently of other causes—but they may have most effectively suppressed nationalist identities, in my view, by limiting access to education. There may well have been more resentment among indigenous settler populations in these colonies, but resentment does not amount to nationalism—a specific program, a specific set of ideas. Nationalism, rather, requires certain experiences, ones to which settler societies limited the access of indigenous peoples.

Let us consider structural skepticism yet a little differently. Other strata, other forces besides the middle class and the structures that advanced or inhibited their plight might have furthered nationalism and protest—the proletariat and the peasantry, for instance. Perhaps dispossession of peasant land and peasants' migration to the cities are better linked to nationalism. Up to and through World War II, a major force of social change in Africa as well as Asia was the migration of native peoples away from their villages and toward cities and mines—peoples who were prodded or lured by the seizure of their tribal lands, by forced labor practices in rural areas, and by better wage opportunities. During World War II and afterward, the rate of urban growth across both African and Asian colonies multiplied rapidly.[45] Those who were wage earners organized into trade unions, a trend that also accelerated in British colonies during World War II and afterward.[46] Once in the cities, the proletariat may well have come to view colonial independence as a means of improving its condition. Increasing urbanization, then, brings nationalism, the argument runs. The peasantry who remained in the countryside also had reasons for overturning colonial structures, rooted in certain oppressive practices: onerous property laws, dispossession, and other colonial impositions that increased during the war.

Peasants and proletarians did not generally become nationalists, cognizant of the European national idea and convinced of the rightness of their colony's becoming like a European state. There is no identity formation to be explained here. But they did engage in social protest to improve their economic station, and were often an important part of coalitions that led to independence. As peasants and proletarians were not converts to nationalism, nationalism could not have motivated their social power. Changes in their social surroundings suggest plenty of reasons, structural reasons, behind their protest. Was the protest an alternative form of social power? Was it alone sufficient to elicit the colonies' pressure on the British Cabinet? These strata contributed to protest, at least sporadically, sometimes importantly. They were perhaps most important in Kenya, where they comprised the troops of the Mau Mau rebellion. Urban workers also formed the ranks of strikes and protests in West Africa in the late 1940s and in East and Central Africa in the late 1950s. Both urban and rural people participated in India's boycotts and demonstrations as well. An ideas account, though, allows that the social power of those motivated by material grievances may contribute to revolutions in sovereignty, but it only denies this power's sufficiency. The crucial organization, direction, and coordination of protest in every case came from nationalists, converted nationalists. Their leadership was essential. It led and coordinated the Mau Mau rebellion and carried on protest after the rebellion was crushed; it coordinated the strikes and protests in other parts of Africa; and it was the impetus behind the formation of political parties, the most vocal and organized advocates of independence. "To nationalism itself, whether in its modes, ideas, or intentions, the 'urbanized' multitudes contributed relatively little, while the still ruralized multitudes contributed still less," Davidson writes.[47]

But perhaps our consideration of structuralism has been too narrow. The middle class, the peasantry, the proletariat—perhaps the focus on these separate strata, their conditions, their demands, misses a larger structural story, one that construes social change as economic change for an entire colony, as a creator of grievance or opportunity for all levels—middle class, proletariat, and peasantry. Aggregate economic change might encourage nationalism in two ways. National identities and social protest could either be the product of the frustrations associated with economic decline, or they could be the product of a revolution of rising expectations created by economic growth. At different times, both trends occurred uniformly across the colonies. During the Depression, a decline in exports and production occurred; during World War II, austerity measures, inflation, and shortages were common. The decade after World War II, though, brought colonies a rise in export-led growth.[48] That nationalist social protest increased most sharply right after World War II suggests the influence of either economic trend. Was nationalism the effect of accumulating frustration or of rising expectations? Or both? It is possible that it was a combination of frustration and expectation that brought the desire for revolt. We can hypothesize that some combination of the two was responsible for the nationalist identities of the middle class and the social protest of the middle class, the proletariat, and the peasantry during the time of these changes and shortly afterward.

On the scale of the entire colony, we can also inquire into another influence that we might call "structural political change," meaning change in the institutional structure of the colonial regime. The subject here would be the "Second Colonial Occupation" in Africa, a metropolitan effort just after World War II to promote economic development through far-reaching reform. The chief source of grievance would have been a restructuring of the colonial administration that required officials to exercise control over agricultural and other policy much more locally, heavily, and intrusively than they had before.[49]

The rise of strikes in Africa during the Depression, mass involvement in African politics after World War II, an increase in mass involvement in politics in India during the 1930s, the rise of African rural discontent over colonial impositions during the Second Colonial Occupation—all of these correlate well with these aggregate political and economic eclipsing circumstances. Although these circumstances might explain much of the discontent that led swaths of society to protest, we still cannot account for this protest apart from the key leadership and coordinating role of converted nationalists. Some of these nationalists may have come to their ideas, or have been radicalized to more extreme ideas, as a result of the same political and economic change. But African and Asian nationalists were around well before the Depression and the war, and those who came to their beliefs during the Depression and war years were the same leaders who encountered the circumstances of reflection that I have discussed. Aggregate structural change does not explain when nationalist leaders arose or supplant the role of intellectually defining circumstances.

One other structural influence is worth considering. It is one to which I have alluded, but which deserves fuller consideration. It is the presence and oppression of large populations of European white settlers, who lived in East Africa and Central Africa. The settlers' influence was both social and political. As I have mentioned, the size of the middle class and the nature of structures of exclusion are related closely to the existence of settler populations. In the settler colonies, discrimination against Africans was most pervasive. The settlers were mostly deeply conservative farmers and miners who, in establishing their farms and mines from the nineteenth century onward, brought enormous upheaval to the lives of Africans. Farmers seized most of the fertile land and created a division of holdings much like the pattern in South Africa, where a minority of 10 percent or less of the population would own 70 percent or more of the land. Especially in the late nineteenth and early twentieth centuries, the white settlers practiced forced labor and created taxation schemes that gave Africans little choice but to leave their villages and enter the mines. Color bars and thousands of forms of petty discrimination were prevalent, and access to government positions were much more restricted, in settler colonies than they were elsewhere. Whites held majorities in legislatures, even though they were popular minorities, and they were slow to give Africans real power. True majority rule was the whites' pervading fear. Educational opportunities for Africans were also much more restricted, as were opportunities to hold middle-class occupations. Especially harsh in their discrimination were lower-class white settlers, who were closest to the African laborers in economic privileges.[50]

A. G. Hopkins, one of the leading economic historians of Africa, remarks that of all the dimensions along which African colonies might be compared, the settler variable accounts most powerfully for political and economic differences.[51] Does it explain nationalism? Nationalism was everywhere; only some colonies were settler colonies; settler populations, then, are not a necessary condition of nationalism. They may have been one source of economic and political grievances, just as other economic, political, and social structures were, but they were not necessary factors. In several respects, though, their presence affected the pattern of nationalism—the size and intensity of identity formation and protest. Because fewer Africans could be educated in settler colonies, nationalists were also fewer there and their organizational initiatives weaker. Denied opportunity more harshly in settler colonies, these nationalists were also likely to harbor a greater proportion of social concerns in their alloy of grievances. In these colonies, nationalists were also more willing to cooperate with masses of peasants and workers who had not developed nationalist identities, but were willing to resist. Peasants and workers (per capita) willing to revolt were also more numerous, as there was more occasion for their misery. Generally, the national and social struggle converged greatest in the settler colonies.

The appearance of resistance in settler colonies was also likely to come later than in colonies that were similarly situated economically and socially, largely because protest was much more restricted by the colonial government, making it more difficult for anticolonialists to organize. The independence movements of East and Central Africa, then, came after those of West Africa. Finally, the transition to independence was much rougher and more violent in settler colonies. White Settlers deeply feared being outnumbered by Africans in an independent state; Africans were more likely to be militant where settlers were reluctant to compromise. It was in Kenya that Britain fought one of its few short wars for colonial independence. When Britain was granting independence and fostering a transition to African rule elsewhere, it failed to grant such concessions to Southern Rhodesia, which instead unilaterally seceded from the British Empire in 1965. Settlers, then, influenced the pattern of nationalist resistance, although they were not necessary for its occurrence.

Conclusions

The influence of the middle class, the oppression of the middle class, the growth of the middle class, the grievances of peasants and proletariats, changing economic fortunes, the political structures of oppression, and the injustices that white settlers inflicted all helped to form nationalists and to elicit the protest that precipitated the British Cabinet's decision for colonial independence. Other critics of colonialism, the United States, the Soviet Union, and nonaligned states, sought the decline of the British Empire in part for strategic and economic reasons. Together, class, political structures, and the international balance of power account for an important part of the pressures to which the British Cabinet responded by granting its colonies independence. But I argue that they supplement, not supplant, that they assist, not obviate, the influence of ideas. Ideas, performing the complex logic of reputational social power, were both autonomous and efficacious in bringing about the British portion of this revolution in sovereignty. They explain Britain's momentous decision, and the peaceful pattern of its implementation.

The case for the reputational social power of ideas becomes even stronger through a contrast with an altogether different empire, with different features. It is one whose established ideas were closed to criticism of its colonialism, where ideas thus had to translate their influence into the bloody use of arms. The French Empire is the subject of chapter 12. Here again, I aim to demonstrate the influence of ideas, their autonomy and their efficacy, although this time through a very different kind of social power.

TWELVE

THE FALL OF GREATER FRANCE

FRANCE GAVE UP the bulk of its colonial empire in the late 1950s and early 1960s, its possessions in West and Equatorial Africa, in Madagascar, and in Algeria. By the mid-1950s, it had granted independence to Indochina, Tunisia, and Morocco, a prelude to the later crescendo. In the timing and sweep of its releases, France was a grand partner to Britain in creating the new constitution of colonial independence. France, I want to argue, also lost its empire through the same crisis of pluralism, the same surge of anticolonial ideas after World War II, the same contradiction between revolutionary ideas and the norm of colonial rule, that defeated Britain. That ideas brought colonial independence, France corroborates.

How ideas brought colonial independence, though, could hardly have been more different in the two empires. In comparison to France's experience, Britain's release of empire was a massive technical problem, carried out through stops and starts, through negotiations, not always careful or controlled, accompanied to be sure by shootings and by dispatches of troops and police, but in the end accomplishing a gradual and smooth relinquishment. France, by contrast, let go of its empire in a histrionic seizure, through the sensational drama of long and severe wars in Algeria and Indochina, the killing of thousands in Madagascar, skirmishes in Tunisia and Morocco, and through the collapse and rebuilding of its very constitutional republic. In these opposite experiences were diverging forms of the social power of ideas. Ideas defeated the British Empire through a thousand irritations, an outbreak of itchy protests and incidents. Ideas slew the French Empire; they forced it into a bloody and politically convulsive collapse.

In 1962 the British Foreign Secretary, the Earl of Home, wrote a memorandum to the British Cabinet recommending against pulling out of the United Nations Committee of Seventeen, where nonaligned states were heavily criticizing Britain for its slowness in freeing its colonies. He contrasted Britain's plight with France's. A few years earlier, he noted, France had ignored UN criticisms of its war with Algeria. France, he pointed out, faced neither the domestic criticism or Commonwealth criticism that Britain faced, and was prepared to disregard the reproach of the United States and the criticism of the UN majority.[1] He recommended against

Britain showing similar disdain. A surrounding storm of protest would undermine Britain's interests.

The Earl of Home's enduring insight is France's divergent approach to anticolonial criticism. Behind this approach was a very different established ideal. France's aim in Algeria and its disdain for international criticism reflected its vision of assimilating its colonies into a Greater France. To challenge this ideal, far more hostile to colonial independence than Britain's ideal of gradual self-government, champions of anticolonial ideas could not apply the reputational power of rhetorical criticism: France did not espouse a justification, or maintain a reputation, to which they could appeal. Instead, anticolonialists—colonial nationalists in particular—had to translate their ideas into the currency of arms, forcing France to pay the high price of war for empire. It was ultimately the cost of fighting a rebellion in Algeria, the constitutional collapse and threat of a right-wing generals' coup in France itself, that brought the renunciation of empire under the leadership of Charles de Gaulle. In France, the precipitate of anticolonial ideas mixed with a different established ideal, yielding a very different kind of imperial demise.

That colonial incorporation was France's established ideal, that colonial nationalists translated revolutionary anticolonial ideas into arms, that France was unresponsive to anticolonial criticism, that the crisis of the contradiction between revolutionary ideas and established ideas brought about the end of the French Empire, are all claims that I seek to defend in this chapter. The role of ideas in the French case, just as in the British case, is also subject to structural skepticism. Perhaps it was changes in France's relative economic and strategic power that brought it to give up its colonies; perhaps France had a deeper economic and strategic interest in its colonies than Britain, explaining its tighter grip on empire; perhaps the anticolonial ideas that challenged the French Empire were the product of the economic and political interests of its colonists. All of this skepticism, I will seek to answer.

That France did not relinquish its empire until anticolonial nationalists wielded the power of armed resistance is an argument that ideas brought the occurrence of colonial independence. That France's imperial ideal meant that resistance would take the form of arms is an argument about the pattern of colonial independence. The two arguments reinforce each other, as in the British case. My argument about the French case, though, is generally simpler. The social power of armed ideas is more direct, less complex, than the reputational social power of ideas; there are fewer linkages to describe and defend. I tell the story, then, more briefly—in one chapter, rather than three.[2]

The Uncompromising but Unsuccessful Project of Greater France

That colonies were not destined for independence, but were to remain a part of a greater French Union in which the government of France remained sovereign, was the French established ideal of empire, the ideal that France espoused in its public justifications. Colonists were taught the French language and French ideas; eventually, they would become French citizens. France centralized its colonial administration in Paris with the aim of governing all aspects of colonial life, unlike Britain, which preferred to govern through locals whenever possible, and with more limited ambitions. Unlike British colonists, French colonists were represented in the French National Assembly, not in proportion to their numbers, especially in the case of indigenous Africans and Asians, but nevertheless incorporated into a greater political whole. A classical argument of the French ideal was that individual colonists could come to enjoy greater rights and economic benefits of being citizens in a greater French Empire, but that as groups they would be denied provisions for governing themselves, much less independence.

This ideal was widely held in France, supported by a wide swath of the political spectrum between World War II and the end of the Fourth Republic in 1958, indeed by all parties except for the Communists. France pursued the policy by tightening its imperial grip only further after World War II, finally deciding to release its colonies only after first seeking to suppress nationalism militarily, then paying a dear price for this suppression: defeat in two long, destructive wars, and the collapse of its constitutional republic over domestic divisions that resulted from war. Unlike Britain, France did not react to unrest in its colonies through rapid concessions of self-government. Its policy, rather, was what Raymond Aron described in 1957: "Once indecision and unauthorized acts together had brought on the explosion, the official slogan became 'hold on' (just as at Verdun)."[3] In not every case did France fight a war where it eventually granted independence. To its West and Equatorial African colonies, it conceded freedom smoothly. Even here, though, France's forfeiture was a reaction to military rout and political collapse, an initiative toward a more successful policy in the wake of defeat elsewhere.

France's ideal of incorporation and assimilation—which I will herein call Greater France—finds its roots in its late-nineteenth-century imperial explosion, its vast expansion of its empire in Africa and Asia.[4] French nationalism, whether or not it was a central cause of this imperialism, was closely associated with the ideal. As cabinets, legislators, armies, missionaries, and businessmen commanded and carried out the carving up of Africa and Asia, they spoke of the greatness of the French nation, the importance of empire to a Great Power's status, and the need to recover the prestige lost in France's defeat to Germany in 1871. They also voiced the humanitarian ideal of improving the conditions of the inhabitants of these stretches, bringing them civilization. Both nationalism and humanitarianism were cast French. Asians and Africans were to be taught not merely self-government and "civilized" Western ways, but were to be given French civilization and, most importantly, the French language. As historians Christopher Andrew and A. S. Kanya-Forstner describe it, "Natives fortunate enough to find themselves under French rule were potential Frenchmen destined for full integration into the universal values of French civilization, irrespective of colour, creed, or cultural traditions."[5] The most enthusiastic advocates of these ideals were several small citizens' organizations, known as the "Colonial Party," and dedicated to the spread of empire. Although they never numbered more than 10,000 before 1914, they lobbied and shaped the thinking of top government officials, including colonial officials.[6]

After World War I, French officials, like British officials, softened their nationalist appeals and strengthened the humanitarian justification for empire—this, in response to criticism of colonialism implied in the formation of the League of Nations mandate system and voiced strongest by U.S. President Woodrow Wilson. Parallel to Lord Lugard's tract announcing a mission of colonial development in Britain, former colonial official Albert Saurrat wrote the widely read *La Mise en valeur des colonies* (*The Development of the Colonies*), with roughly the same message.[7] In colonial circles, some officials began to speak of "association," rather than "assimilation," suggesting the development of limited government institutions for colonial peoples, but even this notion was much less progressive than the British ideal of gradual self-government.[8] Voices in the Socialist Party espoused a notion of gradual self government much like the British one, which proclaimed independence as an eventual goal for the colonies. But gradual self-government never became an officially proclaimed ideal. Greater France remained central to France's official imperial purpose.

After World War II, French officials brought the Greater France ideal right into the heart of their justifications for colonialism. Like Britain, France began a program of economic development in many of its colonies after World War II, but it was loath to yield political concessions, usually doing so when organized rebellion had taken place or was imminent, and, until the end, hoping to achieve lasting imperial stability. France offered no rationale of gradual self-government, stated no end of independence. The French ideal was closely associated with French national greatness and status, articulated most famously by Charles de Gaulle. Not everyone voiced the ideal. Communists and the left wing of the Socialist Party did in fact advocate colonial independence—of a gradual British sort—and criticized France's colonial wars; but they were a minority. The vast majority of the public and the National Assembly was part of what scholars have called a French "colonial consensus," a shared ideal of empire.[9]

In the aftermath of World War II, as the British were granting independence to India, Pakistan, Burma, and Ceylon, and negotiating political progress with the Gold Coast and Nigeria, the French began a war with Indochina, killed thousands in Madagascar, passed the Statute of Algeria that reformed Algeria's assembly but brought little political progress for Algerians, and shortly afterward rigged the elections to this assembly. Charles de Gaulle, leading the Free French Resistance during the war, had set the tone. Under his inspiration, high French colonial officials met at Brazzaville, Congo, in early 1944 to make recommendations about colonial affairs to a future Constituent Assembly, aiming both to preserve empire and win the colonies' fealty. The war had proved the economic and strategic value of the colonies, but also their vitality to the status of a great empire that would soon need to recover from humiliating defeat. The conference agreed upon reforms, including economic ones such as development through investment, education, and the abolition of enforced labor, and political ones such as doing away with native legal codes, extending French civil liberties to the empire, increasing collaboration of metropolitan officials with native elites, allowing native representation in the French Constituent Assembly, and creating a "French Federation," which would include representatives of the colonists as well as France, and would promote the welfare of the colonies. But note also the preface to the conference report: "The ends of the colonizing work accomplished by France in the colonies rule out any autonomy, any possibility of evolution outside the French bloc of the empire; the eventual establishment, even in the future, of self-government in the colonies is out of the question."[10] Colonial Commissioner René Pleven explained the rationale:

> In greater colonial France there are neither peoples to free nor racial discriminations to abolish. There are populations who feel French and who want to take, and to whom France wishes to give, a larger and larger part in the life and democratic institutions of the French community . . . but who do not expect to know any other independence than the independence of France."[11]

The end goal for de Gaulle and his colonial officials was not that colonies would be independent, but that they would be French.

The desire of the French to retain France's empire after World War II was linked deeply with their desire to recover the prestige they had lost from their defeat to Hitler. During the war, de Gaulle had lectured U.S. President Roosevelt thus:

> I know that you are preparing to aid France materially, and that aid will be invaluable to her. But it is in the political realm that she must recover her vigor, her self-reliance, and consequently, her role. How can she do this if she is excluded from the organization of the great world powers and their decisions, if she loses her African and Asian territories—in short, if the settlement of the war definitively imposes upon her the psychology of the vanquished?[12]

In Britain, there were conservatives such as Churchill for whom empire was a part of the national heritage and greatness, but these were the sentiments of one party, and increasingly one wing of one party, not an ideal whose reach extended well into the left side of the political spectrum, as it did in France. Neither, of course, had Britain just been defeated in war.[13]

Immediately after World War II, the provisional government decreed many of the liberal reforms promised at Brazzaville, including colonial representation at the planned Constituent National Assembly.[14] Yet in the 1947 Constitution of the Fourth Republic, which set the colonies' status in the new French regime, there was little to please progressive liberals (Communists and left-wing Socialists), despite their advocacy of a more visionary document. The constitution turned the French Empire into a "French Union" in which colonies would have representatives in their local assemblies and in the French National Assembly, but the makeup of the local assemblies, like all important colonial affairs, was to be determined by the National Assembly, while in the National Assembly, colonial representation was far from proportionate. There was no mention of progress toward self-government or future independence.[15]

The spirit of this constitution was being realized in France's contemporary policy toward Indochina. Before the end of the war, on March 24, 1945, de Gaulle's provisional government declared that after Japan's surrender, Indochina (the five countries of Tonkin, Annam, Cochin China, Laos, and Cambodia) would be formed into a federation ruled by a governor-general and a Council of State appointed in Paris, along with a local elected Assembly—a formula for continued French sovereignty. Although a March sixth agreement between Paris and Viet Minh resistance leader Ho Chi Minh hinted at greater autonomy for an emerging Vietnam, both the terms of the Fourth Republic Constitution and the outbreak of war in November 1946 overrode this accord and committed France firmly to defending empire. It was Socialist Prime Ministers Leon Blum and Paul Ramadier who set this course in late 1946 and early 1947. In the words of Ramadier, "Liberty within the French Union: This liberty is the foundation of future relations between France and the people of Indochina. It has no limits but those imposed by the membership of these territories in the French Union."[16] France would pursue this course, fighting to preserve its empire against the guerrilla army of Ho Chi Minh, refusing also to negotiate greater autonomy with non-Communist Bao Dai, until it suffered defeat at Dien Bien Phu in 1954. At that time, it granted independence to a partitioned Vietnam.[17]

In Algeria, too, France flirted with liberalism under the provisional government, but then asserted its sovereignty during the Fourth Republic. In 1947, the National Assembly passed the Statute of Algeria, setting the terms of sovereignty in Algeria. Rejecting a Communist proposal to grant the Algerians greater representation as a way station to independence within the French Union (an arrangement akin to the British Commonwealth), and rejecting a somewhat liberal Socialist proposal that also gave the virtually disenfranchised Algerian Muslims greater representation, the Assembly passed a statute that gave the Muslims only limited representation and kept power over basic economic, political, and administrative affairs in Paris. During the next year, Paris, represented by Socialist Governor-General Marcel-Edmond Naegelen and Interior Minister Jules Moch, rigged elections to the Algerian assembly and refused to implement many of the statute's reforms.[18] Paris's policy remained firm, while Muslims organized politically and began terrorism. By 1954, the conflict escalated into war, one that would not finally end until France granted Algeria its independence in 1962. For France finally to change its policy, it took the tumultuous events of 1958. The fall of the Fourth Republic had complex causes, but chief among them were divisions over the colonial war in Algeria and the near generals' coup that was provoked by its prosecution. Only the return of de Gaulle, with his remarkable prestige and the strengthened presidency of the Fifth Republic, could bring about a de-escalation of the war in Algeria and independence in other colonies, while maintaining domestic stability in France. It took a war and a constitutional crisis, both the product of the armed power of anticolonial ideas, for France to change course.

In West and Equatorial Africa, France introduced limited reforms following the Second World War, extending the franchise and African representation, but it also sent its police to suppress dissent in the late 1940s and early 1950s. In the end, though, France's policy was quite different here. Under the government of Edgar Faure, it extended significant privileges to these colonies in the *Loi Cadre* reforms of 1956, providing a universal franchise and stronger representation in the National Assembly in Paris, but still maintaining French control over foreign policy, defense policy, internal security, and key economic policy, and still showing no intention of allowing independence. Two years later, de Gaulle sharply accelerated this policy, extending independence to these regions. There was never an armed insurrection here; France never fought a war here. Even de Gaulle did not grant the Equatorial and West Africans independence immediately. In 1958, he tried to convince them to remain within a "Communauté," in which France would still decide matters of foreign policy, defense, economic planning, and raw materials policy. At first, each of the equatorial colonies except for Guinea voted to join the federation, but then, over the next couple of years, opted for independence within a French Union, an arrangement like the British Commonwealth that would give them full sovereignty.[19]

It is not clear whether France would have extended independence to these colonies if it had not been for the coup and installation of de Gaulle. In granting the *Loi Cadre* reforms, France was adopting a much more deeply reformist approach than it had ever had before. It could be that this was a stage toward independence, just as Britain often conceded significant constitutional reforms in bringing its colonies closer to independence. The decision made first by President Edgar Faure to grant these reforms was part of a new approach to colonial affairs that he and the previous prime minister Pierre Mendès-France shared, one that accompanied the pullout of troops in Indochina, Tunisia, and Morocco (but not Algeria). There is little evidence, though, that either Faure or Mendès-France intended to grant these colonies independence. Faure's and Mendès-France's turn away from armed suppression (except, again, for Algeria) was itself motivated by a conviction that France was overextended, that it had sent troops to too many locales at once, and that the military policy was not proving successful. It was de Gaulle, the architect of France's embrace of colonial freedom, who actually granted them independence, and even he did so only after first trying to convince them to remain in the "Communauté." France's change broadly followed its pattern of extending reform or independence only after attempting, and being frustrated by, military suppression—the social power of armed ideas.[20]

Tunisia and Morocco, the other Maghreb states, both gained their independence in 1956—also without a major war and before de Gaulle's accession, but only after armed resistance movements had formed and France had sent troops. Though not wars on the scale of Indochina and Algeria, these experiences were closer to the broad French pattern than to the British one. In the later 1940s, France showed little willingness to concede reforms in these colonies, and installed the reactionary General Juin as governor-general in Morocco. It was only after both sides had formed and deployed armed movements, after the intense terrorism of resistance forces and the counterterrorism of French settlers, that the French governments under Mendès-France and Faure even considered undertaking the negotiations that led to independence. Independence here was a part of the Faure/Mendès-France turn. This turn, again, was motivated by frustration with armed suppression, as it was in virtually every other French colony after World War II.

The Upholders of the Colonial Consensus

"Greater France" was French official policy from the Second World War until de Gaulle's presidency. Successive Cabinets carried it out consistently (with a slightly more reformist version under the Mendès-France and Faure governments), and solid majorities in the National Assembly consistently supported it—this despite the complex party structure, the constantly shifting coalitions, and the frequently revolving governments of the Fourth Republic. The reason for this consistency, quite simply, was that the established ideal was widely held, by a significant portion of the Socialist Party on rightward. The contrast with Britian is clear. There, a Labour Party that grew opposed to colonialism during the 1950s prevented any similar colonial consensus and provided a strong source of domestic criticism.

The Socialists formed the linchpin of this ideal, for it was their dissent from the consensus that could conceivably destroy its force. The Communists advocated the end of empire, but they left the government in 1947, no longer to return. The Socialists, by contrast, often participated in Cabinet coalitions, and when they did so they upheld the ideal. Exactly why they upheld the ideal is one of the lively debates in the scholarship on the end of the French Empire. One view, which blames the colonial wars on a weak constitutional system, claims that Socialists supported empire because, unwilling to join the Communists, they could only join a coalition with the right in order to share in governing. Colonial policy was thus hijacked by right-wing parties.[21] An opposing view claims, rather, that Socialists were committed to the colonial consensus by their very outlook, and supported empire prior to the demands of coalitional politics.[22]

What is at stake in this debate for a theory of ideas? If it were the case that the Socialists supported empire for opportunistic coalitional reasons, the width and depth of the ideal would be diminished, for here would be a party that adhered to it only weakly. Yet even then it would remain true that to the right of the Socialists, the ideal was strong enough to serve as the standard with which the Socialists would have to ally. But is the coalitional theory compelling? We must concede it some validity. In some respects, the Socialists were less enthusiastic about empire outside of power than they were in power. Between 1951 and 1956, when the Socialists did not take part in the Cabinet, they established connections with the liberal opposition forces to colonial rule in Tunisia, supported Mendès-France and Faure as they negotiated independence with Tunisia and Morocco, and, in several party platforms, advocated advances in political representation for Muslims in Algeria. By contrast, when they held the premiership or participated in the Cabinet, they supported imperial war.[23]

For several reasons, though, it is difficult to explain Socialist positions apart from the commitment of many Socialists to the Greater France ideal and the commitment of comparatively few to anticolonial ideas. Even when they were out of power, the Socialists spoke of economic and political advance, but were generally reluctant to use the terms "independence" or "secession," especially toward Algeria (although they indeed supported the Mendèsist policy on Tunisia and Morocco). Often, the party put forth the dual goals of "reform" and "order," colonial desiderata that were to guarantee empire's persistence. By 1955, three parliamentary factions on the issue of decolonization were apparent. First, there were the liberals, led by Alain Savary; second were the "nationalists," led by Max Lejeune, who had been condemning North African nationalism and any form of "separatism" since the early 1950s; and third was a middle faction, which might side with either of the other two. Even when out of power, the party was far from dominated by the colonial critics.[24]

The Socialists' positions while in power are also difficult to explain through coalitional dynamics. Before World War II, the party's stance in government was hardly one of ardent anti-imperialism; as far back as Juarès, it had advocated a nationalist policy of continuing empire, although also calling for progressive reforms.[25] Early after World War II, the party continued to emphasize the glory of empire.[26] As Socialists, the party spoke of Marxism, but it was, as Miles Kahler notes, a "pre-Leninist Marxism," one that included no ideal of self-determination and anticolonialism.[27] Socialists often spoke of empire using the same rhetoric as conservatives, as when Socialist Governor-General Naegelen insisted that whereas there would be no progress in Algeria for collective rights, there might be advances for individual rights.[28] Even before the Communists had disappeared from government in 1947, leaving them unavailable as coalition partners, the Socialist Party was well to the right of the Communists in its treatment of the Congress of Black Africans, its policy in Indochina, its position on the Statute of Algeria, and its support for the brutal repression of the Madagascar uprising in March and April 1947.[29] When Socialists held the premiership, they showed little propensity even to test the limits of coalition and steer either the party or France to a more reformist colonial policy. It was Socialist Premiers Blum and Ramadier who initiated armed repression in Indochina. The Socialist proposal for the Statute of Algeria was not far from the one that the Assembly adopted; the Socialists supported their fellow partisan Naegelen; and it was Socialist Premier Guy Mollet who abandoned a reformist policy in Algeria and increased the number of troops there from 200,000 to 500,000 in 1956 for "pacification."[30] During his tenure as premier, Mollet held tenaciously to a policy of crushing the Algerian rebellion, protecting French citizens, especially the *petits blancs*, advocating individual liberty over collective political rights, arguing that independence was "not a Socialist solution," allowing elections only once order had been restored, and in the meantime pushing social and economic reforms, not political ones—all key tenets of the Greater France ideal.[31]

Meanwhile, as long as the Socialists were participating in government, those in the party who did oppose empire rarely opposed colonial policy publicly in the National Assembly; their sentiments were never strong enough to break ranks. At one point, the liberal colonial faction attempted to rally the party against Mollet's war in Algeria, but got little response. Anticolonial sentiment was always of low salience in the Socialist Party: Whenever Socialists withdrew from Cabinets during the Fourth Republic, it was always over social and economic issues.[32] Critics who did voice dissent came from the party's rank and file at National Party Councils and Congresses, but even here, imperial opponents were a minority. At the height of the war in Algeria, only 30 percent of them supported anticolonial resolutions.[33]

The Socialists did much, both in and out of government and in and out of the premiership, to convert France's imperial ideal to policy, marshaling it on behalf of continuing empire—the norm of colonial rule. Socialist opponents of empire did little that was effective to oppose it, either. Part of the Socialists' net influence can be attributed to their desire to ally with parties to the right and form a governing coalition, and part of it to the party's electoral base among the French settlers in Algeria. But much of it can only be explained by the commitment of many Socialists to empire.

To the right of the Socialists were several Fourth Republic factions, all of which were staunch opponents of colonial independence. The staunchest were the Gaullists (from 1947, the Rassemblement du Peuple Français), who coupled empire with the prestige and independence of France. When de Gaulle himself left politics in 1952, they became even more devoted to empire. Even after the election of 1956, which they lost heavily, they generally remained hostile opponents to colonial independence—many, to the Fourth Republic regime itself—although there was a tiny faction of liberal Gaullists who advocated a negotiated resolution in Algeria. Meanwhile, de Gaulle became increasingly liberal on colonial issues from the time he left politics in 1952 to his three years of public silence beginning in 1955. When he returned in 1958, he was prepared to negotiate with the Front of National Liberation (FLN) in Algeria, and he would eventually agree to independence. His followers still needed to be converted, but most of them would come around under his urging. Only one force could lead the Gaullists to agree to the end of empire: de Gaulle.[34]

Aside from the Gaullists, conservatives ranging over several parties were generally consistent supporters of empire, especially toward Algeria. Less ideologically supportive of empire, but not a convinced opponent of it either, was the Radical Party. As a small party, it was a potential coalition

TABLE 12.1
Public Opinion Poll on Favored Solution for Algeria

Question	*Percentage*
Among the Three Following Solutions, Which Do You Favor for Algeria?	
Treat Algeria like a group of regular French departments; that is, that all inhabitants, Muslim or French, have rights equal to those of the French of France	36
Grant Algeria much internal autonomy, although keeping her within the French Republic	34
Grant Algeria complete independence; that is, abandon Algeria completely with a more or less long delay	18
No opinion expressed	12

Source: Sondages, Revue Française de l'Opinion Publique 1 (1957):41, published by the Institut Français d'Opinion Publique, Paris; reprinted in Tony Smith, *The French Stake in Algeria, 1945–62* (Ithaca: Cornell University Press, 1978), 151.

partner for other parties wanting to form a majority, and thus more flexible in its ideology. It was the Radicals Mendès-France and Faure who shifted France's policy somewhat by pulling out of Indochina, Tunisia, and Morocco. French historian Jean-Baptiste Duroselle describes Faure and Mendès-France as part of a more pragmatic strain in French politics, one committed to national grandeur, and more prone to emphasize economic expansion and the preservation of military security. Such a party could support colonial independence when holding colonies became extremely costly.[35]

What about the political landscape beyond parties—public opinion, voters? Is there any particular evidence that they, too, were a part of the colonial consensus? Colonial issues were never highly salient among the French public, as among the British public, until substantial numbers of French troops began to fight in Algeria. It is evidence for the public consensus on empire, then, that as France was increasing its armed commitment to Algeria in 1957, solid majorities supported maintaining political leadership in Algeria in some form, as the public opinion poll in table 12.1 shows.

Besides the Communists, the only exception to this consensus was a stratum of French intellectuals who grew increasingly critical of the war in Algeria after 1956, when reports of French torture began to appear in public. France had a lively tradition of "engaged" intellectuals, commenting on public events, but except for those who identified with communism or the extreme left, these intellectuals generally did not call for independence in Algeria until the end of the 1950s. Some supported France's war there enthusiastically, while a middle layer was reformist, calling for France to act more justly, but not to relinquish Algeria. The turn of more intellectuals against the war itself in the late 1950s detracted significantly from the colonial consensus, and took away popular support for the war. But this turn did not occur until roughly the time of the attempted coup and the return of de Gaulle.[36]

Domestic criticism of empire in France was much weaker than it was in Great Britain, and support for empire was much stronger. The British Labour Party became officially critical of empire during the 1950s, and was united in its opposition to it, whereas the French Socialists supported the empire when they were in power and were divided over the issue when out of power. Not only was support for empire wider in France, but the very concept of "empire" represented something far more ambitious, far more muscular, something that was supposed to last a lot longer than the "empire" in Britain. In Britain, anticolonial ideas opposed the established ideal but also could appeal to it. In France, anticolonial ideas proposed something altogether different than the established ideal; here, there was much more tension and much more friction between the two notions. More widely supported and more intransigent, the ideal of Greater France was much more difficult for anticolonialists to crack than was the British ideal of gradual self-government.

Anticolonial Ideas: Effective Only When Armed

With a different established ideal of empire, France reacted very differently to anticolonial criticism. As the width of the French colonial consensus implies, the French Cabinet had far fewer, far less powerful domestic anticolonial critics than Britain. It showed little sympathy for international critics, either—the United States, the United Nations, and others. Without a goal of eventual national independence for France's colonies, clenching its perpetual empire as a plank of its national greatness, the French Cabinet brooked little sympathy for those who reproved its unprogressive character. French colonial nationalists, too, could not rely upon rhetoric, protest, and mild unrest as such nationalists had done to impel Britain. Only through arms could they, did they, bring the French government to change its course.

The International Context

Virtually every major historian of the period agrees that a major theme of French foreign policy during this period was resistance to direction from the United States or the United Nations.[37] After being defeated in World War II, France strove to assert its independence and regain its Great Power status. Empire here was key. De Gaulle rallied French prestige after World War II; Gaullists continued the cause and found the support of other conservative parties, of many if not most Socialists, and of a large majority of the public.[38]

Prestige demanded that France could never subordinate itself to the United States. France would develop no "special relationship" to America, and would scantly heed its criticism. An allied rivalry between France and the United States began in World War II through mutual enmity between Roosevelt and de Gaulle, and it continued throughout colonial independence. Political scientist Alfred Grosser describes as a "reluctant choice" France's decision to ally with the United States and the Atlantic Alliance. "From one end to the other, from 1947–49 until 1958, the element of anti-Americanism, springing from a feeling of dependence, seems undeniable to me. This anti-Americanism grew stronger with the impression of greater dependence upon the United States," wrote Grosser.[39] France did join the Atlantic Alliance, but it fought the Americans on several postwar issues—the Marshall Plan, the European Defense Community, the nuclear shield, and the giving of American money for the war in Indochina.[40] Britain, losing less prestige in the war and having less to regain, relied more heavily upon the United States for its security, and yet worried less about dependence.

As for communism, the French regarded it as a threat, but a different sort of threat than the British perceived. Not so much as competitors in a global contest for reputation in the eyes of the nonaligned world, the Soviets were seen as the source of subversion within the French colonies, and for that matter within the French Republic itself. Quite often in the war in Algeria, French politicians would appeal to the public and each other by pointing out the threat of communism in Algeria.[41] The effect was the exact opposite of pressure for colonial independence. Communist insurrection, a threat to the empire's integrity, to its established ideal, was instead to be militarily crushed.

France also shunned criticism from the United Nations. As historian D. Bruce Marshall claims, France saw the UN Charter, and especially the UN Trusteeship system, as deep challenges to the principle of colonial authority. De Gaulle believed that "like all ideologies, [the UN Trusteeship system] was simply a facade meant to conceal the true interests of its sponsors, whom he suspected of harboring 'malevolent intentions toward the French Union.' "[42] A French colonial minister, Giacobbi, had even harsher words:

> [The ideas of a trusteeship system and a mandate system] are ideas that are current in the press. The government attaches no more importance to them than it ought; but the government owes it to itself to say that the territories that have been shaped, civilized, enriched [fécondés] by the blood and the

> sweat of its children are out of the question and could not in any way become the object of other attentions than those which emanate from French sovereignty, which intend to exercise themselves for the good of all those who live in those territories.[43]

The prerogatives of French sovereignty that Giacobbi described, France's view of itself as the "patron of civilization" within its empire, entirely contradicted the UN's view of colonies—that they were somewhere in between dependent colonies and independent states, and that their progress toward statehood was to be a matter for international oversight.[44]

France lived its attitude toward the United Nations during the Algerian conflict. Britain, though irritated by the UN's criticism, decided again and again to avoid a walkout or anything that would appear altogether to shun the United Nations. France walked out or refused to attend on several occasions. From 1952 onward, France would not sit in the United Nations whenever that body discussed questions dealing with France's possessions in the Mahgreb. The French delegation walked out in 1955 when a resolution against France's role in Algeria was passed, and it subsequently sought to shun discussions of Algeria.[45] Such action would make little sense if France was concerned about its reputation in the same way that Britain was.

The Colonial Context

Efficacious anticolonial ideas came only from the colonies, and were only efficacious when armed. In France, as in Britain, it was the social power of colonists that sparked the chain of events leading to independence. In French colonies, revolutionary ideas were behind this social power, and were the force that brought about the revolution. Here, too, the European idea converted colonists into nationalists; here, too, it was nationalist converts who were behind the effective social power. In France, as in Britain, ideas that arose in the colonies led to the occurrence of colonial independence.

That French colonists resorted to arms, though, made the French experience vastly different in character. In all of the French colonies, anticolonial ideas spread, and in all of the major ones except for West Africa, they turned into armed insurrection. By this, I mean organized fighting forces, not rioting mobs or demonstrating protesters. In response, France sent its own troops to these colonies, fought drawn-out wars and small skirmishes, but eventually granted independence, usually after its military efforts had been frustrated. The British, by contrast, faced rebellions only in Kenya and Malaya, and put down both of them rather easily. In no case was organized insurrection the precipitant that led the British to yield independence.

French colonists initiated armed conflict because they became convinced that France would not compromise with any of their demands for political progress. Their decision to take up arms reciprocated France's intransigent ideal. Indeed, the disposition to fight was rarely inherent in the ideas of French colonial nationalists. Rather, they took up arms only when France refused to mete out any significant portion of self-government. In almost all cases, resistance appeared or gained steam after France's initial round of refusals following World War II. This implies that there were possibilities for France to negotiate, that nationalists in French colonies might have settled in the short term for significant concessions short of independence, and that had France's approach been similar to Britain's, so could its colonies' transition to independence have been similar, too.

In each colony to which France granted independence, educational, religious, and wartime experiences—circumstances of reflection—led colonists to convert to nationalist ideas or Western ideas of political progress, just as in the British colonies. Similar to nationalists in British colonies, French colonial nationalists also played a key leadership role in organizing armed resistance or, in the case of French West Africa, social protest.

In the Maghreb colonies, Algeria, Tunisia, and Morocco, European political ideas infiltrated earlier than anywhere else in Africa. They fused with Islamic ideas, emphasizing the concept of *asabiyya*, or community solidarity, among Muslims, which had also made its way into the Maghreb from the Middle East via Egypt. Since educated Islamic men in the latter areas were much more numerous than Christian intellectuals in British Africa and French West Africa, nationalism could better mix with religion, and thus spread more widely through it. By the early 1900s, many Muslims had accepted the European political form; through European state institutions, the old community of Islam would be restored. At this stage, though, the Muslims envisioned developing these institutions under European tutelage.[46]

In Algeria, a few Muslims began to take on more radical ideas in the 1920s. They received them in Paris, in part from the French Communist Party, which encouraged the African Muslims, but with which they would later break in 1933. The leader of the African Muslims was Messali Hajd, who launched the Etoile Nord-Africaine party to advance a program that called for workers' rights and Islamic defiance against French assimilation. Most politically aware Muslims of the interwar period, however, were liberal reformers, desiring greater access to Algerian political institutions, better representation for Muslims, obligatory education for Muslims, and abrogation of laws requiring Muslims to renounce their religion before becoming French citizens (although this cause was one over which liberals would split). Most of these liberals were bourgeois and were among the few educated Muslim Algerians, having received a secondary or college education in French-run schools between roughly 1915 and 1925. In these schools, they adopted French ideas of equality. At the end of World War I, about 1,000 of these liberals, practicing middle-class professions such as law, medicine, and teaching, formed the Young Algerians, an organization that advocated reform. In 1931, a separate, more religiously oriented liberal group, the Algerian Association of Ulma, also formed, this one reflecting the conviction of many Algerian liberals that theirs was a nation with Islamic roots, whose future would lie in a destiny separate from France.[47]

During the 1930s, many of the bourgeois youth completing secondary and college educations came to hold more radical versions of European ideas of equality. By the end of the decade, many had joined the new Parti du Peuple Algérien (PPA), which formed in 1937 and came to advocate independence in the Manifesto of the Algerian People in 1943. Their radicalism was due in part to the failure of previous liberals to secure any meaningful reforms, and in part to certain French refusals such as the salient failure in 1938 of the Leon Blum government to pass the Blum-Viollette proposal for relaxing the renunciation of Islam as a requirement for French citizenship. Still more radical were other Algerian Muslims, who first became convinced that revolution was the only means of forcing the French to budge. Most of these eventual revolutionaries were lower in social class than their bourgeois fellow activists and generally had less education. Their strong common experience was serving in the Algerian army during World War II. Fighting with French soldiers, and generally treated respectfully, they then became disillusioned upon returning to civilian society to find themselves again subordinated.[48]

Each of the above groups of converts to nationalism, in their differing levels of radicalism, would be organizers and leaders of nationalist resistance. It was nationalists who led the Etoile Nord-Africaine, nationalists who led the PPA, and nationalists who formed the Friends of the Manifesto in 1944, which called for Algeria to become an immediately autonomous federated republic. It was also nationalists who formed the Mouvement pour le Triomphe des Libertés Démocratiques (MTLD), out of which formed the clandestine paramilitary group, the Organisation Spéciale (OS) in 1947. In 1954, a minority of these politically active Algerian Muslims launched an uprising that would turn into the eight-year struggle for independence. Much more so than movements in West Africa or even Kenya, this struggle took on a social character. The rebellion became a popular movement involving the peasantry, the proletariat, and the petty bourgeoisie. Resistance had indeed developed this breadth as early as 1945, when uprisings broke out among crowds of thousands in Algiers, Oran, Guélm, and Sétif. As was the case in British Africa and India, though, even this popular resistance was coordinated and instigated by nationalist leaders, whose views had been formed in schools, in the army, and through religious influences.[49]

It was not until 1952 that Algerian Muslims formed an armed guerrilla movement, under Ben Bella, which would take the field two years later. They did not turn to military resistance until the French had again and again refused to concede political progress or even negotiate; even then, only a minority of politically active Algerian Muslims initially took up arms in the struggle. In May 1945, French police fired upon protesting crowds in Algiers, Oran, Guélm, and Sétif, arresting and killing thousands. Nine years of nationalist party professions and demands followed, all of which France answered by rejection and repression, its French National Assembly passing only the thinly generous Statute of Algeria. Eight years of fighting ensued; France finally granted Algeria independence in 1962.[50] During the same period, by contrast, Britain had granted independence to India, Burma, and Ceylon, and was close to granting it to the Gold Coast and Nigeria.

In Tunisia and Morocco, nationalist identities formed through a closely parallel path. In the early 1920s, there arose a group of bourgeois liberals advocating reform, liberals who had been exposed to many of the same influences as Algeria's liberals. They formed the Liberal Constitutional Party, also known as the Destour. In the 1930s, a less moderate constitutional party, the Néo-Destour, formed under the guidance of Habib Bourguiba and other nationalists. During the 1930s, an alliance between the national struggle and the social struggle, somewhat along the lines of the one in Algeria, also began to take shape. Tunisian workers had founded a trade union in 1924, which managed to survive into the 1930s, when it allied with the Néo-Destour party in protesting colonial injustices. In 1937, there was a general strike in Tunis and widespread resistance to colonial rules and regulations. In Morocco, too, proto-parties urging reform emerged, beginning in 1933. Most prominent was the Action du Peuple, under the guidance of nationalists whose identities formed through Muslim and Western influences. In urban areas, working-class protest arose, as well as protest against French efforts to stamp out the influence of Islam. The year 1937 was, in historian Basil Davidson's words, a "highpoint in convergence between bourgeois nationalists and urban masses."[51]

In both Tunisia and Morocco, the level of social protests increased throughout the 1940s and into the 1950s. Bourguiba's Néo-Destour party grew in numbers and strength, and allied closely with a federation of Tunisian trade unions. An important moment was the decision of the Bey of Tunis, the major Muslim leader in Tunisia, to grant support to the Néo-Destour in 1947, giving the party added legitimacy in Muslim eyes. By the late 1940s, several general strikes and demonstrations resulted in

French dispatches of troops. In 1952, France disbanded the Néo-Destour party and imprisoned Bourguiba. With nationalist leaders in prison, a guerrilla movement of 2,500 peasants sprang up and began an armed struggle that would bring in over 70,000 French troops. Like nationalists elsewhere, Bourguiba was wary of allying too closely with peasants, but it turned out that their rebellion worked to his advantage without any bargaining on his part. In 1954, the French decided to set Bourguiba free and negotiate independence, extricating themselves from the conflict and allowing Bourguiba to negotiate without the help of peasant leaders.[52]

In Morocco, political activist groups who strongly emphasized Muslim ideals, the Istiqlal, grew up in the early 1940s, and like the Néo-Destour, collaborated with trade unions. They also benefited from the support of Islam, particularly that of the Sultan Mohamed V. A guerrilla army of peasants took up arms in 1955, eliciting at first French troops, but then resulting in negotiations for independence, which was achieved in 1956. In both Tunisia and Morocco, it was only after French refusals to compromise that colonialists took up arms; it was only after they took up arms that France agreed to negotiate.[53]

In Madagascar, two political parties—the Mouvement Démocratique pour le Renouveau Malgache (MRDM) and the Parti des Désinhérités de Madagascar—formed after World War II, and were led by Western-educated nationalists. By 1946, the MRDM was advocating a referendum on Madagascar's political status. The French colonial minister, Marius Moutet, cabled the high commissioner to "fight the MRDM by every means." The Malagasies responded to France's complete rejection of compromise with increased resistance, and by 1947, a rebellion. France silenced it. French reports at the time recorded 80,000 to 90,000 killed; later French figures reported 11,000 dead.[54] Independence in Madagascar diverged from the pattern elsewhere in that it did not happen until long after the resistance leaders had been imprisoned or killed, the fighting had died down, and France had found leaders with whom it could collaborate closely. The pattern of French refusal and colonial armed response, however, rang true.

In Indochina, nationalism and armed resistance appeared much earlier. Ho Chi Minh had formed a substantial Communist Party by the 1930s, after having been educated in Paris. By the end of World War II, his army had won substantial gains, capturing Hanoi and then declaring independence on September 2, 1945. It is plausible, however, that the French and Ho Chi Minh could have reached an acceptable agreement upon Vietnamese independence within some form of French Union around this time. During 1945, the government in Paris showed its willingness to negotiate with the Viet Minh, reaching agreement on an Indochinese Federation, in which Vietnam would be a "free state" with its own government, parliament, army, and treasury, while Paris was to control the foreign relations of the federation. The agreement did not last, however, partly because its terms were ambiguous and understood differently by Paris and Ho Chi Minh, but also because the French High Commissioner, Admiral d'Argenlieu, was determined to subvert it, which he did mainly by declaring Cochin China, a part of Vietnam that the Viet Minh claimed, an independent republic within Indochina. D'Argenlieu's approach was much more typical of France's general colonial policy after World War II. By 1946, Ho Chi Minh's troops and the French army were at war. The French continued to refuse to compromise; the 1947 Fourth Republic Constitution gave Vietnam even less than had the French concessions of 1945. Even Bao Dai, the noncommunist leader in South Vietnam, condemned the French Union's provisions as "purely French texts which do not concern us."[55] The war continued until 1954, when France, defeated at Dien Bien Phu, granted independence to a partitioned Vietnam.

French West and Equatorial African's independence, again, arrived differently, without armed insurrection or French surrender. Why France granted significant reforms in 1956, and then independence in 1958, can be explained by the initial policy turn of Radicals Mendès-France and Faure, by the more radical policy turn of de Gaulle, and by the comparatively mild resistance and greater willingness to cooperate of the African political leaders. Why nationalism was in turn less intense in French Black Africa than in the Maghreb is attributable to aspects of Black Africa's social structure, especially the lack of settler influence. But in French Black Africa, as in British West Africa, nationalist social protest still arose, and was also arguably the result of the influence of ideas.

There were few nationalists in French Black Africa during the interwar period, fewer than in the other French colonies. France exceptionally allowed political participation—parties, local representation—in Senegal, but elsewhere in the region it failed to allow such activity and censored protest. It was in Paris, then, that colonists from this region developed nationalist ideas. According to an official count in 1926, 1,813 of these colonists resided in France, although a similar count in 1932 showed that only 21 of these colonists were students in French universities (compared to 19 Malagasies and 695 Indo-Chinese).[56] Parisian black Africans encountered three nationalist influences. First was the influence of intellectuals from the Antilles (West Indies), whose doctrines were prenationalistic, but which called for the development of Africa along European lines. This was mild reformism, which regarded colonization as a necessary stage to African advancement. Second was the influence of the French Communist Party, which was advocating colonial independence even as early as the interwar period. Although by the early 1930s, most African intellectuals who belonged to the party had become disillusioned with their subordinate position in it, many of them formed their thinking in this context. Third, other African intellectuals formed their thinking separately, either in Parisian universities, or in anticolonialist leagues such as the Ligue pour la Défense de la Race Nègre. Many of these black Africans, even if they did not themselves become involved in the anticolonialist politics of the 1950s, influenced those who did. But before the war, and even well after the war, few of these nationalists spoke of independence, but only of political reforms.[57]

The first major organization for political advancement was the Parti Démocratique de la Côte d'Ivoire (PDCI), formed in 1946 by Felix Houphouët-Boigny, a wealthy planter and physician. The PDCI led grassroots campaigns against many colonial injustices, although it never advocated independence. Also in 1946, Houphouët-Boigny and others who had been influenced by the interwar nationalists formed the Rassemblement Démocratique Africain (RDA), a party that was to represent all of the French Black African territories in the National Assembly in Paris. The RDA allied with the Communists in the Assembly, not so much out of sympathy for communism—Houphouët-Boigny turned out to be rather conservative—but rather because the Communist Party was the only party that advocated colonial political progress. After the French Communists were maneuvered out of the government in Paris in 1947, the RDA became part of the permanent opposition and the French government began repressing it, killing a few dozen African leaders and arresting hundreds. All of this changed when, in 1951, Houphouët-Boigny bargained with Colonial Minister FranÇois Mitterand to abandon the RDA's alliance with the Communists in return for a general promise of progress toward greater political autonomy for West and Equatorial African colonies. Over the next eight years, African nationalists publicly demanded greater autonomy within a French federation. It was not until 1958 that they advocated independence.[58]

Up through the early 1950s, the French took a slow pace toward colonial progress. French police actively silenced too-rapid calls for progress or departures from the ideal of African citizenship in a Greater France, even though only a handful of Africans actually became French citizens. France, though, was willing to reverse course in Black Africa, offering the *Loi Cadre* reforms of 1956, then conceding independence under de Gaulle in 1958. Here, unlike elsewhere, it avoided war. I have argued that France's willingness to concede independence in Black Africa sprung from de Gaulle's change in course when he returned to power in 1958. This change was in turn a response to military defeat elsewhere, an attempt to avoid similar conflict here, all consonant with the French pattern.

Nationalists throughout the French colonies, then, exerted social power on behalf of their ideas through arms, with the exception of West and

Equatorial African nationalists, who protested similarly to their counterparts in most British colonies—through demonstration, organization into parties and lobbies, and occasional small riots. In the French case, like the British case, we also find evidence for ideas' power in shaping nationalist resistance by comparing the timing by which colonial nationalist movements developed. Where colonists were exposed earliest to experiences that led them to a European model of politics, and in those colonies where nationalist ideas attracted the most followers, nationalist struggles also came earliest. More colonists converted to nationalism in the interwar period in the Maghreb than in French Black Africa; movements for independence and the European idea of nationalism appeared earlier in the Maghreb as well. Within the Maghreb, there were also wider networks of nationalists and earlier independence movements in Algeria than in Tunisia and Morocco, also corresponding to the earlier arrival of European nationalism there. In Indochina, too, there was a larger, earlier stratum of nationalists than there was in Black Africa. Here, too, anticolonial opposition was intense and early; here, too, France fought a protracted war. France had been fighting noncommunist nationalist as well as Communist insurgents since the early thirties.[59]

In each of France's colonies, ideas shaped nationalists, and nationalists acted on ideas to mount protest, in most cases by organizing armed forces. Nationalists organized armed forces because France scorned their milder pleas. France scorned them out of its established imperial ideal of Greater France. In 1963, Hubert Deschamps, a former French colonial governor-general and then historian, delivered to a British audience a lecture given in memory of Lord Lugard. In it, he compared the French and the British approaches to empire and offered a tally of each of their results:

> Your system was based on the conviction that peoples are different, and on respect for their own ways. You believed in the possibility of allowing Africa to develop in the forms of the past and with people of the past. This separate existence was bound to lead to separation later. Even if you did not see it consciously, centrifugal movement was the logical consequence of your premisses [*sic*]. The belief of the eighteenth century and the French Revolution . . . postulated by contrast the fundamental similarity of all human beings and their ability to develop according to one and the same concept. Africa should thus have obtained its place in the modern world by means of a swift revolution replacing old structures with new forms. Then there would no longer be any obstacle to assimilation in one and the same political structure. And now let us count up the score: you lost in developing in traditional forms, but you gained in African autonomy. I won in terms of the victory of modern man and institutions. I lost in terms of political assimilation. *Un but à un*, Lord Lugard. *Match nul.* In reality we were both deceived by absolute values. Peo-

> ple are at the same time both similar and different. The Africans reacted in a healthy way: they both demanded the same political forms as those of Europeans, and defended the uniqueness of their culture. In the words of Senghor, they wanted "to assimilate, but not be assimilated."[60]

Professor Deschamps's quotation of Senegalese nationalist Léopold Senghor reveals his understanding of African nationalists' desires. But his statement that France lost only "in terms of assimilation," and that the success of its colonial experience was roughly equal to Britain's seems off the mark. With two decades of war, the collapse of its constitutional republic, and thousands of lives lost—African, Asian, and French—France paid a far heavier price than Britian for an aspiration that was far more ambitious.

Alternative Explanations: Strategy, Economics, and the Interests of French Settlers

It is possible, though, that France's imperial collapse was little more than the Cabinet's response to changes in economic and strategic social power, and that French colonial nationalism was itself the outgrowth of the political and economic interests of colonists, and especially, in this case, the influence of French settlers. In judging structural variables, we profit from a comparison with Britain. Were France's colonies more economically or strategically valuable than Britain's? Were its settlers more numerous or stalwart?

The Economic Argument

One of the explanations of Britain's decision to grant independence was the declining value of its colonies. Is there a similar argument for France? The trend in the value of France's colonies is ambiguous. Over the twentieth century, the imperial share of France's overall trade increased. In the early 1880s, 4.7 percent of French imports were from, and 6.7 percent of its exports were to, its empire. By World War I, the figures were 9.3 percent for imports and 11 percent for exports; by the early 1930s, the percentages were 23 percent of imports and 33 percent of exports; and after a brief decline during World War II, they went up by 1953 to 25 percent of imports and 37 percent of exports.[61] By other indices, though, the colonies were becoming less valuable. An increasing portion of France's trade—like Britain's—was shifting to the European market; France's colonies were not providing it with the foreign exchange benefits for which policymakers had hoped after World War II; and colonies were contributing little to France's important manufacturing growth.[62] The economic ambivalence is also apparent with respect to specific colonies. Algeria, for instance, was consistently France's largest trading partner, accounting in 1953 for 27 percent of France's imports from its colonies (7 percent of France's total imports) and 31 percent of France's colonial imports (11 percent of total exports). Yet, the composition of this trade casts doubt on its overall value. Most of Algeria's exports were agricultural, one-third in wine, and were hardly essential to a state with a large agricultural base like France.[63]

If economic measures are themselves ambivalent, they are even more fuzzily associated with France's policy. As in the British case, it was far from clear that political independence would be inimical to the metropole's economic links—witness France's close economic relationship with Black African states after their independence. There was no strong economic reason for persistence in political control. If economic issues were primary, we would surely expect France to cultivate relationships with local colonial interests, if not by immediately granting them independence, then at least by granting them some concessions, as Britain did. In fact, France's stalwart refusal and armed repression seem, from an economic perspective, the least rational policy it could possibly have chosen.[64]

Another sort of economic argument, however, runs opposite to the economic decline argument, and is based on the comparison with Britain. It holds that France held on to its colonies so tightly because it did in fact value them, and in fact valued them more than Britain valued its colonies, thereby explaining France's relative intransigence. The argument would explain the relatively violent pattern, although not the occurrence, of France's decolonization. It has some merit. Table 12.2 shows that France's colonial exports and imports exceeded Britain's throughout the twentieth century, at least with respect to Africa.

France also exceeded Britain in its levels of government aid and private capital investment in Africa.[65] But neither is this economic argument a strong one. The differences in the figures are real, but not so large that they explain the radically different approach of France to colonial independence. Again, too, France's armed intransigence contradicts a strong positive economic interest in its colonies.

But a structuralist might pose the economic argument yet differently. Perhaps it was not the economic interests of France or Britain as a whole that mattered, but rather the stake that French and British business had in the colonial political relationship, or the degree to which each country's business thought that independence would bring adversity. In his study of metropolitan business interests in the colonies, Miles Kahler concludes, "Overall, the political exposure, and the political resistance, of the French colonial economic interests were generally higher than those of the British."[66]

TABLE 12.2
France's and Britain's Trade With Africa as a Percentage of Their Total Trade

Year	*Britain*	*Year*	*France*
1900		1900	
Exports	5.0	Exports	8.9
Imports	1.4	Imports	5.0
1905		1910	
Exports	5.0	Exports	9.8
Imports	5.4	Imports	9.1
1910		1914	
Exports	5.8	Exports	13.7
Imports	8.1	Imports	7.5
1920		1920	
Exports	22.2	Exports	13.6
Imports	13.5	Imports	5.0
1928		1926	
Exports	11.3	Exports	12.2
Imports	4.6	Imports	9.3
1933		1928	
Exports	10.4	Exports	14.5
Imports	2.2	Imports	10.4
1937		1935	
Exports	13.3	Exports	26.9
Imports	3.8	Imports	20.9
1947		1938	
Exports	13.2	Exports	22.5
Imports	6.3	Imports	20.9
1950		1951	
Exports	12.5	Exports	29.6
Imports	12.5	Imports	14.5
1956		1954	
Exports	12.8	Exports	29.0
Imports	9.8	Imports	18.8

Source: From David K. Fieldhouse, "The Economic Exploitation of Africa: Some British and French Comparisons," in *France and Britain in Africa: Imperial Rivalry and Colonial Rule*, ed. Prosser Gifford and William Roger Louis (New Haven: Yale University Press, 1971), 593–662; 642, 646.

As Kahler points out, though, business interests mattered only if they decisively influenced the state's colonial policy. There is little evidence for this in either France or Britain. In Britain, the Joint East and Central Africa Board, representing colonial businesses, enjoyed some imperialist influence within the British Conservative Party during the 1950s, but was ultimately shunned by Iain Macleod when he advocated independence. A French counterpart, the Comité Central de la France d'Outre-Mer, was even weaker in that it was fragmented and represented only one section of French business. A deeper problem with the business argument, as with other arguments about the comparatively larger French colonial stake, is again the lack of fit with policy. France's repressive approach was hardly conducive to preserving the interests of business, investment, and trade.[67] It is indicative, too, that those who were most in favor of keeping French colonies French—the French colonial settlers—were also the most fiercely opposed to those with business interests, whom they regarded as traitors.[68]

Military and Strategic Interests at Home and Abroad

Perhaps it is strategic interests that explain France's yield of empire, and the difference between France's and Britain's approaches. It is difficult to argue, though, that France gave up its colonies because they declined in strategic value, or that France had substantially greater strategic interests to guard in Africa or Asia than did Britain. Virtually no historian argues that France viewed any of its colonies as key strategic posts. Mahgreb colonies did prove vital to the Free French Resistance against the Nazis in World War II, but World War II was a different strategic world than that of the late 1940s and early 1950s. The importance of these lands may have lingered on in the minds of imperial enthusiasts in the French military, but it would be difficult to separate the strategic assessment from the enthusiasm; that is, devotion to the imperial ideal.

But perhaps the scope of the strategic argument, like the economic argument, is too broad. Perhaps it was not France's general military interests that explain its actions, but the position of the French military within the French government. Whereas the British military was firmly subordinate to the civilian rulers, in France the military was notoriously and historically independent. During the Third Republic, it had conquered western Sudan and Algeria largely on its own initiative, apart from metropolitan guidance. During World War II, when soldiers joined the Free French Resistance in insubordination, they strengthened the military's role in political activity. The practice of giving the military political responsibilities in colonial conflicts added to the trend. But to view the role of the military as only a structural factor would be a mistake; this explains that the military could influence policy, but not why it took the position on the colonial conflict that it did. The close alliance of the French military with colonial settlers, especially in Algeria, and the attempted generals' coup of 1958 can only be explained by the intense devotion to empire within the military. It was perhaps Greater France's strongest proponent, a key participant in the colonial consensus.[69]

Within the Colonies

In France, as in Britain, economic, social, and political structures may also explain nationalist identities and social protest in the colonies themselves. The structural candidates are the same in the French colonies as they are in the British colonies. Most of my conclusions about their efficacy are the same as well, and merit briefer discussion, not belabored argument. Exceptionally, settler populations were numerous and powerful in French colonies, and more strongly challenge the French imperial ideal in explaining France's journey to colonial independence. They deserve more detailed attention.

The size of the French colonial middle classes, like that of the British colonial middle classes, did not change substantially over time. They are thus doubtful eclipsing circumstances for the rise of identities and protest. Unlike the British cases, the size of the middle classes in the French settler colonies—here the Maghreb colonies—was not that different (per capita) than the size of the middle classes in French West Africa or Indochina. In the Maghreb, though, the number of nationalists and the ferocity of their agitation for independence measured much stronger than in West Africa. Something other than the middle class, then, must have influenced nationalism and protest. The middle class also does not explain why, within the Mahgreb, although the middle classes were larger in Tunisia and Morocco, the nationalists were fewer and armed protest less widespread and less intense.[70] In the French colonies, as was true in the British colonies, though, even a positive relationship between the size of the middle-class and the level of nationalist identities and protest would not establish whether middle-class nationalists were influenced by their class interests or by the experiences through which they were exposed to ideas—religion, war, education.

Those structures that impede the advancement of the middle class help in part to explain French colonial nationalism. In Algeria, the structure of the settler population was more oppressive than in any of the other French colonies; here, too, were the most nationalists and the largest-scale armed resistance. It was also here that protest had the largest social component, the largest involvement of peasants and proletarians, who were not necessarily nationalists. In Tunisia and Morocco, the structures of oppression were less oppressive than in Algeria, but more oppressive than in West

Africa; here the level of armed resistance was indeed intermediate. Indochina, however, does not fit the pattern; here, there was a relatively small settler population, but there were many nationalists and an intense armed rebellion. Like the middle class itself, however, oppressive social structures do not necessarily rule out the role of ideas in creating nationalist identities or in motivating nationalists to take up arms. There is also a high correlation between those colonists who became nationalist and those who had identity-forming experiences.[71]

Urbanization, the rise of peasant grievances, and political and economic change influenced social protest in the French colonies similarly to the way they did in the British ones. They characterize all colonies. But in the French colonies, as in the British ones, nationalist converts were vital in organizing and coordinating the protest, which in this case was often armed rebellion.

The most striking feature of French colonies, and a potential explanation for France's experience of decolonization, was their large settler populations. As in British East and Central Africa, large settler communities lived in many French colonies, especially the Mahgreb. The interests of French settlers were like those of the British settlers—they were deeply conservative (many Algerian settlers were fascist under the Vichy government), were frightened for their future safety, and were generally opposed to colonial independence. Again, nationalism and protest arose in both French settler and nonsettler colonies; settlers in colonies are not a necessary condition. But the presence of settlers could well explain different levels of resistance and repression between France's colonies, and why resistance was more violent in French colonies than in British ones. If French settlers were more numerous, more obstructionist, and more influential in their metropolitan capital than British ones, they might explain the French pattern better than the French imperial ideal. French settlers, in fact, made up a larger proportion of their respective colonies' populations than did British settlers, as table 12.3 demonstrates.[72]

Algeria had by far the largest settler population; North African populations were roughly comparable to the British population in the Central African Federation; and all of these populations were larger than the British population in Kenya. The social makeup of the settler populations is also important. Lower-income settlers, agricultural settlers, and civil servants (likely to lose their jobs in an African government) were most likely to resist and to remain loyal to the imperial cause. How did the colonies compare by this measure? The income of Algerian settlers was 20 percent lower than the metropolitan average, while that of Moroccans was 40 percent higher, while the income of Kenyan settlers was still higher than the Moroccans'. Algeria had a large civil-servant class and was proportionately less industrialized and more agricultural than Morocco, Kenya, and

TABLE 12.3
Settler Populations in the Colonies

Territory	*Size of Population (year)*	*Ratio of Non-European to European Populations*
Algeria	984,031 (1954)	9:1
Tunisia	239,000 (1946)	14:1
Morocco	325,271 (1946)	22:1
South Africa	2,641,689 (1951)	4:1
Federation of Rhodesia and Nyasaland	287,300 (1958)	26:1
Southern Rhodesia (Zimbabwe)	207,000 (1958)	13:1
Northern Rhodesia (Zambia)	72,000 (1958)	31:1
Nyasaland (Malawi)	8,300 (1958)	328:1
Kenya	67,700 (1960)	93:1
Tanganyika	22,300 (1960)	408:1

Source: Miles Kahler, *Decolonization in Britain and France* (Princeton: Princeton University Press, 1984), 317.

the Central African Federation. Settler access to the metropolitan government mattered, too. Here, Algerian *colons* were advantaged more than any of the other French settlers or British settlers. The Algerian French had both deputies and senators in the French National Assembly, whereas the Moroccans and Tunisians had only senators. The Algerians also had strong support among the Gaullist party, moderate parties, part of the Socialist Party, and especially the Radical Party, whose loyalty from the Algerians strengthened its role as an intermediary, coalition-holding party. North African settlers also exercised strong influence within the French colonial ministry, where they exercised near-veto power over colonial appointments. Together, all of these features of settler populations help explain why resistance to colonial independence was greater in Algeria than it was in Tunisia or Morocco, or than in the British colonies of the Central African Federation or Kenya, and why it was more intense in all of these locales than in West Africa, where there were only traces of white settlers.[73]

But there are limits to what the presence of settlers explains. It is hard to account for the influence of settlers over colonial policy apart from those persons who gave the settlers access; these were French legislators whose propensity to support settler interests was in turn affected by their commitment to the imperial ideal. How else can one explain why the French settlers had influence within several French parties, while the British settlers—mainly the Rhodesians—had support only within a tiny portion of the British Conservative Party? The imperial ideal remains crucial. In France, as in Britain, the influence of settlers in the government also declined during the fifties. Its wane corresponded to the wax of the French war in Algeria, contrary to the case for its influence. Under Mendès-France and Faure the Radical Party broke from its support for settlers in 1954–1955; and subsequent to the outbreak of insurrection in Algeria in 1954, the French denied the Algerian settlers their representation in the lower chamber of the National Assembly, while dissolving the Algerian Assembly, the *conseils généraux*, and the municipal governments.[74] Finally, the settler explanation has little to say about Indochina, where France fought a war as long as the one in Algeria, but where no significant organized settler movements existed.

In the French case, like the British case, settler populations mattered; social and political and economic structures mattered, too. They helped to create contributors to the armed insurrection that led to colonial independence, and to heighten nationalism and protest. But none of them displace the centrality of ideas in bringing about armed insurrection, and in the case of West and Equatorial Africa, social protest.

Ideas and Empire

Ideas elicited France's contribution to colonial independence by effecting the armed resistance that brought down the French Empire. They shaped the identities of the nationalists who took up arms; these nationalists challenged the imperial ideal whose tenets denied their aspirations. I do not consider here the case for intermediate dynamics of the two roles, for it runs little different than it does in the British case. Generally, the work of ideas was simpler and more direct in France than it was in Britain, but it confirms the more complex argument about how ideas elicited the constitution of colonial independence at large. The established ideal held by heads of polities and their minions will determine what sort of social power revolutionary ideas will have to muster. The established imperial ideal determines whether the heads respond to revolutionary ideas in irritated response or harsh dismissal; and how they respond determines whether the revolution in sovereignty will be conducted through tense conferences, diplomatic exchanges, strikes, and demonstrations, or through guerrillas who bomb cafes and fight in jungles against suppressive imperial troops. An even stronger case for the influence of established ideals upon the work of ideas would involve other imperial demises, those of Belgium, the Netherlands, Portugal, the United States, and others: Did a reactionary ideal correspond with armed struggle, a progressive ideal with a smoother transition? I have focused on Britain and France because their grants of independence constituted the preponderance of the practice of the new constitution of colonial independence. It is in the end of these two empires that we see ideas expanding the sovereign states system to the rest of the globe even more subtly than they did in bringing it to Europe at Westphalia.

PART FOUR

THE REVOLUTIONS CONSIDERED TOGETHER

THIRTEEN

CONCLUSION: TWO REVOLUTIONS, ONE MOVEMENT

THE TWO REVOLUTIONS, Westphalia and colonial independence, are separated by three centuries, and by expression and circumstance. The Swedish Lutherans and the Dutch Calvinists who protested and fought against the Catholic Church and the Holy Roman Empire understood their struggle through arguments, incidents, grievances, theologies, languages, images, and tropes, and they pursued it through technologies, armies, economies, polities, organizations, and networks that Mahatma Gandhi, Kwame Nkrumah, Ho Chi Minh, British Socialists, and John Foster Dulles might well have found foreign and peculiar. But the claims of both revolutions' partisans are not wholly alien, untranslatable, or incommensurable. In this concluding chapter, I probe the commonality between the two revolutions and between the two sets of ideas behind them. For all of the differences, we can yet view the revolutions in sovereignty as part of a common movement toward a global system of sovereign states, and the revolutions in ideas as part of an unfolding logic of liberation. I also want to suggest ironic connections between the ideas that brought us the sovereign state and those that may well lie behind a second historical movement, the circumscription of the sovereign state.

The Sovereign State System's Global Conquest: A Movement of Liberation

What both sets of revolutionaries fought for was sovereign authority, the claim of a single body—monarch, theocrat, postcolonial dictator, liberal constitutional regime—to supremacy within a bounded territory. The commonality of the claim is not trivial. Sovereign states, or sovereign state systems, are not a natural form of authority or an inevitable equilibrium. As I argued in chapter 2, medieval Europe, the Islamic world, the world's great historical empires, and wandering tribal societies have all construed the relationship between political authority and territory quite diversely. Sovereign state systems are only one of many schemes of international society. That revolutionaries in both struggles would seek the same organization of politics links them across substantial space and time.

Not only did both sets of revolutionaries claim sovereignty, but both also claimed sovereignty in a similar moral fashion, on behalf of a similar value—freedom. At least freedom of a certain sort. Both revolutions sought sovereign authority as protection for a people, for their local prerogatives, for their immunities, for their autonomy, all of this as a shield from the impositions of a more universal entity, in both cases an empire—Holy Roman, Catholic, British, French. In the languages, tropes, and imagery of both sets of revolutionaries lie the theme of liberation. In Protestant cartoons and sermons, the Catholic Church or the empire was a beast, a colossus, a monstrosity, a foreign power, a distant central authority, a denier of local prerogatives, or of ancient liberties, and of the right of local churches to live out the pure Gospel. In the rhetoric of nationalists, we hear of colonial autocrats, oppressors of races, imperialists—all of these being reactionaries pitted against liberation struggles, pursuers of freedom, seekers of racial equality, and dominated races.

Freedom, autonomy, a protective shield—what this amounts to is a logic of liberation. Liberation, here too, is liberation of a certain sort. Neither set of revolutionaries articulated the full-blown modern liberal state with its panoply of individual rights and democratic institutions. Such a conception is anachronistic to the Reformation and was not even the deep aspiration of many colonial nationalists. Rather, the kind of liberation for which all revolutionaries of sovereignty fought, even if early modern Protestants did not yet so name it, was self-determination: the assertion of groups of people to freedom from the oppression of some larger, centralized authority. Colonial nationalists knew and used the term, appealing to its presence in the Atlantic Charter, the League of Nations Covenant, the United Nations Charter, and the promises of Woodrow Wilson. Self-determination, too, was the substance of the Peace of Augsburg, and of Augsburg as it was modified at Westphalia. Here, religious groups—although only certain groups, as allowed by princes and defined by treaties—gained legal freedom to practice their beliefs.

In both revolutions, then, sovereignty procured freedom in this limited, but important, sense: the holder of sovereignty was immune from rival claims to authority from both within and without its territory. Recall the definition of sovereignty in chapter 2: supreme authority within a territory. The words "supreme" and "within" imply exaltation and enclosure, the sealed space for governance that sovereignty bequeaths. The sovereign space of the early modern European prince required his autonomy from the Church and the empire; the sovereign space of the colonial nationalist, his independence from the colonial metropole. Holders of sovereignty, of course, have ranged profoundly in their provision of freedoms other than self-determination. In the three and a half centuries since Westphalia, liberal democratic constitutions have been a distinct minority among sovereigns. Early modern sovereigns far antedated such constitutions. Liberated colonies more often than not collapsed into authoritarian states. The governments of Adolf Hitler, Joseph Stalin, and Pol Pot, sovereign over rivals to their regimes, but more formidably totalitarian within their sovereign space, attained a fullness of absolutism that medieval Europeans could not but begin to conceive. Both revolutions, then, promoted a form of polity with freedom from territorial rivals, but one in which the sovereign had enjoyed the authoritative space to provide or deny liberal freedoms to the inhabitants of the territory. The provision has been fragile, the denial sometimes quite cruel.

What is remarkable about this form of polity, the sovereign state, is how thoroughly it spread. Westphalia began and colonial independence completed an unprecedented feat—the extension of the sovereign state to the entire land surface of the globe. It is the only form of polity in history to attain such universality. The two revolutions in sovereignty, as diverse as they may be, form a common story, a single movement, that culminated in this exceptional state of affairs.

Skeptical of this story of single movements toward global results will be those who are awed most by the contingency, complexity, and fragmentariness of history. They will question the parsing, the discreteness, and the exhaustiveness of the two revolutions. The history of the sovereign state system did not simply stop in 1648, only to resume after World War II. What of all the states who joined the system in the interim? And what of the arrangements between sovereign states, voluntary or coerced, that have not conformed to their sovereignty—the Soviet domination of Eastern Europe, the International Monetary Fund's oversight into the economic policies of states, and many other aberrant schemes? What of the many violations of sovereignty, the military interventions, coerced debt enforcements, withholding of loans to governments that violate human rights, and the like? What of Hitler and Napoleon and Tojo, who forced their regions of the world into sustained contestation of sovereignty? And what of arrangements like the Concert of Europe, constitutional agreements between great powers to intervene in revolutionary states? We must acknowledge all such phenomena, which qualify an account of an inexorable, monistic, singly progressive direction of history. In chapter 2, I explained them as violations, exceptions, periods of contestation, and short-lived constitutions. But in magnitude, sweep, and foundational importance, all of these anomalies are all overshadowed by the two revolutions in sovereignty that I have described. Each of these revolutions achieved what none of these other arrangements did. They created a lasting international constitution, restructuring the basic authority of polities. The first one fashioned a system of sovereign states for the European continent; the second one replicated this system everywhere. The exceptions, the violations, the contestations all qualify, but do not annul, the collective movement of the two revolutions, the movement by which the sovereign state system took over the globe.

I have sought to explain this epic movement, its component revolutions, their causes. I have searched for the genesis of a structure of authority that states today usually take for granted when they fight wars, make alliances, and negotiate agreements, and which their citizens take for granted when they observe, and sometimes seek to influence, states so endeavoring. The bulk of academic scholarship on international relations today also takes for granted the constitution of the system of sovereign states, assuming its existence as it explains the pursuits of states—their wars, their alliances, their efforts to cooperate in trade, monetary affairs, and the provision of economic stability and growth, their construction of weapons, and their many other ends. This scholarship then locates the causes of these pursuits in the distribution of power in the international system and in international law, international institutions, shared norms and culture, and forces in domestic politics, including the structure of the state, sectors of society, culture, and public opinion. But most of the analyses pay little attention to how we came to have a system in which these pursuits, these causes, carry on in the first place. Significant exceptions lie in several fine works on sovereignty over the past decade that explore the concept of sovereignty or the way in which it shapes relations among states. But none of these aspires to a general explanation of the movement, the revolutions, through which a global sovereign state system came to be.

So, why did this particular form of a constitution of international society arise, appearing first in early modern Europe, then wildly succeeding in occupying the globe? The liberal logic of self-determination that unfolded through the two constitutional revolutions intimates the answers that I have put forth. Behind these revolutions in international constitutions were two revolutions in ideas. Each of the revolutionary ideas proposed the liberation that resulted. Protestantism envisioned a political space free from the temporal authority of the Catholic Church, governed by the sovereign prince. Colonial nationalism asserted statehood for colonies, immunity from the authority of their imperial metropole. Each proposition advocated liberation from a larger political entity, contradicting the established idea that legitimated it, creating a crisis of pluralism, causing the revolution. For all their difference in context and meaning, the two ideas converged upon self-determination as freedom, amounting, then, to their own unfolding logic, a movement of ideas behind the movement toward sovereignty.

How did the ideas bring the revolutions? It is here that I introduce the two roles of ideas. Closest to each revolution, most plainly associated with it, most clearly causing it, is social power. In both revolutions, those who defined their identities according to revolutionary ideas empowered or exerted pressure on heads of their polity, leading them to adopt an interest for the polity in pursuing the new constitution, the revolution in sovereignty. In the revolution at Westphalia, Protestants exercised social power first through their practice of new rites and doctrines, through their disregard of Catholic authority, and through their cooperation with leaders who formed new churches that gave no obeisance to the Catholic hierarchy. More crudely, Protestants took up arms. They fought against the prince or king who would not assent to the Reformation, as in the Netherlands, France, and some German principalities. They fought on behalf of the prince who cooperated with the Reformation, but then had to fight off foreign Catholic powers, as in Sweden, some German principalities, the Dutch United Provinces once they were independent, and post–civil war *politique* France. Where heads of polities favored and supported the Reformation, they could use the social power of their office to seize prerogatives from Catholic authority.

What was distinctive about the revolution of colonial independence was the role of reputational social power. To dissolve the British Empire, its anticolonial critics exercised the power of their revolutionary ideas through public criticism of the British Cabinet, pressuring its reputation for politically progressive colonial governance and forcing it to face the prospect of strategic and electoral losses. France's intransigent imperial ideas of assimilation, by contrast, nullified the prospects for the reputational power of ideas. In the Reformation struggle, the conditions for reputational power were absent. Here, established ideas—a Catholic European social and political order—starkly opposed revolutionary ideas, and were closed to their appeal. Those princes who supported the Reformation and sovereignty did so either under the duress of threat, out of the prospect of gain, or from sympathy for the ideas. In no case did they act to avoid losing their reputation for some other ideal that they held. Those princes who opposed the Reformation were either powerful enough to suppress its social power, or like colonial France, were attached to an opposing established ideal. Reputational social power requires an established ideal that is open to, but not identical to, the criticism of revolutionary ideas.

In both revolutions, it was through social power that proponents of ideas brought the liberation that their ideas demanded. Almost all of the swelling academic literature on the role of ideas in international politics over the past decade focuses on the social power of ideas. It asks, How do ideas, once people adopt them, translate into war, peace, foreign aid, balancing, failure to balance, economic cooperation, weapons policies, intervention, support for human rights, or any policy that a state pursues? International relations scholars have paid less attention to how people arrive at their ideas in the first place. But this first role, shaping identities, is important, for in an ideas explanation, people must adopt ideas into their stable identities before they demand and pursue the political ends that the ideas prescribe. Without accounting for this role, an explanation of politics rooted in ideas will always be vulnerable to structural skepticism. Perhaps the idea came from the material and political circumstances of its holder. Of course, a complete genealogical account of the origin of an idea is impossible. Every idea has its parentage in previous ideas and circumstances; the parentage has progenitors, too, and so on, back to the Garden of Eden. But such an account is not my aim here. I am concerned, rather, with how it is that people come to adopt new ideas. I have argued that we cannot explain this adoption through structural circumstances alone, but that the adoption involves a significant measure of reflection. I have stressed that reflection, too, responds to circumstances. But some circumstances are entirely compatible with, and indeed encourage, reflection, and are even evidence for reflection. Both revolutions in ideas were propelled by circumstances of reflection. The Reformation was powerfully assisted by the sermon and the pamphlet, trends in late medieval theology, the print media, rising literacy, and the perceived corruption of the Catholic Church. Colonial nationalism was fostered by education, religion, and the experience of war. Such circumstances encourage, assist, and provoke, but do not override, reflection upon ideas—the ideas that demanded the liberation of a people through sovereignty.

The recent literature on ideas also stresses the role of several couriers that are involved in bringing ideas into politics—publics, networks of activists, intellectual communities, institutions, heads of polities and the "international context" of heads of polities and their underling officials, meeting with, speaking with, and negotiating with one another. It is not my aim here to assert the importance of any single one of these couriers. Rather, I note the role of several of them—in both revolutions, in both roles of ideas. In both revolutions, publics were important. It took masses of Protestants to disregard Catholic authority, participate in new practices, and join armies in order for the Reformation to occur and to assert social power. In the revolution of colonial independence, French and British public opinion affected the course of decolonization in each country, while in the colonies, large swaths of colonial publics joined nationalist protest and rebellion. Intellectual communities were crucial in both revolutions, too. It was in the universities, indeed, through a transnational network of scholars, that Reformation theology and protest first developed and spread. European universities were also an important breeding ground for colonial nationalists, sending them back to colonies all across Asia, Africa, and Central America. In the revolution of colonial independence, other networks of activists shaped opinion and exerted power, too: British lobbies, colonial nationalist parties. It is also to this revolution that the notion of "institutionalization" of ideas best applies. Britain's and France's established ideals of empire were ensconced as "norms of appropriateness" in government bureaucracies, where officials learned them, espoused them, and, most of all, used them to publicly justify empire. It is also in the revolution of colonial independence, especially in the British case, that the international context of interacting elite officials mattered most. American and Soviet heads of state and diplomats, along with nonaligned states speaking in the United Nations, were crucial in placing stress upon Britain's reputation for fostering gradual self-government. Finally, in both revolutions, heads of polities themselves were important conveyors and fortifiers of ideas. In the Westphalia revolution, key princes and kings often furthered and encouraged the Reformation and led armies against its Catholic opponents, sometimes out of their deep Protestant convictions. In the colonial independence revolution, heads of state were the most important upholders of established ideals, ensuring that these ideals would expedite or obstruct the revolution as they did in each case. All of these couriers and dynamics were the agents of the conversion and social power through which ideas brought each of the two revolutions in sovereignty.

In both cases, ideas alone were not enough. Material structures conspired with ideas to bring about both revolutions in sovereignty. In the Westphalia case, sovereign states had already developed in some parts of Europe, partially accomplishing the revolution in sovereignty, prior to the Reformation, the revolution in ideas. I do not want to concede the irrelevance of ideas to this development, but I must acknowledge powerful explanations rooted in economic and military technological change. In the colonial revolution, European empires had granted many colonies independence prior to the sweeping changes of the years around 1960, concessions for which there are both plausible material and ideas-based explanations, but ones that I have left unevaluated.

In both cases, changes in the international balance of material power helped to bring the revolution. The Westphalia revolution was caused in part by the seventeenth-century relative decline of Spain and the Habsburgs and the rise of challenger states, in their armies and economies, independently of ideas. Few would dispute that Britain's and France's weakened positions following World War II contributed to their concessions of empire. In both cases, too, middle-class interests helped to shape the identities of revolutionaries, both Protestant and colonial nationalist. Finally, I have noted the role of what I have called intermediate dynamics—not the strong form of ideas as captured in the two roles, but not wholly skeptical of ideas, either—in several places in both revolutions. Ideas served as focal points, for instance, in the negotiations leading up to the Peace of Westphalia; they operated as resolvers of uncertainty in established imperial ideals.

What I have sought to challenge, though, are arguments for large-scale historical structural changes being sufficient or even primary causes of the revolutions in sovereignty. For these would claim that what caused the revolutions, and eventually the global system of sovereign states, was not the unfolding of ideas demanding sovereignty as a people's liberation from empire, but the unfolding of changes in markets, class structure, military technology, and the international balance of power, all making the state the optimal organization of politics. These sorts of explanations, as I have discussed, have enjoyed a prominent place in political science and sociology, and are found in Realism, especially Structural Realism, in much of historical sociology, in Marxist analyses, and in the bulk of the literature on the formation of the state. Together, they tell of a different kind of movement propelled by a force other than revolutions in ideas. Against their skepticism, I have argued for the revolutions.

The Circumscription of the Sovereign State System: A Movement of Liberation

In the brief history of revolutions in sovereignty in chapter 3, I described what has amounted to a second movement in sovereignty, one that has proceeded through three revolutions in sovereignty since the late nineteenth century, and that advances opposite to the single movement, the two revolutions, that I have described in this book. It progresses away from sovereignty, toward the circumscription of the sovereign state, and it gives constitutional authority to institutions other than the state, and enables states to have oversight into one another's affairs. This movement also began in Europe, but eventually produced authority with claims reaching potentially across the globe. Briefly, again, the revolutions were first, the growth of minority treaties in Europe in the nineteenth and early twentieth centuries, culminating in League of Nations sponsorship and oversight mechanisms after World War I; second, the rise of European integration after World War II; and third, the rise of intervention sanctioned by international institutions after the Cold War. Plausibly, ideas caused these revolutions, too.

In both of the grand historical movements, the revolutionary ideas were ones of liberation. But this seems paradoxical: How can ideas of liberation both build the sovereign state up and then peel away its prerogatives? The answer lies in the sovereign state's concurrent provision of freedom—for a people, from an empire—and its potential, imperial denial of freedom to the individuals of its own territory. In the nineteenth and twentieth centuries, ideas of liberation came to challenge the denial, to reject the sovereign state's suppression of freedoms for individuals, and to demand institutions that could protect these freedoms from the outside. These ideas were modern liberalism. Although they differed in their nineteenth- and twentieth-century versions, and in their socialist and classical liberal versions, these ideas generally favored individual rights and democratic institutions. The minority treaties demanded that Eastern European countries protect the rights of their religious and ethnic minorities to worship, language, and education. Their advocates were parties and lobbies in Britain and France, President Wilson and his supporters in America, and other framers of the League of Nations. European integration was at first limited to institutions for common governance of coal and steel, but even at its inception, its purpose was much more. Its strongest and most consistent proponents were Christian Democratic parties that, inspired by the social teachings of the Catholic Church, opposed the "heresy" of the absolutely sovereign state and envisioned a unified federal Europe, governed by liberal democratic principles, held together by institutions that transcended national loyalties. International intervention after the Cold War has also aimed to establish and secure liberal democratic values—the delivery of humanitarian supplies, the settlement of civil war, the rebuilding of failed states, the enforcement of human rights and elections, and the arrest and trial of war criminals. Its chief advocates have been liberals, in bureaucracies, parties, public opinion, international lobbies, and the media.

All of these claims about the impact of ideas upon further revolutions in sovereignty amount to hypotheses. They need defense, the sort of defense I have offered for the two revolutions in this book. Of course, structural hypotheses would also claim to explain them as the product of changes in the balances of power, markets, technology, and the like, and these would also have to be considered. But should ideas here turn out to be efficacious and autonomous, then an irony would emerge. Notions of liberation would be responsible for displacing the sovereign state, and are vigorously displacing it today, just as they established it in the first place.

There is a final irony. Persisting through the revolutions in both movements is not only liberation, but another courier with another set of ideas, one that was profoundly resistant to the revolution at Westphalia, but quite in favor of the sovereignty-stripping twentieth-century revolutions. It is a shadow tradition of critique, one that preceded, then witnessed and sometimes participated in, the revolutions in sovereignty I have described. I have in mind the Catholic Church. Recall from chapter 5 Pope Innocent X's condemnation of the settlement at Westphalia. He called it "null, void, invalid, iniquitous, unjust, damnable, reprobate, inane, empty of meaning and effect for all time." After Westphalia, the Church continued to regard the absolutely sovereign state as a heresy. As late as the end of the nineteenth century, it still banned the writings of Hugo Grotius, one of the earliest articulators of the sovereign state system, and condemned international law as a "Protestant science." To European secular liberals, of course, the Catholic Church's condemnation was little more than reactionary medievalism. Indeed, the Church seemed not to support the liberation that the sovereign state's proponents claimed for it. But then, in the twentieth century, the Church, as well as Christian Democratic parties inspired by the Church's social teachings, became powerful advocates of European integration. Following the Second Vatican Council, the Church has also come to strongly support human rights and the institutions that would enforce them across borders.

Is there a link here? Or is this simply a different Church in a different time? Doubtless the doctrine of the Catholic Church developed. Only in its twentieth-century social teaching did it come to embrace liberalism and democracy. But there is continuity in its criticism, too. It is found in a logic other than liberation, one that sometimes resonates with it, sometimes opposes it. All along, the Church has condemned the absolutely sovereign state as an idolatrous claimant to godlike status, an affront to a moral order and to a natural law, whose authority lies ultimately far outside the borders of the state. Fixed and unchanging, this order is much like an established idea. Yet, it leaves intact no earthly status quo. To the sovereign state, it offers this abiding reproach: supreme political authority, within borders, anywhere, of a mortal person, of any sort of human institution, is something to which nobody ought to make claim. Supremacy lies instead in the fixed order. Standing in critical judgment, always calling the state to account, this fixed order is indeed much like a revolutionary idea.

NOTES

CHAPTER ONE
INTRODUCTION:
REVOLUTIONS IN SOVEREIGNTY

1. John Gerard Ruggie, "Continuity and Transformation in the World Polity: Towards a Neorealist Synthesis," in Robert O. Keohane, ed., *Neorealism and Its Critics* (New York: Columbia University Press, 1986), 141.

2. In his essay in a commemorative conference and art exhibition on the Peace of Westphalia held in 1998–1999, historian Heinz Duchhardt notes that though Westphalia "represents a crucial turning-point in European history," it has never achieved the status of a *lieu de mémoire*, or a publicly acknowledged historical event. See Duchhardt, "The Peace of Westphalia as *Lieu de Mémoire* in Germany and Europe," in Klaus Bussmann and Heinz Schilling, eds., *1648—War and Peace in Europe* (Münster, Germany: Westfalisches Landesmuseum, 1998), 41.

3. John Vasquez, *The Power of Power Politics: A Critique* (New Brunswick, N.J.: Rutgers University Press, 1983), chap. 5. Published in 1983, the analysis is somewhat outdated, but the magnitude of the figures is nevertheless striking.

4. For Durkheim, the relationship between structure and superstructure was not entirely one way. Politics, religion, and philosophy, mostly shaped by the division of labor, could also exercise a shaping influence of their own. See Emile Durkheim, *The Division of Labor In Society*, trans. W.D. Halls (New York: Free Press, 1984).

5. Classics in historical sociology are Theda Skocpol, *States and Social Revolutions* (Cambridge: Cambridge University Press, 1979); Barrington Moore, *Social Origins of Dictatorship and Democracy* (Boston: Beacon Press, 1966). For a contemporary overview of the literature, see Ira Katznelson, "Structure and Configuration in Comparative Politics," in Mark Irving Lichbach and Alan Zuckerman, eds., *Comparative Politics: Rationality, Culture, and Structure* (Cambridge: Cambridge University Press, 1997), 81–112. On Realism and ideas, see the discussion in chapter 5.

6. See, for instance, the essays in Peter Katzenstein, ed., *The Culture Of National Security: Norms and Identity in World Politics* (New York: Columbia University Press, 1996).

7. See Samuel Huntington, *The Clash of Civilizations and the Remaking of World Order* (New York: Simon & Schuster, 1996). The original thesis appeared as "The Clash of Civilizations?" *Foreign Affairs* 72, no. 3 (Summer 1993): 22–49. In the preface of his book, Huntington noted that the article, "according to *Foreign Affairs* editors, stirred up more discussion in three years than any other article they had published since the 1940s." Huntington is not the only exception among political scientists. See Benjamin Barber, *Jihad vs. McWorld* (New York: Times Books, 1995); Douglas Johnston and Cynthia Sampson, eds., *Religion, The Missing Dimension of Statecraft* (Oxford: Oxford University Press, 1994); the work of Sohail Hashmi, for instance, "International Society and Its Islamic Malcontents,"

Fletcher Forum 20 (1996): 13–29; and a special issue of *Orbis: A Journal of World Affairs* devoted to faith and statecraft (Vol. 42, No. 2, Spring 1998). Sociologists generally treat religion more seriously; many of its practitioners have strongly challenged the "secularization thesis" of the 1950s and 1960s. See, among others, Mark Juergensmeyer, *The New Cold War? Religious Nationalism Confronts the Secular State* (Berkeley: University of California Press, 1993).

8. Gilles Kepel, *The Revenge of God: The Resurgence of Islam, Christianity, and Judaism in the Modern World*, trans. Alan Braley (University Park: Pennsylvania State University Press, 1994).

CHAPTER TWO
THE CONSTITUTION OF INTERNATIONAL SOCIETY

1. On the construction of internal and external spheres of authority, see Alexander Wendt, "Anarchy Is What States Make of It," *International Organization* 46, no. 2: 391–425; Jens Bartelson, *A Genealogy of Sovereignty* (Cambridge: Cambridge University Press, 1995), 88–136; R.B.J. Walker, *Inside/Outside: International Relations as Political Theory* (Cambridge: Cambridge University Press, 1993).

2. Hedley Bull and Adam Watson, "Introduction," in Hedley Bull and Adam Watson, eds., *The Expansion of International Society* (Oxford: Oxford University Press, 1984), 1. For other key works in the English School, see Hedley Bull, *The Anarchical Society: A Study of Order in World Politics* (New York: Columbia University Press, 1977); Martin Wight, *Systems of States* (London: Leicester University Press, 1977); Martin Wight, *Power Politics* (Harmondsworth, U.K.: Penguin, 1979); Herbert Butterfield and Martin Wight, eds., *Diplomatic Investigations* (London: Allen and Unwin, 1966); Adam Watson, *The Evolution of International Society: A Comparative Historical Analysis* (London: Routledge, 1992); Barry Buzan, "From International System to International Society: Structural Realism and Regime Theory Meet the English School," *International Organization* 47 (1993): 327–52; Martin Shaw, "There Is No Such Thing as Society: Beyond Individualism and Statism in International Security Studies," *Review of International Studies* 19 (1993): 159–75; and Chris Brown, "International Theory and International Society: The Viability of the Middle Way?" *Review of International Studies* 21 (1995): 183–96.

3. On the historical variety of polities, systems of polities, and the authority structures that constitute them, see Yale H. Ferguson and Richard W. Mansbach, *Polities: Authority, Identities, and Change* (Columbia: University of South Carolina Press, 1996).

4. Wight, *Systems of States*, 24–25. I have relied heavily in this section on Watson, *The Evolution of International Society.*

5. See Adam Watson, *Evolution of International Society*, 112–19.

6. For skeptics of stable definitions of sovereignty, see Lassa Oppenheim, *International Law*, Vol. 1 (London: Longmans, Green, and Co., 1905), 103; Richard Falk, "Sovereignty," in *Oxford Companion to Politics of the World* (Oxford: Oxford University Press, 1993), 854; Jens Bartelson, *A Genealogy of Sovereignty*; S. Benn,

"Sovereignty." in *Encyclopedia of Philosophy* 7 (1955): 501–5; and E. H. Carr, *The Twenty Years' Crisis* (New York: Harper and Row, 1964).

7. The oldest citation of "sovereignty" in the *Oxford English Dictionary* is dated 1290. See *Oxford English Dictionary*, Vol. 16, ed. J. A. Simpson and E.S.C. Weiner (Oxford: Clarendon Press, 1989), 77–79.

8. There are many scholars who share roughly the definition of sovereignty that I develop herein. See J. L. Brierly, *The Law of Nations* (New York: Oxford University Press, 1963), 13; Robert O. Keohane, "Sovereignty, Interdependence, and International Institutions," in Michael Joseph Smith and Linda Miller, eds., *Ideas and Ideals: Essays in Honor of Stanley Hoffmann* (Boulder, Colo.: Westview Press, 1993), 91–107; Kenneth Waltz, *Theory of International Politics* (Lexington, Mass.: Addison-Wesley, 1979), 96; Hans Morgenthau, *Politics Among Nations: The Struggle for Power and Peace*, 6th ed. (New York: Alfred A. Knopf, 1985), 133. Michael Fowler and Julie Marie Bunck, *Law, Power, and the Sovereign State* (University Park: Pennsylvania State University Press, 1995); John Gerard Ruggie, "Territoriality and Beyond: Problematizing Modernity in International Relations," International Organization 47, no. 1 (1993): 139–74; Friedrich Kratochwil, "Of Systems, Boundaries, and Territoriality: An Inquiry into the Formation of the States-System," *Word Politics* 39 (1986): 27–52; and Thomas J. Biersteker and Cynthia Weber, "The Social Construction of State Sovereignty," in Biersteker and Weber, eds., *The Social Construction of State Sovereignty* (Cambridge: Cambridge University Press, 1996), 2. For recent sophisticated explication of sovereignty in international relations, see Stephen Krasner, *Sovereignty: Organized Hypocrisy* (Princeton: Princeton University Press, 1999); and J. Samuel Barkin and Bruce Cronin, "The State and the Nation: Changing Norms and the Rules of Sovereignty in International Relations," *International Organization* 48, no. 1 (Winter 1994): 107–30.

9. R. P. Wolff, "The Conflict Between Authority and Autonomy," in Joseph Raz, ed., *Authority* (Oxford: Basil Blackwell, 1990), 20.

10. I use legitimacy here in its descriptive sense, not to mean justified or morally defensible, but as Max Weber meant it: Something is legitimate if it is assented to, or at least regarded as part of the normal, proper, state of affairs. For Weber, authority attains its legitimacy either because it has behind it either tradition, emotional power, rationality, or legality. See Max Weber, "The Theory of Social and Economic Organization," in Talcott Parsons, ed., *Max Weber: The Theory of Social and Economic Organization* (New York: Free Press, 1947), 124–32.

11. William Shakespeare, *King Richard II*, act 4, scene 1, lines 248–51.

12. On the importance of territoriality to sovereignty, see Ruggie, "Territoriality and Beyond," 148–52; and Hendrik Spruyt, *The Sovereign State and Its Competitors* (Princeton: Princeton University Press, 1994), 34–36.

13. See Jean Bodin, *On Sovereignty* (Cambridge: Cambridge University Press, 1992); and Thomas Hobbes, *Leviathan* (Harmondsworth, U.K.: Penguin, 1968).

14. See F. H. Hinsley, *Sovereignty*, 2d ed. (Cambridge: Cambridge University Press, 1986); Michael Wilks, *The Problem of Sovereignty in the Middle Ages* (Cambridge: Cambridge University Press, 1964); Jacques Maritain, *Man and the State* (Chicago: University of Chicago Press, 1951).

15. This is not to deny that you can have one without the other. For instance, a state that is in the midst of civil war, but whose authority is unchallenged from the outside, might have external sovereignty but not internal sovereignty. But when sovereignty is realized, both aspects are present.

16. See UN Charter, Article 2(4); J. L. Brierly, *The Law of Nations*; Ian Brownlie, *Principles of Public International Law*, 3d. ed. (Oxford: Oxford University Press, 1979); Michael Akehurst, *A Modern Introduction to International Law*, 5th ed. (London: George Allen and Unwin, 1984); Alan James, *Sovereign Statehood* (London: Allen and Unwin, 1986).

17. Alan James, "The Practice of Sovereign Statehood in Contemporary International Society," *Political Studies* 47, no. 3 (1999): 460–62.

18. See Friedrich Kratochwil, "Sovereignty as *Dominium*: Is There a Right of Humanitarian Intervention?" in Gene Lyons and Michael Mastanduno, eds., *Beyond Westphalia?* 21–43; John Gerard Ruggie, "Continuity and Transformation in the World Polity: Toward a Neorealist Synthesis," in Robert O. Keohane, ed., *Neorealism and Its Critics* (New York: Columbia University Press, 1986), 131–57.

19. James, "The Practice of Sovereign Statehood," 462–64.

20. In fact, this must be somewhat qualified even in the case of Bodin, for whom the sovereign is bound by natural law, is under a duty to respect the liberties and property of subjects as they are entitled to them, and is obligated to abide by his contracts with private citizens. There is no right to resistance, however, to correspond to these duties. See Bodin, *On Sovereignty*, and J. H. Franklin, *Jean Bodin and the Rise of Absolutist Theory* (Cambridge: Cambridge University Press, 1973).

21. See Sohail Hashmi, "International Society and Its Islamic Malcontents," *The Fletcher Forum* (1996), 13–29.

22. See Fred Israel, ed., *Major Peace Treaties in Modern History, 1648–1967*, Vol. 1 (New York: McGraw-Hill, 1967).

23. Hinsley, *Sovereignty*, 193–95; Emeric de Vattel, *The Law of Nations* (Philadelphia: T. & J. W. Johnson, 1844).

24. On core constitutive principles, see Stephen A. Kocs, "Explaining the Strategic Behavior of States: International Law as System Structure," *International Studies Quarterly* 38 (1994): 535–56; and Antonio Cassese, *International Law in a Divided World* (1986), 129–57.

25. Similar to my argument about the third face of authority, Christian Reus-Smit argues that the "constitutional structure of international society" defines "pure procedural justice." See Christian Reus-Smit, "The Constitutional Structure of International Society," *International Organization* 51 (1997): 568–70. On constitutional norms, see also Nicholas Greenwood Onuf, *World of Our Making: Rules and Rule in Social Theory and International Relations* (Columbia: University of South Carolina Press, 1989).

26. Of course, norm has many meanings for social scientists, ranging from patterns of behavior that result from the fear of sanctions, to customary behavior, to moral beliefs, to standards that constitute the very identities of actors, whether they are tribespeople or states. On the variety of definitions of norms in international relations, see J. Thomson, "Norms in International Relations: A Conceptual Analysis," *International Journal of Group Tensions* 23 (1993): 67–83; and Ronald L. Jepperson, Alexander Wendt, and Peter J. Katzenstein, "Norms, Identity, and Cul-

ture in National Security, in Katzenstein, ed., *The Culture of National Security*, 54. Norms there are "collective expectations about proper behavior for a given identity."

27. On customary law, see J. L. Brierly, *The Law of Nations*, 5th ed. (Oxford: Oxford University Press, 1963), 59–62; and Anthony Clark Arend, *Legal Rules and International Society* (New York: Oxford University Press, 1999).

28. See Walter Wriston, *The Twilight of Sovereignty* (New York: Scribners, 1992); Kenichi Ohmae, *The End of the Nation State* (New York: HarperCollins, 1995); Raymond Vernon, *Sovereignty at Bay* (New York: Basic Books, 1971); Richard Cooper, *The Economics of Interdependence: Economic Policy in the Atlantic Community* (New York: McGraw-Hill, 1968). For a good discussion of the relationship between sovereignty and power, see Harry Gelber, *Sovereignty Through Interdependence* (London: Kluwer Law, 1997).

29. See Alexander Wendt, "Collective Identity Formation and the International State," *American Political Science Review* 88 (1994): 384–96; and Reus-Smit, "The Constitutional Structure."

30. Generally agreeing that sovereignty should be separated from power are theorists as diverse as Brierly, *The Law of Nations*, 13; Waltz, *Theory of International Politics*, 96; Morgenthau, *Politics Among Nations*, 333; and Keohane, "Sovereignty, Interdependence, and International Institutions," 92–93.

31. Keohane develops a separate term for the set of obligations that states occur through their treaty commitments—"operational sovereignty." See Keohane, "Sovereignty, Interdependence, and International Institutions."

32. On the compromise of sovereignty, see Krasner, *Sovereignty*.

33. I draw these examples from Fowler and Bunck, *Law, Power, and the Sovereign State*, 83–125.

34. Closely related would be an institutional theory of norms, arguing that norms help polities achieve interests that they are prevented from achieving because of problems of mistrust and cheating. See Robert O. Keohane, *After Hegemony* (Princeton: Princeton University Press, 1984); and Stephen D. Krasner, "Structural Causes and Regime Consequences: Regimes as Intervening Variables," in Stephen D. Krasner, ed., *International Regimes* (Ithaca: Cornell University Press, 1983), 1–22.

CHAPTER THREE
A BRIEF HISTORY OF CONSTITUTIONS OF INTERNATIONAL SOCIETY IN THE WEST

1. For examples of such histories, see Paul Kennedy, *The Rise and Fall of the Great Powers* (New York: Random House, 1987); Robert Gilpin, *War and Change in World Politics* (Cambridge: Cambridge University Press, 1981).

2. For these histories, see Adam Watson, *The Evolution of International Society: A Comparative Historical Analysis* (London: Routledge, 1992).

3. Andreas Osiander, *The States System of Europe, 1640–1990* (Oxford: Oxford University Press, 1994), 27.

4. Martin Wight, *Systems of States* (London: Leicester University Press, 1977), 24–25.

5. On the Ottomans, see Thomas Naff, "The Ottoman Empire and the European States System," in Hedley Bull and Adam Watson, eds., *The Expansion of International Society* (Oxford: Oxford University Press, 1984), 143–70; and Hedley Bull, "The Emergence of a Universal International Society," in Bull and Watson, eds., *The Expansion*, 117–26.

6. See Adam Watson, "European International Society and Its Expansion," in Bull and Watson, eds., *The Expansion*, 13–32; Hedley Bull, "The Emergence of an International Society"; Stephen Krasner, "Compromising Westphalia," *International Security* 20, no. 3: 115–51.

7. For an insightful analysis of institutional forms of the denial of sovereignty, see David Strang, "Contested Sovereignty: The Social Construction of Colonial Imperialism," in Thomas J. Biersteker and Cynthia Weber, eds., *The Social Construction of State Sovereignty* (Cambridge: Cambridge University Press, 1996), 22–49.

8. See Robert Klein, *Sovereign Equality among States: The History of an Idea* (Toronto: University of Toronto Press, 1974).

9. On Japan, see Gerrit Gong, *The Standard of Civilization in International Society* (Oxford: Oxford University Press, 1984), 28–29.

10. Gong, *The Standard*, 14–15.

11. On weak sovereign states, see Robert Jackson, *Quasi-States: Sovereignty, International Relations, and the Third World* (Cambridge: Cambridge University Press, 1990).

12. General Assembly Resolution 1514, United Nations Declaration on the Granting of Independence to Colonial Peoples and Countries.

13. For an argument that economic subordination actually diminishes former colonies' sovereignty, see Naeem Inayatullah, "Beyond the Sovereignty Dilemma: Quasi-States as Social Construct," in Thomas J. Biersteker and Cynthia Weber, eds., *State Sovereignty as Social Construct* (Cambridge: Cambridge University Press, 1996), 50–80.

14. Daniel Froats and Stephen Krasner, "Minority Rights and the Westphalia Model," in David A. Lake and Donald S. Rothchild, eds., *The International Spread of Ethnic Conflict: Fear, Diffusion, and Escalation* (Princeton: Princeton University Press, 1998). On minority treaties, see Inis Claude, *National Minorities: An International Problem* (Cambridge: Harvard University Press, 1955); Raymond Pearson, *National Minorities in Eastern Europe, 1848–1945* (London: Macmillan, 1983); C. A. Macartney, *National States and National Minorities* (New York: Russell and Russell, 1968).

15. Froats and Krasner, "Minority Rights."

16. Froats and Krasner, "Minority Rights."

17. After the Cold War, minority rights have resurfaced through some international agreements and institutions, although mechanisms for oversight and implementation are weak. These agreements include the 1992 General Assembly Declaration on the Rights of Person Belonging to National or Ethnic, Religious, and Linguistic Minorities, in the 1990 CSCE/OSCE Copenhagen Document for Europe, and in the 1991 Charter of Paris for a New Europe. In its mediation of the breakup of Yugoslavia, the European Community's Arbitration Commission made respect for minority rights a provision of the recognition of new republics.

18. See Robert Keohane and Stanley Hoffmann, "Institutional Change in Europe in the 1980's," in Robert Keohane and Stanley Hoffmann, eds., *The New European Community: Decisionmaking and Institutional Change* (Boulder, Colo.: Westview Press, 1991), 1–39.

19. For helpful accounts of contemporary intervention, see Oliver Ramsbotham and Tom Woodhouse, *Humanitarian Intervention in International Conflict* (Cambridge: Cambridge University Press, 1996); Kelly Kate Pease and David Forsythe, "Human Rights, Humanitarian Intervention, and World Politics," *Human Rights Quarterly* 15 (1993): 290–314; Shashi Tharoor, "United Nations Peacekeeping in Europe," *Survival* 37, no. 2: 121–34; and Lori Fisler Damrosch, ed., *Enforcing Restraint: Collective Intervention in Internal Conflicts* (New York: Council on Foreign Relations Press, 1993).

20. See Paul Taylor, "The United Nations in the 1990s: Proactive Cosmopolitanism and the Issue of Sovereignty," *Political Studies* 47 (special issue, 1997): 538–65.

21. Article 2(4) prohibits unilateral intervention in the form of "the threat or use of force against territorial integrity or political independence of any state, or in any other manner consistent with the Purposes of the United Nations," whereas Article 2(7) is directed against the intervention of the United Nations in matters that are in states' domestic jurisdictions. The two articles, then, seem to leave some room for UN-endorsed intervention—if, that is, it is "consistent with the Purposes of the United Nations" or, if not, a matter in states' domestic jurisdictions. Subsequent UN Documents even more directly condemn intervention, especially unilateral intervention. For arguments that UN law forbids intervention, see Lori Damrosch, "Commentary on Collective Military Intervention to Enforce Human Rights," in Lori Damrosch and David Scheffer, eds., *Law and Force in the New International Order* (Boulder, Colo.: Westview Press, 1991), 215–23.

22. UN Doc. S/RES/688 (1991). On the significance of 688, See David Scheffer, "Toward a Modern Doctrine of Humanitarian Intervention," *University of Toledo Law Review* 23 (winter 1992): 253–94.

23. Here, I rely heavily in the interpretation of Gregory H. Fox, "New Approaches to International Human Rights: The Sovereign State Revisited," in Sohail H. Hashmi, ed., *State Sovereignty: Change and Persistence in International Relations* (University Park: Pennsylvania State University Press, 1997), 105–130.

24. A possible exception is the 1999 Kosovo intervention, which was not authorized by a specific Security Council resolution, but which China attempted to block by passing a resolution condemning the intervention by NATO. The Security Council, however, voted down the resolution.

25. On interpretations of Security Council resolutions on intervention, see David Scheffer, "Toward a Modern Doctrine of Humanitarian Intervention," *University of Toledo Law Review* 23 (1992): 253–94; Jarat Chopra and Thomas Weiss, "Sovereignty Is No Longer Sacrosanct: Codifying Humanitarian Intervention," *Ethics and International Affairs* 6 (1992): 95.

26. See Krasner, "Compromising Westphalia," 125; Jack Donnelly, *International Human Rights* (Boulder, Colo.: Westview Press, 1992); and David Forsythe, *Human Rights and World Politics* (Lincoln: University of Nebraska Press, 1989), 19.

27. On the Concert of Europe, see E. V. Gulick, *Europe's Classical Balance of Power* (Ithaca: Cornell University Press, 1955).

28. On the history of self-determination, see Alfred Cobban, *National Self-Determination* (Oxford: Oxford University Press, 1945); Hurst Hannum, *Autonomy, Sovereignty, and Self-Determination: The Accommodation of Conflicting Rights* (Philadelphia: University of Pennsylvania Press, 1990).

CHAPTER FOUR
HOW REVOLUTIONS IN IDEAS BRING REVOLUTIONS IN SOVEREIGNTY

1. By "active pursuits," I imply that interests are what states determine to achieve once they have taken into account all of the relevant factors, including the nature of the international distribution of power, as opposed to "pre-strategic interests," which are what they may desire prior to taking the international milieu into account. Interests are also distinct from what I call "strategies," which are tactics for achieving an interest—e.g., entering an alliance, building up an army, spreading democratic propaganda. For a discussion of these issues (not necessarily equivalent to my own), see Andrew Moravcsik, "Taking Preferences Seriously: A Liberal Theory of International Politics," *International Organization* 51, no. 4: 513–54.

2. Here, I concur with the constructivist insight that states' interests are not fixed and to be considered as given, but are constructed and shaped through domestic politics. See Peter J. Katzenstein, ed., *The Culture of National Security: News and Identity in World Politics* (New York: Columbia University Press, 1986); and Martha Finnemore, *National Interests in International Society* (Ithaca: Cornell University Press, 1996).

3. Marx's starkest view of ideas is in "The German Ideology," in *The Marx-Engels Reader*, ed. Robert C. Tucker, 2d ed. (New York: W.W. Norton & Co., 1972), 110–64.

4. Max Weber, "The Social Psychology of the World Religions," in *From Max Weber: Essays in Sociology*, ed., trans., and intro. H. H. Gerth and C. Wright Mills (New York: Oxford University Press, 1946), 267–301.

5. A few works predate the trend. See, for instance, John Odell, *U.S. Monetary Policy: Markets, Power, and Ideas as Sources of Change* (Princeton: Princeton University Press, 1982); Jack Snyder, *The Ideology of the Offensive* (Ithaca: Cornell University Press, 1984); and Stephen Van Evera, "The Cult of the Offensive and the Origins of the First World War," *International Security* 9, no. 1. (summer 1984): 58–107. For works that describe and broadly represent the trend, see Judith Goldstein and Robert O. Keohane, eds., *Ideas and Foreign Policy: Beliefs, Institutions, and Political Change* (Ithaca: Cornell University Press, 1993); Katzenstein, ed., *The Culture of National Security*; Peter Hall, ed., *The Political Power of Economic Ideas* (Princeton: Princeton University Press, 1989); Mark Blyth, "Any More Bright Ideas?: The Ideational Turn of Comparative Political Economy," *Comparative Politics* 29 (1997); John Kurt Jacobson, "Much Ado About Ideas: The Cognitive Factor in Economic Policy," *World Politics* 47 (1995); Michael Mann, *The Sources of Social Power*, vol. 1 (Cambridge: Cambridge University Press,

1986). For "constructivist" works, see most prominently the work of Alexander Wendt, set forth in "Collective Identity Formation and the International State," *American Political Science Review* 88 (1994): 384–96, and in "Anarchy Is What States Make of It: The Social Construction of Power Politics," *International Organization* 46 (1992): 395–421.

6. In the first category, see Mlada Bukovansky, "American Identity and Neutral Rights from Independence to the War of 1812," *International Organization* 51 (1997); Richard Price, "Reversing the Gun Sights: Transnational Civil Society Targets Land Mines," *International Organization* 52 (1998); Richard Price and Nina Tannenwald, "Norms and Deterrence: The Nuclear and Chemical Weapons Taboo," in Peter J. Katzenstein, ed., *The Culture of National Security* (New York: Columbia University Press, 1996); Audie Klotz, *Norms in International Relations: The Struggle Against Apartheid* (Ithaca: Cornell University Press, 1995); Martha Finnemore and Kathryn Sikkink, "International Norm Dynamics and Political Change," *International Organization* 52, no. 4, (1998): 898. In the second category, see, for examples, the essays in Goldstein and Keohane, *Ideas and Foreign Policy. Beliefs, Institutions, and Political Change*; and most of the essays in Katzenstein, ed., *The Culture of National Security.*

7. See Ronald L. Jepperson, Alexander Wendt, and Peter J. Katzenstein, "Norms, Identity, and Culture in National Security," in Peter J. Katzenstein, ed., *The Culture of National Security* (New York: Columbia University Press, 1996), 58–60.

8. Such versions adopt a variety of strategies, ranging from showing how utility functions are specified by ideas, culture, or psychological schema, to asserting the rationality of the attempts of "norms entrepreneurs" to construct common knowledge and to alter others' utility functions in accordance with their commitments, to devising models of how ideas modify the pursuit of rational action as "focal points" or "resolvers of uncertainty," and to charting the social context of rational action. See Finnemore and Sikkink, "International Norm Dynamics and Political Change," 909–15; Goldstein and Keohane, "Ideas and Foreign Policy: An Analytical Framework," 3–30; Miles Kahler, "Rationality in International Relations," *International Organization* 52, no. 4 (1998): 933–38; James G. March and Johan Olsen, "The Institutional Dynamics of International Political Orders," *International Organization* 52, no. 4 (1998): 952–54; Jon Elster, *Nuts and Bolts for the Social Sciences* (Cambridge: Cambridge University Press, 1989); Jon Elster, *Political Psychology* (Cambridge; Cambridge University Press, 1993). For a more skeptical view of the reconcilability of constructivist and rationalist traditions, see John Gerard Ruggie, "What Makes the World Hang Together? Neo-Utilitarianism and the Social Constructivist Challenge," *International Organization* 52, no. 4 (1998): 883–85.

9. See the essays in Thomas J. Biersteker and Cynthia Weber, *State Sovereignty as Social Construct* (Cambridge: Cambridge University Press, 1996); Jepperson, Wendt, and Katzenstein, "Norms, Identity, and Culture in National Security," 45–46; John Gerard Ruggie, "Territoriality and Beyond: Problematizing Modernity in International Relations," *International Organization* 47, no. 1 (1993): 139–74; Ruggie, "What Makes the World Hang Together? Neo-Utilitarianism and the

Social Constructivist Challenge," 870; Wendt, "Anarchy Is What States Make of It: The Social Construction of Power Politics," 412–15.

10. Rodney Bruce Hall, *National Collective Identity: Social Constructs and International Systems* (New York: Columbia University Press, 1999), 51–58.

11. Jeffrey T. Checkel, "The Constructivist Turn in International Relations Theory," *World Politics* 50: 340–42; Janice Thomson, "State Sovereignty in International Relations: Bridging the Gap Between Theory and Empirical Research," *International Studies Quarterly* 39 (1995). See also John Gerard Ruggie's comment, "Social constructivists in international relations have not yet managed to devise a theory of constitutive rules," in Ruggie, "What Makes the World Hang Together? 872.

12. Robert Dahl's classic "intuitive idea of power" is that "*A* has power over *B* to the extent that he can get *B* to do something that *B* would not otherwise do," found in Dahl, "The Concept of Power," *Behavioral Science*, 2 (1957): 201–15. For a notion of power friendly to the first role, see Steven Lukes, *Power: A Radical View* (London: Macmillan, 1974).

13. For examples of constructivists who also emphasize the shaping of identities, see Mlada Bukovansky, "American Identity and Neutral Rights from Independence to the War of 1812" Richard Price, "Reversing the Gun Sights; Richard Price and Nina Tannenwald, "Norms and Deterrence; Audie Klotz, *Norms in International Relations*; and Martha Finnemore and Kathryn Sikkink, "International Norm Dynamics and Political Change," 898. Calling for an emphasis on the persuasive and discursive powers of ideas is Albert Yee, "The Causal Effects of Ideas on Policies," *International Organization* 50 (1996): 69–108.

For a macrosociological works on the origins of intellectual ideas, see Randall Collins, *The Sociology of Philosophies* (Cambridge: Harvard University Press, 1988); and Robert Wuthnow, *Communities of Discourse* (Cambridge: Harvard University Press, 1989).

14. For a definition of identity, see Jepperson, Wendt, and Katzenstein, "Norms, Identity, and Culture in National Security," 59. There, they define identities as "images of individuality and distinctiveness" ("selfhood") held and projected by an actor and formed (and modified over time) through relations with significant "others."

15. Concerned with the adoption of ideas into identities, the first role is distinguished from psychological theories, which focus on mental processes—biases, perception, attribution, and the like. For an overview of the role of these processes in international politics, see Robert Jervis, *Perception and Misperception in International Politics* (Princeton: Princeton University Press, 1976).

16. This perception of the person is found in "common morality" philosophies, and in philosophies of the free will. See Alan Donagan, *The Theory of Morality* (Chicago: University of Chicago Press, 1977); and Harry Frankfurt, "Freedom of the Will and the Concept of the Person," *Journal of Philosophy* 68 (1971): 5–20. For a fascinating account by a social scientist who seeks to defend a notion of the person as holding a moral "perspective" that cannot be reduced to sociocultural, economic, biological, or psychological factors, see Kristen Renwick Monroe, *The Heart of Altruism: Perceptions of a Common Humanity* (Princeton: Princeton University Press, 1996).

17. The "diffusion of ideas" also plays a prominent role in Emanuel Adler and Peter Haas, "Conclusion: Epistemic Communities, World Order, and the Creation of a Reflective Research Program," *International Organization* 46 (1992): 378–81.

18. Some works on ideas have noted the central role of systemic "shocks," such as economic collapse or systemic war. An example of the emergence of Keynesianism after World War II is Peter Hall, ed., *The Political Power of Economic Ideas.*

19. On the role of "social facts," see Peter L. Berger and Thomas Luckmann, *The Social Construction of Reality* (New York: Doubleday, 1966). The term is originally from Emile Durkheim, in "The Rules of Sociological Method," in *The Rules of Sociological Method*, ed. Steven Lukes, trans. W. D. Halls (New York: Free Press, 1982), 35–38.

20. I have not listed the types of circumstances of reflection exhaustively, and there could be others: means of communication such as the printing press, for instance.

21. On Durkheim, see Emile Durkheim, "Marxism and Sociology: The Materialist Conception of History," in *The Rules of Sociological Method*, ed. Steven Lukes, trans. W. D. Halls (New York: Free Press, 1982), 171; Emile Durkheim, *The Division of Labor in Society*, intro. Lewis A. Coser, trans. W. D. Halls (New York: Free Press, 1984); Emile Durkheim, *The Elementary Forms of the Religious Life*, trans. Joseph Ward Swain (New York: Free Press, 1915); and Emile Durkheim, "The Contribution of Sociology to Psychology and Philosophy," in Durkheim, *The Rules of Sociological Method*, ed. and intro. Steven Lukes, trans. W. D. Halls (New York: Free Press, 1982), 236–40.

22. That is, I do not examine structures that consist of ideas themselves—discourse, languages, and so on. The closest I come is in allowing "social facts" to be circumstances of reflection, as I described in the previous section. For a discussion of this kind of structure, see, for instance, Terence Hawkes' work on linguistic structuralism, *Structuralism and Semiotics* (Los Angeles: University of California Press, 1977).

23. For a stark notion of ideas as "hooks," adopted instrumentally, see Kenneth Shepsle, "Comment," in *Regulatory Policy and the Social Sciences*, ed. Roger Noll (Berkeley: University of California Press, 1985), 231–37.

24. On the tenets of rational choice theory and the role of ideas in relation to them, see Michael Taylor, "Structure, Culture and Action in the Explanation of Social Change," *Politics and Society* 17 (1989): 115–62.

25. The term is from Goldstein and Keohane, who develop the concept in *Ideas and Foreign Policy*, 13. See also Ann Swidler's idea of culture as a "tool-kit," a subtle, creative variation of this, in her "Culture in Action: Symbols and Strategies," *American Sociological Review* 51 (1986): 273–86.

26. Weber, "The Social Psychology of the World Religions," 280.

27. Most ideas that function as resolvers of uncertainty will be instrumental ideas. An example would be "strategic culture," a set of ideas that specify how to maximize military security or power. For a discussion of the concept, see Alastair Iain Johnston, "Thinking About Strategic Culture," *International Security* 19 (1995): 32–64.

28. Other social theories that posit ideas as a form of social power that is separable from, but not exclusive of, other forms of social power, include Jürgen Habermas, *Legitimation Crisis*, trans. Thomas McCarthy (Boston: Beacon Press, 1975); and Michael Mann, *The Sources of Social Power*, vol. 1 (Cambridge: Cambridge University Press, 1986). Mann's notion of "ideological power," which he uses to categorize social power in societies across history, is especially helpful here. For the concept, see pp. 22–24. For a viewpoint that stresses the essential role of power in constructing norms of sovereignty, see Thomas J. Biersteker and Cynthia Weber, "The Social Construction of State Sovereignty," in Biersteker and Weber, *State Sovereignty as Social Construct* (Cambridge: Cambridge University Press, 1996), 1–21. For works in the recent political science literature on ideas that emphasize the social power of ideas, see the essays in Judith Goldstein and Robert O. Keohane, eds., *Ideas and Foreign Policy: Beliefs, Institutions, and Political Change*; and most of the essays in Peter J. Katzenstein ed., *The Culture of National Security.*

29. Rational-choice theories, of course, are not inherently hostile to ideas explanations. Ideas may shape the preferences that define the form of utility that an actor seeks to maximize.

30. On the tradition of Realism, its commonality and variation, see Michael Doyle, *Ways of War and Peace* (New York: W. W. Norton and Company, 1997), 41–201.

31. In Morgenthau's pithy formulation, "The main signpost that helps political realism to find its way through the landscape of international politics is the concept of *interest defined in terms of power*," Hans J. Morgenthau, *Politics Among Nations: The Struggle for Power and Peace*, 6th ed., rev. Kenneth W. Thompson (New York: Alfred A. Knopf, 1985), 11. Morgenthau is somewhat vague on exactly what power is—in the beginning of *Politics Among Nations*, he writes that power is "anything that establishes and maintains the control of man over man," 11. It is later, in a chapter entitled "Elements of National Power," that he discusses power as the resources to fight war, 127–69. There, he lists among the "elements of national power" geography, natural resources, industrial capacity, population, and military preparedness, as well as "softer" elements such as national character, national morale, and the quality of government, which also contribute to effective combat. Similar notions of power are put forth by Kenneth Waltz, *Theory of International Politics* (Lexington, Mass.: Addison-Wesley, 1979); and Robert Gilpin, *War and Change in World Politics* (Cambridge: Cambridge University Press, 1981), 13–14. Gilpin's definition, though, is slightly more restricted: "Power refers simply to the military, economic, and technological capabilities of states," 13.

For helpful interpretations and critiques of Morgenthau's notion of power, see David Baldwin, "Neoliberalism, Neorealism and World Politics," in *Neorealism and Neoliberalism*, ed. David Baldwin (New York: Columbia University Press, 1993), 3–28. Helpful criticisms of Morgenthau on this point are also in Stanley Hoffmann, *Janus and Minerva: Essays in the Theory and Practice of International Politics* (Boulder, Colo.: Westview Press, 1987), 78; Michael Joseph Smith, *Realist Thought from Weber to Kissinger* (Baton Rouge: Louisiana State University Press, 1986), 141–47; and Robert O. Keohane, "Realism, Neorealism, and the Study of World Politics," in *Neorealism and Its Critics*, ed. Robert O. Keohane (New York: Columbia University Press, 1986), 11.

32. When I use the term "power" in discussions of Realism, I mean the Realist version of power: the resources to fight war. I do not, of course, intend to depart from my earlier contention that power does not necessarily mean material power, and that ideas, too, can be a form of power.

33. Keohane points out the continuity of the rationality assumption in Realist thought: "Morgenthau's sophisticated use of the rationality assumption was consistent both with that of Thucydides and those of later realists and neorealists, including Waltz." He also offers a helpful definition of the assumption, which he argues is implicit in Morgenthau and most carefully elaborated in neoclassical economics: "To say that governments act rationally in this sense means that they have consistent, ordered preferences, and that they calculate the costs and benefits of all alternative policies in order to maximize their utility in light both of those preferences and of their perceptions of the nature of reality" See Robert O. Keohane, "Realism, Neorealism and the Study of World Politics," 11–12. See also Michael Joseph Smith, *Realist Thought*, 221.

34. See the realism set forth in Fareed Zakaria, *From Wealth to Power: The Unusual Origins of America's Role* (Princeton: Princeton University Press, 1998).

35. See Smith, *Realist Thought*, 219.

36. The relationship between anarchy and states' interests and power is not a causal theory that I intend to test, but it is a corresponding assumption of Realism. Most Realists, however, including Waltz, Morgenthau, and others, assert that there is a relationship between anarchy, interests, and power of the sort that I describe here. It is important, too, that not all Realists are Structural Realists. Some place a greater emphasis on the domestic factors that shape a state's pursuit of power.

37. See Thomas Hobbes, *Leviathan*, ed. and intro. C. B. MacPherson (Harmondsworth, U.K.: Penguin Books, 1968). On Hobbes in international relations thought, see Hoffmann, *Janus and Minerva*, 26–33; and Doyle, *Ways of War and Peace*, 111–36.

38. See Smith, *Realist Thought*, 220–24. See Morgenthau on ideologies: "The actor on the political scene cannot help 'playing an act' by concealing the true nature of his political actions behind the mask of a political ideology. The more removed the individual is from a particular power struggle, the more likely he is to understand its true nature. So it is not by accident that foreigners have often a better understanding of the politics of a particular country than have the natives, and that scholars are better equipped than politicians to understand what politics is all about. On the other hand, politicians have an ineradicable tendency to deceive themselves about what they are doing by referring to their policies not in terms of power but in terms of either legal or ethical principles or biological necessities. In other words, while all politics is necessarily pursuit of power, ideologies render involvement in the at contest for power psychologically and morally acceptable to the actors and their audience," in Morgenthau, *Politics Among Nations*, 102. See also his treatment of morality, mores, and law on pp. 243–48. For Waltz, see *Theory of International Politics*, 82–87.

39. Carr: "Current theories of morality have been designed to perpetuate [the] supremacy of the English-speaking peoples," in E. H. Carr, *The Twenty Years' Crisis, 1919–39* (New York: Harper and Row, 1964), 69. "What matters is that these

supposedly absolute and universal principles were not principles at all, but the unconscious reflections of national interests at a particular time," 87.

40. Carr, *The Twenty Years' Crisis*, 93.

41. Morgenthau, *Politics Among Nations*, 31, 260–74.

42. Gilpin, *War and Change*, 34, 35.

43. Henry Kissinger, *A World Restored* (Boston: Houghton Mifflin, 1957). For a treatment of Realism, arguing that it does allow for ethical ideals to be important, see James Lee Ray, "The Abolition of Slavery and the End of International War," *International Organization* 43 (1989): 405–39.

44. Smith, *Realist Thought*, 72

45. Morgenthau, *Politics Among Nations*, 5, 31, 102–3, 260–74.

46. Kissinger allows a greater role for ideas in his *Diplomacy* (New York: Simon and Schuster, 1994).

47. Morgenthau, *Politics Among Nations*, chapters 15–19.

48. Carr, *The Twenty Years' Crisis*, 132–45.

49. John Hall raises the problem in "Ideas and the Social Sciences," in *Ideas and Foreign Policy: Beliefs, Institutions, and Political Change*, ed. Judith Goldstein and Robert Keohane (Ithaca: Cornell University Press, 1993), 31–54, 39. On this point, Hall cites Patricia Crone, *Pre-Industrial Societies* (Oxford: Basil Blackwell, 1989), 138.

50. The closest is Gilpin, who explains the "rules of the system" according to Realist logic, Gilpin, in *War and Change*.

51. Occasionally, Realists acknowledge more complexity: Morgenthau asserts that during its four centuries of existence, international law has mostly been observed scrupulously. But he is referring to law that governs the movement of merchant vessels and diplomats, not troops, and he insists again and again that law itself does not alter fundamental interests or how states pursue them. *Politics Among Nations*, 296–97.

52. This is an implication of the argument of Stephen Krasner that the "Westphalian model is an analytic assumption for realism. For realism the ontological givens in the international system are Westphalian states, understood as unitary rational actors operating in an anarchic setting and striving to enhance their well being and security." See Stephen Krasner, "Compromising Westphalia," *International Security* 20, no. 3: (1995/96) 115–51.

53. Barrington Moore, *The Social Origins of Democracy and Dictatorship* (Boston: Beacon Press, 1966); Theda Skocpol, *States and Social Revolutions: A Comparative Analysis of France, Russia, and China* (Cambridge: Cambridge University Press, 1979); Brian Downing, *The Military Revolution and Political Change: Origins of Democracy and Autocracy in Early Modern Europe* (Princeton: Princeton University Press, 1992). For a helpful recent essay on the tradition of macrohistorical sociology, see Ira Katznelson, "Structure and Configuration in Comparative Politics," in *Comparative Politics: Rationality, Culture and Structure*, ed. Mark Irving Lichbach and Alan S. Zuckerman (Cambridge: Cambridge University Press, 1997), 81–112.

54. See Geoffrey Garret and Barry R. Weingast, "Ideas, Interests, and Institutions: Constructing the European Community's Internal Market," in *Ideas and*

Foreign Policy, ed. Judith Goldstein and Robert Keohane (Ithaca: Cornell University Press, 1993), 173–206.

55. Thomas Risse-Kappen, "Ideas Do Not Float Freely: Transnational Coalitions, Domestic Structures, and the End of the Cold War," *International Organization* 48 (1994): 185–214.

56. On the role of publics, see David Lumsdaine, *Moral Vision in International Politics* (Princeton: Princeton University Press, 1993); and Robert McElroy, *Morality and American Foreign Policy* (Princeton: Princeton University Press, 1992).

57. In the contemporary political science literature, one sort of intellectual community, which political scientists Emmanuel Adler and Peter Haas have mapped, is the "epistemic community," made up of natural scientists or social scientists, who create and provide technical knowledge by which they influence issues like environmental politics or arms control. Adler and Haas, "Conclusion"; see also Ernst Haas, *When Knowledge Is Power: Three Models of Change in International Organizations* (Berkeley: University of California Press, 1991). See also the work of G. John Ikenberry, "Creating Yesterday's New World Order: Keynesian 'New Thinking' and the Anglo-American Postwar Settlement," in *Ideas and Foreign Policy*, ed. Judith Goldstein and Robert Keohane (Ithaca: Cornell University Press, 1993), 57–86.

58. This is similar to reputational social power. On these networks, see Kathryn Sikkink and Margaret F. Keck, Activists Beyond Borders: Advocacy Networks: International Politics (Ithaca: Cornell University Press, 1998).

59. Judith Goldstein, *Ideas, Institutions, and American Trade Policy* (Ithaca: Cornell University Press, 1993), 3.

60. On rules of appropriateness and organizational theory in general, see James G. March and Johan P. Olsen, *Rediscovering Institutions: The Organizational Basic of Politics* (New York: Free Press, 1989). See also P. J. Dimaggio and W. W. Powell, "The Iron Cage Revisited: Institutional Isomorphism and Collective Rationality in Organizational Fields," *American Sociological Review* (April 1983): 147–60, whose approaches to explaining "institutional isomorphism" incorporate in many ways both roles of ideas as well as structural explanations.

61. See Goldstein, *Ideas, Interests, and American Trade Policy*, 3. In her work, it is this second dynamic that she calls institutionalization.

62. My focus on a particular set of actors renders my definition of international society narrower than the traditional one of Hedley Bull in Bull, *The Anarchical Society* (New York: Columbia University Press, 1977), 13.

63. John W. Meyer, "The World Polity and the Authority of the Nation-State," *Studies of the Modern World System*, ed. A. Bergeson (New York: Academic Press, 1980), 109–38. Similarly, Alexander Wendt proposes three international causal mechanisms found in the international system: "structural contexts," "systemic processes," and "strategic practice," which play a role similar to Meyer's world polity. See Alexander Wendt, "Collective Identity Formation and the International State," 384–96.

64. In her empirical work on international society, Martha Finnemore shows how an international social structure of norms influenced the policies of states toward science issues, humanitarian conduct in wartime, and development assistance. She traces carefully how members of international organizations "teach"

norms to members of state institutions, reconstituting their identities—what looks a lot like ideas' first role—but she also acknowledges the role of political, especially bureaucratic, influence in affecting policy—social power. Martha Finnemore, *National Interests in International Society.*

65. On these criteria, see Philip E. Tetlock and Aaron Belkin, "Counterfactual Thought Experiments in World Politics: Logical, Methodological, and Psychological Perspectives," in Philip E. Tetlock and Aaron Belkin, eds., *Counterfactual Thought Experiments in World Politics* (Princeton: Princeton University Press, 1996), 21–25. Their "minimal-rewrite-of-history" rule holds that in the alternative counterfactual world, one can imagine the proposed cause—here, ideas—being absent, while the proposed effect—here, revolutions in sovereignty—still results. That is, the proposed cause (ideas) and the alternative imagined cause (structures alone) were not themselves so tightly causally linked that we could not imagine the simultaneous absence of one and presence of the other. I hold that it is plausible that even had ideas had no influence, structures alone could plausibly have produced the same outcome. Structures were not so dependent upon ideas themselves that in the absence of the ideas, the structures would have disappeared or have been altered out of recognition. In historical fact, as I suggest, structures *were* affected by ideas. But for the counterfactual to be valid we only need to accept that structures could plausibly have operated completely independently of ideas.

66. The comparison of the effects of ideas across separate times and places within a single revolution of sovereignty is what Gary King, Robert O. Keohane, and Sidney Verba, in their work on political science methodology, refer to as the strategy of "making many observations from few." See *Designing Social Inquiry* (Princeton: Princeton University Press, 1994), 217–28. It is also reflected in Tetlock and Belkin's sixth criterion, "projectability." See *Counterfactual Thought Experiments*, 30–31.

67. See King, Keohane, and Verba, *Designing Social Inquiry*, 28–29.

68. See King, Keohane, and Verba's definition of causation in *Designing Social Inquiry*, 81–82. A vital methodological point: I am not here proposing a general covering law, "it takes a revolution in ideas to bring a revolution in sovereignty," and am not, for methodological purposes, proposing the two revolution as instances, or tests, of a single law. Rather, I present ideas as a form of what Jon Elster calls a "causal mechanism," a manner of exerting influence, in Elster's words "a specific causal pattern that can be recognized after the event but rarely foreseen." Ideas will not, then, be captured through the "nomological" method, through "covering laws" that take the form "if (certain) ideas occur, then we will have a (certain) political result." We can, however, assert that *this* causal mechanism (ideas) rather than *that* causal mechanism (structure alone) is behind *that* observed political event (revolutions in sovereignty). Once we have seen that a revolution in sovereignty has occurred, we can then sort out the claims of ideas and structure through the types of comparisons over time and place that I have described. Jon Elster, *Political Psychology*, 2–3.

Of course, as I outlined in chapters 2 and 3, I view both cases as "revolutions in sovereignty," since they revise at least one face of sovereignty. But they are not similar enough phenomena to be viewed as members of the same category of event to be explained causally. I treat them idiographically, not nomothetically. Each revolution represents a separate counterfactual claim. I seek to break down each counterfactual claim, though, into separate "cases" of polities that can be compared over time and space. It is at this level that I seek generalization through the comparative method. For the basis of such reasoning, see Belkin and Tetlock, *Counterfactual Thought Experiments*, 10–12.

CHAPTER FIVE
WESTPHALIA AS ORIGIN

1. William Shakespeare, *Richard II*, ed. Michael Clamp (Cambridge: Cambridge University Press, 1992), act 4, scene 2, lines 247–50. For a discussion of Shakespeare's theory of kingship, see Ernst Kantorowicz, *The King's Two Bodies* (Princeton: Princeton University Press, 1957), 24–42.

2. William Shakespeare, *King Henry V*, ed. Andrew Gurr (Cambridge: Cambridge University Press, 1992), act 2, scene 2, lines 170–76.

3. To be more precise, the law by which the king ruled was internally sovereign. By this law, in both England and France, the king was still limited by parliament in some respects. The age of absolute monarchy had not yet arrived. On the transition from the medieval to the modern idea of kingship, see Geoffrey Barraclough, *The Medieval Empire: Ideal and Reality* (London: G. Philip, 1950).

4. See Friedrich Meinecke, *Machiavellianism: The Doctrine of Raison d'Etat and Its Place in Modern History*, trans. Douglas Scott (Boulder, Colo.: Westview Press, 1984).

5. Emeric de Vattel, *The Law of Nations* (Philadelphia: T. & J. W. Johnson, 1844).

6. Leo Gross, "The Peace of Westphalia, 1648–1948," *American Journal of International Law* 42 (1948): 28; Hans Morgenthau, *Politics Among Nations: The Struggle For Power and Peace*, 6th ed. (New York: Alfred A. Knopf, 1985), 328–30; Kalevi J. Holsti, *Peace and War: Armed Conflicts and International Order, 1648–1989* (Cambridge: Cambridge University Press, 1991).

7. See especially Stephen Krasner, "Westphalia and All That," in *Ideas and Foreign Policy: Beliefs, Institutions, and Political Change*, ed. Judith Goldstein and Robert O. Keohane (Ithaca: Cornell University Press, 1993), 235–64; and Krasner, "Compromising Westphalia," *International Security* 20, no. 3 (1995/96): 115–51.

8. For a similar view, see Martin Wight, *Systems of States* (London: Leicester University Press, 1977); and Charles Tilly, *Coercion, Capital, and European States AD 990–1992* (Oxford: Basil Blackwell. 1992), 161–83.

9. On the body of Christ metaphor, see Ernst Kantorowicz, *The King's Two Bodies*, 193–272.

10. John Gerard Ruggie, "Continuity and Transformation in the World Polity: Toward a Neorealist Synthesis," in *Neorealism and its Critics*, ed. Robert O. Keohane (New York: Columbia University Press, 1986), 141–48. See also Hendrik Spruyt, *The Sovereign State And Its Competitors* (Princeton: Princeton University Press, 1994), 34–36; Brian Tierney, *Crisis of Church and State* (Englewood Cliffs, N.J.: Prentice-Hall, 1964); Michael Wilks, *The Problem of Sovereignty in the Middle Ages* (Cambridge: Cambridge University Press, 1964).

11. The vast body of medieval scholarship ranges from works that emphasize the role of common norms and ideals to works of a Marxist/structuralist perspective. But even the latter sort of works do not omit the role of norms. See, for instance, Marc Bloch, *Feudal Society*, 2 vols., trans. L. A. Manyon (Chicago: University of Chicago Press, 1960). Similarly, the study of Georges Duby on the mâconnaise region of France, which emphasizes constant war, recognizes the role of norms. See his *La société aux XIe et XIIe siècles dans la région mâconnaise* (Paris: Ecole des Hautes Etudes, 1953). For a recent work that emphasizes common norms and ideals, see Susan Reynolds, *Kingdoms and Communities in Western Europe, 900–1300* (Oxford: Clarendon Press, 1984). See also Tierney, *Crisis of Church and State*. On medieval historiography, see Norman Cantor, *Inventing the Middle Ages: The Lives, Works, and Ideas of the Great Medievalists of the Twentieth Century* (New York: W. Morrow, 1991).

12. See, for instance, Markus Fischer, "Feudal Europe, 800–1300: Communal Discourse and Conflictual Practices," *International Organization* 46 (1992): 427–66. See also the response to Fischer by Rodney Bruce Hall and Friedrich Kratochwil, "Medieval Tales: Neorealist 'Science' and the Abuse of History," *International Organization* 47 (1993): 479–91.

13. Duby, *La société*.

14. See Reynolds, *Kingdoms and Communities*; and Gianfranco Poggi, *The Development of the Modern State: A Sociological Introduction* (Stanford: Stanford University Press, 1978).

15. See Joseph R. Strayer, *The Medieval Origins of the Modern State* (Princeton: Princeton University Press, 1970); Joseph R. Strayer and Dana C. Munro, *The Middle Ages, 395–1500*, 4th ed. (New York: Appleton-Century-Crofts, Inc., 1959); John H. Mundy, *Europe in the High Middle Ages, 1150–1309* (New York: Basic Books, 1973); Reynolds, *Kingdoms and Communities*; and Walter Ullman, *Principles of Government and Politics in the Middle Ages* (New York: Barnes & Noble, 1966). For a helpful piece by an international relations scholar on power, ideas, and authority in the Middle Ages, see Rodney Bruce Hall, "Moral Authority as a Power Resource," *International Organization* 51, no. 4 (1997): 591–622.

16. Strayer, *The Medieval Origins of the Modern State*; Garret Mattingly, *Renaissance Diplomacy* (Boston: Houghton-Mifflin, 1955), 56–57; Wight, *Systems of States*.

17. See also Spruyt, *The Sovereign State System and Its Competitors*, for a nonlinear account of the origins of the state system.

18. Wight, *Systems of States*; and Tilly, *Coercion, Capital and European States*, 77–78.

19. Robert A. Kann, *A History of the Habsburg Empire* (Berkeley: University of California Press, 1974), 1–24; H. G. Koenigsberger, *Estates and Revolutions: Essays in Early Modern European History* (Ithaca: Cornell University Press, 1971); J. Berenger, *History of the Habsburg Empire* (London: Berenger, 1994); Johannes Arndt, "The Emperor and the Reich (1600–1648)," in Klauss Bussmann and Heinz Schilling, eds., *1648—War and Peace in Europe* (Münster, Germany: Westfalisches Landesmuseum, 1998), 69.

20. Jonathan Israel, *The Dutch Republic: Its Rise, Greatness, and Fall, 1477–1806* (Oxford: Oxford University Press, 1995), 9–40; Pieter Geyl, *The Revolt of the Netherlands, 1555–1609* (London: Williams and Norgate, 1932).

21. Gerald Strauss, *Law, Resistance, and the State: The Opposition to Roman Law in Reformation Germany* (Princeton: Princeton University Press, 1986), 136–64; Hajo Holborn, *A History of Modern Germany*, Vol. I: *The Reformation* (New York: Alfred A. Knopf, 1959); John Gagliardo, *Germany Under the Old Regime, 1600–1790* (London: Longmans, 1991); Geoffrey Barraclough, *The Origins of Modern Germany* (Oxford: Basil Blackwell, 1947).

22. Koenigsberger, *Estates and Revolutions*; Barraclough, *The Origins of Modern Germany*, 355–405; Holborn, *A History of Modern Germany*, 284–338; Johannes Burkhardt, "The Summitless Pyramid: War Aims and Peace Compromise among Europe's Universalistic Powers," in Klaus Bussmann and Heinz Schilling, eds., *1648—War and Peace in Europe*, Münster, Germany: Westfalisches Landesmuseum, 1998), 54, 56.

23. Sovereignty at Augsburg was qualified, though. First, only Catholic and Lutheran regions were included in the settlement: Zwinglian and Calvinist "sacramentarians" and Anabaptist "sectarians" were not to be tolerated. Second, also included was an "ecclesiastical reservation" stating that principalities would retain whatever faith they had at the time of the settlement; if a bishop or an archbishop were to convert to Protestantism, he would lose his office and a Catholic would replace him. Finally, there was to be no toleration for dissenting individuals or congregations within principalities. On the terms of Augsburg, see Holborn, *A History of Modern Germany*, 243–46; and Barraclough, *The Origins of Modern Germany*, 371.

24. John Elliott, "War and Peace in Europe, 1618–1648," in Bussmann and Schilling, eds., *1648—War and Peace in Europe*, 24.

25. Elliott, "War and Peace," 23.

26. It is important to note that France and Spain failed to settle their war, which they continued to fight until the Peace of the Pyrenees in 1659.

27. Historian Heinhard Steiger explains that the participants in the negotiations saw it as imperative that they achieve a "unitary peace." See Heinhard Steiger, "Concrete Peace and General Order: The Legal Meaning of the Treaties of 24 October 1648," in Bussmann and Schilling, eds., *1648—War and Peace in Europe*, 444.

28. Volker Gerhardt, "On the Historical Significance of the Peace of Westphalia: Twelve Theses," in Bussmann and Schilling, eds., *1648—War and Peace in Europe*, 485.

29. Gerhardt, "On the Historical Significance," 485; Konrad Repgen, "Negotiating the Peace of Westphalia: A Survey with an Examination of the Major Problems," in Bussmann and Schilling, eds., *1648—War and Peace in Europe*, 355–56. Elliott, "War and Peace," 37.

30. Repgen, "Negotiating the Peace of Westphalia," 355.

31. Andreas Osiander, *The States System of Europe, 1640–1990* (Oxford: Clarendon Press, 1994), 27.

32. Steiger, "Concrete Peace and General Order, 440.

33. Steiger, "Concrete Peace and General Order," 442.

34. Osiander, *The States System*, 72. For the text of the treaties, see Fred L. Israel, ed., *Major Peace Treaties of Modern History, 1648–1967* (New York: Chelsea House Publishers, 1967), for the Treaty of Münster; and Clive Parry, ed., *The Consolidated Treaty Series* (Dobbs Ferry, N.Y.: Oceana Publications, 1981), 198–269, for the Treaty of Osnabrück. On the settlement in general, see Fritz Dickmann, *Der Westphaelische Frieden* (Münster, Germany: Aschendorff, 1965); Fritz Dickmann, Kiremhild Goronzy, Emil Shieche, Hans Wagner, and Ernst Manfred Wermter, eds., *Acta Pacis Westphalicae* (Münster, Germany: Aschendorff, 1962); Fritz Dickmann, "Rechtsgedanke und Machtpolitik bei Richelieu: Studienen neu endeckten Quellen," *Historische Zeitschrift* 196 (1963): 265–319; George Pages, *The Thirty Years' War*, trans. David Maland and John Hooper (New York: Harper and Row, 1970); Geoffrey Parker, *The Thirty Years' War* (London: Routledge, Kegan, and Paul, 1997); J. V. Polisensky, *The Thirty Years' War*, trans. Robert Evans (Berkeley: University of California Press, 1971); T. K. Rabb, ed., *The Thirty Years' War: Problems of Motive, Extent, and Effect* (Boston: D. C. Heath and Company, 1964).

35. Heinz Schilling, "War and Peace at the Emergence of Modernity—Europe Between State Belligerence, Religious Wars, and the Desire for Peace," in Bussmann and Schilling, eds., *1648—War and Peace in Europe*, 20.

36. Heinz Duchhardt, "The Peace of Westphalia as *Lieu de Mémoire* in Germany and Europe," in Bussmann and Schilling, eds., *1648—War and Peace in Europe*, 41.

37. Steiger, "Concrete Peace and General Order," 440.

38. Gerhardt, "On the Historical Significance," 487.

39. Osiander, *The States System*, 72. On the settlement in general, see Dickmann et al., *Acta Pacis Westphalicae*; Dickmann, *Der Westphaelische Frieden*; Dickmann, "Rechtsgedanke"; Pages, *The Thirty Years' War*; Parker, *The Thirty Years' War*; Polisensky, *The Thirty Years' War*; and Rabb, ed., *The Thirty Years' War.*

40. F. H. Hinsley, *Sovereignty*, 2d ed. (Cambridge: Cambridge University Press, 1986; Jens Bartelson, *A Genealogy of Sovereignty* (Cambridge: Cambridge University Press, 1995).

41. Osiander, *The States System*, 51–66.

42. Dieter Wyduckel, "The Imperial Constitution and the Imperial Doctrine of Public Law: Facing the Institutional Challenge of the Peace of Westphalia," in Bussmann and Schilling, eds., *1648—War and Peace in Europe*, 77.

43. Wyduckel, "The Imperial Constitution," 80.

44. Fred Israel, ed., *Major Peace Treaties*, 27.

45. Osiander, *The States System*, 46–47.

46. On the views of the diplomats, see Osiander, *The States System*, 27, 41, 77–89; Michael Roberts, *Gustavus Adolphus*, 2 vols. (London: Longmans, Green, 1958); Michael Roberts, *Essays in Swedish History* (London: Weidenfeld and Nicolson, 1967), 82–110; Carl J. Burckhardt, *Richelieu and His Age*, trans. Bernard Hoy (New York: Harcourt, Brace, Jovanovich, 1970), 262–450; Robert Knecht, *Richelieu* (London: Longmans, 1991), 84–118; Armand-Jean du Plessis, duc de Richelieu, *The Political Testament of Cardinal Richelieu: The Significant Chapters and Supporting Selections*, trans. Henry Bertram Hill (Madison: University of Wisconsin Press, 1981).

47. William F. Church, *Richelieu and Reason of State* (Princeton: Princeton University Press, 1972), 283–349; Victor-L. Tapié, *France in the Age of Louis XIII and Richelieu*, trans. and ed. D. McN. Lockie (Cambridge: Cambridge University Press, 1984), 133–34; and Klaus Malettke, "France's Imperial Policy during the Thirty Years' War and the Peace of Westphalia," in Bussmann and Schilling, eds., *1648—War and Peace in Europe*, 184.

48. Quoted in Holsti, *Peace and War*, 27, from Geoffrey Symcox, ed., *War Diplomacy, and Imperialism, 1618–1763* (New York: Walker, 1974), 103–5.

49. Quoted in Parker, *The Thirty Years' War*, 184, from C. T. Odhner, *Die Politik Schwedens im Westphälische Friedens congress und die Gründung der schwedischen Herrschaft in Deutschland* (Gotha, 1877), 163.

50. Duchardt, "The Peace of Westphalia as *Lieu de Mémoire*," 44.

51. Johannes Arndt, "The Emperor and the Reich," 74.

52. Quoted in David Maland, *Europe in the Seventeenth Century* (London: Macmillan, 1966), 16; see also Mattingly, *Renaissance Diplomacy*, and Klaus Jaitner, "The Popes and the Struggle for Power during the Sixteenth and Seventeenth Centuries," in Bussmann and Schilling, eds., *1648—War and Peace in Europe*, 61.

53. Kann, *A History of the Habsburg Empire*, 52; Osiander, *The States System*, 46; Barraclough, *The Origins of Modern Germany*, 381–87.

54. Kann, *A History of the Habsburg Empire*, 54; Arndt, "The Emperor and the Reich," 75.

55. Gagliardo, *Germany Under the Old Regime*, 45.

56. Roger Wines, "The Imperial Circles, Princely Diplomacy, and Imperial Reform, 1681–1714," *Journal of Modern History* 39, no. 1 (1967): 1–29.

57. Steiger, "Concrete Peace and General Order," 440.

58. Osiander, *The States System*, 40; Holborn, *A History of Modern Germany*, 368–69.

59. Osiander, *The States System*, 40–42; Maland, *Europe in the Seventeenth Century*, 184.

60. Parker, *The Thirty Years' War*, 196–97; Holborn, *A History of Modern Germany*; Barraclough, *The Origins of Modern Germany*; Rabb, ed., *The Thirty Years' War*; Maland, *Europe in the Seventeenth Century*; Holsti, *Peace and War*, 46–59.

61. Holsti, *Peace and War*, 46–59. See also Evan Luard, *War in International Society: A Study in International Sociology* (London: I. B. Tauris, 1986), 35–52; Osiander, *The States System*, 49; Barraclough, *The Origins of Modern Germany*, 381–87.

62. Quoted in Schilling, "War and Peace at the Emergence of Modernity, 22.

63. Steiger, "Concrete Peace and General Order," 443.

64. Osiander, *The States System*, 122,

65. Holsti, *Peace and War*, 56.

66. Ibid., 92.

67. Rodney Bruce Hall describes the period 1555–1648 in European history as a "dynastic-sovereign" one. That is, the authority of princes was both sovereign and dependent on dynastic legitimacy. After Westphalia, he argues, the territorial principle eclipsed the dynastic principle. See Rodney Bruce Hall, *National Collective Identity: Social Constructs and International Systems* (New York: Columbia University Press, 1999), 32–35.

68. For a leading, comprehensive text, see James Crawford, *The Creation of States in International Law* (Oxford: Clarendon Press, 1979). The Montevideo criteria, I quote on p. 36. His general discussion of criteria falls on pp. 31–76. See also John Dugard, *Recognition and the United Nations* (Cambridge: Grotius Publications, Ltd., 1987).

69. Stephen D. Krasner, *Sovereignty. Organized Hypocrisy* (Princeton: Princeton University Press, 1999), 14–20.

70. See Gerrit Gong, *The Standard of "Civilization" in International Society* (Oxford: Clarendon Press, 1984).

71. Gong, *The Standard of Civilization*, 14–15.

72. Crawford, *The Creation of States in International Law*, 131–34

73. See Krasner, *Sovereignty*, 14–25.

74. An excellent source on the principle is R. J. Vincent, *Non-Intervention and International Order* (Princeton: Princeton University Press, 1974). Another helpful exploration, though limited to the context of the Americas, is Ann Van Wynen Thomas and A. J. Thomas, Jr., *Non-Intervention. The Law and Its Import in the Americas* (Dallas: Southern Methodist University Press, 1956).

75. Schilling, "War and Peace at the Emergence of Modernity," 17.

CHAPTER SIX
THE ORIGIN OF WESTPHALIA

1. Max Weber, *The Protestant Ethic and the Spirit of Capitalism* (New York: Charles Scribner's Sons, 1958); R. H. Tawney, *Religion and the Rise of Capitalism* (London: John Murray, 1936). On the Weber controversy, see Gianfranco Poggi, *Calvinism and the Capitalist Spirit* (London: Macmillan, 1983); Hartmut Lehmann and Gunther Roth, *Weber's Protestant Ethic: Origins, Evidence, and Context* (Cambridge: Cambridge University Press, 1993).

2. For historians, see, for example, Hajo Holborn, *A History of Modern Germany*, vol. 1: *The Reformation* (New York: Alfred A. Knopf, 1959); and Geoffrey Baraclough, *The Origins of Modern Germany* (Oxford: Basil Blackwell, 1947). Some social scientists have acknowledged this influence, if briefly. See Rodney Bruce Hall, *National Collective Identity: social Constructs and International Systems* (New York: Columbia University Press, 1999), 51–58; Bruce Porter, *War and the Rise of the State* (New York: Free Press, 1994), 68–69; and Michael Mann, *The sources of Social Power*, vol. 1 (Cambridge: Cambridge University Press, 1986), 463–72

3. See Charles Tilly, *Coercion, Capital, and European States AD 990–1992* (Oxford: Basil Blackwell 1992).

4. Hendrik Spruyt, *The Sovereign State and Its Competitors* (Princeton: Princeton University Press, 1994), 153–80.

5. Otto Hintze, *The Historical Essays of Otto Hintze* (Oxford: Oxford University Press, 1975); Richard Bean, "War and the Birth of the Nation-State," *Journal of Economic History* 33 (1973): 203–21; Bruce Porter, *War and the Rise of the State* (New York: Free Press, 1994); Tilly, *Coercion, Capital, and European States.* The *locus classicus* on the military revolution is Michael Roberts, *Essays in Swedish History* (London: Weidenfeld and Nicolson, 1967), 195–225. An impressive recent

work on the long-term political results of the military revolution is I ing, *The Military Revolution and Political Change* (Princeton: Prince sity Press, 1992), 56–74. For a critique of the military revolution thesi frey Parker, "The 'Military Revolution,' 1550–1660—A Myth?" *Modern History* 48 (1976): 195–214; Geoffrey Parker, *The Military* (Cambridge: Cambridge University Press, 1988).

6. Douglass C. North and R. P. Thomas, *The Rise of the Western World* (Cambridge: Cambridge University Press, 1973); Spruyt, *The Sovereign State and Its Competitors*.

7. Immanuel Wallerstein, *The Modern World System: Capitalist Agriculture and the Origins of the European World-Economy in the Sixteenth Century* (New York: Academic Press, 1974); Perry Anderson, *Lineages of the Absolutist State* (London: Verso, 1974); Thomas Ertman, *Birth of the Leviathan: Building States and Regimes in Medieval and Early Modern Europe* (Cambridge: Cambridge University Press, 1997).

8. Hendrik Spruyt, *The Sovereign State and Its Competitors*.

9. See Paul Kennedy, *The Rise and Fall of the Great Powers: Economic Change and Military Conflict from 1500 to 2000* (New York: Random House, 1987), 31–73; Aristide Zolberg, "Origins of the Modern World System: A Missing Link," *World Politics* 23 (1981): 253–58; Ludwig Dehio, *The Precarious Balance*, trans. Charles Fulman (New York: Knopf, 1962); S. H. Steinberg, "The Thirty Years' War and the Conflict for European Hegemony," in T. K. Rabb, ed., *The Thirty Years' War: Problems of Motive, Extent, and Effect* (Boston: D. C. Heath, 1964); Robert Gilpin, *War and Change* (Cambridge: Cambridge University Press, 1981).

10. See Stephen Ozment, ed., *Reformation Europe: A Guide to Research* (St. Louis, Mo.: Center for Reformation Research, 1982); R. Po-Chia Hsia, ed., *The German People and the Reformation* (Ithaca: Cornell University Press, 1988).

11. Martin Luther, *Bondage of the Will*, ed. Philip S. Watson, trans. Philip S. Watson and Benjamin Drewery, Vol. 33, *Luther's Works* (Philadelphia: Westminster Press, 1972), 175.

12. Martin Luther, *Bondage of the Will*; Martin Luther, *The Freedom of a Christian*, ed. Harold J. Grimm, trans. W. A. Lambert, Vol. 31, *Luther's Works* (Philadelphia: Westminster Press, 1957), Quentin Skinner, *The Foundations of Modern Political Thought*, Vol. 2: *The Age of the Reformation* (Cambridge: Cambridge University Press, 1978); Euan Cameron, *The European Reformation* (Oxford: Oxford University Press, 1991), 99–198; Heiko Oberman, *Luther: Man Between God and the Devil* (New Haven: Yale University Press, 1989); Stephen Ozment, *Protestants: The Birth of a Revolution* (New York: Doubleday, 1992), 43–86; Louis Bouyer, *The Spirit and Forms of Protestantism* (London: Harville Press, 1955), Alistair McGrath, *Reformation Thought: An Introduction* (Oxford: Oxford University Press, 1988).

13. See McGrath, *Reformation Thought*; Heiko Oberman, *The Harvest of Medieval Theology: Gabriel Biel and Late Medieval Nominalism* (Cambridge: Harvard University Press, 1963).

14. Quoted in Cameron, *The European Reformation*, 147.

15. Ibid.

16. Ozment, *The Age of Reform*, 48.

17. For descriptions of the Church's role in contemporary social life, see Cameron, *The European Reformation*, 20–37, 145–55.

18. Ozment, *Protestants*, 118–48.

19. Romans 13:1–7.

20. Cameron, *The European Reformation*, 153.

21. Cameron, *The European Reformation*, 152–53; Martin Luther, *Temporal Authority: To What Extent It Should Be Obeyed*, ed. Walter I. Brandt, trans. J. J. Schindel, Vol. 45, *Luther's Works* (Philadelphia: Westminster Press, 1967); Ozment, *Protestants*, 122–40; Skinner, *The Foundations of Modern Political Thought*.

22. Cameron, *The European Reformation*, 70–78.

23. Ibid.

24. G. R. Elton, *Reformation Europe* (London: Collins, 1963), 56; Owen Chadwick, *The Reformation* (London: Penguin, 1964), 67–71; John M. Todd, *The Reformation* (New York: Doubleday, 1971), 230–39.

25. Barraclough, *The Origins of Modern Germany*, 374.

26. Elton, *Reformation Europe*, 148; Todd, *Reformation*, 236–38. The Confession omitted disputed matters such as purgatory, transubstantiation, and the priesthood of all believers, and mentioned justification by faith but not "alone."

27. Holborn, *A History of Modern Germany*, 137–39, 158, 162, 374; Chadwick, *The Reformation*, 67–71; Todd, *Reformation*, 230–39; A. G. Dickens, *Reformation and Society in Sixteenth Century Europe* (London: Thames and Hudson, 1966), 87–106; Elton, *Reformation Europe*; Barraclough, *The Origins of Modern Germany*.

28. John Gagliardo, *Germany Under the Old Regime, 1600–1790* (London: Longmans, 1991), 14; Cameron, *The European Reformation*, 210–91; Elton, *Reformation Europe*; Holborn, *A History of Modern Germany*, 284–95.

29. Holborn, *A History of Modern Germany*, 37–51; Barraclough, *The Origins of Modern Germany*, 363–67; Gagliardo, *Germany Under the Old Regime*, 2–4.

30. See Cameron, *The European Reformation*, 199–313.

31. Simon Groenveld, "The Treaty of Münster as the Culmination of a Progressive Revolution," in Bussmann and Schilling, eds., *1648–War and Peace in Europe*, 123.

32. Parker, *The Dutch Revolt* (Ithaca: Cornell University Press, 1977), 19–40; J.H. Elliot, *Europe Divided, 1559–1598* (London: Collins, 1968), 124–45.

33. Elliot, *Europe Divided*, 124–45; Parker, *The Dutch Revolt*; Pieter Geyl, *The Revolt of the Netherlands, 1555–1609* (London: Williams and Norgate, Ltd., 1932).

34. Elliot, *Europe Divided*, 124–45; Parker, *The Dutch Revolt*, 169–224; George L. Smith, *Religion and Trade in the New Netherlands: Dutch Origins and American Development* (Ithaca: Cornell University Press, 1973).

35. Joseph R. Strayer, *The Medieval Origins of the Modern State* (Princeton: Princeton University Press, 1970).

36. John Lynch, *Spain Under the Habsburgs* (New York: Oxford University Press, 1965); H. G. Koenigsberger and George L. Mosse, *Europe in the Sixteenth Century* (New York: Holt, Rinehart, and Winston, 1968); Elliot, *Europe Divided*, 11–29.

37. Skinner, *Foundations of Modern Political Thought*, Vol. 2; William F. Church, *Constitutional Thought in Sixteenth Century France* (Cambridge: Harvard University Press, 1941).

38. Friedrich Meinecke, *Machiavellianism: The Doctrine of Raison d'Etat and Its Place in Modern History*, trans. Douglas Scott (Boulder, Colo.: Westview Press, 1984), 1.

39. Armand-Jean du Plessis, duc de Richelieu, *The Political Testament of Cardinal Richelieu*, trans. Henry Bertram Hill (Madison: University of Wisconsin Press, 1981). It is uncertain whether Richelieu actually wrote the work. On the question of authorship, see William F. Church, *Richelieu and Reason of State* (Princeton: Princeton University Press, 1972), 480–82.

40. Osiander, *The States System*, 27–29; Meinecke, *Machiavellianism*, 1; Church, *Richelieu and Reason of State*, 283–340, 480–82; Richelieu, *The Political Testament.*

41. Roberts, *Essays in Swedish History*; Michael Roberts, *The Early Vasas: A History of Sweden, 1523–1611* (Cambridge: Cambridge University Press,1968); Michael Roberts, *Gustavus Adolphus and the Rise of Sweden* (London: English Universities Press,1973); Ole Peter Grell, "Scandinavia," in *The Early Reformation in Europe*, ed. A. Pettegree (Cambridge: Cambridge University Press, 1992), 94–119.

42. Parker, *The Thirty Years' War*, 155.

43. Ibid.

44. Ibid.

CHAPTER SEVEN
THE POWER OF PROTESTANT PROPOSITIONS

1. The method proposed here—charting out the events by which the two roles exercise the influence already suggested by a broad correlation—is what Alexander George calls "process tracing." See Alexander George, "Case Studies and Theory Development: The Method of Structured Focused Comparisons," in Paul Gordon Lauren, ed., *Diplomacy: New Approaches in History, Theory, and Policy* (New York: Free Press, 1979).

2. Robert Wuthnow, *Communities of Discourse* (Cambridge: Harvard University Press, 1989), 131.

3. Ibid., 129–40.

4. Euan Cameron, *The European Reformation*, Ithaca: Cornell University Press, 1971), 99–110, 199–318; Stephen Ozment, *Protestants: The Birth of a Revolution* (New York: Doubleday, 1992), 43–86.

5. Cameron, *The European Reformation*, 199–318.

6. Cameron, *The European Reformation*, 210–92. On threat theory, see Stephen Walt, *The Origin of Alliances* (Ithaca: Cornell University Press, 1987).

7. For Calvin's theology and political ideas, see John Calvin, *Institutes of the Christian Religion*, trans. Henry Beveridge (Grand Rapids, Mich.: Wm. Eerdmans Publishing Company, 1989). See also Quentin Skinner, *The Foundations of Modern Political Thought*, vol. 2, *The Age of the Reformation* (Cambridge: Cambridge

University Press, 1978), 225–38. For Huguenot doctrines of revolt, see Skinner, *Foundations*, vol. 2, 239–301.

8. Quote from A. G. Dickens, *Reformation and Society in Sixteenth Century Europe* (London: Thames and Hudson, 1966), 167. On Calvinist revolts, see also H. G. Koenigsberger, "Organization of Revolutionary Parties in France and the Netherlands During the Sixteenth Century," in H. G. Koenigsberger, *Estates and Revolutions: Essays in Early Modern European History* (Ithaca: Cornell University Press, 1971), 224–53.

9. J. H. Elliot, *Europe Divided, 1559–1598* (London: Collins, 1968), 34–36; Geoffrey Parker, *The Dutch Revolt*, Ithaca: Cornell University Press, 1977), 30–41; Dickens, *The Reformation and Society*, 99–104; Pieter Geyl, *The Revolt of the Netherlands, 1555–1609* (London: Williams and Nargate, 1932).

10. Jonathan Israel, "The Dutch-Spanish War and the Holy Roman Empire (1568–1648)," in Bussmann and Schilling, eds., *1648—War and Peace in Europe*, 112.

11. Israel, "The Dutch-Spanish War," 111.

12. Ibid., 112.

13. Parker, *The Dutch Revolt*, 126–68; Geoffrey Parker, *Spain and the Netherlands, 1559–1659* (Glasgow: Fontana Press, 1990), 52–53; John Lynch, *Spain and the Habsburgs* (New York: Oxford University Press, 1964).

14. Bruce Porter, *War and the Rise of the State* (New York: Free Press, 1994), 73.

15. Dickens, *Reformation and Society*, 164–87; Elliot, *Europe Divided*, 116–25.

16. On the *politiques*, see Skinner, *The Foundations of Modern Political Thought*, Vol. 2, 249–54; and William F. Church, *Constitutional Thought in Sixteenth-Century France* (Cambridge: Harvard University Press, 1941), 194–271. For Bodin, see Jean Bodin, *On Sovereignty: Four Chapters from Six Books of the Commonwealth*, ed. and trans. Julian Franklin (Cambridge: Cambridge University Press, 1992). On Bodin, see also Julian H. Franklin, *Jean Bodin and the Rise of Absolutist Theory* (Cambridge: Cambridge University Press, 1973).

17. Elliot, *Europe Divided*, 5–4; H. G. Koenigsberger and George L. Mosse, *Europe in the Sixteenth Century* (New York: Holt, Rinehart, and Winston, 1968).

18. On the religious wars in France, see James Westfall Thompson, *The Wars of Religion in France, 1559–1576* (New York: Frederick Ungar Publishing Co., 1909).

19. Victor-L. Tapié, *France in the Age of Louis XIII and Richelieu*, trans. D. McN. Lockie (Cambridge: Cambridge University Press, 1984); William F. Church, *Richelieu and Reason of State* (Princeton: Princeton University Press, 1972), 81–102.

20. Quoted in Church, *Richelieu*, 376.

21. Michael Roberts, *The Swedish Imperial Experience, 1516–1718* (Cambridge: Cambridge University Press, 1979), 64.

22. Michael Roberts, *The Early Vasas: A History of Sweden, 1523–1611* (Cambridge: Cambridge University Press, 1968), 68–70; N. K. Anderson, "The Reformation in Scandinavia and the Baltic," in *The New Cambridge Modern History*, ed. G. R. Elton (Cambridge: Cambridge University Press, 1958), 146–53.

23. Roberts, *Essays in Swedish History*, 78; Michael Roberts, *Gustavus Adolphus*, 2 vols. (London: Longmans, Green, 1958); Hedley Bull, "The Importance of Grotius in the Study of International Relations," in *Hugo Grotius and International Relations*, ed. Hedley Bull, Benedict Kingsbury, and Adam Roberts (Oxford: Clarendon Press, 1990).

24. Roberts, *Essays in Swedish History*, 84.

25. Roberts, *The Swedish Imperial Experience*, 67–70.

26. Heinhard Steiger, "Concrete Peace and General Order: *The Legal Meaning of the Treaties* of 24 October 1648," in Klauss Bussmann and Heinz Schilling, eds., *1648—War and Peace in Europe* (Münster, Germany; Westfalisches Museum, 1998), 439.

27. For histories of the Thirty Years' War, see George Pages, *The Thirty Years War*, trans. David Maland (New York: Harper and Row, 1970); Geoffrey Parker, *The Thirty Years' War* (London: Routledge, Kegan and Paul, 1997). C. V. Wedgewood, *The Thirty Years' War* (New Haven: Yale University Press, 1939). For scholarly opinion on the war, see T. K. Rabb, ed., *The Thirty Years' War: Problems of Motive, Extent, and Effect* (Boston: D. C. Heath, 1964).

28. Kenneth Shepsle, "Comment," in *Regulatory Policy and the Social Sciences*, ed. Roger Noll (Berkeley: University of California Press, 1985).

29. For an argument along these lines, see Skinner, *Foundations*, Vol. 2, 65–108.

30. Cameron, *The European Reformation*, 294–99; F. L. Carsten, *Princes and Parliaments in Germany from the Fifteenth to the Eighteenth Century* (Oxford: Oxford University Press, 1959); A. G. Dickens, *The German Nation and Martin Luther* (London: Edward Arnold. 1974); Thomas Brady, "In Search of the Godly City: The Domestication of Religion in the German Urban Reformation," in R. Po-Chia Hsia, ed., *The German People and the Reformation* (Ithaca: Cornell University Press, 1988), 14–32.

31. Alister McGrath, *The Intellectual Origins of the European Reformation* (Oxford: Basil Blackwell, 1987); Heiko Oberman, *The Harvest of Medieval Theology: Gabriel Biel and Late Medieval Nominalism* (Cambridge: Harvard University Press, 1963).

32. Spruyt, *The Sovereign State and Its Competitors*, 22–33.

33. For these accounts, see chapter 6.

34. David Kaiser, *Politics and War: European Conflict from Philip II to Hitler* (Cambridge: Harvard University Press, 1990); Geoffrey Parker and Lesley M. Smith, eds., *The General Crisis of the Seventeenth Century* (London: Routledge and Kegan Paul, 1978); Trevor Aston, ed., *Crisis in Europe, 1560–1660* (London: Routledge and Kegan Paul, 1965); John H. Kautsky, *The Politics of Aristocratic Empires* (Chapel Hill: University of North Carolina Press, 1982), 341–46.

35. Brian Downing, *The Military Revolution and Political Change* (Princeton: Princeton University Press, 1992); John Gagliardo, *Germany Under the Old Regime 1600–1790* (London: Longmans, 1991). Geoffrey Barraclough, *The Origins of Modern Germany* (Oxford: Basil Blackwell, 1947), 376–80; Carl Cipolla, *The Fontana Economic History of Europe: The Sixteenth and Seventeenth Centuries* (Glasgow: William Collins Sons, 1974); Gerald Strauss, *Law, Resistance, and the State: The Opposition to Roman Law in Reformation Germany* (Princeton: Princeton

University Press, 1986); Bernd Moeller, *Imperial Cities and the Reformation*, trans. H. C. Erik Middlefort and Mark U. Edwards Jr. (Philadelphia: Fortress Press, 1972); Carsten, *Princes and Parliaments*, 165–78.

36. Jonathan Israel, *The Dutch Republic: Its Rise, Greatness, and Fall, 1477–1806* (Oxford: Oxford University Press, 1995), 241.

37. Geoffrey Parker, "The 'Military Revolution,' 1550–1660—A Myth?" *Journal of Modern History* 48 (1976): 206; Israel, *The Dutch Republic*, 106–230; Jan DeVries, *The Dutch Rural Economy in the Golden Age, 1500–1700* (New Haven: Yale University Press, 1974); Henri Pirenne, *Early Democracies in the Low Countries: Urban Society and Political Conflict in the Middle Ages and Renaissance* (New York: Harper and Row, 1963); J. W. Smit, "The Present Position of Studies Regarding the Revolt of the Netherlands," in *Britain and the Netherlands*, ed. J. S. Bromley and E. H. Kossman (Groningen: Wolters, 1960); Geyl, *The Revolt of the Netherlands.*

38. Parker, "The Military Revolution," 206; Richard Bonney, *Political Change in France Under Richelieu and Mazarin, 1624–1661* (Oxford: Oxford University Press, 1978); Richard Bonney, *The King's Debts: Finance and Politics in France, 1589–1661* (Oxford: Oxford University Press, 1981); Richard Bonney, *Society and Government in France Under Richelieu and Mazarin, 1624–1661* (London: Collier-Macmillan, 1988); Church, *Richelieu and Reason of State*, 81–102, 283–340; Elliot, *Europe Divided*, 11–29; Martin Wolfe, *The Fiscal System of Renaissance France* (New Haven: Yale University Press, 1972); Porter, *War and the Rise of the State*, 74; Tapié, *France in the Age of Louis XIII and Richelieu*; Robin Briggs, *Early Modern France, 1560–1715* (Oxford: Oxford University Press, 1977); David Buisseret, *Sully and the Growth of Centralized Government in France, 1598–1610* (London: Eyre and Spottiswoode, 1968).

39. Parker, "The 'Military Revolution,' " 206; Roberts, *Essays in Swedish History*, 78; Roberts, *Gustavus Adolphus.*

40. Parker, "The 'Military Revolution,' " 206.

41. Thomas Ertman, *Birth of the Leviathan: Building States and Regimes in Medieval and Modern Europe* (Cambridge: Cambridge University Press, 1997), 110–24, 267–304; J. H. Elliot, *Imperial Spain, 1469–1716* (London: Edward Arnold, 1963); J. H. Elliot, "The Decline of Spain," in *Crisis in Europe 1560–1660: Essays from Past and Present* (London: Routledge and Kegan paul, 1965); Henry Kamen, *Spain 1469–1714: A Society in Conflict* (London: Longmans, 1983); J. H. Elliot, *Richelieu and Olivares* (Cambridge: Cambridge University Press, 1984).

42. For the idea of "imperial overstretch," see Paul Kennedy, *The Rise and Fall of the Great Powers: Economic Change and Military Conflict from 1500 to 2000* (New York: Random House, 1957). On Spain's relative decline, see J. H. Elliot, "The Decline of Spain"; and Kamen, *Spain 1469–1714.*

43. Ozment, *The Age of Reform, 1220–1550: An Intellectual and Religious History of Late Medieval and Reformation Europe* (New Haven: Yale University Press, 1980), 222–23; Ozment, *Protestants*, 9–86; Cameron, *The European Reformation*, 20–37, 79–93.

44. Alister McGrath, *Reformation Thought: An Introduction* (Oxford: Oxford University Press, 1988); McGrath, *The Intellectual Origins*; Oberman, *The Harvest*

of Medieval Theology; Heiko A. Oberman, *Masters of the Reformation: The Emergence of a New Intellectual Climate in Europe* (Cambridge: Cambridge University Press, 1981).

45. Wuthnow, *Communities of Discourse*, 25–51; Andrew Pettegree, *The Early Reformation in Europe* (Cambridge: Cambridge University Press, 1991), 11–15; Bernd Moeller, *Imperial Cities and the Reformation*; Brady, "In Search of the Godly City"; R. W. Scribner, *Popular Culture and Popular Movements in Reformation Germany* (London: Hambledon Press, 1987), 123–242.

46. McGrath, *The Intellectual Origins*; Oberman, *The Harvest of Medieval Theology*.

47. Wuthnow, *Communities of Discourse*, 25–51; Pettegree, *The Early Reformation*; Bob Scribner, Roy Porter, and Mikulcs Teich, eds., *The Reformation in National Context* (Cambridge: Cambridge University Press, 1994).

48. H. R. Trevor-Roper, *Religion, the Reformation, and Social Change* (New York: Harper and Row, 1956).

49. R. M. Hartwell, *The Industrial Revolution and Economic Growth* (London: Methuen, 1971), 303.

50. In this section, I rely heavily upon Timothy B. Shah, "Making the World Safe for Liberalism: The Taming of Religion from Hugo Grotius to John Rawls," paper presented at the Annual Meeting of the American Political Science Association, 1997.

CHAPTER EIGHT
IDEAS AND THE END OF EMPIRE

1. On Latin American states and sovereignty, see chapter 3. See also Stephen D. Krasner, "Compromising Westphalia," *International Security* 20, no. 3 (1995/96): 115–51.

2. For a helpful summary of these natural-law protests of colonization, see Lynn Berat, *Walvis Bay: Decolonization and International Law* (New Haven: Yale University Press, 1990), 104–8. Berat also provides a useful discussion of the legal rationales that European states gave for holding colonies. See pp. 108–21.

3. For good analyses of the differences between empires' styles of rule, see David Fieldhouse, *The Colonial Empires* (New York: Dell, 1966); and David Strang, "The Inner Incompatibility of Empire and Nation: Popular Sovereignty and Decolonization," *Sociological Perspectives* 35 (1992): 367–85.

4. Quoted in Brian Lapping, *End of Empire* (London: Granada, 1985), xiv. For an excellent analysis of the concept of empires with respect to sovereignty, see Michael Doyle, *Empires* (Ithaca: Cornell University Press, 1986).

5. This must be slightly qualified by the fact that, at times, one European power would fight for the independence of another European power's colony. The French, for instance, allied themselves with the American colonists against the British. But this occurred only once a colonial revolt was under way, and it was always directed only toward the independence of a particular colony, never toward a general norm of colonial independence. European powers' disrespect of one an-

other's prerogatives toward their colonies was a violation of the Westphalian norm, not an attempt at its revision.

6. The phrase is from Franz Ansprenger, *The Dissolution of Colonial Empires* (London: Routledge, 1989), 251.

7. From David Strang, "Global Patterns of Decolonization, 1500–1987," *International Studies Quarterly* 35 (1991): 429–54. See particularly pp. 435, 444–52.

8. Quoted in Berat, *Walvis Bay*, 143.

9. UN GAOR Res. 1514 (1960).

10. UN GAOR Res. 1541 (1960).

11. Do these documents transform self-determination from its status as a guiding principle in the UN Charter into customary law, which is a positive obligation of states? Following international lawyer Lynn Berat, I believe there is some merit to the argument. Later General Assembly resolutions, declarations, and treaties condemning colonialism combine with the 1960 Declaration to form a strong claim that colonies' right to independence is a matter of law: examples are the 1966 Covenants on Civil and Political Rights and Economic and Social Rights, the General Assembly's 1970 Declaration on Principles of International Law Concerning Friendly Relations and Cooperation Among States (UN GAOR Res. 2628 [1970]), and the Assembly's Programme of Action for the full implementation of the Declaration on the Granting of Independence to Colonial Peoples of the same year. The latter states that "the further continuation of colonialism in all its forms and manifestations [is] a crime which constitutes a violation of the Charter of the United Nations, the Declaration on the Granting of Independence to Colonial and Peoples and the principles of international law," (UN GAOR Res. 2621 [1970]). Berat notes that by the time of the Declaration, there had arisen a debate over the legal status of General Assembly Resolutions. She writes that "by 1966, it was settled that U.N. resolutions were not binding per se. They had the force of law only when they restated a binding rule of international law, when they had been incorporated into state practice, or when they had been so often repeated over time and had been accepted by the majority of the states of the world as binding that they had become a rule of customary international law. Thus, although the General Assembly resolutions were persuasive rather than binding, the principle of self-determination, because it was frequently cited and was accepted by most states, had become a right of peoples everywhere, a rule of customary international law," Berat, *Walvis Bay*, 144.

For an opposing legal interpretation, see Leo Gross, "The Right of Self-Determination in International Law," in *New States in the Modern World*, ed. Martin Kilson (Cambridge: Harvard University Press, 1975), 136–57. For other discussions of self-determination and decolonization, see Inis L. Claude Jr., "Domestic Jurisdiction and Colonialism," in *New States in the Modern World*, ed. Martin Kilson (Cambridge: Harvard University Press, 1975), 121–35; and Heather Wilson, *International Law and the Use of Force by National Liberation Movements* (Oxford: Oxford University Press, 1988).

12. See David A. Kay, "The Politics of Decolonization," in *International Organization: Politics and Process*, ed. Leland Goodrich and David A. Kay (Madison: University of Wisconsin Press, 1973), 307–32, 314.

13. Berat describes the terms of acquisition by occupation: "This required the settlement of terra nullius with the object of incorporating that territory into the national domain and exercising sovereignty over it. The two conditions of occupation were that the occupied territory had to be terra nullius and that the occupation had to be real or effective. In defining terra nullius, the views of the positivists prevailed [which meant that terra nullius was territory whose inhabitants were not members of the family of nations and subject to international law]. Accordingly, Europeans did not recognize the sovereignty of 'noncivilized' peoples to the lands they occupied at the time the Europeans encountered them. . . . For effective occupation, it was not essential that the occupying power have sufficient force to repel foreign intrusion or that it be effectively exploiting the land. It was necessary only that the Europeans exercise sufficient governmental control over the land to protect life and property there," Berat, *Walvis Bay*, 118.

14. Hedley Bull, "European States and African Political Communities," in *The Expansion of International Society*, ed. Hedley Bull and Adam Watson (Oxford: Oxford University Press, 1984), 99–114, 110. Quote is from the Berlin Final Act text, which may be found in Sir Edward Hertslet, *The Map of Africa by Treaty*, vol. 1 (London: Harrison and Sons, 1896).

15. William Roger Louis, "The Era of the Mandates System and the Non-European World," in *The Expansion of International Society*, ed. Hedley Bull and Adam Watson (Oxford: Oxford University Press, 1984), 201–213, 201–2.

16. The "non-self-governing territories" are dealt with in Chapter XI of the United Nations Charter, the "trust" territories in Chapters XII and XIII.

17. Berat, *Walvis Bay*, 140–42.

18. Other European states, Belgium and Portugal, for instance, also released colonies around this time. But the size of their empires and the number of colonies to which they granted independence (two apiece) were dwarfed by Britain and France.

I also want to stress a similarity in the structure of my argument with the Westphalia case. I do not present here an argument for decolonization in general. My question is not, What are the conditions under which an empire will release a colony? Nor do I see this case as an instance of a general law prescribing a set of conditions for a revolution in sovereignty to occur. Rather, I seek to explain this revolution in sovereignty as a historically unique revolution in the constitution of international society. Here again, though, I do find cases within the revolution, and employ comparisons across time and place.

19. Other scholars have constructed general accounts of decolonization emphasizing ideas, but with significant differences from my own. See David Strang, "The Inner Incompatibility of Empire and Nation"; Strang, "Global Patterns of Decolonization, 429–54. Neta Crawford, "Decolonization as an International Norm: The Evolution of Practices, Arguments, and Beliefs," in *Emerging Norms of Justified Intervention*, ed. Laura W. Reed and Carl Kaysen (Cambridge, Mass.: The Committee on International Security Studies, American Academy of Arts and Sciences, 1993), 37–62; Robert H. Jackson, "The Weight of Ideas in Decolonization: Normative Change in International Relations," in *Ideas and Foreign Policy: Beliefs, Institutions, and Political Change*, ed. Judith Goldstein and Robert O. Keohane (Ithaca: Cornell University Press, 1993), 111–38; and Ronald Robinson, "The

Moral Disarmament of African Empire, 1919–1947," *Journal of Imperial and Commonwealth History* 7, no. 1 (1979): 86–104.

20. For an excellent explication of nationalism, see David Miller, *On Nationality* (Oxford: Clarendon Press, 1995), 21–27.

21. On the content of anticolonial ideas, see Stephen Howe, *Anticolonialism in British Politics: The Left and the End of Empire, 1918–1964*, Oxford Historical Monographs (Oxford: Oxford University Press, 1993).

22. For this concept, see chapter 4.

23. For large-*n* analyses of the role of norms, see David Strang, "From Dependency to Sovereignty: An Event History Analysis of Decolonization, 1870–1987," *American Sociological Review* 55, no. 6 (1990): 846–60; Gary Goertz, *Contexts of International Politics* (Cambridge: Cambridge University Press, 1994), 250–67. More qualitative studies of the role of norms are Martha Finnemore, "Constructing Norms of Humanitarian Intervention," in Peter Katzenstein, ed., *The Culture of National Security: News and Identity in World Politics* (New York: Columbia University Press, 1996), 153–85; and Neta Crawford, "Decolonization as an International Norm, 37–62.

24. I note these works with respect to Britain and France in chapters 11 and 14 respectively. There are a few works, though, that give general, economically oriented, structural accounts of the rise and fall of empires. See Christopher Chase-Dunn and Richard Rubinson, "Toward a Structural Perspective on the World-System," *Politics and Society* 7, no. 4 (1977): 453–76; Terry Boswell, "Colonial Empires and the Capitalist World-Economy: A Time Series Analysis of Colonization, 1640–1960," *American Sociological Review* 54 (1989) 180–96; and Albert Bergesen and Ronald Schoenberg, "The Long Waves of Colonial Expansion and Contraction, 1415–1970," in Albert Bergesen, ed., *Studies of the Modern World System* (New York: Academic Press, 1980).

25. On the importance of perceptions of power, see Aaron Friedberg, *The Weary Titan: Britain and the Experience of Relative Decline, 1895–1905* (Princeton: Princeton University Press, 1988); Robert Jervis, *Perception and Misperception in International Politics* (Princeton: Princeton University Press, 1976); Charles Kupchan, *The Vulnerability of Empire* (Ithaca: Cornell University Press, 1994); and William Curtis Wohlforth, *The Elusive Balance: Power and Perceptions During the Cold War* (Ithaca: Cornell University Press, 1993).

CHAPTER NINE
THE END OF THE BRITISH EMPIRE: CASHING OUT THE PROMISE OF SELF-GOVERNMENT

1. See Brian Lapping, *End of Empire* (New York: St. Martin's Press, 1985), 16.

2. Other scholars have offered arguments about British decolonization that employ some version of an ideas argument, or some element of the account I have just outlined. For histories that are quite sympathetic to British policymakers, portraying the end of empire, planned according to a script rooted in Britain's colonial ideals, see Clement Attlee, *Empire into Commonwealth* (Oxford: Oxford University Press, 1961); D. J. Morgan, *The Official History of Colonial Development*, 5 vols. (London: Macmillan, 1980); J. Strachey, *The End of Empire* (Lon-

don: Gollancz, 1959). For more sophisticated accounts, see John Darwin, *Britain and Decolonisation* (New York: St. Martin's Press, 1988); John Darwin, *The End of the British Empire* (Oxford: Oxford University Press, 1991); David Goldsworthy, "Britain and the International Critics of British Colonialism, 1951–56," *Journal of Commonwealth and Comparative Politics* 29 (1991): 1–24; Ronald Robinson, "The Moral Disarmament of African Empire, 1919–1947," *Journal of Imperial and Commonwealth History* 7, no. 1 (1979); and Tony Smith, "A Comparative Study of French and British Decolonization," *Comparative Studies in Society and History* 20 (1978): 70–102.

3. For structural arguments along these lines, see P. J. Cain and A. G. Hopkins, *British Imperialism: Crisis and Deconstruction, 1914–1990* (London: Longmans, 1993); Bernard Porter, *The Lion's Share: A Short History of British Imperialism, 1850–1970* (London: Longmans, 1996); Colin Cross, *The Fall of the British Empire, 1918–1968* (London: Hodder and Stoughton, 1975); Correlli Barnett, *The Collapse of British Power* (Atlantic Highlands, N.J.: Humanities Press International, 1972). On the historiography of British decolonization, see Paul Kennedy, *Strategy and Diplomacy, 1870–1945* (London: Allen and Unwin, 1983), 197–218; A. N. Porter and A. J. Stockwell, *British Imperial Policy and Decolonization, 1938–1964*, vol. 1: 1938–1951 (New York: St. Martin's Press, 1987), 3–7; and John Darwin, *The End of The British Empire.*

4. On the public view of empire, see John Darwin, *The End of the British Empire*, 16. Several prime ministers, foreign secretaries, defense ministers, and others dissented from the pace of colonial advancement that the Colonial Office advocated. In the Labour Government, Foreign Secretary Bevin was an enthusiastic advocate of empire; Churchill's love of Empire was widely known. On Bevin's imperialist views, see Parthi Sarathi Gupta, *Imperialism and the British Labour Movement, 1914–64* (New York: Homes and Meier Publishers, 1975), 388; and Ronald Hyam, "Introduction," in Ronald Hyam, ed., *The Labour Government and the End of Empire*, series A, volume 2, of the British Documents on the End of Empire (London: Her Majesty's Stationery Office, 1992), Part 1: *High Policy and Administration*, 321–22. On Churchill, see David Goldsworthy, *Colonial Issue in British Politics* (Oxford: Clarendon Press, 1971), 376.

5. Examples of colonial memoirs or retrospective writing are A. Milner, *England in Egypt* (London: Arnold, 1920); and F. D. Lugard, *The Dual Mandate in British Tropical Africa* (London: Blackwood and Sons, 1922).

6. John Gallagher and Ronald Robinson, "The Imperialism of Free Trade," *Economic History Review* 6, no. 1 (1953): 1–15, reprinted in J. A. Gallagher, *The Decline, Revival, and Fall of the British Empire* (Cambridge: Cambridge University Press, 1982), 1–18.

7. Tony Smith, "A Comparative Study," p. 73.

8. Quoted in Franz Ansprenger, *The Dissolution of Colonial Empires* (London: Routledge, 1989), 64.

9. Smith, "A Comparative Study," 73.

10. John Darwin, *Britain and Decolonisation*, 30–33.

11. See J. G. Darwin, "The Fear of Falling: British Politics and Imperial Decline Since 1900," In *Transactions of the Royal Historical Society*, vol. 36 of the 5th series (1986), 27–44.

12. Goldsworthy, *Colonial Issues in British Politics*, 376.

13. Gupta, *Imperialism and the British Labour Movement*, 390–91.

14. H.T. Boudillon, "Reflections on Colonial Office Organisation," note for CO Organisation Committee, CO 866/49, no. 1, COOC/1, in Hyam, ed., Part 1, 321–22.

15. Hyam, "Introduction," xxx, xxxii.

16. CO 866/49, no. 27, COOC 23, October 23, 1948, quoted in Hyam, "Introduction," xxxii.

17. CO 866/49, no. 23, COOC 19, paper on Colonial Office objectives and functions, 1948, quoted in Hyam, "Introduction," xlvi.

18. Hyam, "Introduction," xxxiv.

19. See, for example, "[Local government]: circular dispatch from Mr. Creech Jones to the African governors," February 25, 1947, CO 847/35/6, nos. 15–24, in Hyam, ed., Part 1, 119–29 (see note 4).

20. This is apparent in a minute concerning the Gold Coast written by deputy under-secretary of state Sir Charles Jeffries, October 10, 1949, CO 96/800/1, quoted in Hyam, Part 1, "Introduction," xxxvi.

21. "Report of the [CO Agenda] Committee on the Conference of African Governors," May 22, 1947, CO 847/36/1, no. 9, in Hyam, ed., Part 1, 203–4.

22. Morrison quoted in the *Manchester Guardian*, June 11, 1943, quoted in Hyam, "Introduction," xxxv.

23. David Goldsworthy, "Introduction," in *The Conservative Government and the End of Empire, 1951–57*, ed. David Goldsworthy, series A, volume 3, of the British Documents on the End of Empire (London: Her Majesty's Stationery Office, 1994), xlv–liii.

24. "Commonwealth Membership": Cabinet memorandum by Lord Swinton, October 11, 1954, Appendix, paragraph 3, CAB 129/71, C(54)307, in David Goldsworthy, ed., Part 2: *Politics and Administration*, 33–34.

25. "Africa: The Next Ten Years," CAB 134/1355, May 1959, 16–18.

26. Iain Macleod, "Britain's Future Policy in Africa," *Weekend Telegraph*, March 12, 1965.

27. Iain Macleod, "Trouble in Africa," signed editorial, *Spectator*, January 31, 1964, 127.

28. William Roger Louis, *Imperialism at Bay: The United States and the Decolonization of the British Empire, 1914–45* (Oxford: Oxford University Press, 1978), 475.

29. Below, in the section on alternative explanations, I will also consider the importance of the strategic relationship. On the relationship between Britain and the United States in general, see Phillip Darby, *Three Faces of Imperialism: British and American Approaches to Asia and Africa, 1870–1970* (New Haven: Yale University Press, 1987), 169–89; John Lewis Gaddis, *We Now Know: Rethinking Cold War History* (Oxford: Oxford University Press, 1997), 155–58; John Darwin, *The End of the British Empire*, 60–61. For accounts of U.S.-British wartime diplomacy, see Christopher Thorne, *Allies of a Kind: The United States, Britain, and the War against Japan, 1941–45*, (New York: Oxford University Press, 1978); William Roger Louis, *Imperialism at Bay*.

30. On the United Nations as a source of legitimacy, see Inis L. Claude Jr., "Collective Legitimation as a Political Function of the United Nations," in *International Organization: Politics and Process*, ed. Leland Goodrich and David A. Kay (Madison: University of Wisconsin Press, 1973), 287–306.

31. Harold Jacobson, "The United Nations and Colonialism," 288; and David A. Kay, "The Politics of Decolonization," in *International Organization: Politics and Process*, ed. Leland Goodrich and David A. Kay (Madison: University of Wisconsin Press, 1973), 308–9.

32. "The Colonial Empire Today: Summary of our Main Problems and Policies": CO International Relations Department Paper," May 1950, CO 537 /5968, par. 75, in Hyam, ed., Part 2, 354–55.

33. "The Colonial Empire Today, par. 79, in Hyam, ed., Part 2, 355.

34. "The Colonial Empire Today," par. 86, in Hyam, ed., Part 2, 359.

35. Hyam, ed., "Introduction," li.

36. Goldsworthy, ed., "Introduction," xl–xli.

37. Goldsworthy, "Introduction," xl.

38. Ibid., xli-xlii.

39. Darwin, *The End of the British Empire*, 71–72. In addition, see the essays in William Roger Louis and R. Owen, *Suez 1956: The Crisis and Its Consequences* (Oxford: Oxford University Press, 1989).

40. "Africa: The Next Ten Years," 30.

41. The memo was circulated to colonial governors and several others, and was signed by Sir Hilary Poynton, September 29, 1960, CO 936/678.

42. Earl of Home to J.H.A. Watson, January 25, 1962, FO 371/161 358.

43. The anti-Communist purpose of the report is mentioned in a memo of January 15, 1959, CAB 134/1353 (AF(59)1).

44. "Africa: The Next Ten Years," 5–6.

45. See memo of September 29, 1960, CO 936/678.

46. Darwin, *Britain and Decolonisation*, 227; see also Miles Kahler, *Decolonization in Britain and France* (Princeton: Princeton University Press, 1984), 142–50.

47. "Africa: The Next Ten Years," 29.

48. "Africa: The Next Ten Years," 29.

49. Colonial Office memorandum to the Prime Minister, March 17, 1957, PREM 11/3239 (PM(57)92).

50. Note to the Prime Minister, February 23, 1957, PREM 11/3239 (PM(57)9).

51. See letter from Norman Brook to the Prime Minister, February 25, 1957, PREM 11/3239 (PM(57)92), and "British Colonial Policy: United States Attitude," PREM 11/3239 (PM(57)9).

52. "Steering Committee: Democracy in Backward Countries," June 11, 1959, FO 371/143 695, (SC(59)26).

53. Letter circulated to Colonial Governors from the Secretary of State, " 'Draft Dispatch' to Governors of All African Colonies and Aden," May 29, 1957, PREM 11/3239.

54. Note to the Prime Minister, February 23, 1957.

55. " 'Draft Dispatch' to Governors of All African Colonies and Aden," May 29, 1957, PREM 11/3239.

56. "United Kingdom Policy on Colonial Matters in the United Nations," February, 1961, CO 936/679.

57. See, for example, a note from Duncan Sandys to the Prime Minister, October 9, 1961, PREM 11/3594.

58. Memorandum by the Secretary of State for Foreign Affairs, "Colonial Issues at the United Nations," May 30, 1962, CAB 129/109 (C(62)73).

59. In a 1960 memorandum on Malta, Colonial Secretary Ian Macleod wrote, "On grounds of general policy, having regard to opinion in Malta and on both sides of the House of Commons and also to the inevitable attacks that will come in the United Nations, we cannot continue further with direct rule," May 25, 1960, PREM 11/3240 (PM(60)35). See also a memorandum written by Macleod on February 28, 1961, CAB 128/35, (CC(61)10). On Cyprus, see for example the record of a Cabinet meeting on July 16, 1957, where "it was suggested that the proposed arrangements would not be as acceptable to opinion in the United States and the United Nations as they would be if they contained some reference to the ultimate possibility of self-determination for the island as a whole," CAB 128/31 (CC(57)52). On Rhodesia, evidence of world public opinion playing a role is in a memorandum written by R. A. Butler, the First Secretary of State, on February 7, 1963, CAB 128/37 (CC(63)10).

60. Darwin, *Britain and Decolonisation*, 258.

61. Stephen Howe, *Anticolonialism in British Politics: The Left and the End of Empire, 1918–1964* (Oxford: Oxford University Press, 1993), 171. On the two streams of Labour, see also David Goldsworthy, *Colonial Issues in British Politics*, 377–78.

62. This is not to deny that Communists actively organized, only that the Cabinet did not mention them. Certainly they added to the chorus of colonial critics. See Howe, *Anticolonialism in British Politics*, 53–66, 117–26, 159–66.

63. Miles Kahler, *Decolonization*, 243–47.

64. Goldsworthy, *Colonial Issues in British Politics*, p. 337. See Kahler, *Decolonization*, 246–48.

65. See Howe, *Anticolonialism in British Politics*, 318–19, and his analysis of parliamentary debates in chap. 6. See also Goldsworthy, *Colonial Issues*, chap. 3.

66. See Kahler, *Decolonization*, 129–50; Goldsworthy, *Colonial Issues*, 364–70; J. G. Darwin, "The Fear of Falling."

67. See minutes for March 11, 1959 (CC(59)16, March 17, 1959 (CC(59)17), March 23, 1959 (CC(59)19), March 25, 1959 (CC(59)20), June 4, 1959 (CC(59)33), July 16, 1959 (CC(59)42), July 20, 1959 (CC(59)43), December 3, 1959 (CC(59)61), in CAB 128/33, October 6, 1960, (AF(M)(60)); and a memorandum by Ian Macleod on "Colonial Policy Committee Detention Legislation in Nyasaland," February 19, 1960, CAB 134/1362, (CPC(60)4).

68. See a report to the Prime Minister from Ian Macleod, March 31, 1960, PREM 11/3240 (PM(60)35); a telegram from New York to the Foreign Office (United Kingdom Mission to the United Nations), CO 936/679; record of a conversation between Harold Macmillan and Averell Harriman at Admiralty House on Monday, February 27, 1961, CO 936/668; a Foreign Office report of June 11, 1959, FO 371/143 695 (SC(59)26); a memorandum by the Secretary of State for Commonwealth Relations, "Federation of Rhodesia and Nyasaland," October

25, 1957, (C(57)248), CAB 129/87; a memorandum by the Secretary of State for Commonwealth Relations, November 12, 1958 (C(58)232), CAB 129/95; and record of a Cabinet meetings of April 12, 1960 (C(60)66), May 30, 1962 (C(62)73), CAB 129/109.

69. For an account of Macleod's political efforts, see Goldsworthy, *Colonial Issues in British Politics*, 364–70.

70. On the lack of colonial issues in the 1959 election, see D. E. Butler and Richard Rose, *The British General Election of 1959* (London: Macmillan, 1960).

71. The first brackets are the author's, the second, mine. Goldsworthy, *Colonial Issues in British Politics*, 364.

CHAPTER TEN
REVOLUTIONARY IDEAS IN THE BRITISH COLONIES

1. John Darwin, *Britain and Decolonisation: The Retreat from Empire in the Post-War World* (New York: St. Martin's Press, 1988), 249–70; Geoffrey Barraclough, *Survey of International Affairs* (London: Oxford University Press, 1964); Gary Wasserman, *The Politics of Decolonization* (Cambridge: Cambridge University Press, 1976).

2. On the lack of an ambition for political change of many tribal and religious leaders, see Edward Shils, "The Intellectuals in the Political Development of the New States," *World Politics* 12, no. 3 (April 1960): 329–68, 331.

3. For prominent analyses of colonial nationalism, see Elie Kedourie, *Nationalism in Asia and Africa* (New York: World Publishing Company, 1970); Benedict Anderson, *Imagined Communities*, 2d ed. (London: Verso, 1991).

4. Basil Davidson, *Let Freedom Come: Africa in Modern History* (Boston: Little, Brown, 1978), 139–40.

5. Ibid., 223. For characteristics of the nationalist elite, see also Shils, "The Intellectuals," 332–38.

6. Davidson, *Let Freedom Come*, 165–68. On Pan-Africanism, see J. Ayodele Langley, *Pan-Africanism and Nationalism in West Africa, 1900–1945: A Study in Ideology and Social Class* (Oxford: Clarendon Press, 1972).

7. Thomas Hodgkin, *Nationalism in Colonial Africa* (London: Frederick Muller Ltd., 1956), 114–15; Davidson, *Let Freedom Come*, 157–58.

8. Davidson, *Let Freedom Come*, 178; H. S. Wilson, *West African Nationalism* (London: Macmillan, 1969); Langley, *Pan-Africanism and Nationalism in West Africa*.

9. Davidson, *Let Freedom Come*, 200.

10. Ibid. 199.

11. Michael Crowder, "The 1939–45 War and West Africa," in *History of West Africa*, ed. J.F.A. Ajayi (London: Longmans, 1987), 665–92, 682.

12. Davidson, *Let Freedom Come*, 202–4.

13. Crowder, "The 1939–45 War."

14. On stages of evolution of the colonial idea, see Shils, "The Intellectuals," 354–61.

15. Davidson, *Let Freedom Come*, 165–80.

16. J. B. Webster, "African Political Activity in French West Africa," in *History of West Africa*, ed. J.F.A. Ajayi, (London: Longmans, 1987), 635–64, 642–43, 655–59; Hodgkin, *Nationalism in Colonial Africa*, 93–114.

17. Webster, "African Political Activity in West Africa," 635–38.

18. Davidson, *Let Freedom Come*, 232–33.

19. Ian Henderson, "The Origins of Nationalism in East and Central Africa: The Zambian Case," *Journal of African History* 11 (1970): 591–603, 593.

20. See T. O. Ranger, "Connexions between 'Primary Resistance' Movements and Modern Mass Nationalism in East and Central Africa: Parts 1 and 2," *Journal of African History* 9 (1968): 437–53, 631–41, 634–41.

21. On the growth of Indian nationalism, see Bipan Chandra, *India's Struggle for Independence* (Harmondsworth, U.K.: 1989); Gordon Johnson, *Provincial Politics and Indian Nationalism* (Cambridge: Cambridge University Press, 1973); Anil Seal, "Imperialism and Nationalism in India," in *Locality, Province and Nations*, ed. John Gallagher, Gordon Johnson, and Anil Seal (Cambridge: Cambridge University Press, 1973); Richard Sisson and Stanley Wolpert, eds., *Congress and Indian Nationalism*, (Berkeley: University of California Press, 1988); and Stanley Wolpert, *A New History of India*, 4th ed. (Oxford: Oxford University Press, 1993).

22. Darwin, *The End of the British Empire*, 89.

23. On the "national struggle" vs. "social struggle" theme, see Davidson, *Let Freedom Come*, 227.

24. Olajide Aluko, "Politics of Decolonisation in British West Africa," in *History of West Africa*, ed. J.F.A. Ajayi (London: Longmans, 1974, 1987), 693–735, 698–700; Davidson, *Let Freedom Come*, 232–34.

25. Aluko, "Politics of Decolonisation," 703–10.

26. Davidson, *Let Freedom Come*, 262–65.

27. Ibid., 262–67; Henderson, "The Origins of Nationalism in East and Central Africa"; J. M. Lonsdale, "Some Origins of Nationalism in East Africa," *Journal of African History* 9, no. 1 (1968): 119–46; D. A. Low and A. Smith, eds., *History of East Africa*, vol. 3 (Oxford: Clarendon Press, 1976), iii; C. Rosberg and J. Nottingham, *The Myth of "Mau Mau": Nationalism in Kenya* (Stanford: Stanford University Press, 1966).

28. See Bipan Chandra, *The Rise and Growth of Economic Nationalism in India* (New Delhi: People's Publishing House, 1996); Gordon Johnson, *Provincial Politics and Indian Nationalism*; and Stanley Wolpert, *A New History of India*.

CHAPTER ELEVEN
BRITAIN'S BURDEN OF EMPIRE

1. Hugh Tinker, *Race, Conflict, and the International Order* (London: Macmillan, 1977).

2. On Britain's relative decline, see Paul Kennedy, *The Rise and Fall of the Great Powers: Economic Change and Military Conflict from 1500 to 2000* (New York: Random House, 1987); and Joseph S. Nye, *Bound to Lead* (New York: Basic Books, 1990).

3. My typology corresponds with that of John Darwin, *The End of the British Empire* (Oxford: Oxford University Press, 1991), 41–43.

4. Raymond F. Betts, *France and Decolonisation, 1900–1960* (New York: St. Martin's Press, 1991), 23.

5. Examples of these neocolonialist explanations include Immanuel Wallerstein, "Three Stages of African Involvement in the World Economy," in *The Political Economy of Contemporary Africa*, ed. Peter C. W. Gutkind and Immanuel Wallerstein (Beverly Hills, Calif.: Sage, 1985); and G. Wasserman, *The Politics of Decolonization* (Cambridge: Cambridge University Press, 1976).

6. David Goldsworthy, "Introduction," in David Goldsworthy, ed., *The Conservative Government and the End of Empire, 1951–57* (London: Her Majesty's Stationery Office, 1994), xxv.

7. Darwin, *The End of the British Empire*, 44. On Britain's currency policy, see Susan Strange, *Sterling and British Policy* (Oxford: Oxford University Press, 1971).

8. Rondald Hyam, "Introduction," in Ronald Hyam, ed., *The Labour Government and the End of Empire* (London: HMSO, 1992), xlii.

9. Goldsworthy, "Introduction," xxvi.

10. Sidney Pollard, *The Development of the British Economy: 1914–1980*, 3d ed. (London: Edward Arnold, 1983), 352.

11. Hyam, "Introduction," 43.

12. Goldsworthy, "Introduction," xxv.

13. *Annual Statistical Abstract* 93 (1956): 238, in Allister E. Hinds, "Imperial Policy and Colonial Sterling Balances, 1943–56," *Journal of Imperial and Commonwealth History* 19 (1991): 30.

14. Darwin, *The End of the British Empire*, 48; C. H. Lee, *The British Economy Since 1700: A Macroeconomic Perspective* (Cambridge: Cambridge University Press, 1986), 223–26.

15. Hyam, "Introduction," xliv.

16. See " 'Defence: Outline of Future Policy,' Extracts from Cmnd. 124, February 1957, *PP* 23 (1956–57): 489, par. 6, in A. N. Porter and A. J. Stockwell, *British Imperial Policy and Decolonization, 1938–1964*, vol. 2: 1951–1964 (London: Macmillan, 1987), 453. There had been previous memoranda issuing a similar conclusion. See, for instance, " 'British Overseas Obligations': Cabinet Memorandum by Mr. Eden," June 18, 1952, CAB 129/53 (C(52)202), in Goldsworthy, ed., Part 1, 4–12.

17. Goldsworthy, "Introduction," xxvii.

18. Hyam, ed., "Introduction," pp. xxv-xxix.

19. See S. Newton, "Britain, the Sterling Area and European Integration," in *Money, Finance, and Empire 1790–1960*, ed. A. N. Porter and R. F. Holland (London: Frank Cass, 1985); and Darwin, *The End of the British Empire*, 45.

20. Hyam, "Introduction," xlii.

21. Hyam, "Introduction," xlii. On the vital nature of the colonies for Britain's economic position, see "[Economic Development in Africa]: speech by Sir S. Cripps (minister for economic affairs) to the African Governors' Conference (paper AGC 22)," November 12, 1947, CO 847/36/4, no. 24, in Hyam, ed., Part 1, 298–302.

22. Hyam, "Introduction," xlvii, lx.

23. Goldsworthy, "Introduction," lvii.

24. Cmnd 827 (1959), *Report of the Committee on the Working of the Monetary System*, in Darwin, *The End of the British Empire*, 49.

25. Porter and Stockwell, *British Imperial Policy and Decolonization, 1938–64*, 35.

26. Goldsworthy, "Introduction," liv, lvi.

27. Quoted in D. J. Morgan, *The Official History of Colonial Development*, 5 vols. (London: Macmillan, 1980), 102.

28. Hyam, "Introduction," xlv.

29. Goldsworthy, "Introduction," xlv, xlvi.

30. Goldsworthy, xxvi, xxvii–xxxix.

31. Darwin, *The End of the British Empire*, 48.

32. Ibid., 50.

33. Goldsworthy, "Introduction," xxxix–xl.

34. Darwin, *Britain and Decolonisation*, 262.

35. See Tony Smith, *America's Mission: The United States and the Worldwide Struggle for Democracy in the Twentieth Century* (Princeton: Princeton University Press. 1994).

36. See John Lewis Gaddis, *We Now Know: Rethinking Cold War History* (Oxford: Oxford University Press, 1997), 155–58.

37. See Stephen Walt, *The Origins of Alliances* (Ithaca: Cornell University Press, 1987).

38. See J. Strachey, *The End of Empire* (London: Gollancz, 1959); and A. P. Thornton, *The Imperial Idea and Its Enemies: A Study in British Power* (London: Macmillan, 1959). For a discussion of such arguments, see Darwin, *The End of the British Empire*, 14.

39. On the association between the middle class and nationalist beliefs, see Basil Davidson, *Let Freedom Come: Africa in Modern History* (London: Longmans, 1978), 128, and T. Hodgkin, *Nationalism in Colonial Africa* (London: Frederick Mueller, Ltd., 1956), 116.

40. Some of the relevant historical works addressing this issue are J. F. Ade Ajayi, "The Continuity of African Institutions under Colonialism," in *Emerging Themes in African History*, ed. T. O. Ranger (London: Heinemann, 1968); J. F. Ajayi and Michael Crowder, eds., *History of West Africa*, 2d ed. (London: Longmans, 1987); E. A. Ayandele et al., eds., *The Making of Modern Africa* (London: Longmans, 1968, 1971); Elliot Berg, "The Economic Basis of Political Choice in French West Africa," *American Political Science Review* 54 (1960): 391–405; Bipan Chandra, *The Rise and Growth of Economic Nationalism in India* (New Delhi: People's Publishing House, 1966); Robin Cohen, *Labour and Politics in Nigeria, 1945–1971* (London: William Heinemann, 1974); Michael Crowder, *Colonial West Africa* (London: H. Cass, 1978); Michael Crowder, "The 1939–45 War and West Africa"; Michael Crowder and Donal Cruise O'Brien, "Politics of Decolonisation in French West Africa," in *History of West Africa*, 2d ed., J.F.A. Ayayi (London: Longmans, 1987); Davidson, *Let Freedom Come;* R. O. Ekundere, *An Economic History of Nigeria, 1860–1960* (London: Methuen, 1973); Roland Oliver and Gervase Matthew, eds., *History of East Africa* vol. 1 (Oxford: Oxford University Press, 1963); A. G. Hopkins, *An Economic History of West Africa* (New York: Columbia University Press, 1973); J. A. Iliffe, *A Modern History of Tangan-*

yika (Cambridge: Cambridge University Press, 1979); D. A. Low, and A. Smith, eds., *History of East Africa*, 3 vols. (Oxford: Clarendon, 1976); Robert Rotberg, *The Rise of Nationalism in Central Africa* (Cambridge: Harvard University Press, 1966); H. S. Wilson, *Origins of West African Nationalism* (London: Macmillan, 1969); G. Johnson, *Provincial Politics and Indian Nationalism* (Cambridge: Cambridge University Press, 1973); Stanley Wolpert, *A New History of India*, 4th ed. (Oxford: Oxford University Press, 1993).

41. I derive this conclusion from a broad array of sources. See note 40.

42. See E. P. Thompson, *The Making of the English Working Class* (New York: Pantheon Books, 1964).

43. Again, the evidence is comparative. See note 40.

44. William Quandt, *Revolution and Political Leadership: Algeria, 1954–1958* (Cambridge: MIT Press, 1969).

45. For statistical and descriptive evidence, see Hodgkin, *Nationalism in Colonial Africa*, 67, and Davidson, *Let Freedom Come*, 212.

46. Hodgkin, *Nationalism in Colonial Africa*, 118.

47. Davidson, *Let Freedom Come*, 215. On the attitudes and activities of the urbanized proletariat, see P. C. Lloyd, *Power and Independence: Urban Africans' Perception of Social Inequality* (London: Routledge, 1974). See also A. G. Hopkins, *An Economic History of West Africa*, 242.

48. For description and statistics on growth and slump, see Hopkins, *An Economic History.*

49. On the Second Colonial Occupation's importance in Africa, see Crowder, "The 1939–45 War and West Africa," 678–81, and D. A. Low and J. M. Lonsdale, "Introduction: Towards the New Order, 1945–63," in *History of East Africa*, vol. 3, ed. D. A. Low and J. M. Lonsdale (Oxford: Clarendon Press, 1976).

50. On the settlers, see Davidson, *Let Freedom Come*, 260–70; J. M. Lonsdale, "Some Origins of Nationalism in East Africa," *Journal of African History* 9, no. 1 (1968): Ian Henderson, "The Origins of Nationalism in East and Central Africa: The Zambian Case," *Journal of African History* 11, no. 4 (1970): 591–603; Low and Lonsdale, "Introduction: Towards the New Order, 1945–63."

51. Hopkins, *An Economic History.*

CHAPTER TWELVE
THE FALL OF GREATER FRANCE

1. "Colonial Issues at the United Nations," a memorandum by the Secretary of State for Foreign Affairs, May 30, 1962, CAB 129/109 (C(62)73).

2. The state of scholarship on Britain and France during this period bears out this relative simplicity. On France, there are many works on specific topics such as the Algeria conflict, France's West Africa policy, and so on, but few works on the general subject of "the end of empire," whereas many works on the British case address the subject in this broad form. France's imperial policy must be understood through specific conflicts, especially the Algerian conflict. The connection between these specific conflicts and the end of empire, however, is not deeply controversial.

3. See Raymond F. Betts, *France and Decolonisation, 1900–1960* (New York: St. Martin's Press, 1991), 23.

4. There were many terms used to characterize this ideal, many of which, such as "French Union," corresponded to particular policy proposals. For inclusivity, I will use the term "Greater France," implying France's continued sovereignty in its empire. The term "la plus grande France" was in fact often used to describe France's empire.

5. Christopher Andrew and A. S. Kanya-Forstner, *The Climax of French Imperial Expansion, 1914–1924* (Stanford: Stanford University Press, 1981), 26.

6. See Andrew and Kanya-Forstner, *The Climax*, 9–32; C. M. Andrew and A. S. Kanya-Forstner, "The French 'Colonial Party': Its Composition, Aims and Influence, 1885–1914," *Historical Journal* 14. no. 1 (1971): 99–128; and Henri Brunschwig, *French Colonialism, 1871–1914. Myths and Realities* (New York: Frederick A. Praeger, 1964), 20–30, 167–81.

7. Betts, *France and Decolonisation, 1900–1960*, 23.

8. See Hubert Deschamps, "French Colonial Policy in Tropical Africa Between the Two World Wars," in *France and Britain in Africa: Imperial Rivalry and Colonial Rule*, ed. Prosser Gifford and William Roger Louis (New Haven: Yale University Press, 1971), 543–70; Leonard Thompson, "France and Britain in Africa: A Perspective," 777–84; William Cohen, "The French Colonial Service in West Africa," in *France and Britain in Africa: Imperial Rivalry and Colonial Rule*, ed. Prosser Gifford and William Roger Lewis (New Haven: Yale University Press, 1971), 777–84.

9. The colonial consensus is the major theme of Tony Smith's *The French Stake in Algeria, 1945–62* (Ithaca: Cornell University Press, 1978).

10. Smith, *The French Stake in Algeria*, 60. Quote from *Brazzaville: 30 janvier-8 fevrier 1944*, published by the Ministère des Colonies, p. 32, in Smith, *The French Stake*, 60.

11. *Brazzaville*, p. 22, quoted in Smith, *The French Stake*, 60.

12. Charles de Gaulle, *The Complete Memoirs of Charles de Gaulle* (New York: Simon and Schuster, 1967), 574.

13. Of course, France's defeat was what Marc Bloch termed, in the title of a book, a "strange defeat" (Marc Bloch, *Strange Defeat: A Statement of Evidence Written in 1940*, trans. Gerard Hopkins [New York: Norton, 1968]), one that was reversed by its allies, leaving France to rebuild free from occupation or loser's penalty.

14. The colonies received 64 seats out of 586; about half of these belonged to settler deputies. Smith, *The French Stake*, 61.

15. Smith, *The French Stake*, 68.

16. Ibid., 73.

17. Ibid., 58–73.

18. Ibid., 116–18.

19. I have relied here on Rudolf von Albertini, *Decolonization* (New York: Holmes and Meyer, 1982), 425–42.

20. See Miles Kahler, *Decolonization in Britain and France* (Princeton: Princeton University Press, 1984), 327–30; and Charles-Robert Ageron, *La décolonisation française* (Paris: Armand Colin, 1994).

21. Tony Smith writes: "In response to the question of *why* the process of decolonization was so difficult, the most general response has been to point to the mani-

fold structural shortcomings of the governmental system under the Fourth Republic," in Smith, *The French Stake*, 31. In support of this claim, he cites several authors on the weakness of the Fourth Republic, including Philip Williams, *Crisis and Compromise: Politics in the Fourth Republic* (London: Longmans, 1964); Nicholas Wahl, "The French Political System," in *Patterns of Government*, ed. Samuel Beer and Adam Ulam (New York: Random House, 1962); Nathan Leites, *On the Game of Politics in France* (Stanford: Stanford University Press, 1959); Michael Crozier, *The Bureaucratic Phenomenon* (Chicago: University of Chicago Press, 1964).

22. This is the view of Tony Smith, *The French Stake in Algeria*. Kahler argues that it is partially true. Kahler, *Decolonization*, 161–14.

23. Kahler, *Decolonization*, 183–88.

24. Ibid., 190, 191–94.

25. Smith, *The French Stake*, 54–57; see also D. Bruce Marshall, *The French Colonial Myth and Constitution-Making in the Fourth Republic* (New Haven: Yale University Press, 1973).

26. Kahler, *Decolonization*, 167; see also Philip Williams, *Crisis and Compromise.*

27. Kahler, *Decolonization*, 171.

28. Ibid., 178.

29. Smith, *The French Stake*, 130.

30. Smith, *The French Stake*, 133; Kahler, *Decolonization*, 173–78; see also Michael Clark, *Algeria in Turmoil: A History of the Rebellion* (Praeger: New York, 1959).

31. Kahler, *Decolonization*, 199–200.

32. Ibid., 225–26.

33. Ibid., 215.

34. Kahler, *Decolonization*, 79–106; Duncan MacRae, *Parliament, Parties, and Society in France, 1946–1958* (New York: St. Martin's Press, 1967).

35. Jean-Baptiste Duroselle, "Changes in French Foreign Policy Since 1945," in *In Search of France*, ed. Stanley Hoffmann (Cambridge: Harvard University Press, 1963), 305–58, 344–45.

36. Paul Sorum, *Intellectuals and Decolonization in France* (Durham: University of North Carolina Press, 1977), 238–44.

37. See, for instance, Anton W. De Porte, *De Gaulle's Foreign Policy, 1944–1946* (Cambridge: Harvard University Press, 1968); Alfred Grosser, *French Foreign Policy Under De Gaulle*, trans. Lois Ames Pattison (Boston: Little, Brown, 1965); Jean LaCouture, *Charles de Gaulle* (New York: Norton, 1990–1992); Stanley Hoffmann, ed., *In Search of France* (Cambridge: Harvard University Press, 1963).

38. See De Porte, *De Gaulle's Foreign Policy.*

39. Grosser, *French Foreign Policy*, 7.

40. Smith, *The French Stake*, 165–66.

41. Smith, *The French Stake*; Dorothy Pickles, *Algeria and France: From Colonialism to Cooperation* (New York: Frederick A. Praeger, 1963).

42. Quoted in Marshall, *The French Colonial Myth*, 182–83.

43. Marshall, *The French Colonial Myth*, 183.

44. Ibid., 187–88.

45. Pickles, *Algeria and France*, 47–48.

46. See William Quandt, *Revolution and Political Leadership: Algeria, 1954–1958* (Cambridge: MIT Press, 1969), 25–86; Davidson, *Let Freedom Come*, 163–64.

47. See Quandt, *Revolution*, 25–38.

48. Ibid., 43–86.

49. See Quandt, *Revolution*; Pickles, *Algeria and France*; Smith, *The French Stake in Algeria*.

50. Davidson, *Let Freedom Come*, 247–48. See also Samir Amin, "Underdevelopment and Dependence," *Journal of Modern African Studies* 10 (1972): 503–24; and Samir Amin, *The Maghreb in the Modern World*, trans. Michael Perl (Harmondsworth, U.K.: Penguin Books, 1970).

51. Davidson, *Let Freedom Come*, 194.

52. Ibid., 243–45.

53. See Stephane Bernard, *The Franco-Moroccan Conflict, 1943–1956* (New Haven: Yale University Press, 1968); and Davidson, *Let Freedom Come*, 245–46.

54. Quote and figures are from Basil Davidson, *Modern Africa: A Social and Political History* (London: Longmans, 1994), 131.

55. Quoted in Henri Grimal, *Decolonization: The British, French, Dutch and Belgian Empires, 1919–1963*, trans. Stephan De Vos. (Boulder, Colo.: Westview Press, 1978), 251.

56. Davidson, *Let Freedom Come*, 189.

57. On the intellectual development of black African nationalists, see Michael Crowder and Donal Cruise O'Brien, "Politics of Decolonisation in French West Africa," *History of West Africa*, ed. J.F.A. Ajayi (London: Longman, 1987), 736–60, 736–37; Wesley Johnson, "African Political Activity in French West Africa," in *History of West Africa*, ed. J.F.A. Ajayi (London: Longmans, 1987), 608–34, 629–34.

58. African nationalists debated hotly among themselves what form such a federation would take, particularly over whether it would be two large federations, one for western Africa, one for equatorial Africa, as more radical nationalists advocated, or one in which each of the colonies would be represented separately, as relative conservatives like Houphouët-Boigny desired. On nationalist politics during this period, see Crowder and O'Brien, "Politics of Decolonisation in French West Africa," 740–60; and Davidson, *Let Freedom Come*, 251–56.

59. Indochina raises a special sort of issue, however, because here it may have been not only the strength of the anticolonial opposition that mattered in the struggle against colonial rule, but also the content of anticolonial ideas—namely communism. That Indo-Chinese nationalists were Communists does not detract from the ideas-based explanation of anticolonial resistance, but it does call into question whether it was France's imperial ideal that was operative for policymakers in Paris. Was it instead France's anticommunism, rather than its imperial ideal, that drove it to fight eight years in Indochina? Doubtless the antipathy to communism of French governments, both before and after World War II, influenced its policy. But France's desire to maintain its empire was essential, too. The crucial evidence for this is France's refusal to cooperate or compromise with the Vietnamese non-Communist leader Bao Dai, with whom France might have effectively countered Ho Chi Minh, but who also wanted Vietnamese independence. The

contrast with the British policy toward communists in Malaya is instructive. Although the communist opposition in Malaya was weaker than Ho Chi Minh, Britain was willing to cooperate, and benefited from cooperating with the Alliance Party, a noncommunist alternative that helped Britain to crush communist opposition relatively quickly. Tony Smith makes the same comparison in "A Comparative Study of French and British Decolonization," *Comparative Studies in Society and History* 20, no. 1 (1978): 94. On Indochina, see also A. W. Cameron, *Vietnam Crisis* (Ithaca: Cornell University Press, 1971).

60. Quoted in Franz Ansprenger, *The Dissolution of Colonial Empires* (London: Routledge, 1989), 65–66.

61. Figures are from Smith, *The French Stake*, 157.

62. Kahler, *Decolonization*, 309–10.

63. Smith, *The French Stake*, 158.

64. Of course, France did not adopt this strategy in Black Africa, due to the different approach of Charles de Gaulle. It is doubtful, too, that the variation can be explained economically, for the Maghreb states were more valuable to France than the Black African ones.

65. Between 1956 and 1964, British government spending on colonies was $2.867 billion to France's $6.811 billion; and British private investment was $2.791 billion to France's $2.853 million. Figures are quoted from David K. Fieldhouse, "The Economic Exploitation of Africa: Some British and French Comparisons," in *France and Britain in Africa: Imperial Rivalry and Colonial Rule,* ed. Prosser Gifford and William Roger Louis (New Haven: Yale University Press, 1971), 593–662, 633–34.

66. Kahler, *Decolonization*, 300.

67. Ibid., 299–308.

68. Smith, *The French Stake*, 161.

69. John Stewart Ambler, *The French Army in Politics, 1945–1962* (Columbus: Ohio State University Press, 1962); Kahler, *Decolonization*, 348–53.

70. See Amin, *The Maghreb in the Modern World.*

71. See Davidson, *Let Freedom Come*; Amin, "Underdevelopment and Dependence"; Amin, *The Maghreb in the Modern World*; Crowder and O'Brien, "Politics of Decolonisation in French West Africa"; Johnson, "African Political Activity in French West Africa"; Pickles, *Algeria and France.*

72. In Madagascar, the settler community numbered 60,000 in the late 1940s—smaller than North Africa, about the size of the Kenya community—but was reported to have tight access to the colonial administration. See Davidson, *Let Freedom Come*, 249–51.

73. I have borrowed here heavily from Kahler, *Decolonization*, 316–35, 344–48.

74. Kahler, *Decolonization*, 327–28.

BIBLIOGRAPHY

ARCHIVAL SOURCES

Public Records Office, London.

WORKS CITED

"Treaty of Münster." *Major Peace Treaties in Modern History, 1648–1967.* Ed. Fred Israel. New York: Chelsea House Publishers, 1967.

"Treaty of Osnabrück." *The Consolidated Treaty Series.* Vol. 1. Ed. Clive Parry. Dobbs Ferry, N.Y.: Oceana Publications, 1981.

Adler, Emanuel, and Peter Haas. "Conclusion: Epistemic Communities, World Order, and the Creation of a Reflective Research Program." *International Organization* 46 (winter 1992): 367–90.

Ageron, Charles-Robert Ageron. *La décolonisation française.* Paris: Armand Colin, 1994.

Ajayi, J. F., and Michael Crowder, eds. *History of West Africa.* 2d ed. London: Longmans, 1987.

Ajayi, J. F. Ade. "The Continuity of African Institutions under Colonialism." In *Emerging Themes in African History.* Ed. T. O. Ranger. London: Heinemann, 1968.

Akehurst, Michael. *A Modern Introduction to International Law*, 5th ed. London: George Allen and Unwin, 1984.

Albertini, Rudolf von. *Decolonization.* New York: Holmes and Meyer, 1982.

Aluko, Olajide. "Politics of Decolonisation in British West Africa." *History of West Africa.* Ed. J.F.A. Ajayi. London: Longmans, 1974, 1987.

Ambler, John Stewart. *The French Army in Politics, 1945–1962.* Columbus: Ohio State University Press, 1962.

Amin, Samir. *The Maghreb in the Modern World.* Harmondsworth, U.K.: Penguin Books, 1970.

———. "Underdevelopment and Dependence." *Journal of Modern African Studies* 10, no. 4 (1972): 503–24.

Anderson, Benedict. *Imagined Communities*, 2d ed. London: Verso, 1991.

Anderson, N. K. "The Reformation in Scandinavia and the Baltic." *The New Cambridge Modern History.* Ed. G. R. Elton. Vol. 2 *The Reformation, 1520–1559*, 134–60. Cambridge: Cambridge University Press, 1958.

Anderson, Perry. *Lineages of the Absolutist State.* London: Verso, 1974.

Andrew, Christopher, and A. S. Kanya-Forstner. *The Climax of French Imperial Expansion 1914–1924.* Stanford, Calif.: Stanford University Press, 1981.

Andrew, C. M., and A. S. Kanya-Forstner. "The French 'Colonial Party': Its Compositions, Aims and Influence," 1885–1914, *Historical Journal* 14 (March 1971): 99–128.

Ansprenger, Franz. *The Dissolution of Colonial Empires.* London: Routledge, 1989.

Arndt, Johannes, "The Emperor and the Reich (1600–1648)." In 1648–War and Peace in Europe. Ed. Klaus Bussmann and Heinz Schilling. 69–76. Münster, Germany: Westfalisches Landesmuseum, 1998.

Aston, Trevor, ed. *Crisis in Europe, 1560–1660.* London: Routledge and Kegan Paul, 1965.

Attlee, Clement. *Empire into Commonwealth.* Oxford: Oxford University Press, 1961.

Ayandele, E. A., et al., eds. *The Making of Modern Africa.* London: Longmans, 1968, 1971.

Baldwin, David. "Neoliberalism, Neorealism and World Politics." In *Neorealism and Neoliberalism.* Ed. David Baldwin. 3–28. New York: Columbia University Press, 1993.

Barber, Benjamin. *Jihad vs. McWorld.* New York: Time Books, 1995.

Barnett, Correlli. *The Collapse of British Power.* Atlantic Highlands, N.J.: Humanities Press International, 1972.

Barraclough, Geoffrey. *The Origins of Modern Germany.* Oxford: Basil Blackwell, 1947.

———. *The Medieval Empire: Ideal and Reality.* London: G. Philip, 1950.

———. *Survey of International Affairs.* London: Oxford University Press, 1964.

Bartelson, Jens. *A Genealogy of Sovereignty.* Cambridge: Cambridge University Press, 1995.

Bean, Richard. "War and the Birth of the Nation-State." *Journal of Economic History* 33 (1973): 203–21.

Benecke, Gerhard. *Society and Politics in Germany, 1500–1750.* London: Routledge and Kegan Paul, 1974.

Benn, Stanley. "Sovereignty." *Encyclopedia of Philosophy* 7, no. 8 (1967): 501–5.

Berat, Lynn. *Walvis Bay: Decolonization and International Law.* New Haven: Yale University Press, 1990.

Berenger, J. *History of the Habsburg Empire.* London: Berenger, 1994.

Berg, Elliot. "The Economic Basis of Political Choice in French West Africa." *American Political Science Review* 54 (1960): 391–405.

Berger, Peter L., and Thomas Luckmann. *The Social Construction of Reality.* New York: Doubleday, 1966.

Bergesen, Albert, ed. *Studies of the Modern World-System.* New York: Academic Press, 1980.

Bernard, Stephane. *The Franco-Morrocan Conflict 1943–1956.* New Haven: Yale University Press, 1968.

Betts, Raymond F. *France and Decolonisation 1900–1960.* New York: St. Martin's Press, 1991.

Biersteker, Thomas J., and Cynthia Weber, "The Social Construction of State Sovereignty." In *State Sovereignty as Social Construct.* Ed. Thomas J. Biersteker and Cynthia Weber. Cambridge: Cambridge University Press, 1996.

Biersteker, Thomas J., and Cynthia Weber, eds. *State Sovereignty as Social Construct.* Cambridge: Cambridge University Press, 1996.

Bloch, Marc. *Feudal Society.* Trans. L. A. Manyon. 2 Vols. Chicago: University of Chicago Press, 1960.

———. *Strange Defeat: A Statement of Evidence Written in 1940.* Trans. Gerard Hopkins. New York: Norton, 1968.

Blyth, Mark. "Any More Bright Ideas?: The Ideational Turn of Comparative Political Economy." *Comparative Politics* 29 (1997): 229–50.

Bodin, Jean. *On Sovereignty: Four Chapters from Six Books of the Commonwealth.* Trans. Julian Franklin. Cambridge: Cambridge University Press, 1992.

Bonney, Richard. *Political Change in France Under Richelieu and Mazarin 1624–1661.* Oxford: Oxford University Press, 1978.

———. *The King's Debts: Finance and Politics in France, 1589–1661.* Oxford: Oxford University Press, 1981.

———. *Society and Government in France Under Richelieu and Mazarin 1624–1661.* London: Collier-Macmillan, 1988.

Boswell, Terry. "Colonial Empires and the Capitalist World-Economy: A Time Series Analysis of Colonization, 1640–1960." *American Sociological Review* 54 (1989): 180–96.

Bouyer, Louis. *The Spirit and Forms of Protestantism.* London: Harville Press, 1955.

Brady, Thomas. "In Search of the Godly City: The Domestication of Religion in the German Urban Reformation." In *The German People and the Reformation.* Ed. R. Po-Chia Hsia. Ithaca: Cornell University Press, 1988.

Brierly, J. L. *The Law of Nations.* New York: Oxford University Press, 1963.

Briggs, Robin. *Early Modern France, 1560–1715.* Oxford: Oxford University Press, 1977.

Brown, Chris. "International Theory and International Society: The Viability of the Middle Way?" *Review of International Studies* 21 (1995): 183–96.

Brownlie, Ian. *Principles of Public International Law.* 3d ed. Oxford: Oxford University Press, 1979.

Brunschwig, Henri. *French Colonialism, 1871–1914: Myths and Realities.* New York: Praeger, 1966.

Buisseret, David. *Sully and the Growth of Centralized Government in France 1598–1610.* London: Eyre & Spottiswoode, 1968.

Bukovansky, Mlada. "American Identity and Neutral Rights from Independence to the War of 1812." *International Organization* 51 (1997): 209–47.

Bull, Hedley. *The Anarchical Society.* New York: Columbia University Press, 1977.

———. "The Emergence of a Universal International Society." In *The Expansion of International Society.* Ed. Hedley Bull and Adam Watson. 117–26. Oxford: Oxford University Press, 1984.

———. "The Importance of Grotius in the Study of International Relations." In *Hugo Grotius and International Relations.* Ed. Hedley Bull, Benedict Kingsbury, and Adam Roberts. 65–90. Oxford: Clarendon Press, 1990.

Bull, Hedley, and Adam Watson, eds. *The Expansion of International Society.* Oxford: Oxford University Press, 1984.

Burckhardt, Carl J. *Richelieu and His Age.* Trans. Bernard Hoy. New York: Harcourt, Brace, Jovanovich, 1970.

Burckhardt, Johannes, "The Summitless Pyramid: War Aims and Peace Compromise among Europe's Universalist Powers." In *1648–War and Peace in Europe.*

Ed. Klaus Bussmann and Heinz Schilling. 51–60. Münster, Germany: Westfalisches Landesmuseum, 1998.

Bussmann, Klaus, and Heinz Schilling, eds. *1648—War and Peace in Europe.* Münster, Germany: Westfalisches Landesmuseum, 1998.

Butler, D. E., and Richard Rose. *The British General Election of 1959.* London: Macmillan, 1960.

Butterfield, Herbert, and Martin Wight, eds. *Diplomatic Investigations.* London: Allen and Unwin, 1966.

Buzan, Barry. "From International System to International Society: Structural Realism and Regime Theory Meet the English School" *International Organization* 47 (1993): 327–52.

Cain, P. J., and A. G. Hopkins. *British Imperialism: Crisis and Deconstruction, 1914–1990.* London: Longmans, 1993.

Calvin, John. *Institutes of the Christian Religion.* Grand Rapids, Mich.: Wm. Eerdmans Publishing Company, 1989.

Cameron, A.W. *Vietnam Crisis.* Ithaca: Cornell University Press, 1971.

Cameron, Euan. *The European Reformation.* Oxford: Oxford University Press, 1991.

Cantor, Norman. *Inventing the Middle Ages: The Lives, Works, and Ideas of the Great Medievalists of the Twentieth Century.* New York: W. Morrow, 1991.

Carr, E. H. *The Twenty Years' Crisis.* New York: Harper and Row, 1964.

Carsten, F. L. *Princes and Parliaments in Germany from the Fifteenth to the Eighteenth Century.* Oxford: Oxford University Press, 1959.

Chadwick, Owen. *The Reformation.* London: Penguin, 1964.

Chandra, Bipan. *India's Struggle for Independence.* Harmondsworth, U.K.: Penguin, 1989.

———. *The Rise and Growth of Economic Nationalism in India.* New Delhi: People's Publishing House, 1996.

Chase-Dunn, Christopher. "Interstate System and Capitalist World-Economy: One Logic or Two?" *International Studies Quarterly* 25 (1982): 19–42.

Chase-Dunn, Christopher, and Richard Rubinson. "Toward a Structural Perspective on the World-System." *Politics and Society* 7, no. 4 (1977): 453–76.

Checkel, Jeffrey T. "The Constructivist Turn in International Relations Theory." *World Politics* 50 (1998): 324–48.

Chopra, Jarat, and Thomas Weiss, "Sovereignty Is No Longer Sacrosanct: Codifying Humanitarian Intervention," *Ethics and International Affairs* 6 (1992): 95–117.

Church, William F(arr). *Constitutional Thought in Sixteen-Century France.* Cambridge: Harvard University Press, 1941.

Church, William F. *Richelieu and Reason of State.* Princeton: Princeton University Press, 1972.

Cipolla, Carl, ed. *The Fontana Economic History of Europe: The Sixteenth and Seventeenth Centuries.* Glasgow: William Collins Sons, 1974.

Clark, Michael. *Algeria in Turmoil: A History of the Rebellion.* Praeger: New York, 1959.

Claude, Inis. *National Minorities: An International Problem.* Cambridge: Harvard University Press, 1955.

Claude, Inis L. Jr. "Collective Legitimation as a Political Function of the United Nations." In *International Organization: Politics and Process.* Ed. Leland Goodrich and David A. Kay. 287–306. Madison: University of Wisconsin Press, 1973.

Cobban, Alfred. *National Self-Determination.* Oxford: Oxford University Press, 1945.

Cohen, R. *Labour and Politics in Nigeria, 1945–1971.* London: Heinemann, 1974.

Cohen, William. "The French Colonial Service in West Africa." In *France and Britain in Africa: Imperial Rivalry and Colonial Rule.* Ed. Prosser Gifford and William Roger Louis. 777–84. New Haven: Yale University Press, 1971.

Collins, Randall. *The Sociology of Philosophies.* Cambridge: Harvard University Press, 1988.

Cooper, Richard. *The Economics of Interdependence: Economic Policy in the Atlantic Community.* New York: McGraw-Hill, 1968.

Crawford, James. *The Creation of States in International Law.* Oxford: Clarendon Press, 1979.

Crawford, Neta. "Decolonization as an International Norm: The Evolution of Practices, Arguments, and Beliefs." In *Emerging Norms of Justified Intervention.* Ed. Laura W. Reed and Carl Kaysen. 37–62. Cambridge, Mass.: The Committee on International Security Studies, American Academy of Arts and Sciences, 1993.

Cross, Colin. *The Fall of the British Empire.* London: Hodder and Stoughton, 1968.

Crowder, Michael. *Colonial West Africa.* London: H. Cass, 1978.

———. "The 1939–45 War and West Africa." In *History of West Africa.* Ed. J.F.A. Ajayi. 665–92. London: Longmans, 1987.

Crowder, Michael, and Donal Cruise O'Brien. "Politics of Decolonisation in French West Africa." In *History of West Africa.* Ed. J.F.A. Ajayi. 736–60. London: Longman, 1987.

Crozier, Michel. *The Bureaucratic Phenomenon.* Chicago: University of Chicago Press, 1964.

Dahl, Robert. "The Concept of Power." *Behavioral Science* 2 (1957): 201–15.

Damrosch, Lori. "Commentary on Collective Military Intervention to Enforce Human Rights." In *Law and Force in the New International Order.* Ed. Lori Damrosch and David Scheffer. 215–23. Boulder, Colo.: Westview Press, 1991.

Damrosch, Lori Fisler, ed. *Enforcing Restraint: Collective Intervention in Internal Conflicts.* New York: Council on Foreign Relations Press, 1993.

Darby, Phillip. *Three Faces of Imperialism: British and American Approaches to Asia and Africa 1870–1970.* New Haven: Yale University Press, 1987.

Darwin, J. G. "The Fear of Falling: British Politics and Imperial Decline Since 1990." In *Transactions of the Royal Historical Society.* 27–44. Vol. 36 of the 5th Series. London: Royal Historical Society, 1986.

Darwin, John. *Britain and Decolonisation: The Retreat from Empire in the Post-War World.* New York: St. Martin's Press, 1988.

———. *The End of the British Empire.* Oxford: Oxford University, 1991.

Davidson, Basil. *The Africans: An Entry to Social and Cultural History.* London: Longmans, 1969.

Davidson, Basil. *Let Freedom Come: Africa in Modern History.* Boston: Little, Brown and Company, 1978.

de Gaulle, Charles. *The Complete Memoirs of Charles de Gaulle.* New York: Simon and Schuster, 1967.

Dehio, Ludwig. *The Precarious Balance.* Trans. Charles Fulman. New York: Knopf, 1962.

De Porte, Anton W. *De Gaulle's Foreign Policy, 1944–1946.* Cambridge: Harvard University Press, 1968.

Deschamps, Hubert. "French Colonial Policy in Tropical Africa Between the Two World Wars." In *France and Britain in Africa: Imperial Rivalry and Colonial Rule.* Ed. Prosser Gifford and William Roger Louis. 543–70. New Haven: Yale University Press, 1971.

DeVries, Jan. *The Dutch Rural Economy in the Golden Age, 1500–1700.* New Haven: Yale University Press, 1974.

Dickens, A. G. *Reformation and Society in Sixteenth Century Europe.* London: Thames and Hudson, 1966.

———. *The German Nation and Martin Luther.* London: Edward Arnold, 1974.

Dickmann, Fritz. "Rechtsgedanke und Machtpolitik bei Richelieu: Studienen neu endeckten Quellen." *Historische Zeitschrift* 196 (1963): 265–319.

———. *Der Westphaelische Frieden.* Münster, Germany: Aschendorff, 1965.

Dickmann, Fritz, et al., eds. *Acta Pacis Westphalicae.* Münster: Aschendorff, 1962.

Dimaggio, P. J., and W. W. Powell. "The Iron Cage Revisited: Institutional Isomorphism and Collective Rationality in Organizational Fields." *American Sociological Review* (April 1983): 147–60.

Donagan, Alan. *The Theory of Morality.* Chicago: University of Chicago Press, 1977.

Downing, Brian. *The Military Revolution and Political Change: Origins of Democracy and Autocracy in Early Modern Europe.* Princeton: Princeton University Press, 1992.

Doyle, Michael, *Empires.* Ithaca: Cornell University Press, 1986.

———. *Ways of War and Peace.* New York: W. W. Norton and Company, 1997.

Duby, Georges. *La société aux XIe et XIIe siècles dans la région mâconnaise.* Paris: Ecole Pratique des Hautes Etudes, 1953.

Duchhardt, Heinz, "The Peace of Westphalia as *Lieu de Mémoire* in Germany and Europe." In *1648–War and Peace in Europe.* Ed. Klaus Bussmann and Heinz Schilling, 41–50. Münster, Germany: Westfalisches Landesmuseum, 1998.

Dugard, John. *Recognition and the United Nations.* Cambridge: Grotius Publications, Ltd., 1987.

Durkheim, Emile. *The Elementary Forms of the Religious Life.* Trans. Joseph Ward Swain: New York: Free Press, 1915.

———. "The Contribution of Sociology to Psychology and Philosophy." In *The Rules of Sociological Method.* Ed. and intro. Steven Lukes. Trans. W. D. Halls. 236–40. New York: Free Press, 1982.

———. "Marxism and Sociology: The Materialist Congestion of History." In *The Rules of the Sociological Method.* Ed. and intro. Steven Lukes. Trans. W.D. Halls. New York: Free Press, 1982.

———. "The Rules of Sociological Method." In *The Rules of Sociological Method.* Ed. Steven Lukes. Trans. W. D. Halls. 31–163. New York: Free Press, 1982.

———. *The Division of Labor in Society.* Intro. Lewis A. Coser. Trans. W.D. Halls. New York: Free Press, 1984.

Duroselle, Jean-Baptiste. "Changes in French Foreign Policy Since 1945." In *In Search of France.* Ed. Stanley Hoffmann. 305–58. Cambridge: Harvard University Press, 1963.

Ekundere, R. O. *An Economic History of Nigeria, 1860–1960.* London: Methuen, 1973.

Elliott, J. H. *Imperial Spain, 1469–1716.* London: Edward Arnold, 1963.

———. "The Decline of Spain." In *Crisis in Europe 1560–1660: Essays from Past and Present.* Ed. Trevor Aston. London: Routledge and Kegan Paul, 1965.

———. *Europe Divided, 1559–1598.* London: Collins, 1968.

———. *Richelieu and Olivares.* Cambridge: Cambridge University Press, 1984.

Elliott, John, "War and Peace in Europe, 1618–1648." In *1648—War and Peace in Europe.* Ed. Klaus Bussmann and Heinz Schilling. 23–40. Münster, Germany: Westfalisches Landesmuseum, 1998.

Elster, Jon. *Nuts and Bolts for the Social Sciences.* Cambridge: Cambridge University Press, 1989.

———. *Political Psychology.* Cambridge: Cambridge University Press, 1993.

Elton, G. R. *Reformation Europe, 1517–1559.* London: Collins, 1963.

Ertman, Thomas. *Birth of the Leviathan: Building States and Regimes in Medieval and Early Modern Europe.* Cambridge: Cambridge University Press, 1997.

Evera, Stephen Van. "The Cult of the Offensive and the Origins of the First World War." *International Security* 9, no. 1 (1984): 58–107.

"Faith and Statecraft." *Orbis* vol. 42, no. 2 (special issue, 1998).

Falk, Richard. "Sovereignty." In *Oxford Companion to Politics of the World.* Ed. Joel Krieger. Oxford: Oxford University Press, 1993.

Fieldhouse, David. *Colonial Empires.* New York: Dell, 1966.

Fieldhouse, David K. "The Economic Exploitation of Africa: Some British and French Comparisons." In *France and Britain in Africa: Imperial Rivalry and Colonial Rule.* Ed. Prosser Gifford and William Roger Louis. 593–662. New Haven: Yale University Press, 1971.

Finnemore, Martha. "Constructing Norms of Humanitarian Intervention." In *The Culture of National Security.* Ed. Peter Katzenstein. 153–85. New York: Columbia University Press, 1983.

———. *National Interests in International Society.* Ithaca: Cornell University Press, 1996.

Finnemore, Martha, and Kathryn Sikkink. "International Norm Dynamics and Political Change." *International Organization* 52, no. 4 (1998): 887–917.

Fischer, Markus. "Feudal Europe, 800–1300: Communal Discourse and Conflictual Practices." *International Organization* 46 (1992): 427–66.

Forsythe, David. *Human Rights and World Politics.* Lincoln: University of Nebraska Press, 1989.

Foucault, Michel. *Discipline and Punish: The Birth of the Prison.* New York: Vintage, 1979.

Fowler, Michael Ross, and Julie Marie Bunck. *Law, Power, and the Sovereign State.* University Park: Pennsylvania State University Press, 1995.

Fox, Gregory H. "New Approaches to International Human Rights: The Sovereign State Revisited." In *State Sovereignty: Change and Persistence in International Relations.* Ed. Sohail H. Hashmi. University Park: Pennsylvania State University Press, 1997.

Frankfurt, Harry. "Freedom of the Will and the Concept of the Person." *Journal of Philosophy* 68 (January 1971).

Franklin, Julian. *Jean Bodin and the Sixteenth Century Revolution in the Methodology of Law and History.* New York: Columbia University Press, 1963.

Friedberg, Aaron. *The Weary Titan: Britain and the Experience of Relative Decline, 1895–1905.* Princeton: Princeton University Press, 1988.

Froats, Daniel, and Stephen Krasner. "Minority Rights and the Westphalia Model." In *The International Spread of Ethnic Conflict: Fear, Diffusion, and Escalation.* Ed. David A. Lake and Donald S. Rothchild. Princeton: Princeton University Press, 1998.

Gaddis, John Lewis. *We Now Know: Rethinking Cold War History.* Oxford: Oxford University Press, 1997.

Gagliardo, John. *Germany Under the Old Regime 1600–1790.* London: Longmans, 1991.

Gallagher, J. A. *The Decline, Revival, and Fall of the British Empire.* Cambridge: Cambridge University Press, 1982.

Gallagher, John, and Ronald Robinson. "The Imperialism of Free Trade." *Economic History Review* 6, no. 1 (1953): 1–15.

Garret, Geoffrey, and Barry R. Weingast. In "Ideas, Interests, and Institutions: Constructing the European Community's Internal Market." In *Ideas and Foreign Policy Beliefs, Institutions, and Political Change.* Ed. Judith Goldstein and Robert Keohane. 173–206. Ithaca: Cornell University Press, 1993.

Gelber, Harry. *Sovereignty Through Interdependence.* London: Kluwer Law, 1997.

George, Alexander. "Case Studies and Theory Development: The Method of Structured, Focused Comparisons." In Paul Gordon Lauren, ed. *Diplomacy: New Approaches in History, Theory, and Policy.* New York: Free Press, 1979.

Gerhardt, Volker, "On the Historical Significance of the Peace of Westphalia: Twelve Theses." In Klaus Bussmann and Heinz Schilling. *1648–War and Peace in Europe.* 485–91. Münster, Germany: Westfalisches Landesmuseum, 1998.

Geyl, Pieter. *The Revolt of the Netherlands, 1555–1609.* London: Williams and Norgate, 1932.

Gilpin, Robert. *War and Change in World Politics.* Cambridge: Cambridge University Press, 1981.

Goertz, Gary. *Contexts of International Politics.* Cambridge: Cambridge University Press, 1994.

Goldstein, Judith. *Ideas, Institutions, and American Trade Policy.* Ithaca: Cornell University Press, 1993.

Goldstein, Judith, and Robert O. Keohane. "Ideas and Foreign Policy: An Analytical Framework." In Judith Goldstein and Robert O. Keohane, eds. *Ideas and Foreign Policy: Beliefs, Institutions, and Political Change.* 330. Ithaca: Cornell University Press, 1993.

Goldstein, Judith, and Robert O. Keohane, eds. *Ideas and Foreign Policy: Beliefs, Institutions, and Political Change*. Ithaca: Cornell University Press, 1993.

Goldsworthy, David. *Colonial Issues in British Politics*. Oxford: Clarendon Press, 1971.

———. "Britain and the International Critics of British Colonialism, 1951–56." *Journal of Commonwealth and Comparative Politics* 29, no. 1 (1991).

Goldsworthy, David, ed. *The Conservative Government and the End of Empire*. 3 vols. London: Her Majesty's Stationery Office, 1994.

Gong, Gerrit. *The Standard of 'Civilization' in International Society*. Oxford: Clarendon Press, 1984.

Grimal, Henri. *Decolonization: The British, French, Dutch, and Belgian Empires, 1919–1963*. Trans. Stephan De Vos. Boulder, Colo.: Westview Press, 1978.

Groenveld, Simon, "The Treaty of Münster as the Culmination of a Progressive Revolution." In *1648–War and Peace in Europe*. Ed. Klaus Bussmann and Heinz Schilling. 123–32. Münster, Germany: Westfalisches Landesmuseum, 1998.

Gross, Leo. "The Peace of Westphalia, 1648–1948." *American Journal of International Law* 42 (1948): 20–41.

———. "The Right of Self-Determination in International Law." In *New States in the Modern World*. Ed. Martin Kilson. Cambridge: Harvard University Press, 1975.

Grosser, Alfred. *French Foreign Policy under De Gaulle*. Trans. Lois Ames Pattison. Boston: Little, Brown and Company, 1965.

Grotius, Hugo. *The Truth of the Christian Religion*. Oxford: Law and Whittaker, 1818.

———. *The Law of War and Peace*. Westport: Hyperion, 1993.

Gulick, E. V. *Europe's Classical Balance of Power*. Ithaca: Cornell University Press, 1955.

Gupta, Partha Sarathi. *Imperialism and the British Labour Movement, 1914–1964*. New York: Holmes and Meier Publishers, 1975.

Haas, Ernst. *When Knowledge Is Power: Three Models of Change in International Organizations*. Berkeley: University of California Press, 1991.

Habermas, Jurgen. *Legitimation Crisis*. Trans. Thomas McCarthy. Boston: Beacon Press, 1975.

Hall, John. "Ideas and the Social Sciences." In *Ideas and Foreign Policy: Beliefs, Institutions, and Political Change*. Ed. Judith Goldstein and Robert Keohane. 31–54. Ithaca: Cornell University Press, 1993.

Hall, Peter, ed. *The Political Power of Economic Ideas*. Princeton: Princeton University Press, 1989.

Hall, Rodney Bruce. "Moral Authority as a Power Resource." *International Organization* 51, no. 4 (1997): 591–622.

———. *National Collective Identity: Social Constructs and International Systems*. New York: Columbia University Press, 1999.

———, and Friedrich Kratochwil. "Medieval Tales: Neorealist 'Science' and the Abuse of History." *International Organization* 47 (1993): 479–91.

Hannum, Hurst. *Autonomy, Sovereignty, and Self-Determination: The Accommodation of Conflicting Rights*. Philadelphia: University of Pennsylvania Press, 1990.

Hartwell, R. M. *The Industrial Revolution and Economic Growth.* London: Methuen, 1971.

Hashmi, Sohail. "International Society and its Islamic Malcontents." *Fletcher Forum* 20 (1996): 13–29.

Hashmi, Sohail, ed. *State Sovereignty: Change and Persistence in International Relations.* University Park: Pennsylvania State University Press, 1997.

Henderson, Ian. "The Origins of Nationalism in East and Central Africa: The Zambian Case." *Journal of African History* 11, no. 4 (1970): 591–603.

Hertslet, Sir Edward. *The Map of Africa by Treaty.* Vol. 1. London: Harrison and Sons, 1896.

Hinds, Allister E. "Imperial Policy and Colonial Sterling Balances, 1943–56." *Journal of Imperial and Commonwealth History* 19, no. 1 (1991): 24–44.

Hinsley, F. H. *Sovereignty,* 2d ed. Cambridge: Cambridge University Press, 1986.

Hintze, Otto. *The Historical Essays of Otto Hintze.* Oxford: Oxford University Press, 1975.

Hobbes, Thomas. *Leviathan.* Harmondsworth, U.K.: Penguin, 1968.

Hodgkin, T. *Nationalism in Colonial Africa.* London: Frederick Muller, Ltd., 1956.

Hoffmann, Stanley. *Janus and Minerva: Essays in the Theory and Practice of International Politics.* Boulder, Colo.: Westview Press, 1987.

Holborn, Hajo. *A History of Modern Germany.* Vol. I: *The Reformation.* New York: Alfred A. Knopf, 1959.

Holsti, Kalevi. *Peace and War: Armed Conflicts and International Order 1648–1989.* Cambridge: Cambridge University Press, 1991.

Hopkins, A. G. *An Economic History of West Africa.* New York: Columbia University Press, 1973.

Howe, Stephen. *Anticolonialism in British Politics: The Left and the End of Empire, 1918–1964.* Oxford Historical Monographs. Oxford: Oxford University Press, 1993.

Hsia, R. Po-Chia, ed. *The German People and the Reformation,* Ithaca: Cornell University Press, 1988.

Huntington, Samuel, "The Clash of Civilizations?" *Foreign Affairs* 72, no. 3 (Summer 1993): 22–49.

———. *The Clash of Civilizations and the Remaking of World Order.* New York: Simon and Schuster, 1996.

Hyam, Ronald, ed. *The Labour Government and the End of Empire.* 3 vols. London: Her Majesty's Stationery Office, 1992.

Ikenberry, G. John. "Creating Yesterday's New World Order: Keynesian 'New Thinking' and the Anglo-American Postwar Settlement." In *Ideas and Foreign Policy Beliefs, Institutions, and Political Change.* Ed. Judith Goldstein and Robert Keohane. 57–86. Ithaca: Cornell University Press, 1993.

Iliffe, J. *A Modern History of Tanganyika.* Cambridge: Cambridge University Press, 1979.

Israel, Fred. L., ed. *Major Peace Treaties of Modern History, 1648–1967.* New York: Chelsea House Publishers, 1967.

Israel, Jonathan. *The Dutch Republic: Its Rise, Greatness, and Fall, 1477–1806.* Oxford: Oxford University Press, 1995.

———. "The Dutch-Spanish War and the Holy Roman Empire (1568–1648)." In Klaus Bussmann and Heinz Schilling, eds. *1648–War and Peace in Europe.* 111–22. Münster, Germany: Westfalisches Landesmuseum, 1998.

Jackson, Robert. *Quasi-States: Sovereignty, International Relations, and the Third World.* Cambridge: Cambridge University Press, 1990.

———. "The Weight of Ideas in Decolonization: Normative Change in International Relations." In *Ideas and Foreign Policy: Beliefs, Institutions, and Political Change.* Ed. Judith Goldstein and Robert O. Keohane. 111–39. Ithaca: Cornell University Press, 1993.

Jacobson, John Kurt. "Much Ado About Ideas: The Cognitive Factor in Economic Policy." *World Politics* 47 (1995): 283–310.

Jaitner, Klaus, "The Popes and the Struggle for Power during the Sixteenth and Seventeenth Centuries." In Klaus Bussmann and Heinz Schilling, eds. *1648—War and Peace in Europe.* 61–68. Münster, Germany: Westfalisches Landesmuseum, 1998.

James, Alan. *Sovereign Statehood.* London: Allen and Unwin, 1986.

———. "The Practice of Sovereign Statehood in Contemporary International Society." *Political Studies* 47, no. 3 (1999): 457–73.

Jepperson, Ronald L., Alexander Wendt, and Peter J. Katzenstein. "Norms, Identity, and Culture in National Security." In *The Culture of National Security.* Ed. Peter J. Katzenstein. 33–75. New York: Columbia University Press, 1996.

Jervis, Robert. *Perception and Misperception in International Politics.* Princeton: Princeton University Press, 1976.

Johnson, G. *Provincial Politics and Indian Nationalism.* Cambridge: Cambridge University Press, 1973.

Johnson, Wesley. "African Political Activity in French West Africa." In *History of West Africa.* Ed. J.F.A. Ajayi. 608–34. London: Longmans, 1987.

Johnston, Alastair Iain. "Thinking About Strategic Culture." *International Security* 19 (1995): 32–64.

Johnston, Douglas, and Cynthia Sampson, eds. *Religion: The Missing Dimension of Statecraft.* Oxford: Oxford University Press, 1994.

Juergensmeyer, Mark. *The New Cold War? Religious Nationalism Confronts the Secular State.* Berkeley: University of California Press, 1993.

Kahler, Miles. *Decolonization in Britain and France.* Princeton: Princeton University Press, 1984.

———. "Rationality in International Relations." *International Organization* 52, no. 4 (1998): 933–38.

Kaiser, David. *Politics and War: European Conflict from Philip II to Hitler.* Cambridge: Harvard University Press, 1990.

Kamen, Henry. *Spain 1469–1714: A Society in Conflict.* London and New York: Longmans, 1983.

Kann, Robert A. *A History of the Habsburg Empire.* Berkeley: University of California Press, 1974.

Kantorowicz, Ernst. *The King's Two Bodies.* Princeton: Princeton University Press, 1957.

Katzenstein, Peter, ed. *The Culture of National Security: News and Identity in World Politics.* New York: Columbia University Press, 1996.

Katznelson, Ira. "Structure and Configuration in Comparative Politics." In *Comparative Politics: Rationality, Culture, and Structure*. Ed. Mark Irving Lichbach and Alan Zuckerman. 81–112. Cambridge: Cambridge University Press, 1997.

Kautsky, John H. *The Politics of Aristocratic Empires*. Chapel Hill: University of North Carolina Press, 1982.

Kay, David A. "The Politics of Decolonization." In *International Organization: Politics and Process*. Ed. Leland Goodrich and David A. Kay. 307–32. Madison: University of Wisconsin Press, 1973.

Kedourie, Elie. *Nationalism in Asia and Africa*. New York: World Publishing Company, 1970.

Kennedy, Paul. "Why Did the British Empire Last So Long?" In *Strategy and Diplomacy, 1870–1945*. 197–218. London: Allen and Unwin, 1983.

———. *The Rise and Fall of the Great Powers: Economic Change and Military Conflict from 1500 to 2000*. New York: Random House, 1987.

Keohane, Robert O. "Realism, Neorealism, and the Study of World Politics." In *Neorealism and Its Critics*. Ed. Robert O. Keohane. 1–26. New York: Columbia University Press, 1986.

Keohane, Robert O. *International Institutions and State Power*. Boulder, Colo.: Westview Press, 1989.

———. "Sovereignty, Interdependence, and International Institutions." In *Ideas and Ideals: Essays on Politics in Honor of Stanley Hoffmann*. Ed. Linda B. Miller and Michael Joseph Smith. Boulder, Colo.: Westview Press, 1993.

Keohane, Robert, and Stanley Hoffmann. "Institutional Change in Europe in the 1980's." In *The New European Community: Decisionmaking and Institutional Change*. Ed. Robert Keohane and Stanley Hoffmann. 1–39. Boulder, Colo.: Westview Press, 1991.

Kepel, Gilles. *The Revenge of God: the Resurgence of Islam, Christianity, and Judaism in the Modern World*. Trans. Alan Braley. University Park: Pennsylvania State University Press, 1994.

King, Gary, Robert O. Keohane, and Sidney Verba. *Designing Social Inquiry*. Princeton: Princeton University Press, 1994.

Kissinger, Henry. *A World Restored*. Boston: Houghton Mifflin, 1957.

———. *Diplomacy*. New York: Simon and Schuster, 1994.

Klein, Robert. *Sovereign Equality Among States: The History of an Idea*. Toronto: University of Toronto Press, 1974.

Klotz, Audie. *Protesting Prejudice: Apartheid and the Politics of Norms in International Relations*. Ithaca: Cornell University Press, 1995.

Knecht, Robert. *Richelieu*. London: Longmans, 1991.

Koenigsberger, H. G. *Estates and Revolutions: Essays in Early Modern European History*. Ithaca: Cornell University Press, 1971.

———. "Organization of Revolutionary Parties in France and the Netherlands During the Sixteenth Century." In H. G. Koenigsberger, *Estates and Revolutions: Essays in Early Modern European History*. 224–53. Ithaca: Cornell University Press, 1971.

Koenigsberger, H. G., and George L. Mosse. *Europe in the Sixteenth Century*. New York: Holt, Rinehart, and Winston, 1968.

Krasner, Stephen, D. "Structural Causes and Regime Consequences: Regimes as Intervening Variables." In *International Regimes.* Ed. Stephen Krasner. 1–22. Ithaca: Cornell University Press, 1983.

———. "Sovereignty: An Institutional Perspective." *Comparative Political Studies* 21 (1988): 66–94.

———. "Westphalia and All That." In *Ideas and Foreign Policy: Beliefs, Institutions, and Political Change.* Ed. Judith Goldstein and Robert O. Keohane. 253–64. Ithaca: Cornell University Press, 1993.

———. "Compromising Westphalia." *International Security* 20, no. 3 (1995/96): 115–51.

———. *Sovereignty: Organized Hypocrisy.* Princeton: Princeton University Press, 1999.

———, ed. *International Regimes.* Ithaca: Cornell University Press, 1983.

Kratochwil, Friedrich. "Of Systems, Boundaries, and Territoriality: An Inquiry into the Formation of the States-System." *World Politics* 39 (1986): 27–52.

———. "Sovereignty as 'Dominium': Is There a Right to Humanitarian Intervention?" In *Beyond Westphalia: National Sovereignty and International Intervention.* Ed. Michael Mastanduno and Gene Lyons. chap. 2. Baltimore: Johns Hopkins University Press, 1995.

Kupchan, Charles. *The Vulnerability of Empire.* Ithaca: Cornell University Press, 1994.

LaCouture, Jean. *Charles de Gaulle.* New York: Norton, 1990–1992.

Langley, J. Ayodele. *Pan-Africanism and Nationalism in West Africa, 1900–1945: A Study in Ideology and Social Class.* Oxford: Clarendon Press, 1972.

Lapping, Brian. *End of Empire.* London: Granada, 1985.

Lauren, Paul Gordon, ed. *Diplomacy: New Approaches in History, Theory, and Policy.* New York: Free Press, 1979.

Lee, C. H. *The British Economy Since 1700: A Macroeconomic Perspective.* Cambridge: Cambridge University Press, 1986.

Lehmann, Hartmut, and Gunther Roth. *Weber's Protestant Ethic: Origins, Evidence, and Context.* Cambridge: Cambridge University Press, 1993.

Leites, Nathan. *On the Game of Politics in France.* Stanford: Stanford University Press, 1959.

Lloyd, P. C. *Power and Independence: Urban Africans' Perception of Social Inequality.* London: Routledge, 1974.

Lonsdale, J. M. "Some Origins of Nationalism in East Africa." *Journal of African History* 9, no. 1 (1968): 119–46.

Louis, William Roger. *Imperialism at Bay: The United States and the Decolonization of the British Empire, 1941–45.* Oxford: Oxford University Press, 1978.

———. "The Era of the Mandates System and the Non-European World." In *The Expansion of International Society.* Ed. Hedley Bull and Adam Watson. 201–13. Oxford: Oxford University Press, 1984.

Louis, William Roger, and R. Owen. *Suez 1956: The Crisis and Its Consequences.* Oxford: Oxford University Press, 1989.

Low, D. A., and J. M. Lonsdale. "Introduction: Towards the New Order, 1945–1963." In *History of East Africa.* Vol. 3, 1–64. Ed. D. A. Low and J. M. Lonsdale. Oxford: Clarendon Press, 1976.

Low, D. A., and A. Smith, eds. *History of East Africa.* 3 vols. Oxford: Clarendon Press, 1976.

Luard, Evan. *War in International Society: A Study in International Sociology.* London: I. B. Tauris, 1986.

Lugard, F. D. *The Dual Mandate in British Tropical Africa.* London: W. Blackwood and Sons, 1922.

Lukes, Stephen. *Power: A Radical View.* London: Macmillan, 1974.

Lumsdaine, David. *Moral Vision in International Politics.* Princeton: Princeton University Press, 1993.

Luther, Martin. *The Freedom of a Christian.* Ed. Harold J. Grimm. Trans. W. A. Lambert. Vol. 31, *Luther's Works.* Philadelphia: Westminster Press, 1957.

———. *Temporal Authority: To What Extent It Should Be Obeyed.* Ed. Walther I. Brandt. Trans. J. J. Schindel. Vol. 45, *Luther's Works.* Philadelphia: Westminster Press, 1967.

———. *Bondage of the Will.* Ed. Philip S. Watson. Trans. Philip S. Watson and Benjamin Drewery. Vol. 33, *Luther's Works.* Philadelphia: Westminster Press, 1972.

Lynch, John. *Spain Under the Habsburgs.* New York: Oxford University Press, 1965.

Macartney, C. A. *National States and National Minorities.* New York: Russell and Russell, 1968.

Macrae, Duncan. *Parliament, Parties, and Society in France, 1946–1958.* New York: St. Martin's Press, 1967.

Maland, David. *Europe in the Seventeenth Century.* London: Macmillan, 1966.

Malettke, Klaus, "France's Imperial Policy during the Thirty Years' War and the Peace of Westphalia." In Klaus Bussmann and Heinz Schilling, eds. *1648—War and Peace in Europe.* 177–87. Münster, Germany: Westfalisches Landesmuseum, 1998.

Mann, Michael. *The Sources of Social Power.* Vol. 1. Cambridge: Cambridge University Press, 1986.

March, James G., and Johan Olsen. "The New Institutionalism: Organizational Factors in Political Life." *American Political Science Review* 78 (1984).

———. *Rediscovering Institutions: The Organizational Basis of Politics.* New York: Free Press, 1989.

———. "The Institutional Dynamics of International Political Orders." *International Organization* 52, no. 4 (1998): 943–69.

Maritain, Jacques. *Man and the State.* Chicago: University of Chicago Press, 1951.

Marshall, D. Bruce. *The French Colonial Myth and Constitution-Making in the Fourth Republic.* New Haven: Yale University Press, 1973.

Marx, Karl. "The German Ideology." In *The Marx-Engels Reader.* Ed. Robert C. Tucker. New York: W. W. Norton and Co., 1972.

Mattingly, Garret. *Renaissance Diplomacy.* Boston: Houghton-Mifflin, 1955.

McElroy, Robert. *Morality and American Foreign Policy.* Princeton: Princeton University Press, 1992.

McGrath, Alister. *The Intellectual Origins of the European Reformation.* Oxford: Basil Blackwell, 1987.

———. *Reformation Thought: An Introduction.* Oxford: Oxford University Press, 1988.

Meinecke, Friedrich. *Machiavellianism: The Doctrine of Raison d'Etat and Its Place in Modern History.* Trans. Douglas Scott. Boulder, Colo.: Westview Press, 1984.

Miller, David. *On Nationality.* Oxford: Clarendon Press, 1995.

Milner, A. *England in Egypt.* London: Arnold, 1920.

Milner, Helen. "The Assumption of Anarchy in International Relations Theory." *Review of International Studies* 17 (1991): 67–85.

Moeller, Bernd. *Imperial Cities and the Reformation.* Trans. H. C. Erik Middlefort and Mark U. Edwards Jr. Philadelphia: Fortress Press, 1972.

Monroe, Kristen Renwick. *The Heart of Altruism: Perceptions of a Common Humanity.* Princeton: Princeton University Press, 1996.

Moore, Barrington. *The Social Origins of Dictatorship and Democracy.* Boston: Beacon Press, 1966.

Moravcsik, Andrew. "Taking Preferences Seriously: A Liberal Theory of International Politics." *International Organization* 51, no. 4 (1997): 513–54.

Morgan, D. J. *The Official History of Colonial Development.* 5 vols. London: Macmillan, 1980.

Morgenthau, Hans. *Politics Among Nations: The Struggle for Power and Peace.* 6th ed. New York: Alfred A. Knopf, 1985.

Mundy, John H. *Europe in the High Middle Ages, 1150–1309.* New York: Basic Books, 1973.

Naff, Thomas. "The Ottoman Empire and the European States System." *In The Expansion of International Society.* Ed. Hedley Bull and Adam Watson. 143–70. Oxford: Oxford University Press, 1984.

Newton, S. "Britain, the Sterling Area and European Integration." In *Money, Finance, and Empire, 1790–1960.* Ed. A. N. Porter and R. F. Holland. London: Frank Cass, 1985.

North, Douglass C., and R. P. Thomas. *The Rise of the Western World.* Cambridge: Cambridge University Press, 1973.

Nye, Joseph S. *Bound to Lead.* New York: Basic Books, 1990.

Oberman, Heiko. *The Harvest of Medieval Theology: Gabriel Biel and Late Medieval Nominalism.* Cambridge: Harvard University Press, 1963.

———. *Masters of the Reformation: The Emergence of a New Intellectual Climate in Europe.* Cambridge: Cambridge University Press, 1981.

———. *Luther: Man Between God and the Devil.* New Haven: Yale University Press, 1989.

O'Brien, Patrick. "The Costs and Benefits of British Imperialism, 1846–1914." *Past and Present* 120 (1988): 163–200.

Odell, John. *U.S. Monetary Policy: Markets, Power, and Ideas as Sources of Change.* Princeton: Princeton University Press, 1982.

Ohmae, Kenichi. *The End of the Nation State.* New York: Harper Collins, 1995.

Oliver, Roland, and Gervase Matthew, eds. *History of East Africa.* Vol. 1. Oxford: Oxford University Press, 1963.

Oppenheim, Lassa. *International Law.* Vol. 1. London: Longmans, Green, 1905.

Osiander, Andreas. *The States System of Europe, 1640–1990.* Oxford: Clarendon Press, 1994.

Ozment, Steven. *The Age of Reform, 1220–1550: An Intellectual and Religious History of Late Medieval and Reformation Europe.* New Haven: Yale University Press, 1980.

———. *Protestants: The Birth of a Revolution.* New York: Doubleday, 1992.

———, ed. *Reformation Europe: A Guide to Research.* St. Louis, Mo.: Center for Reformation Research, 1982.

Pages, George. *The Thirty Years' War.* Trans. David Maland and John Hooper. New York: Harper and Row, 1970.

Parker, Geoffrey. "The 'Military Revolution,' 1550–1660—A Myth?" *Journal of Modern History* 48 (1976): 195–214.

———. *The Dutch Revolt.* Ithaca: Cornell University Press, 1977.

———. *The Military Revolution.* Cambridge: Cambridge University Press, 1988.

———. *Spain and the Netherlands, 1559–1659.* Glasgow: Fontana Press, 1990.

———. *The Thirty Years' War.* London: Routledge and Kegan Paul, 1997.

Parker, Geoffrey, and Lesley Smith, eds. *The General Crisis of the Seventeenth Century.* London: Routledge and Kegan Paul, 1985.

Parry, Clive, ed. *The Consolidated Treaty Series.* Dobbs Ferry, N.Y.: Oceana Publications, 1981.

Parsons, Talcott, ed. *Max Weber: The Theory of Social and Economic Organization.* New York: Free Press, 1947.

Pearson, Raymond. *National Minorities in Eastern Europe, 1848–1945.* London: Macmillan, 1983.

Pease, Kelly Kate, and David Forsythe. "Human Rights, Humanitarian Intervention, and World Politics." *Human Rights Quarterly* 15 (1993): 290–314.

Pettegree, Andrew. *The Early Reformation in Europe.* New York: Cambridge University Press, 1991.

Pickles, Dorothy. *Algeria and France: From Colonialism to Cooperation.* New York: Frederick A. Praeger, 1963.

Pirenne, Henry. *Early Democracies in the Low Countries: Urban Society and Political Conflict in the Middle Ages and Renaissance.* New York: Harper and Row, 1963.

Poggi, Gianfranco. *The Development of the Modern State: A Sociological Introduction.* Stanford: Stanford University Press, 1978.

———. *Calvinism and the Capitalist Spirit.* London: Macmillan, 1983.

Polisensky, J. V. *The Thirty Years' War.* Trans. Robert Evans. Berkeley: University of California Press, 1971.

Pollard, Sidney. *The Development of the British Economy: 1914–1980.* 3d ed. London: Edward Arnold, 1983.

Porter, A. N., and A. J. Stockwell. *British Imperial Policy and Decolonization, 1938–1964.* 2 vols. Vol. 2, *1951–1964.* London: Macmillan, 1987.

Porter, Bernard. *The Lion's Share: A Short History of British Imperialism, 1850–1970.* London: Longmans, 1996.

Porter, Bruce. *War and the Rise of the State.* New York: Free Press, 1994.

Price, Richard. "Reversing the Gun Sights: Transnational Civil Society Targets Land Mines." *International Organization* 52 (1998): 613–44.

Price, Richard, and Nina Tannenwald. "Norms and Deterrence: The Nuclear and Chemical Weapons Taboo." In *The Culture of National Security.* Ed. Peter J. Katzenstein. 114–52. New York: Columbia University Press, 1996.

Quandt, William. *Revolution and Political Leadership: Algeria, 1954–1958.* Cambridge: MIT Press, 1969.

Rabb, T. K., ed. *The Thirty Years' War: Problems of Motive, Extent, and Effect.* Boston: D. C. Heath, 1964.

Ramsbotham, Oliver, and Tom Woodhouse. *Humanitarian Intervention in International Conflict.* Cambridge: Cambridge University Press, 1996.

Ranger, T. O. "Connexions between 'Primary Resistance' Movements and Modern Mass Nationalism in East and Central Africa: Parts I and II." *Journal of African History* 9 (1968): 437–53, 631–41.

Ray, James Lee. "The Abolition of Slavery and the End of International War." *International Organization* 43 (1989): 405–39.

Repgen, Konrad, "Negotiating the Peace of Westphalia: A Survey with an Examination of Major Problems." In Klaus Bussmann and Heinz Schilling, eds., *1648—War and Peace in Europe.* 355–72. Münster, Germany: Westfalisches Landesmuseum, 1998.

Reus-Smit, Christian. "The Constitutional Structure of International Society." *International Organization* 51 (1997): 568–70.

Reynolds, Susan. *Kingdoms and Communities in Western Europe, 900–1300.* Oxford: Clarendon Press, 1984.

Richelieu, Armand-Jean du Plessis, duc de. *The Political Testament of Cardinal Richelieu: The Significant Chapters and Supporting Selections.* Trans. Henry Bertram Hill. Madison: University of Wisconsin Press, 1981.

Risse-Kappen, Thomas. "Ideas Do Not Float Freely: Transnational Coalitions, Domestic Structures, and the End of the Cold War." *International Organization* 48 (1994): 185–214..

Roberts, Michael. *Gustavus Adolphus.* 2 vols. London: Longmans, Green, 1958.

———. *Essays in Swedish History.* London: Weidenfeld and Nicolson, 1967.

———. *The Early Vasas: A History of Sweden, 1523–1611.* Cambridge: Cambridge University Press, 1968.

———. *Gustavus Adolphus and the Rise of Sweden.* London: English Universities Press, 1973.

———. *The Swedish Imperial Experience, 1560–1718.* Cambridge: Cambridge University Press, 1979.

Robinson, Ronald. "The Moral Disarmament of African Empire, 1919–1947." *Journal of Imperial and Commonwealth History* 7, no. 1 (1979): 86–104.

Rosberg, C., and J. Nottingham. *The Myth of "Mau Mau": Nationalism in Kenya.* Stanford: Stanford University Press, 1966.

Ruggie, John Gerard. "Continuity and Transformation in the World Polity: Toward a Neorealist Synthesis." In *Neorealism and Its Critics.* Ed. Robert O. Keohane. 131–57. New York: Columbia University Press, 1986.

———. "Territoriality and Beyond: Problematizing Modernity in International Relations." *International Organization* 47, no. 1 (1993): 139–74.

Ruggie, John Gerard. "What Makes the World Hang Together? Neo-Utilitarianism and the Social Constructivist Challenge." *International Organization* 52, 4 (1998): 855–85.

Scheffer, David. "Toward a Modern Doctrine of Humanitarian Intervention." *University of Toledo Law Review* 23 (1992): 253–94.

Schilling, Heinz. "War and Peace at the Emergence of Modernity: Europe Between State Belligerence, Religious Wars, and the Desire for Peace." In Klaus Bussmann and Heinz Schilling, eds., *1648—War and Peace in Europe.* 13–22. Münster, Germany: Westfalisches Landesmuseum, 1998.

Scribner, Bob, Roy Porter, and Mikulcs Teich, eds. *The Reformation in National Context.* Cambridge: Cambridge University Press, 1994.

Scribner, R. W. *Popular Culture and Popular Movements in Reformation Germany.* London: Hambledon Press, 1987.

Seal, Anil. "Imperialism and Nationalism in India." In *Locality, Province, and Nations.* Ed. John Gallagher, Gordon Johnson, and Anil Seal. Cambridge: Cambridge University Press, 1973.

Shah, Timothy B. "Making the World Safe for Liberalism: The Taming of Religion from Hugo Grotius to John Rawls." Paper presented at the Annual Meeting of the American Political Science Association, Washington, D.C., 1997.

Shakespeare, William. *King Henry V.* Ed. Andrew Gurr. Cambridge: Cambridge University Press, 1992.

———. *Richard II.* Ed. Michael Clamp. Cambridge: Cambridge University Press, 1992.

Shaw, Martin. "There Is No Such Thing as Society: Beyond Individualism and Statism in International Security Studies." *Review of International Studies* 19 (1993): 159–75.

Shepsle, Kenneth. "Comment." In *Regulatory Policy and the Social Sciences.* Ed. Roger Noll. Berkeley: University of California Press, 1985.

Shils, Edward. "The Intellectuals in the Political Development of New States." *World Politics* (April 1960): 329–68.

Sikkink, Kathryn, and Margaret Keck. *Activists Beyond Borders: Advocacy Networks in International Politics.* Ithaca: Cornell University Press, 1998.

Sisson, Richard, and Stanley Wolpert, eds. *Congress and Indian Nationalism.* Berkeley: University of California Press, 1988.

Skinner, Quentin. *The Foundations of Modern Political Thought.* 2 vols. Vol. 2, The Age of the Reformation. Cambridge: Cambridge University Press, 1978.

Skocpol, Theda. *States and Social Revolutions: A Comparative Analysis of France, Russia, and China.* Cambridge: Cambridge University Press, 1979.

Smit, J. W. "The Present Position of Studies Regarding the Revolt of the Netherlands." In *Britain and the Netherlands.* Ed. J. S. Bromley and E. H. Kossman. Groningen: Wolters, 1960.

Smith, George L. *Religion and Trade in the New Netherlands: Dutch Origins and American Development.* Ithaca: Cornell University Press, 1973.

Smith, Michael Joseph. *Realist Thought from Weber to Kissinger.* Baton Rouge: Louisiana State University Press, 1986.

Smith, Tony. "A Comparative Study of French and British Decolonization." *Comparative Studies in Society and History* 20, no. 1 (1978): 70–102.

———. *The French Stake in Algeria, 1945–62*. Ithaca: Cornell University Press, 1978.

———. *America's Mission: The United States and the Worldwide Struggle for Democracy in the Twentieth Century*. Princeton: Princeton University Press, 1994.

Snyder, Jack. *The Ideology of the Offensive*. Ithaca: Cornell University Press, 1984.

Sorum, Paul. *Intellectuals and Decolonization in France*. Durham: University of North Carolina Press, 1977.

Spruyt, Hendrik. *The Sovereign State and Its Competitors*. Princeton: Princeton University Press, 1994.

Steiger, Heinhard. "Concrete Peace and General Order: The Legal Meaning of the Treaties of 24 October 1648." In *1648—War and Peace in Europe*. 437–46. Ed. Klaus Bussmann and Heinz Schilling. Münster, Germany: Westfalisches Landesmuseum, 1998.

Steinberg, S. H. "The Thirty Years' War and the Conflict for European Hegemony." In *The Thirty Years' War: Problems of Motive, Extent, and Effect*. Ed. T. K. Rabb. Boston: D. C. Heath, 1964.

Strachey, J. *The End of Empire*. London: Gollancz, 1959.

Strang, David. "From Dependency to Sovereignty: An Event History Analysis of Decolonization," 1870–1987." *American Sociological Review* 55, no. 6 (1990): 846–60.

———. "Global Patterns of Decolonization, 1500–1987." *International Studies Quarterly* 35 (1991): 429–54.

———. "The Inner Incompatibility of Empire and Nation: Popular Sovereignty and Decolonization." *Sociological Perspectives* 35, no. 2 (1992): 367–85.

Strange, Susan. *Sterling and British Policy*. Oxford: Oxford University Press, 1971.

Strauss, Gerald. *Law, Resistance, and the State: The Opposition to Roman Law in Reformation Germany*. Princeton: Princeton University Press, 1986.

Strayer, Joseph R. *The Medieval Origins of the Modern State*. Princeton: Princeton University Press, 1970.

Strayer, Joseph R., and Dana Munro. *The Middle Ages 395–1500*. 4th ed. New York: Appleton-Century-Crofts, 1959.

Swidler, Ann. "Culture in Action: Symbols and Strategies." *American Sociological Review* 51 (1986): 273–86

Tapíe, Victor-L. *France in the Age of Louis XIII and Richelieu*. Trans. D. McN. Lockie. Cambridge: Cambridge University Press, 1984.

Tawney, R. H. *Religion and the Rise of Capitalism*. London: John Murray, 1936.

Taylor, Michael. "Structure, Culture, and Action in the Explanation of Social Change." *Politics and Society* 17, no. 2 (1989): 115–62.

Taylor, Paul. "The United Nations in the 1990s: Proactive Cosmopolitanism and the Issue of Sovereignty." *Political Studies* 47 (special issue, 1999): 538–65.

Tetlock, Philip E., and Aaron Belkin. "Counterfactual Thought Experiments in World Politics: Logical, Methodological, and Psychological Perspectives." In *Counterfactual Thought Experiments in World Politics*. Ed. Philip E. Tetlock and Aaron Belkin. Princeton: Princeton University Press, 1996.

Tetlock, Philip E., and Aaron Belkin, eds. *Counterfactual Thought Experiments in World Politics*. Princeton: Princeton University Press, 1996.

Tharoor, Shashi. "United Nations Peacekeeping in Europe." *Survival* 37, no. 2:121–34.

Thomas, Ann Van Wynen, and A. J. Thomas Jr. *Non-Intervention: The Law and Its Import in the Americas.* Dallas: Southern Methodist University Press, 1956.

Thompson, E. P. *The Making of the English Working Class.* New York: Pantheon Books, 1964.

Thompson, James Westfall. *The Wars of Religion in France, 1559–1576.* New York: Frederick Ungar Publishing Company, 1909.

Thomson, Janice E. "Norms in International Relations: A Conceptual Analysis." *International Journal of Group Tensions* 23, no. 1 (1993): 67–83.

Thomson, Janice E. "State Sovereignty in International Relations: Bridging the Gap between Theory and Empirical Research." *International Studies Quarterly* 39, no. 2 (1995): 213–33.

Thorne, Christopher. *Allies of a Kind: The United States, Britain, and the War Against Japan, 1941–45.* New York: Oxford University Press, 1978.

Thornton, A. P. *The Imperial Idea and Its Enemies: A Study in British Power.* London: Macmillan, 1959.

Tierney, Brian. *Crisis of Church and State.* Englewood Cliffs, N.J.: Prentice-Hall, 1964.

Tilly, Charles. *Coercion, Capital, and European States AD 990–1992.* Oxford: Basil Blackwell, 1992.

Tinker, Hugh. *Race, Conflict, and the International Order.* London: Macmillan, 1977.

Todd, John M. *Reformation.* New York: Doubleday, 1971.

Trevor-Roper, H. R. *Religion, the Reformation, and Social Change.* New York: Harper and Row, 1956.

Ullman, Walter. *Principles of Government and Politics in the Middle Ages.* New York: Barnes and Noble, 1966.

Vasquez, John. *The Power of Power Politics: A Critique.* New Brunswick: Rutgers University Press, 1983.

Vattel, Emeric de. *The Law of Nations.* Philadelphia: T. & J. W. Johnson, 1844.

Vernon, Raymond. *Sovereignty at Bay.* New York: Basic Books, 1971.

Vincent, R. J. *Non-Intervention and International Order.* Princeton: Princeton University Press, 1974.

Walker, R.B.J. *Inside/Outside: International Relations as Political Theory.* Cambridge: Cambridge University Press, 1993.

Wallerstein, Immanuel. *The Modern World System: Capitalist Agriculture and the Origins of the European World-Economy in the Sixteenth Century.* New York: Academic Press, 1974.

———. "Three Stages of African Involvement in the World Economy." In *The Political Economy of Contemporary Africa.* Ed. Peter C. W. Gutkind and Immanuel Wallerstein. 30–57. Beverly Hills, Calif.: Sage Publications, 1976.

Walt, Stephen. *The Origins of Alliances.* Ithaca: Cornell University Press, 1987.

Waltz, Kenneth. *Theory of International Politics.* Lexington, Mass.: Addison-Wesley, 1979.

Wasserman, G. *The Politics of Decolonization.* Cambridge: Cambridge University Press, 1976.

Watson, Adam. "European International Society and Its Expansion." In *The Expansion of International Society.* Ed. Hedley Bull and Adam Watson. 117–26. Oxford: Oxford University Press, 1984.

———. *The Evolution of International Society: A Comparative Historical Analysis.* London: Routledge, 1992.

Weber, Max. "The Social Psychology of the World Religions." In *From Max Weber: Essays in Sociology.* Ed., trans., and intro. H. H. Gerth and C. Wright Mills. 267–301. New York: Oxford University Press, 1946.

———. *The Protestant Ethic and the Spirit of Capitalism.* New York: Charles Scribner's Sons, 1958.

Webster, J. B. "African Political Activity in French West Africa." In *History of West Africa.* Ed. J.F.A. Ajayi. 635–64. London: Longmans, 1987.

Wedgwood, C. V. *The Thirty Years' War.* London: J. Cape, 1938.

Wendt, Alexander. "The Agent-Structure Problem in International Relations Theory." *International Organization* 41, no. 3 (1987): 335–70.

———. "Anarchy Is What States Make of It: The Social Construction of Power Politics." *International Organization* 46 (1992): 395–421.

———. "Collective Identity Formation and the International State." *American Political Science Review* 88, no. 2, (June 1994): 384–96.

Wight, Martin. *Systems of States.* Leicester, U.K.: Leicester University Press, 1977.

———. *Power Politics.* Harmondsworth, U.K.: Penguin, 1979.

Wilks, Michael. *The Problem of Sovereignty in the Middle Ages.* Cambridge: Cambridge University Press, 1964.

Wilson, Heather. *International Law and the Use of Force by National Liberation Movements.* Oxford: Oxford University Press, 1988.

Wilson, H. S. *West African Nationalism.* London: Macmillan, 1969.

Wines, Roger. "The Imperial Circles, Princely Diplomacy, and Imperial Reform, 1681–1714." *Journal of Modern History* 39, no. 1 (1967): 1–29.

Wohlforth, William. *The Elusive Balance: Power and Perceptions During the Cold War.* Ithaca: Cornell University Press, 1993.

Wolfe, Martin. *The Fiscal System of Renaissance France.* New Haven: Yale University Press, 1972.

Wolff, R. P. "The Conflict Between Authority and Autonomy." In *Authority.* Ed. Joseph Raz. Oxford: Basil Blackwell, 1990.

Wolpert, Stanley. *A New History of India.* 4th ed. Oxford: Oxford University Press, 1993.

Wriston, Walter. *The Twilight of Sovereignty.* New York: Scribner's, 1992.

Wuthnow, Robert. *Communities of Discourse.* Cambridge: Harvard University Press, 1989.

Wyduckel, Dieter, "The Imperial Constitution and the Imperial Doctrine of Public Law: Facing the Institutional challenge of the Peace of Westphalia." In *1648—War and Peace in Europe.* Ed. Klaus Bussmann and Heinz Schilling. 77–84. Münster, Germany: Westfalisches Landesmuseum, 1998.

Yee, Albert S. "The Causal Effects of Ideas on Policies." *International Organization* 50, no. 1 (1996): 69–108.

Young, Crawford. *The African Colonial State in Comparative Perspective.* New Haven: Yale University Press, 1994.

Zakaria, Fareed. *From Wealth to Power: The Unusual Origins of America's World Role.* Princeton: Princeton University Press, 1998.

Zolberg, Aristide. "Strategic Interactions and the Formation of Modern States: France and England." *International Social Science Journal* 32 (1980): 687–716.

———. "Origins of the Modern World System: A Missing Link." *World Politics* 23 (1981): 253–81.

INDEX

aberrations in constitution of international society. *See* constitution of international society, compromises of
Abjuration, Edict of (1581), 115, 140
absolutism, 139, 144
Action du Peuple, 237
Adolphus, Gustavus, 86, 119, 134, 135
Africa, 36, 175
Africa: The Next Ten Years report, 183, 184
African Governor's Conference, 176
Alba, Duke of, 129
Algeria, 220, 226, 241; conflict with France, 234; and Islam, 235, 237; public opinion poll solution for, 231; settler population of, 246–48; Statute of, 224, 226, 229
Algerian Association of Ulma, 236
Althusius, Johannes, 84
Amboise, Edict of (1563), 131
Anabaptists, 107, 281n.23
anarchy: and external and internal sovereignty, 18; Hobbes' views on, 60–61; and Realism, 64, 275n.36
Andrew, Christopher, 223
anti-colonial ideas, 101; in Algeria, 235–39; in British East and Central Africa, 196, 199–200; in British West Africa, 195–96, 198–99; domestic context of in British case, 186–89; colonial context of in British case, 190–202; colonial context of in French case, 234–42; in French West and Equatorial Africa, 239–41; in India, 196–97, 200; in Indochina, 238–39; international context of in British case, 179–86; international context of in French case, 232–34; in Madagascar, 238; in Tunisia and Morocco, 237–38
anti-colonial nationalism, 161
Aragon, Ferdinand of, 142
Aron, Raymond, 222
asabiyya, 235
Asia, 36, 175
assimilationist ideal. *See* France, imperial ideal of
Atlantic Alliance, 233
Atlantic Charter, 157, 174, 194, 254; Roosevelt's interpretation of, 180
Attlee, Clement, 175
Augsburg, Peace of (1555), 81, 113
Augsburg, Treaty of (1555), 26, 114, 281n.23
Australia, 171
Austria, 127
Autonomy, 254

Baghdad Pact, 184
Banda, Hastings, 193, 199
Barbarossa, Frederick, 79
Bavaria, 127
Bella, Ben, 237
Berger, Peter, 54
Berlin Conference (1885), 157
Bermuda Conference (1957), 184
Bevin, Ernest, 177
Blum, Leon, 225, 229, 236
Blum-Viollette proposal, 236
Bodin, Jean, 16, 17, 19, 84, 117, 130
Bonaparte, Napoleon, 236
bons français. See *Politique*
Bourdillon, H.T., 175–76
Bourguiba, Habib, 237
British Cabinet: effects of international and domestic criticism on, 58, 190, 200, 203, 208, 218, 257; influence of domestic context on, 186–89; influence of international context on, 182–86
British Conservative Party, 245, 249
British East Africa, 199
British Guiana, 187
Brockway, Fenner, 186, 187
Bull, Hedley, 13
Burma, 171, 175
Butler, Richard, 205

Caine, Sydney, 176
Calvin, John, 104
Calvinism: in France, 115–118; in the Netherlands, 114, 115, 127–129; and the Treaty of Augsburg, 281n.23. *See also* Huguenots
Cameron, Euan, 107
Carr, E.H., 61–62

Castille, Isabella of, 142
Cateau-Cambrésis, Peace of (1559), 116, 143
Catholic Church: as a critic of the sovereign state, 261–62; powers of in early modern Europe, 105–6
Catholic states: growth of state institutions in, 142; influence on Christian Democratic Parties, 261. *See also* Habsburgs
causal pathways of the Reformation's influence, 125–27
Central Africa: British control in, 169, 178; nationalists struggle in, 199; settler's influence in, 217
Central African Federation, 178, 187, 190
Central America, 169
Ceylon, 171, 175
Chamberlain, Joseph, 173
Charles V, Holy Roman Emperor, 80–81, 98, 108, 112, 116
Charles XI, King of Sweden, 141
Charles XII, King of Sweden, 141
Checkel, Jeffrey, 51
Chilembwe, John, 193
China, 33
churches, as circumstances of reflection, 193–94
Churchill, Winston, 168, 174, 175, 194
circumstances of reflection, 54, 69, 258; in colonial context, 192–97; definition of, 53; in French colonial context, 235–42; in Reformation, 144–46
Clash of Civilizations, The, 8
Cold War: influence upon British colonial policy, 180–81; influence upon French colonial policy, 232–34
Colonial Development and Welfare Act, 168, 206
Colonial Fabian Bureau, 175, 186
colonial independence, 15, 20, 154–58; argument for in British case, 168–71; argument for cause of, 158–61; argument for in French case, 220–21; geographic extent of, 36; intrinsic significance of, 36; in practice, 155; legitimacy of, 155–57; self-determination and, 156–57; pattern of, 165
colonial nationalse //ism, 70, 161, 258
colonial rule: character of, 34; historical growth of, 34
Columbo Plan, 206
Comité Central de la France d'Outre Mer, 245
Committee of Seventeen, 185, 220
Communist Party, 228, 229, 231, 238, 239
compromises of sovereignty, forms of, 255
Concert of Europe, 43, 255
Congo, 224
Congress of Berlin (1878), 38
Congress of Black Africans, 229
Congress of Vienna (1815), 95
Congress of Vienna Final Act (1815), 37
Constituent National Assembly, 225
Conservative Party, and its stance toward British empire, 187–89
constitution of international society, 11–27; compromises of, 25; in contested form, 26; defined, 12; as distinguished from mere power, 24–25; as distinguished from other agreements, 25; enforcement of norms in, 22; foundational nature of, 12–13; history of, 29–43; interest of polities in, 47–48; and legitimacy, 22; as more than habitual behavior, 22; as more than mere ideas, 23; and practice, 23; principles for distinguishing, 13–14; as set of norms, 21–22
constructivism, 47, 50–51
Contarini, Alvise, 82
Convention People's Party (CPP), 198
conversion of colonial nationalists. *See* first role of ideas
Counter Reformation, 108, 113, 128
counterfactual logic, 70–72; applied to colonial independence, 159–60; applied to Westphalia, 98–102
couriers of ideas, 67–70, 258; and colonial independence, 101; in Reformation, 124
Cuba, 182
Cuius regio, euis religio, 81, 113, 115
customary law, 23

dévots, 133
d'Argenlieu, Admiral, 239
Dai, Bao, 226, 239, 306n.59
Danquah, J.B., 198
Davidson, Basil, 194, 237
Declaration of the granting of independence to colonial countries and peoples, 155
Declaration on Principles of International Law Concerning Friendly Relations and Cooperation Among States (1970), 292n.11

Declaration on the Granting of Independence to Colonial Peoples and the principles of international law (1970), 292n.11
Defence White Paper (1957), 205, 206
Denmark, 111, 120, 126
Deschamps, Hubert, 241
Destour. *See* Liberal Constitutional Party
Devlin Commission, 188
Devlin Report, 191
Downing, Brian, 66
Dual Mandate in British Tropical Africa, The, 174
DuBois, W.E.B., 193, 195
Duby, Georges, 79
Duchardt, Heinz, 84, 263n.2
Dulles, John Foster, 183, 253
Durkheim, Emile, 7, 55, 59, 68, 263n.4
Duroselle, Jean-Baptiste, 231

East Africa, 213, 217
East Indies, 33
eclipsing circumstances: in British colonial context, 212–19; definition of, 55; in French colonial context, 242–49; in Reformation, 146–47
Eden, Anthony, 175
education, as circumstance of reflection in British colonial context, 193
Egypt, 179, 182
epistemic community, 277n.57
Equality, 191. *See also* racial equality
Erastianism, 107
established ideas, 162, 166. *See also* France, imperial ideal of; Great Britain, imperial ideal of
Etoile Nord-Africaine Party, 235, 236
European Coal and Steel Community, 29, 39
European Community's Arbitration Commission, 268n.17
European Convention on Human Rights, 43
European Court of Justice, 40
European Defense Community, 233
European Economic Community, 207
European Union, 39; norms for sovereignty in, 17, 19, 33, 90, 92; and the United Nations Charter, 42
European Unity: geographic extent of, 40; intrinsic significance of, 40; as a revision of first face of authority, 29; as a revision of second face of authority, 40; as a revision of third face of authority, 40; as a revolution in sovereignty, 39–40
exceptions to constitution of international society. See constitution of international society, compromises of

Fanon, Frantz, 161
Faure, Edgar, 226, 227, 228, 249
Ferdinand II, Holy Roman Emperor, 119, 147
Ferdinand, Archduke, 112
Fieldhouse, David, 244
Finnemore, Martha, 277n.64
first face of authority, 15–19; defined at Westphalia, 30–32; in Peace of Westphalia, 90–92; as revised by European unity, 39; as revised by internationally sanctioned intervention, 41; as revised by minority treaties, 38 first role of ideas, 49, 51–55, 257–58; three versions of, 68; in Algeria, 235–37 ;in British East and Central Africa, 196–99; in British West Africa, 195–96; in colonial context, 191–97; in France, 129; in French West and Equatorial Africa, 239–40; in Germany, 125, 127; in India, 196; in Indochina, 238–39; in Madagascar, 238; in Netherlands, 127–29; in Reformation, 123–24; in Sweden, 134–35; in Tunisia and Morocco, 237–38; timing of in colonies, 195–97
focal points: applied to colonial independence, 200–1; applied to Reformation, 136; ideas as, 66–67, 200–1, 259
Fourth Republic (1958), 222; constitution of the (1947), 225, 239
France: colonial consensus in, 228–32; growth of state in, 140–41; imperial ideal of, 222–227; imperial reforms in, 226–27; influence of Reformation ideas in, 127, 129–34; intellectuals of, 231; and interest in sovereign statehood, 115–18; religious wars in, 116–18; Colonial Party of, 223; summarized polity of, 111;
Francis I, king of France, 116, 134
Free French Resistance, 224
French Black Africa, 254
French Catholic League, 132
French Constituent Assembly, 224
French National Assembly, 222
Front of National Liberation (FLN), 230

Gagliardo, John, 87, 113
Gallagher, John, 173
Gandhi, Mahatma, 192, 196, 200, 253
Garrett, Geoffrey, 67, 68
Garvey, Marcus, 193, 195
Gaulle, Charles de, 221; and colonial consensus, 228, 230, 232; and his cooperation with African Political leaders 239, 307n.64; and imperial reforms, 226–227; and the international context 233; and justifications for colonianism, 223–225
General Assembly Declaration on the Rights of Persons Belonging to National or Ethnic, Religious, and Linguistic Minorities (1992), 268n.17
General Assembly Resolution (1514), 155
Gerhardt, Paul, 89
Gerhardt, Volker, 82, 84
German Ideology, The, 55
Germany: Catholic States in, 111; growth of state institutions in, 139–40; influence of Reformation ideas in, 125–27; and interest in sovereign statehood, 112–14; invasion of, 135; Princes in, 31, 86; Protestant States in, 111;
Ghana. *See* Gold Coast
Ghent, Pacification of (1576), 115, 128
Gilpin, Robert, 62
Gold Coast, 171, 176, 178, 196, 198, 213
Goldstein, Judith, 69
Goldsworthy, David, 189
gradual self-government. *See* Great Britain, imperial ideal of
Great Britain: abandonment of imperial idea, 177–79; Colonial Office in, 168, 169, 173, 176, 177, 182, 186; development of colonial policies in, 205–7; development of imperial ideal in, 173–75; economic decline of, 204–5; historical waves of colonial independence in, 171; imperial ideal of, 172–79; international and domestic criticism of, 190; shift to colonial development policy, 175–77, 179; strategic value of colonies in, 207
Greater France. *See* France, imperial ideal of
Gregory VII, Pope, 79
Gross, Leo, 76
Grosser, Alfred, 233
Grotius, Hugo, 135, 148, 261

Habsburgs, 87; decline of, 259; and France, 116–118, 131, 133; and Germany, 135; and Hungary, 111, 120
Habsburg-Valois Wars (1521–1559), 116, 131
Haiti, 21
Hajd, Messali, 235
Hall, Rodney Bruce, 51, 283n.67
Henry II, king of England, 75, 116
Henry IV, king of England, 79, 116, 117, 130
Henry V, king of England, 75
Henry VIII, king of England, 75, 120
heresies, prior to the Reformation, 108–10
Hitler, Adolf, 255
Hobbes, Thomas, 16, 17, 19, 61
Hobson, J.A., 186
Holland, 128
Holsti, Kalevi, 89
Holy Roman Empire: absence of, 91; and the Catholic Church, 106; and France, 115, 117; and Germany, 85; and the Netherlands, 114; and the Peace of Westphalia, 30–31, 33; sovereignty in, 79
Home, Earl of, 183, 220, 221
Hopkins, A.G., 217
Houphouët-Boigny, Felix, 240, 306n.58
Huguenots, 115, 131, 132. *See also* Calvinism, in France
Hungary, 111, 120, 142
Huntington, Samuel, 8
Hus, Jan, 109, 145
Hyam, Ronald, 206

ideas as cause of constitutional independence, 164–66
ideas as focal points. *See* focal points
ideas as forms of social power. *See* second role of ideas
ideas as resolvers of uncertainty. *See* resolvers of
uncertainty
ideas as shapers of identity. *See* first role of ideas
identity formation of colonial nationalists. *See* first role of ideas
identity formation of Protestants. *See* first role of ideas
Imperial Diet, 113; definition of 81
Independent Labour Party, 186
India, 171, 175, 179, 182, 205
India Act, Government of (1935), 174
Indirect Rule, 174
Indochina, 220, 224, 225, 229, 231, 233, 238, 241, 247, 306n.59
Innocent X, Pope, 87, 261

institutionalization, 69, 173; of Britain's imperial ideal, 169
intermediate dynamic of first role of ideas. *See* resolvers of uncertainty
intermediate dynamic of second role of ideas. *See* focal points
international society, 13–15; characteristics of behavior, 24; definition of, 13; expanse of, 14; principle of separation within, 14
intervention: internationally sanctioned, 40–43; intrinsic significance of, 41–42; legitimacy of, 19; limits of, 42–43; as a revision of first face of authority, 41; as a revision of third face of authority, 41
Iraq, 42
Ireland, 171
Islam, international society in, 15; rules of membership in, 20
Israel, Jonathan, 128, 140
Italy, 111, 121

James, Alan, 18
Japan, 225
jihad, 20
Jones, Arthur Creech, 168, 177, 186

Kahler, Miles, 229, 243, 248
Kanya-Forstner, A.S., 223
Kaunda, Kenneth, 190
Kennan, George, 62
Kenya, 169, politics in, 190, 196, 207; rebellion in, 178, 187, 188, 199; settler population in, 248
Kenya African Union, 199
Kenyatta, Jomo, 192, 199
Kepel, Gilles, 9
Kikuyu Central Association, 199
Kissinger, Henry, 62
Korean War, 205
Krasner, Stephen, 93

L'Hôpital, Michel, 130
La Mise en valeur des Colonies (*The Development of the Colonies)*, 223
Labour Cabinet, 168, 183, 205
Labour Party, and criticism of British empire, 186–87, 211, 232
Latin America, 34, 36, 179
Law of Nations, The, 76
Law of War and Peace (1625), The, 148
League of Nations, 31, 92, 223, 260
League of Nations Covenant, 38, 94, 254
Lejeune, Max, 229
Liberal Constitutional Party, 237
liberalism, as a source of movement away from sovereign states system, 209, 260–61
liberation: role of in historical evolution of sovereignty, 253–62; and slavery, 195
Liberia, 195
Ligue pour la Défense de la Race Nègre, 240
Loi Cadre reforms, 226–227, 240
Louis XIII, king of France, 117
Louis XIV, king of France, 82, 139
Louis, William Roger, 180
Luckmann, Thomas, 54
Lugard, Lord, 174, 223, 241
Luther, Martin: political theology of, 104, 106–8, 123; and role in German Reformation, 112–13; "Two Kingdoms Doctrine" of, 106–7
Lyttleton, Oliver, 168

Maastricht Treaty (1991), 39
Macleod, Iain, 177, 178, 187, 188, 189, 245. *See also* Macmillan, Harold
Macmillan, Harold, 175, concern about Soviet influence, 184; and economic concerns, 206; efforts for colonial independence, 177, 178, 187, 188, 189; revolutionary ideas and, 191. *See also* Macleod, Iain
Madagascar, 220, 224, 229
Maghreb colonies, 235, 241
Malaya, 169, 187
Malayan Federation, 178
Malta, 169
Mandate system, 157
Mandela, Nelson, 192
Manifesto of the Algerian People (1943), 236
Marshall Plan, 233
Marshall, D. Bruce, 233
Marx, Karl, 7, 48, 51, 55, 59, 68
Mau Mau Rebellion, 178, 199, 215
Medici, Catherine de, 115, 116, 131
Meinecke, Friedrich, 118
Melanchthon, Philip, 106, 112
Mendès-France, Pierre, 227, 228, 231, 249
Middle Ages, 31, 77–80
millenarianism, 193, 196
Minh, Ho Chi, 225, 238, 253, 306n.59
minority treaties: geographic and temporal extent of, 38; historical examples of, 37, intrinsic significance of, 38–39; in

minority treaties (*cont.*)
League of Nations, 38; and major constitutional revolutions, 31; as revision of three faces of authority, 38; as a revolution in sovereignty, 37–39
Mitterand, François, 240
Moch, Jules, 226
Mohacs, Battle of, 120
Mohamed V, sultan, 238
Mollet, Guy, 229, 230
Monckton Commission, 188, 191
Monday Club, 187
Montevideo Convention (1993), 93
Moore, Barrington, 66
Morgenthau, Hans, 62, 63, 76, 274n.31, 276n.51
Morocco, 220, 231, 235, 246, 248
Morrison, H.S., 177
Mouvement Démocratique pour le Renouveau Malgache (MRDM), 238
Mouvement pour le Triomphe des Libertés Démocratiques (MTLD), 236
movement away from a system of sovereign states, 36–43, 260–62
movement toward a system of sovereign states, 30–36, 253–60

négritude, 193
Néo-Destour, 237
Naegelen, Marcel-Edmond, 226, 229
Nantes, Edict of, 116, 130, 132
Napoleonic Wars, 37
Nasser, Abdul, 183
National Assembly, 226, 230
National Collective Identity, 51
nationalism, conversion to, 192, 214–15, 217
NATO (North Atlantic Treaty Organization), 42, 205
natural law, 154, 262
Navarre, Henry of, 116, 132, 133
Netherlands: growth of state in, 140; influence of Reformation idea in, 126, 127–29; interest in sovereign statehood, 114–15; recognition of independence, 31 summarized polity of, 111
New Zealand, 128, 171
Nigeria: independence of, 171, 176, 178; nationalist protests in, 198, 199, 213
Nkrumah, Kwame, 196, 198, 253
non-intervention, 32, 40, 95
norms (rules) of appropriateness, 69, 162, 173
Nyasaland, 187, 188, 248
Nyasaland African Congress, 190
Nyerere, Julius, 199

Orange, William of, 114–15, 128
Organisation Sp-ciale (OS), 236
Osiander, Andreas, 85, 91
Ottoman Empire, 33
Overseas Development Cooperation, 206
Oxtenstierna, Count Axel Gustafsson, 86

Pact sunt servanda, 21, 33, 95
Pakistan, 171
Pan-Africanism, 193, 195
Papacy, 33, 77
Paris, Treaty of (1865), 38
Parti Démocratique de la Côte d'Ivoire (PDCI), 240
Parti des Désinhérités de Madagascar, 238
Parti du Peuple Algerien (PPA), 236
Paul, Saint, 107
Petits blancs, 229
Philip II, king of Spain, 81, 114, 129
Philippines, 182
Phu, Dien Bien, 226, 239
Pleven, Ren-, 224
Pluralism, crisis of, 256
Poland, 111, 142
Politique, 101, 118; the influence of Reformation ideas, 127; and religious toleration, 130, 132, 133, 134, 140. *See also* religious toleration
Pot, Pol, 255
Process tracing, 287n.1
Protestant Ethic, The, 98
Protestantism. *See* Reformation.
Pufendorf, Samuel 85

Quandt, William, 214

racial equality, 161, 186
Raison d'état, 86, 101, 116, 118, 121, 133, 140. *See also Richelieu, Cardinal*
Ramadier, Paul, 225, 229
Rassemblement D-mocratique Africain (RDA), 240
Rational-choice theories, 68
Realism, 59–66; account of revolutions in sovereignty in, 63–66; and evidence for its influence on Westphalia, 142–44; in-

ternational history according to, 28; and power, 275n.32; and theories of state system, 103, 118; view of ideas in, 61–63, 68. *See also* structural theories, realist.
reason of reflection, 50, 51–53
Reformation: autonomy of ideas in, 144–46; and Catholic polities, 110; conversion and the, 124; effect of on Westphalia, 70, 72, 98–102; from above, 126; from below, 126, influence of on Thirty Years' War, 136; motives of rulers in, 137; political theology of, 104–110; and polities' interest in Westphalia, 110–22; as source of crisis in polities, 110; structural skepticism of autonomy of, 103–4; structural skepticism of efficacy of, 102–4; of towns, 145
religious pluralism, 147–49
religious tolerance: William of Orange's policy of, 114; Pacification of Ghent and, 115, French domestic policy of, 101, 116–17, 125, 130, 131; Treaty of Augsburg and, 147. *See also politique*
reputational power of ideas, 58, 162–64, 202, 257; and anticolonianism, 179; in British colonial independence, 170–71
resolvers of uncertainty, ideas as, 56–57, 68, 173, 201–2, 259
Respublica Christiana, 77
Restitution, Edict of, 119, 135
revolutions in sovereignty: categorization of, 28–29; definition of, 21; history of, 31; "revolutionary" character of, 43–45; origins of, 65
revolutionary ideas, 162, 166; and nationalism, 191
Rhodesia, 187, 196, 199, 248
Richard II, 16, 75
Richelieu, Cardinal: influence of *politique* thought on, 133; interest in Westphalia, 116; military policy and the Thirty Years' War, 140–41; offensive policy of, 117; political vision of, 86
Roberts, Michael, 134, 135
Robinson, Ronald, 173
Rohan, Duke of, 134
Roosevelt, Franklin D., 157, 224
Rousseau, Jean-Jacques, 16, 17

Sartre, Jean-Paul, 161
satyagraha, 200
Saurrat, Albert, 223
Savary, Alain, 229
Saxony, Elector John of, 112
Schilling, Heinz, 83–84
Schmalkaldic League, 112, 119, 120, 135
Second Colonial Occupation, 216
second face of authority, 19–20; defined at Westphalia, 32; in Peace of Westphalia 92–95; as revised by colonial independence, 35–36; as revised by European Unity, 40; as revised by minority treaties, 38, 154–55; revision of Westphalian definition of, 34–35
second role of ideas, 49, 50, 57–58, 256–57; applied to Reformation, 124–25; denial of, 102, and sources of social power, 68; in British East and Central Africa, 199; in British West Africa, 198–99; in colonial context, 161, 197–200; in France, 130–34; in French colonial context, 232–42; in Germany, 125, 127; in Netherlands, 127–29; in Sweden, 135–36; and reputational social power, 162, 182, 219, 257
Second Vatican Council, 262
Security Council, 42, 181; Resolution 688, 42; Resolution 794, 42
self-determination, 36, 43, 156, 254, 256
Senegal, 239
Senghor, L-opold, 242
settler populations: in British empire, 217–18; in French empire, 247–49
Shakespeare, William, 16, 75
Sierra Leone, 178, 195
Single European Act (1986), 67
Skocpol, Theda, 66
Slavery, 159
social power of ideas. *See* second role of ideas
Somalia, 42
South Africa, 171, 248
Soviet Union, 179, 194, 218
sovereignty, 16–19; absolute and non-absolute varieties of, 18–19; defined, 16–17; holders of, 17; internal and external varieties of, 18; pooling of, 39; as procurer of freedom, 254–55; as shield for evil, 33, 37, 260–62; varieties of, 17–19
Spain: decline of, 259; growth of state institutions in, 142; interest in opposing Westphalia, 120–21; summarized polity of, 111
Speyer, Imperial Diet of, (1526), 112

Spruyt, Hendrik, 99, 103
St. Bartholomew's Day Massacre, 115, 131
Stalin, Joseph, 255
Steiger, Heinhard, 84
structural theories: applied to autonomy of Reformation, 103–4; applied to British colonial context, 212–19; applied to French colonial context, 246–49; of British colonial independence, 203–11; of French colonial independence, 242–49; realist, 59–66; role of in revolutions in sovereignty, 259; as skeptical of autonomy of Reformation ideas, 146–47; as skeptical of colonial criticism of British empire, 212–18; as skeptical of first role of ideas, 55–56; as skeptical of ideas' influence on colonial independence, 166–67; as skeptical of international and domestic criticism of British empire, 208–11; as skeptical of second role of ideas, 58–66, 197; as skeptical of social power of Reformation, 102–4, 137–44
Sweden: growth of state institutions in, 141; interest in sovereign statehood in, 119; role of Reformation in, 134–36; reformation from below, 125–126; summarized polity of, 111
Swinton, Lord, 178
Swiss Confederation, 31

Tanganyika, 178, 186, 190, 196, 248
Tanganyika African National Union, 190
Tanzania, 199
Tawney, R.H., 98
Testament Politique, The, 133
third face of authority: as defined at Westphalia, 32, 95–96; as revised in European Unity, 40; as revised in internationally sanctioned intervention, 41–42; as revised in minority treaties, 38
Thirty Year's War, 44, 96, 117, 119; and Westphalia, 65, 77, 85
Thomson, Janice, 51
three faces of authority, 15–21
Tilly, Charles, 102
Transylvania, 111, 120, 126
Treaty of Osnabr_ck, 37, 84, 89
Trent, Council of, 113, 116, 128
Trusteeship, 157
Trusteeship Council, 181
Truth of the Christian Religion (1627), *The*, 148
Tunisia, 220, 231, 235, 246, 248
Twenty Years Crisis, The, 61
two roles of ideas, 48–51; as applied to Reformation, 123–25; in colonial context, 191; three versions of, 68

Uganda, 178, 199
United Gold Coast Association (UGCC), 198
United Nations, 17, 19; and the doctrine of intervention, 43; influence of upon British colonial independence, 181–82; influence of upon French colonial independence, 232–24
United Nations Declaration (1960), 35, 153, 185
United Nations Charter, chapter VII of, 42; and political independence, 18, 35; and statehood, 94
United Provinces. *See* Netherlands
United States: criticism of Britian, 179–80, 182, 184, 194, 208–9, 218
Utrecht, Peace of (1713), 91

Vasa, Gustavus, 119, 134, 135
Vattel, Emeric de, 21, 76
violations of constitutions of international society. *See* constitution of international society, compromises of

war: as circumstance of reflection in the colonies, 194–95, 235. *See also* World War II
Watchtower Fundamentalists, 196
Watson, Adam, 13
Weber, Max, 49, 50, 56, 68, 98, 146, 265n.10
Weekend Telegraph, 178
Weingast, Barry, 67, 68
Wendt, Alexander, 277n.63
West Indian Federation, 178
West Indies, 191
Westphalia, Peace of (1648), 30–33: as defeat of Holy Roman Empire, 84–88; early modern causes of, 80–82; geographic extent of, 32–35; historians' view of, 83–84; intrinsic significance of, 32; legacy of, 89–96; as origin of modern international relations, 76–77, 82–96; principle of autonomy in, 85; principle of equality in, 85; religion in, 31, 88–89; as revolution in sovereignty, 15, 30–33, 75–

77, 82–96; rights of German states in, 85; signers' view of, 85–87; structural theories of, 102–4; in subsequent practice of states, 87–88; underlying principles of, 82
White settlers, 217–18
Wight, Martin, 14, 32
Wilson, Woodrow, 157, 180, 223, 254, 261
Wise, Frederick the, 137
World War II, 160, 200; and anticolonial ideas, 220; as circumstance of reflection in the colonies, 194–95; European integration after, 260; the French after, 224; and Greater France, 228; and the international context, 232; and the structural argument for Britain's embrace of colonial independence, 203–4, 208; and urban growth, 215
Worms, Imperial Diet of (1521), 108
Wycliffe, John, 109, 145
Wyduckel, Dieter, 84

Young Algerians, 236

Zambian African Congress, 190
Zel Domus, 87